ME, MIKKO, AND ANNIKKI

OTHER WORKS BY TIITU TAKALO

Tiitu Takalo: *Tyhmä tyttö* [Stupid girl] (Suuri Kurpitsa 2004)
Pauli Kallio & Tiitu Takalo: *Josefiina leipoo* [Josefiina bakes] (Suuri Kurpitsa 2006)
Tiitu Takalo: *Kehä* [Ring] (Suuri Kurpitsa 2007)
Tiitu Takalo: *Nurin* [Inside out] (Hyeena 2007)
Tiitu Takalo: *Jää* [Ice] (Suuri Kurpitsa 2008)
Tiitu Takalo: *Tuuli ja myrsky* [Wind and storm] (Suuri Kurpitsa 2009)
Pauli Kallio & Tiitu Takalo: *Ottopoikia ja työläistyttöjä* [Foster Sons and Cotton Girls]
(Tampereen museot 2011) *http://tiitutakalo.net/foster-sons-cotton-girls.htm*

ME, MIKKO, AND ANNIKKI

A Community Love Story in a Finnish City

TIITU TAKALO

Translated by Michael Demson and Helena Halmari
Afterword by Paul Buhle

North Atlantic Books
Berkeley, California

Published by
North Atlantic Books
Berkeley, California

Cover art and design by Tiitu Takalo with Jasmine Hromjak
Book design by Noora Federlay with Jasmine Hromjak
Layout: Noora Federlay with Happenstance Type-O-Rama
Printed in the United States of America

Me, Mikko, and Annikki is sponsored and published by the Society for the Study of Native Arts and Sciences (dba North Atlantic Books), an educational non-profit based in Berkeley, California, that collaborates with partners to develop cross-cultural perspectives, nurture holistic views of art, science, the humanities, and healing, and seed personal and global transformation by publishing work on the relationship of body, spirit, and nature.

North Atlantic Books' publications are available through most bookstores. For further information, visit our website at www.northatlanticbooks.com or call 800-733-3000.

Library of Congress Cataloging-in-Publication Data
Names: Takalo, Tiitu, author, illustrator. | Demson, Michael, translator. |
    Halmari, Helena, translator.
Title: Me, Mikko, and Annikki : a community love story in a Finnish city /
    Tiitu Takalo ; translated by Michael Demson and Helena Halmari.
Other titles: Minä, Mikko ja Annikki. Finnish
Description: Berkeley, California : North Atlantic Books, [2019]
Identifiers: LCCN 2019003063 | ISBN 9781623173609 (paperback)
Subjects: LCSH: Finland—Comic books, strips, etc. | Graphic novels. | BISAC:
    COMICS & GRAPHIC NOVELS / Literary. | HISTORY / Europe / Scandinavia.
Classification: LCC PN6790.F53 T3413 2019 | DDC 741.5/94897—dc23
LC record available at https://lccn.loc.gov/2019003063

1 2 3 4 5 6 7 8 9 Versa 24 23 22 21 20 19

North Atlantic Books is committed to the protection of our environment. We partner with FSC-certified printers
using soy-based inks and print on recycled paper whenever possible.

The translation of this book was supported by a sample translation grant awarded by
FILI - Finnish Literature Exchange and by Sam Houston State University's English Department and College of Humanities and Social Sciences.

PREFACE

By Michael Demson

"Visually, Tiitu Takalo has been one of the best Finnish comics artists for years, mastering many drawing techniques. In the 248-page *Minä, Mikko ja Annikki* she has matured as a writer as well. It's a masterpiece and her final breakthrough." —Harri Römpötti

For years Paul Gravett, a British graphic novelist and scholar, has offered annual lists of the best international graphic novels, compiled by international readers, on his popular English-language blog (paulgravett.com). It was there, back in 2014, that I first saw the cover of Tiitu's graphic novel, *Minä, Mikko ja Annikki*. It appeared beside a review by Harri Römpötti, a Helsinki-based freelance journalist, who has written books and curated exhibits on Finnish comics. His praise for the book was hearty, and it piqued my interest.

You now hold in your hands a copy of *Me, Mikko, and Annikki*—in English!—but back in 2014, there was only *Minä, Mikko ja Annikki*. No English translation existed, and, if you had a copy at all, you were particularly lucky because not that many copies were printed.

Römpötti's review so intrigued me that I started searching for an English translation—it took me some time to realize that there was none. But I discovered that Tiitu has a website (tiitutakalo.net), and there I learned a lot more about her work and her vision. It became clear to me why there were so few copies of *Minä, Mikko ja Annikki*: it is a highly personal work, a project that expresses her profound passion for her lover (Mikko), for her city (Tampere, Finland), for Annikki—her wooden housing complex with its cooperative community, the history of which makes up much of the graphic novel—and for her own work as a comic artist and graphic novelist. Every aspect of the book participates in this expression, from the colors of the paper she used to the lettering printed upon it, from the plot and themes of the interweaving stories to the characters and caricatures that animate each panel, from the regional history the book relates to the future it imagines. Every aspect matters to Tiitu. You will feel this as you read and take in the artistry of every page.

I was charmed immediately by the gutsy punky radicalism of Tiitu's website. It's not hard to gather there her interests: comics, feminism, environmentalism, regional history, communal living, and political justice. At that point, however, I didn't know if that would come through in her graphic novel that I so wanted to get my hands on and read. In poking around more on the internet, I discovered that she had already published several graphic novels, had won an impressive range of prizes, and was well known in the world of European comics—I had to get a copy of *Minä, Mikko ja Annikki*!

This is when I turned to my colleague at Sam Houston State University in Huntsville, Texas—Dr. Helena Halmari, who is not only a proud Finn but also the editor of the *Journal of Finnish Studies*. I explained to her what I knew already about the book and asked her if she would be interested in collaborating on an English translation, knowing that she had done previous translations of Finnish texts for an English-speaking audience. To my delight, she agreed! In fact, she knew the city of Tampere well. Helena grew up just twenty kilometers (about twelve and a half miles) south of the city, in a small town called Lempäälä. When she was growing up, Lempäälä had only 13,000 people (though it's bigger now), and Tampere was the second largest city in Finland—Tampere was the place to go to for major shopping, culture, and entertainment. After graduating from high school, Helena was admitted to the University of Tampere to study languages, and she ended up earning two undergraduate degrees and two masters degrees there. "Public transportation between Lempäälä and Tampere," she told me, "was good, with bus number 71 going back and forth three times per hour." So, even though she was a country girl from a small town, Tampere was her larger reference point. She was excited to translate a book about Tampere. I couldn't believe it—this was serendipitous! We decided to contact Tiitu. Helena reached out, and Tiitu agreed to send us copies of the graphic novel as well as other work she had done so that we could become better acquainted with her art and vision.

And we did. We read and reread the graphic novel. *Minä, Mikko ja Annikki* recounts the history of a low-rise, working-class neighborhood, Annikki, in the Finnish city Tampere, and the present-day fight by two residents—young lovers—to arrest the plans of city developers, who would level the neighborhood for more modern developments. In this regard, the graphic novel's appeal is universal: it is a story of resistance to rapid urban development, to the forces of capitalism, which value economic growth over community. However, it also tells the story of the city from its founding to the present day and offers glimpses into the lives of its residents across various periods of its growth. The chapters are interwoven period pieces, each presented in its own particular color palette and style—from traditional European woodblock, to watercolors, to current comic idioms. More impressive still, Tiitu moves between styles effortlessly—sometimes narrating history through a series of conventional panels, sometimes prompting contemplative reflection through arresting splash pages. Part of the beauty of this book is that its innovative style never feels gimmicky or cheap—it's a work of art. There is nothing sensational, nothing objectified; every character and every theme feels authentic.

The rest, as they say, is history. Helena and I worked on the English translation, consulting with Tiitu frequently. On her next return home, Helena visited with Tiitu in Tampere, bringing us all a little closer. In 2015, as Helena and I were working on the translation, Tiitu won the Tampere City Literature Award for *Minä, Mikko ja Annikki*, and Helena and I were awarded a translation grant by FILI, the Finnish Literature Exchange (www.finlit.fi/fili/en/), which promotes the publication of Finnish literature in translation around the world.

I will never forget the excitement that came with opening the box of Tiitu's art that she sent to Helena and me before we began the translation. In offering you this translation, I hope some of that excitement comes through as you turn the pages of this book, which we believe truly is what Harri Römpötti identified it to be: a masterpiece of the genre of the graphic novel.

TO THE READER

In January 2014 the fair trade market, Maailmankauppa Tasajako, closes its store in the Tammela section of Tampere. In the middle of the night, Mikko rescues a table that has been doomed to the dumpster after he notices a text on the bottom of the table's top, written in beautiful round hand: "Hotel Sotkanvirta, February 12, 1955. We lifted the furniture upside down for a thorough cleaning. Movers R. Jalonen, A. Äijälä, H. Vuorinen."

The table gained more significance because it had a story to tell. This book is my story about one block in one city. It is specifically my story. When I spoke with the former inhabitants of the block, I soon realized that everyone had an endless number of reminiscences and stories. First of all, I understood that this block in Tampere is dear and important to many—even to many of those whose home this place has never been.

I became desperate. I would not be able to record in my graphic novel all the colorful turns in the history of the block. I don't even have the ability and strength to collect them. I had to make a decision: the book will be about my Annikki. I hope that one day another book comes out, telling those stories that were left out of this one.

Alone, many things are harder, bigger, impossible. It's difficult to give oneself a triumphant high-five. Love becomes a reality in the plural. One alone cannot build and maintain a community, a family, a sewing circle, or an entire block. It's easier to fulfill dreams together. Everything begins when we say aloud what our dreams are. It is easy to imagine that one's own dreams are not important. Perhaps this was the thinking of the person who decades ago, for the first time, said aloud that it would be nice to preserve the block of wooden houses called Annikki.

While I have been working on this graphic novel, people in the Tammela section of Tampere have argued again about preserving or demolishing old houses. In 2013, the community board accepted a city plan that dooms for demolition the art noveau storage building of the Tammela railroad yard. It was built in 1907. The warehouses next to it, also built around that time, were already torn down back in 2009. The railroad workers community hall, Morkku, located in that same milieu, is also under the threat of demolition.

During December 2013 and January 2014, Morkku was occupied several times. I visited the site a couple of times and crafted for myself a Morkku sleeve badge. Will that be my memory of this culturally and historically significant community hall?

The buildings of our country are young. Less than 2 percent were built before World War I, and 70 percent during the past three decades. Would it finally be time to take care of that 2 percent? Will a captured picture of Morkku in museums' photo archives be enough for future generations? Is it more startling to walk along the warehouse wall where members of the Red Guard were executed in the spring of 1918—or to stroll along a new street, which has taken over the place where the warehouse once stood?

I am not a researcher or a historian. My book will certainly include errors. There are so many details that some of them must be off. My sources contradict one another, and I have surely made mistakes even while drawing and texting the bubbles.

The most important sources for the historical sections included Jarna Pasanen's 2012 history proseminar study, which deals with the first inhabitants of block 247; Matti Wacklin's books *Tammela: Suutarien pääkaupunki* (Tammela: The shoemakers' capital, 2010) and *Tammela: Tarinoita torin kulmilta* (Tammela: Stories from market corners); Arja Jokinen and Kirsi Juhila's 1987 study titled *Asumisen ankeus ja autuus: Tutkimus Puu-Tammelasta ja sen asukkaista* (The gloom and bliss of living: A study on the Wooden Tammela and its inhabitants); the publication by the Tampere museums, edited by Lind, Antila, and Liuttunen, *Tammerkoski ja kosken kaupunki* (Tammerkoski and the city on the rapids, 2011); and, for the recent history of the block, the website annikinkatu.net. The most important source of pictures was the Tampere museums' Siiri information service's photographic treasure trove.

Tiitu

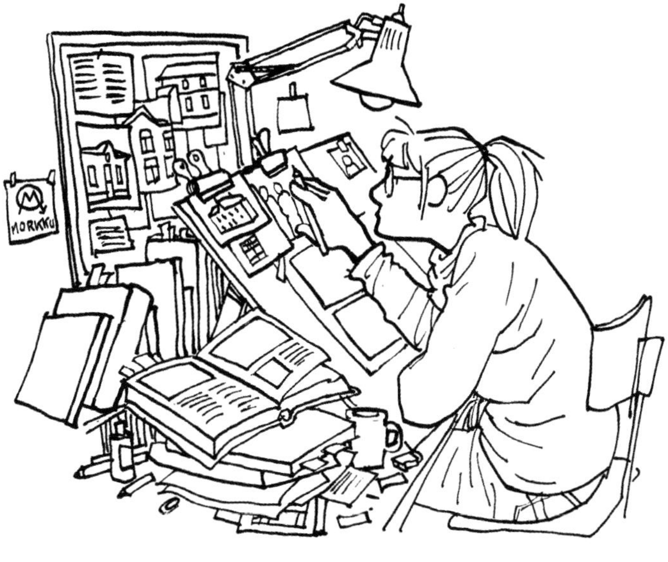
MORKKU

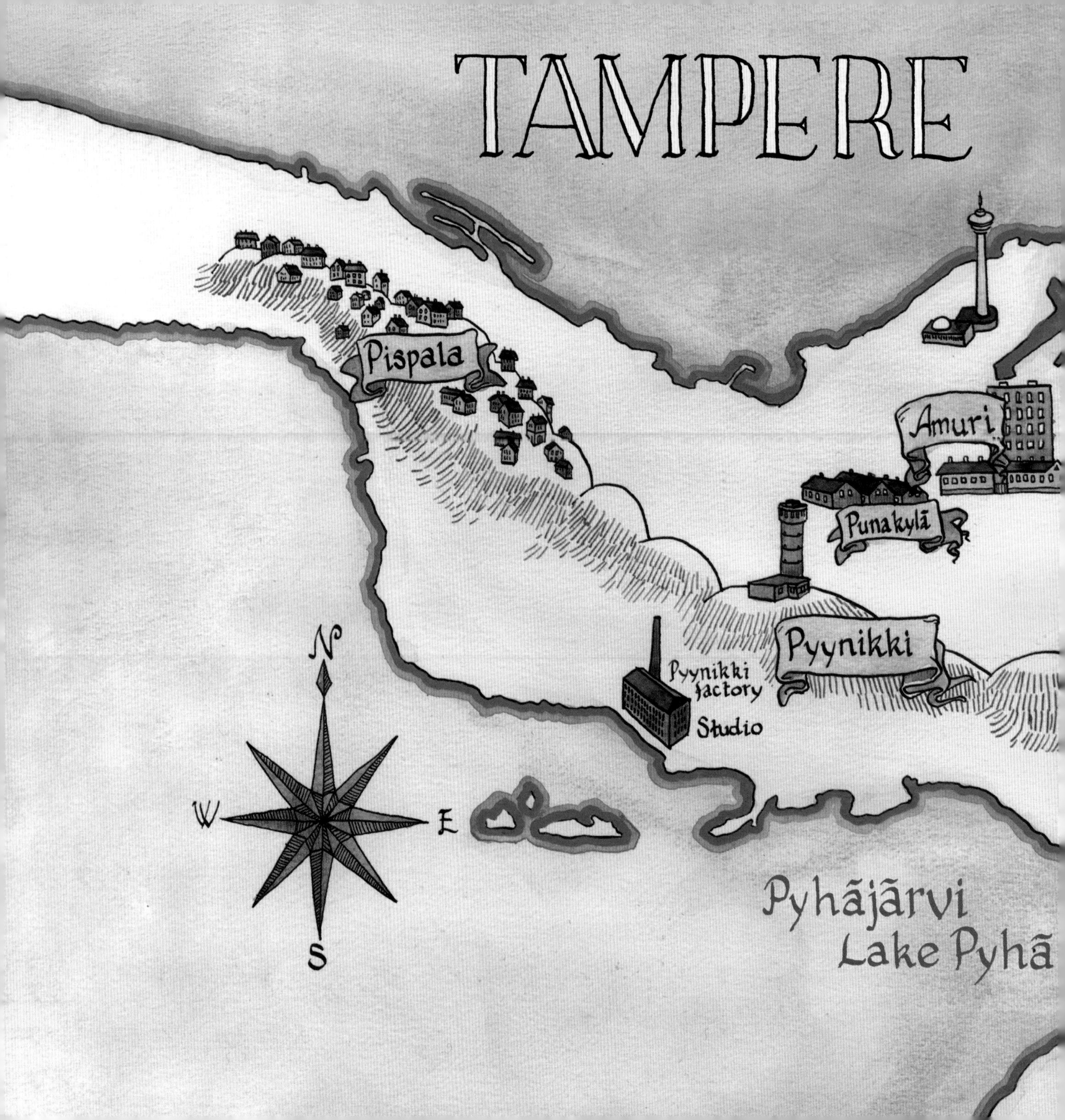
TAMPERE
Pispala
Amuri
Punakylä
Pyynikki
Pyynikki factory
Studio
N
W
E
S
Pyhäjärvi
Lake Pyhä

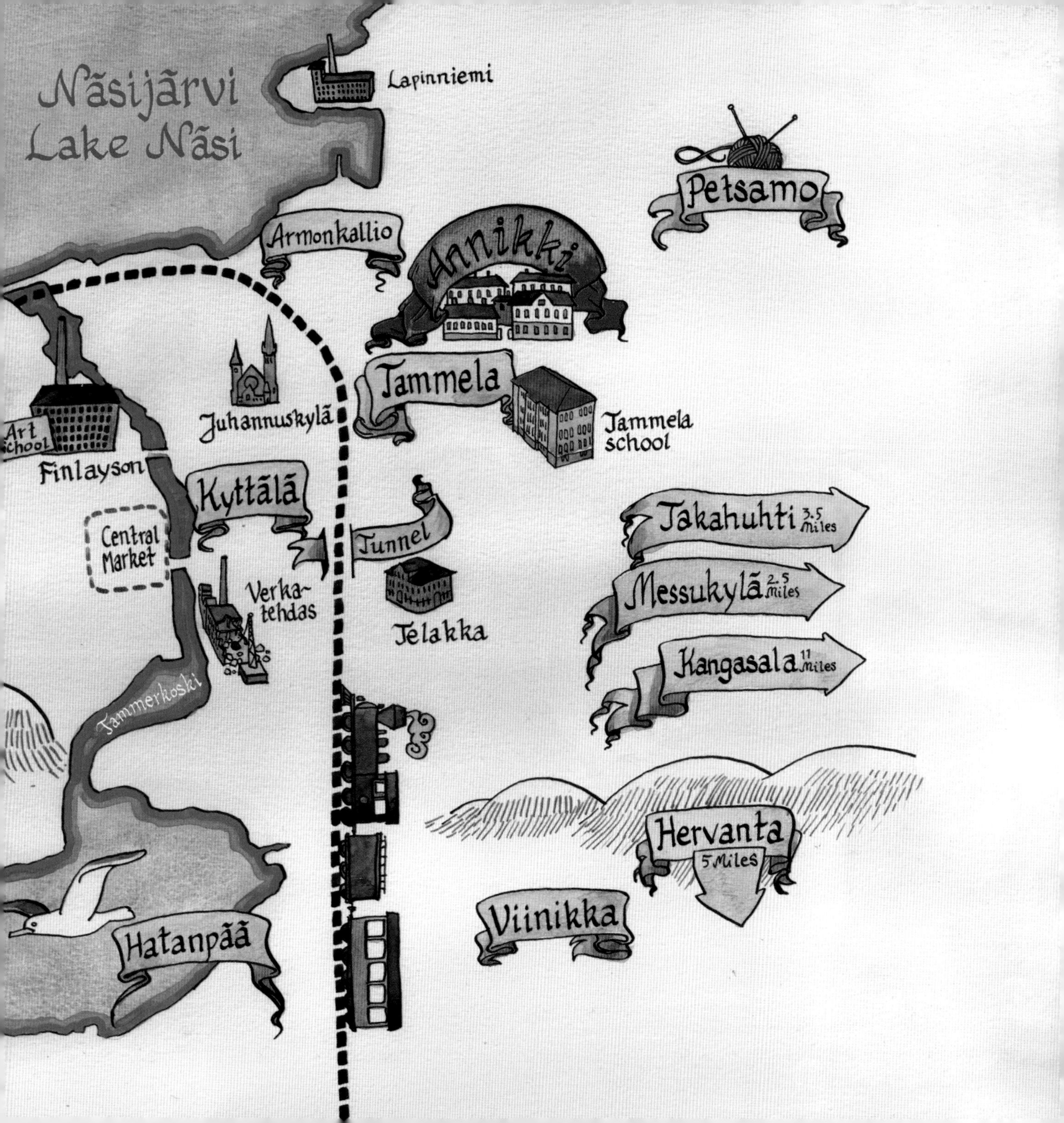

Nāsijārvi
Lake Nāsi
Lapinniemi
Petsamo
Armonkallio
Annikki
Tammela
Tammela school
Juhannuskylā
Art School
Finlayson
Kyttālā
Central Market
Tunnel
Verka-tehdas
Telakka
Takahuhti 3.5 miles
Messukylā 2.5 miles
Kangasala 11 miles
Tammerkoski
Hervanta
5 Miles
Viinikka
Hatanpāā

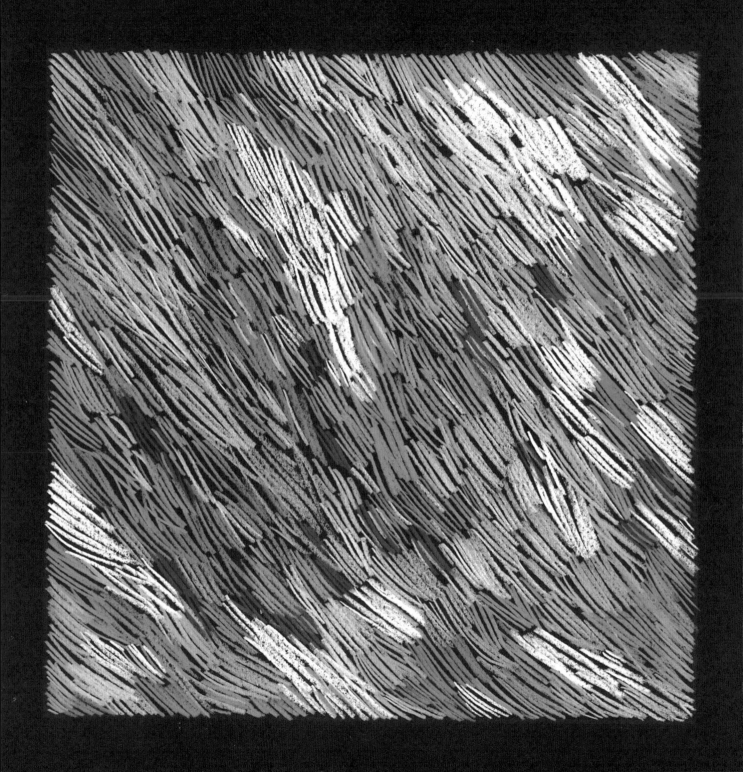

THE ESKER
AND THE RAPIDS

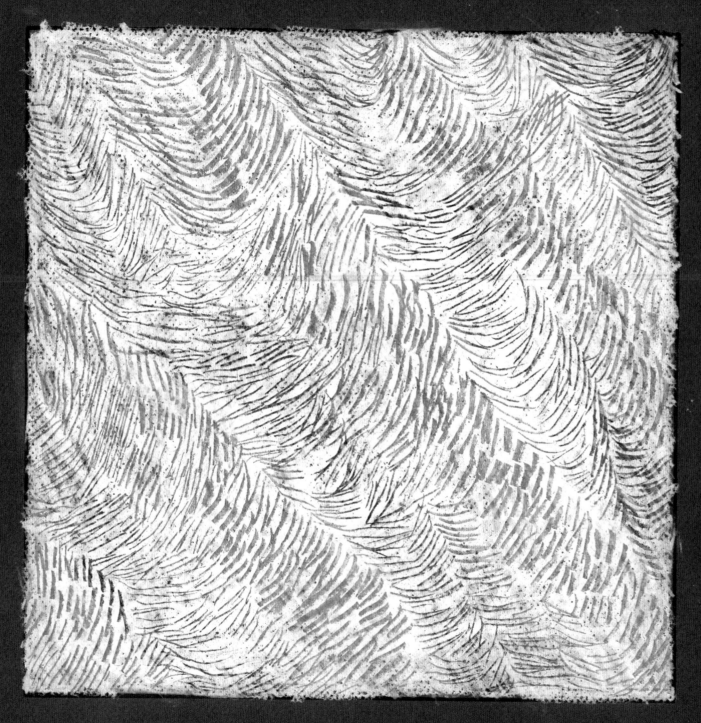

It's about ten thousand years since it happened.

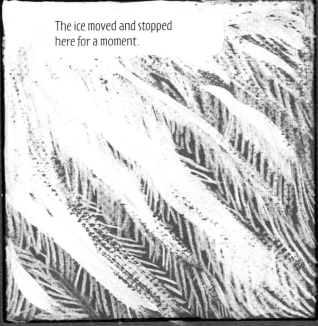

The ice moved and stopped here for a moment.

The rivers formed by melting waters brought with them stones and sand.

In this place the world's highest gravel esker was formed.

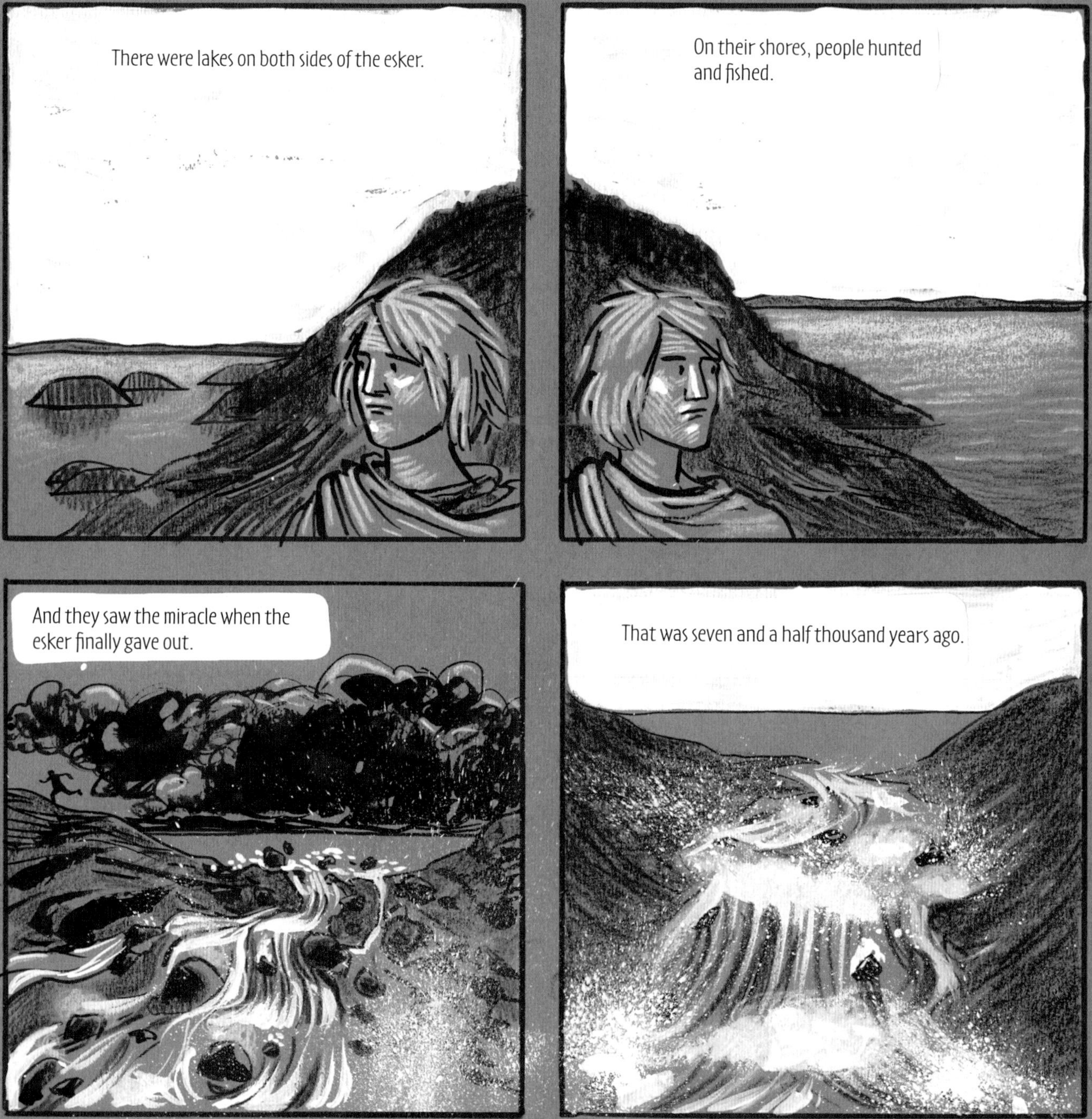
There were lakes on both sides of the esker.
On their shores, people hunted and fished.
And they saw the miracle when the esker finally gave out.
That was seven and a half thousand years ago.

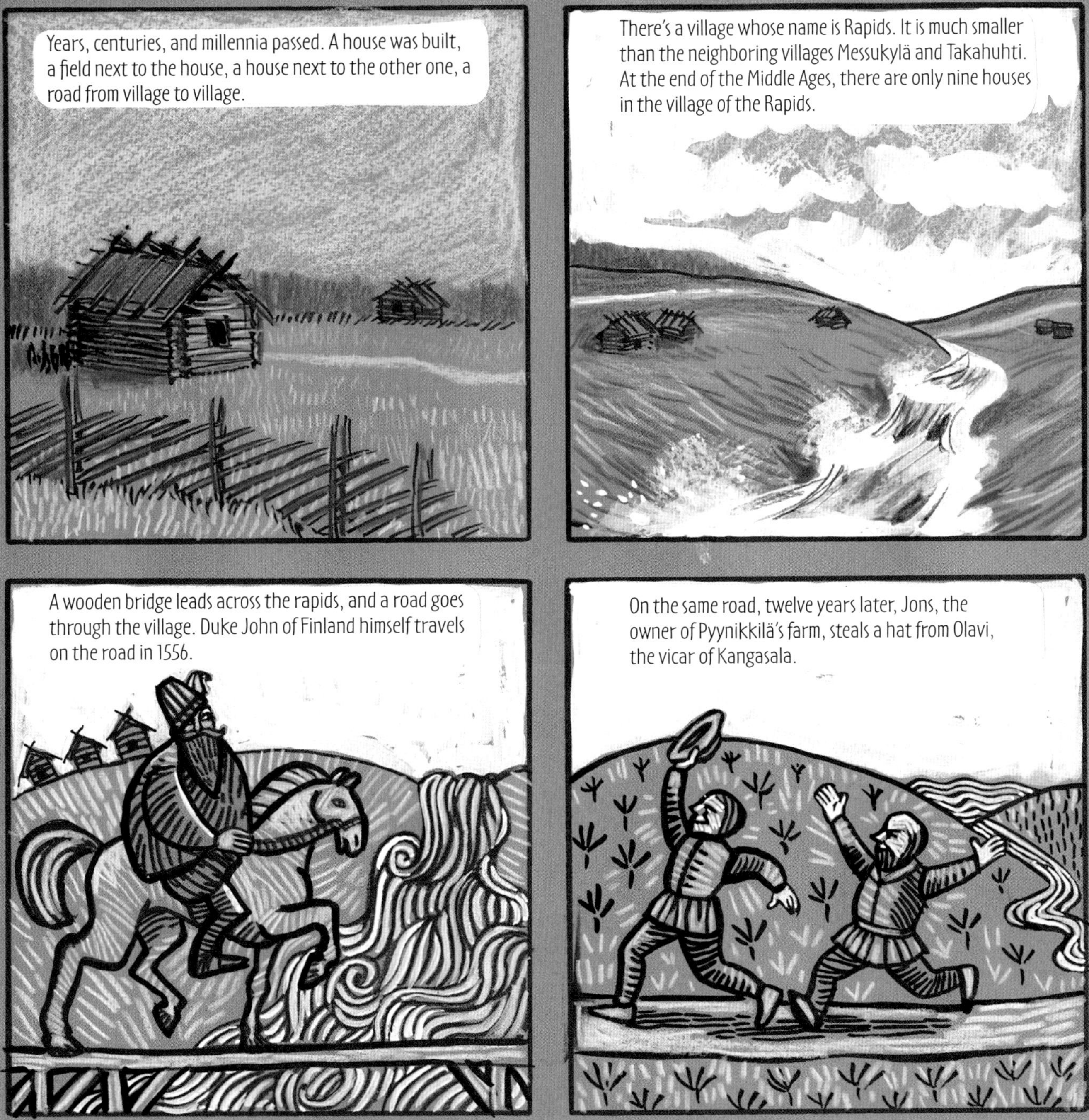
Years, centuries, and millennia passed. A house was built, a field next to the house, a house next to the other one, a road from village to village.
There's a village whose name is Rapids. It is much smaller than the neighboring villages Messukylä and Takahuhti. At the end of the Middle Ages, there are only nine houses in the village of the Rapids.
A wooden bridge leads across the rapids, and a road goes through the village. Duke John of Finland himself travels on the road in 1556.
On the same road, twelve years later, Jons, the owner of Pyynikkilä's farm, steals a hat from Olavi, the vicar of Kangasala.

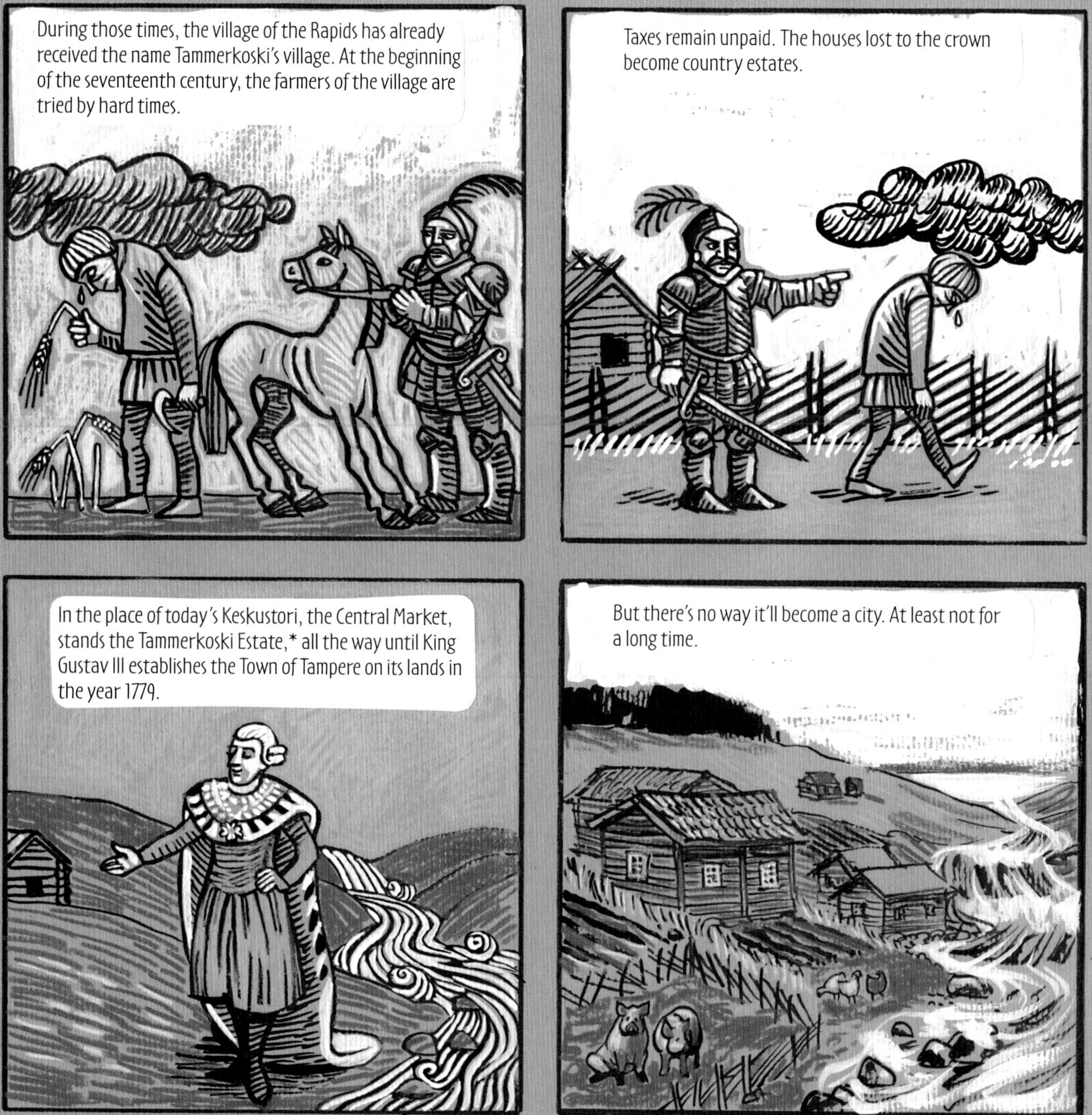
During those times, the village of the Rapids has already received the name Tammerkoski's village. At the beginning of the seventeenth century, the farmers of the village are tried by hard times.
Taxes remain unpaid. The houses lost to the crown become country estates.
In the place of today's Keskustori, the Central Market, stands the Tammerkoski Estate,* all the way until King Gustav III establishes the Town of Tampere on its lands in the year 1779.
But there's no way it'll become a city. At least not for a long time.

*The Swedish name Tammerfors (Tammerkoski in Finnish, Tammer Rapids in English) became Tampere in Finnish.

LOVE SPELL

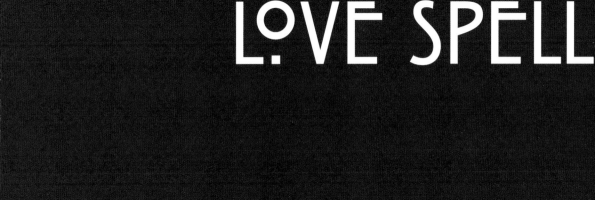

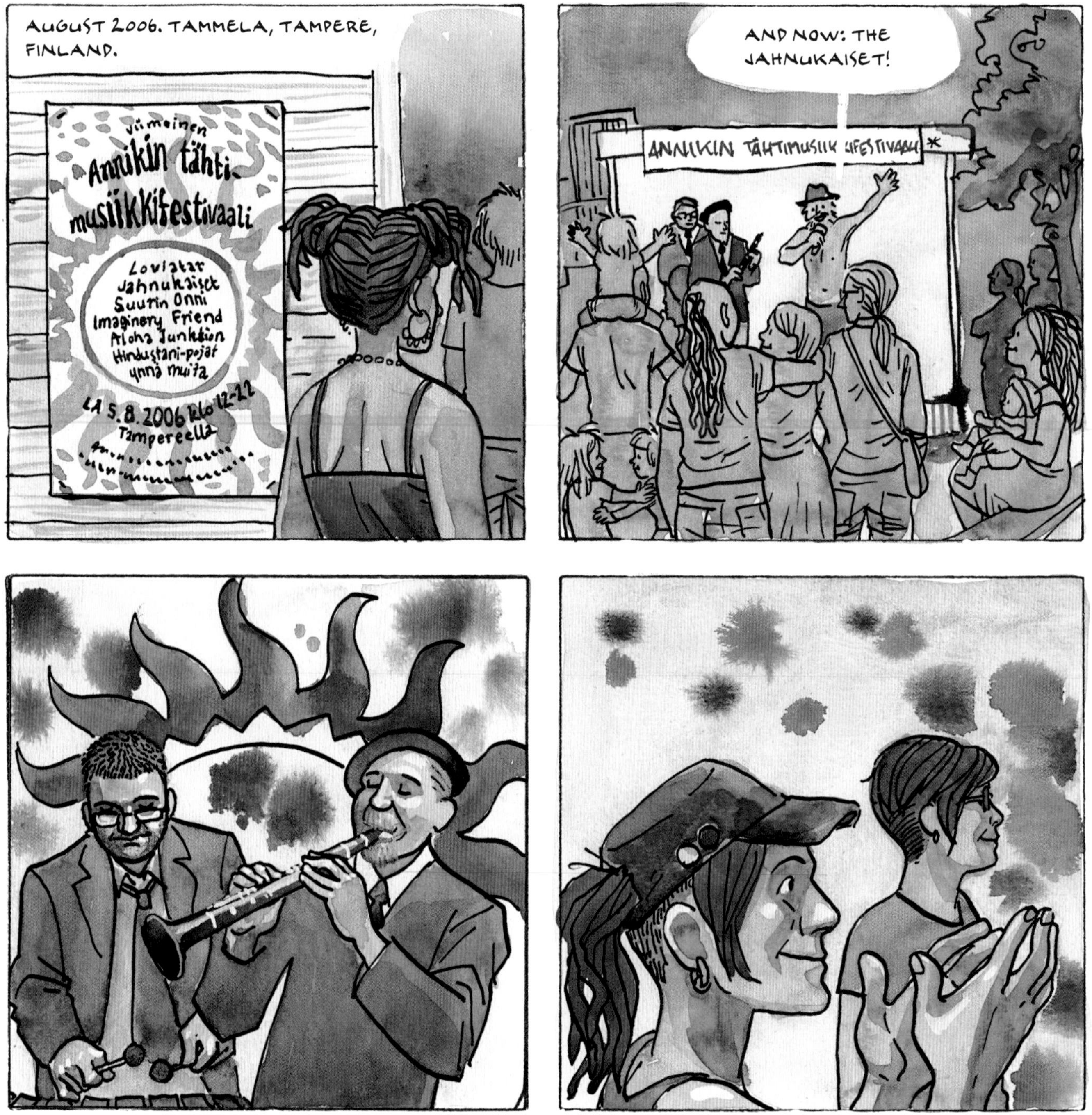
AUGUST 2006. TAMMELA, TAMPERE, FINLAND.
viimeinen
Annikin tähti-
musiikkifestivaali
Loviatar
Jahnukaiset
Suutin Onni
Imaginery Friend
Aloha Junktion
Hindustani-pojat
ynnä muita
LA 5.8.2006 klo 12-22
Tampereella
AND NOW: THE JAHNUKAISET!
ANNIKIN TÄHTIMUSIIKKIFESTIVAALI*

*Star of Annikki Music Festival

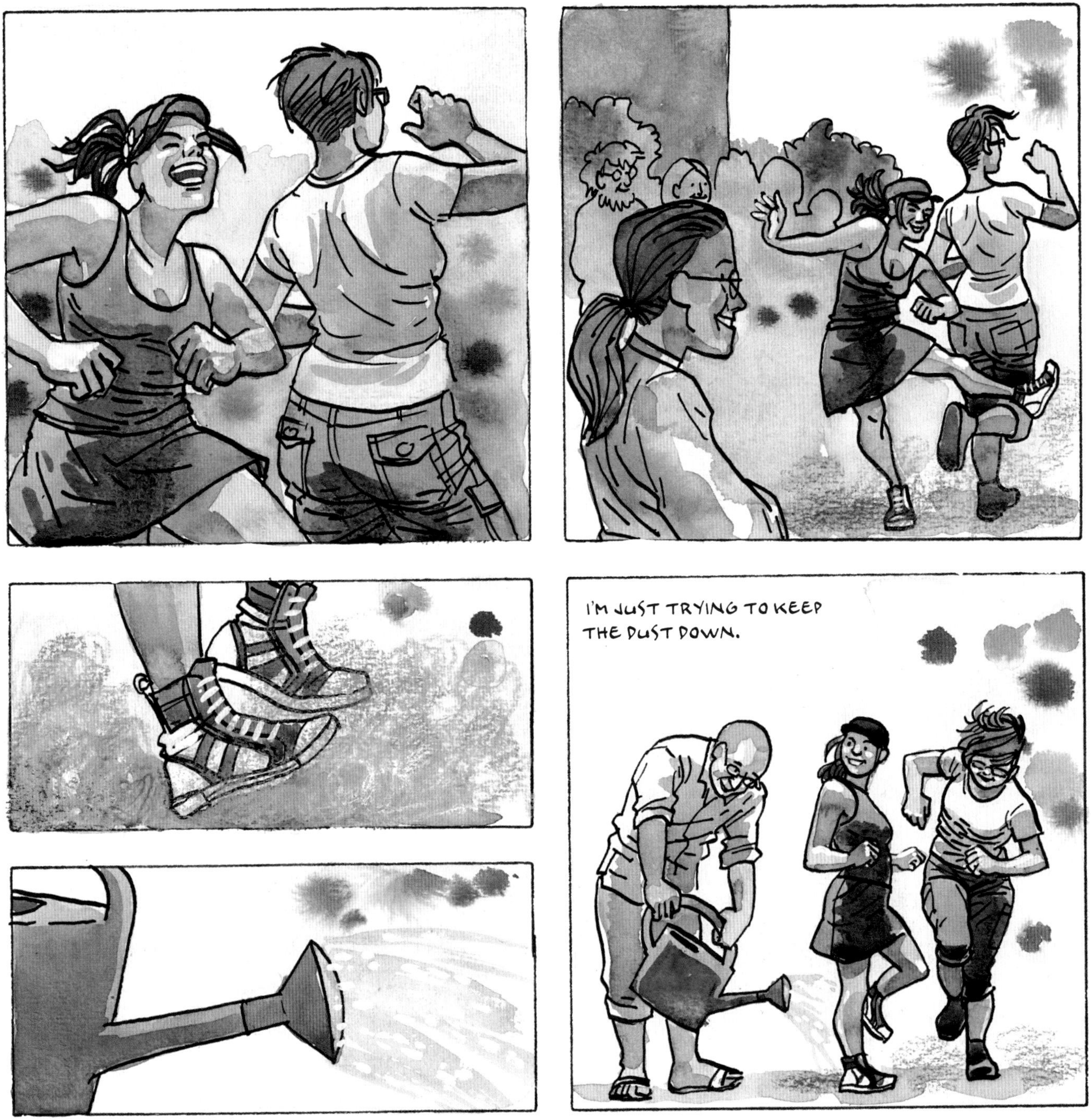
I'M JUST TRYING TO KEEP THE DUST DOWN.

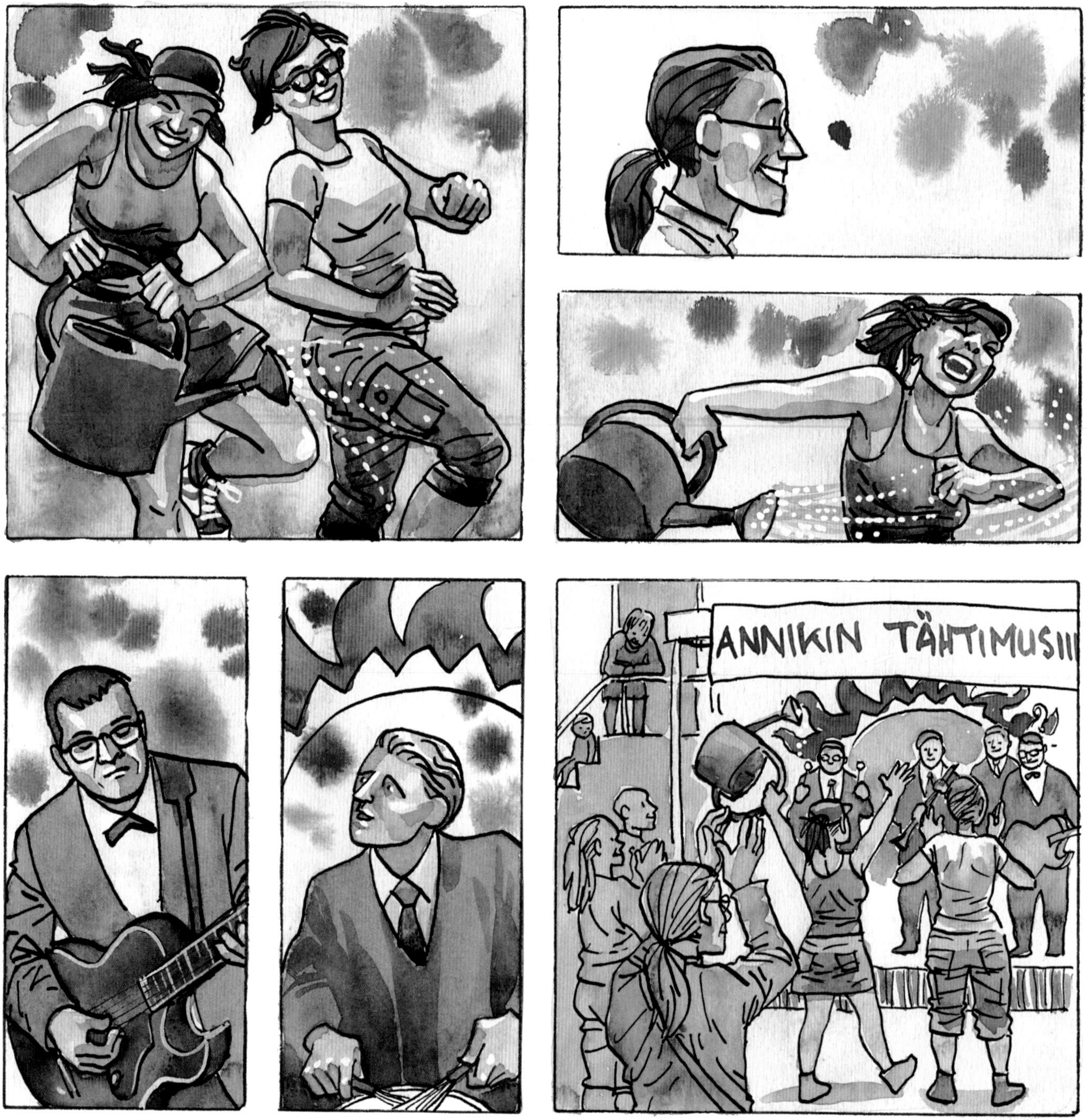
ANNIKIN TÄHTIMUSII

Banner reads: Star of Annikki Music

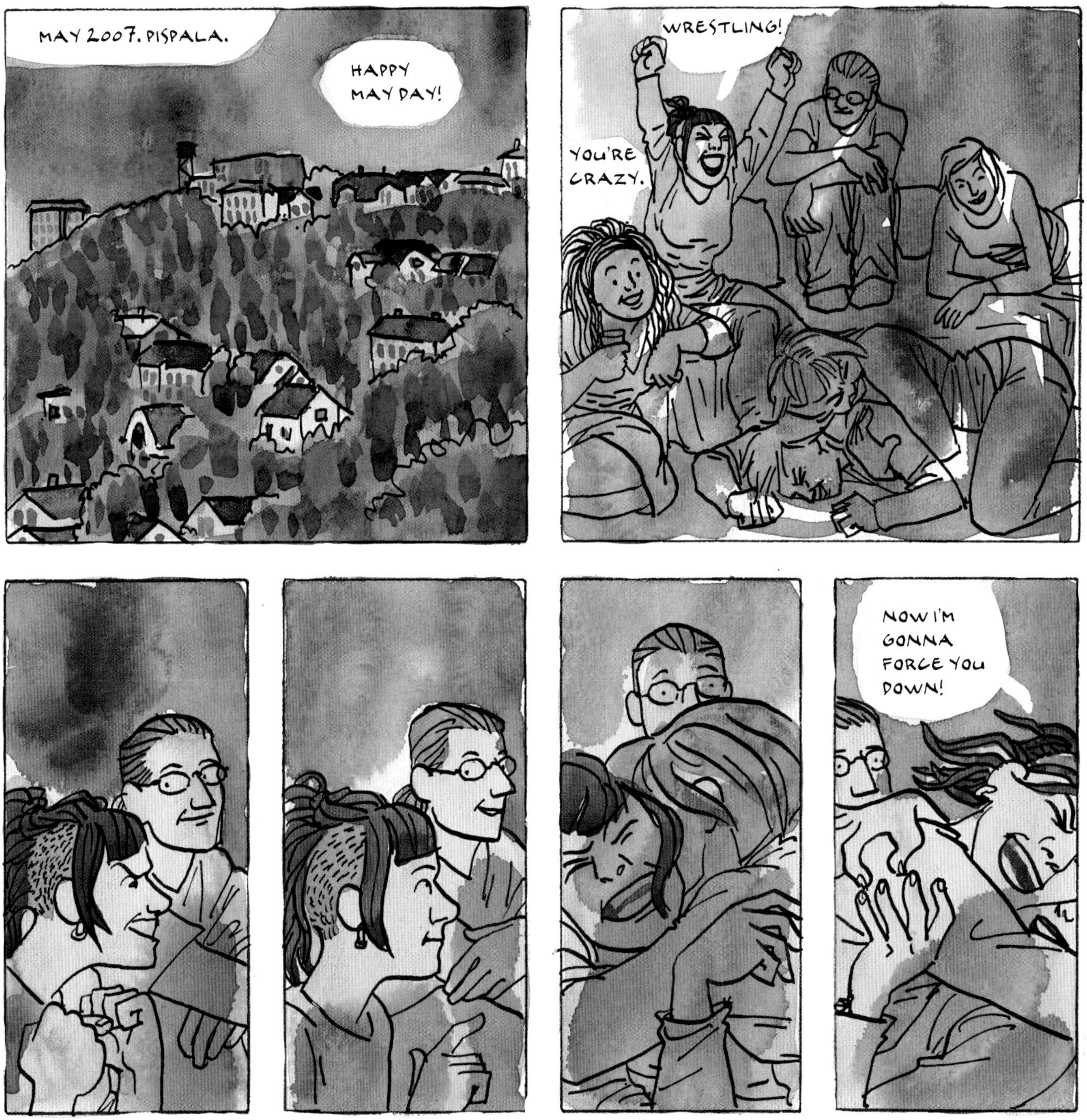
MAY 2007. PISPALA.
HAPPY MAY DAY!
WRESTLING!
YOU'RE CRAZY.
NOW I'M GONNA FORCE YOU DOWN!

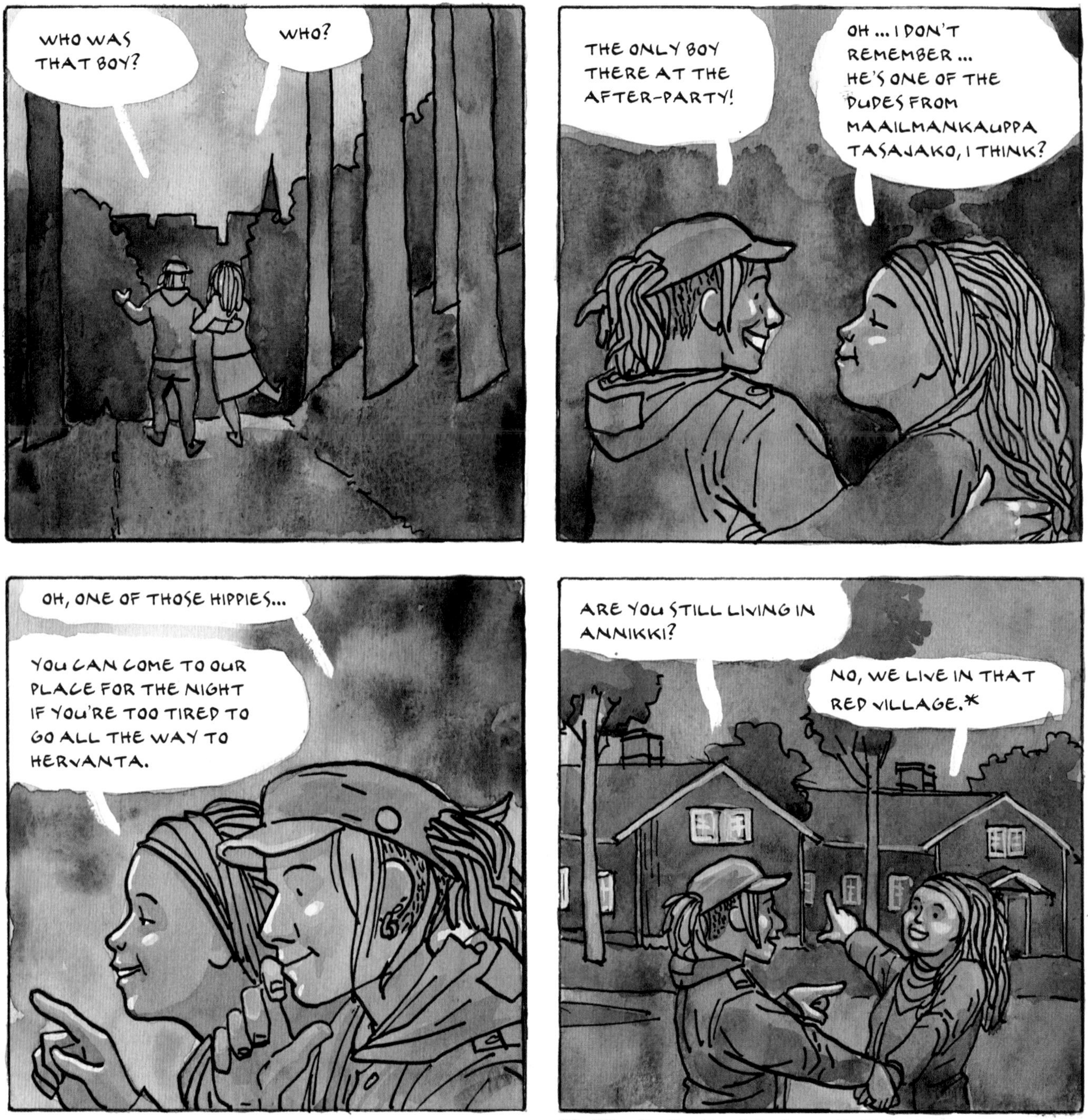
WHO WAS THAT BOY?
WHO?
THE ONLY BOY THERE AT THE AFTER-PARTY!
OH ... I DON'T REMEMBER ... HE'S ONE OF THE DUDES FROM MAAILMANKAUPPA TASAJAKO, I THINK?
OH, ONE OF THOSE HIPPIES...
YOU CAN COME TO OUR PLACE FOR THE NIGHT IF YOU'RE TOO TIRED TO GO ALL THE WAY TO HERVANTA.
ARE YOU STILL LIVING IN ANNIKKI?
NO, WE LIVE IN THAT RED VILLAGE.*

*"Red Village" is a literal translation from the Finnish *Punakylä*, a community in Tampere after Finland's Civil War. Most of the residents were widows of fallen Red soldiers.

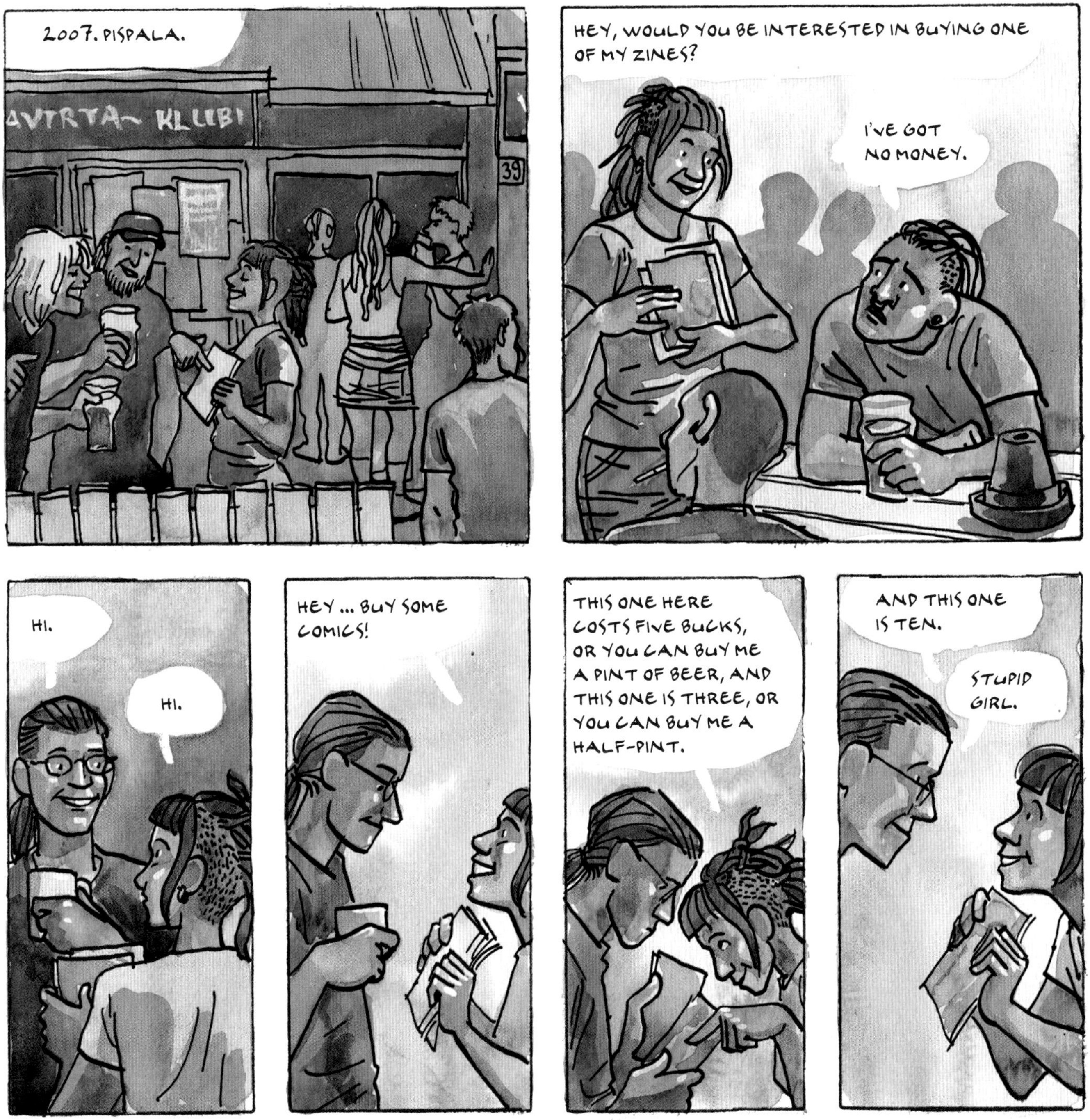
2007. PISPALA.
AVTRTA~ KLUBI
39
HEY, WOULD YOU BE INTERESTED IN BUYING ONE OF MY ZINES?
I'VE GOT NO MONEY.
HI.
HI.
HEY ... BUY SOME COMICS!
THIS ONE HERE COSTS FIVE BUCKS, OR YOU CAN BUY ME A PINT OF BEER, AND THIS ONE IS THREE, OR YOU CAN BUY ME A HALF-PINT.
AND THIS ONE IS TEN.
STUPID GIRL.

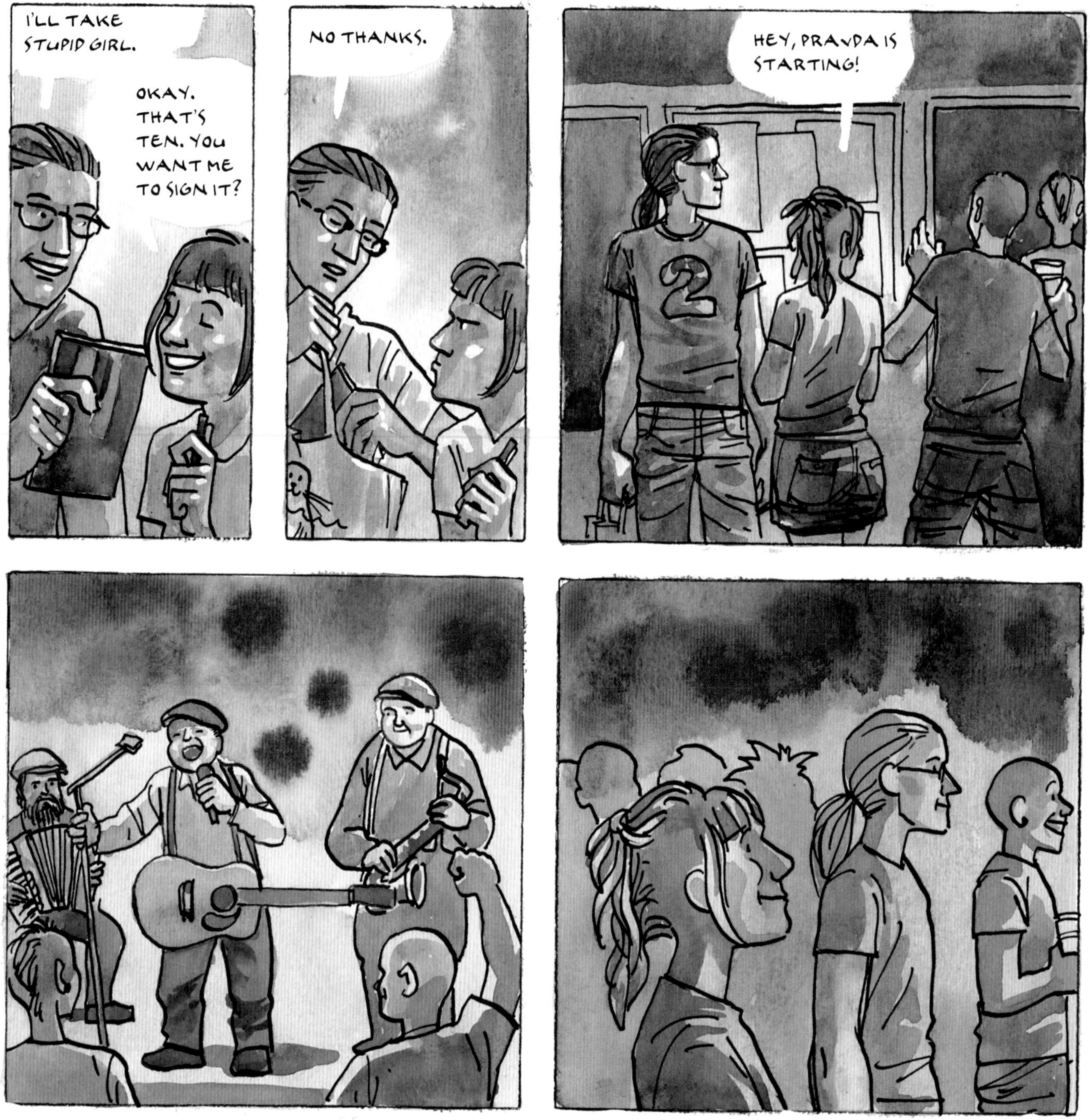
I'LL TAKE STUPID GIRL.
OKAY. THAT'S TEN. YOU WANT ME TO SIGN IT?
NO THANKS.
HEY, PRAVDA IS STARTING!

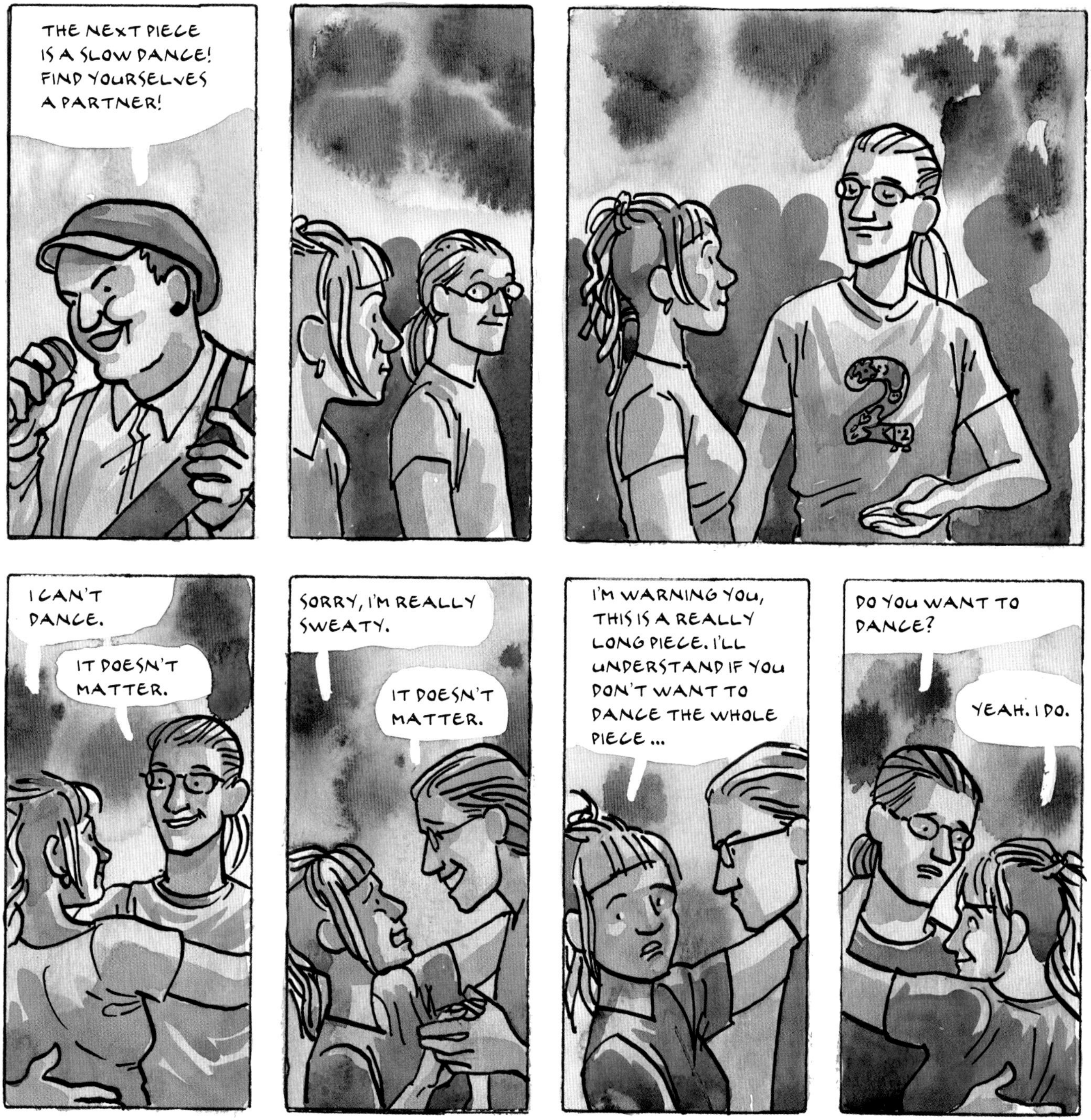
THE NEXT PIECE IS A SLOW DANCE! FIND YOURSELVES A PARTNER!
I CAN'T DANCE.
IT DOESN'T MATTER.
SORRY, I'M REALLY SWEATY.
IT DOESN'T MATTER.
I'M WARNING YOU, THIS IS A REALLY LONG PIECE. I'LL UNDERSTAND IF YOU DON'T WANT TO DANCE THE WHOLE PIECE...
DO YOU WANT TO DANCE?
YEAH. I DO.

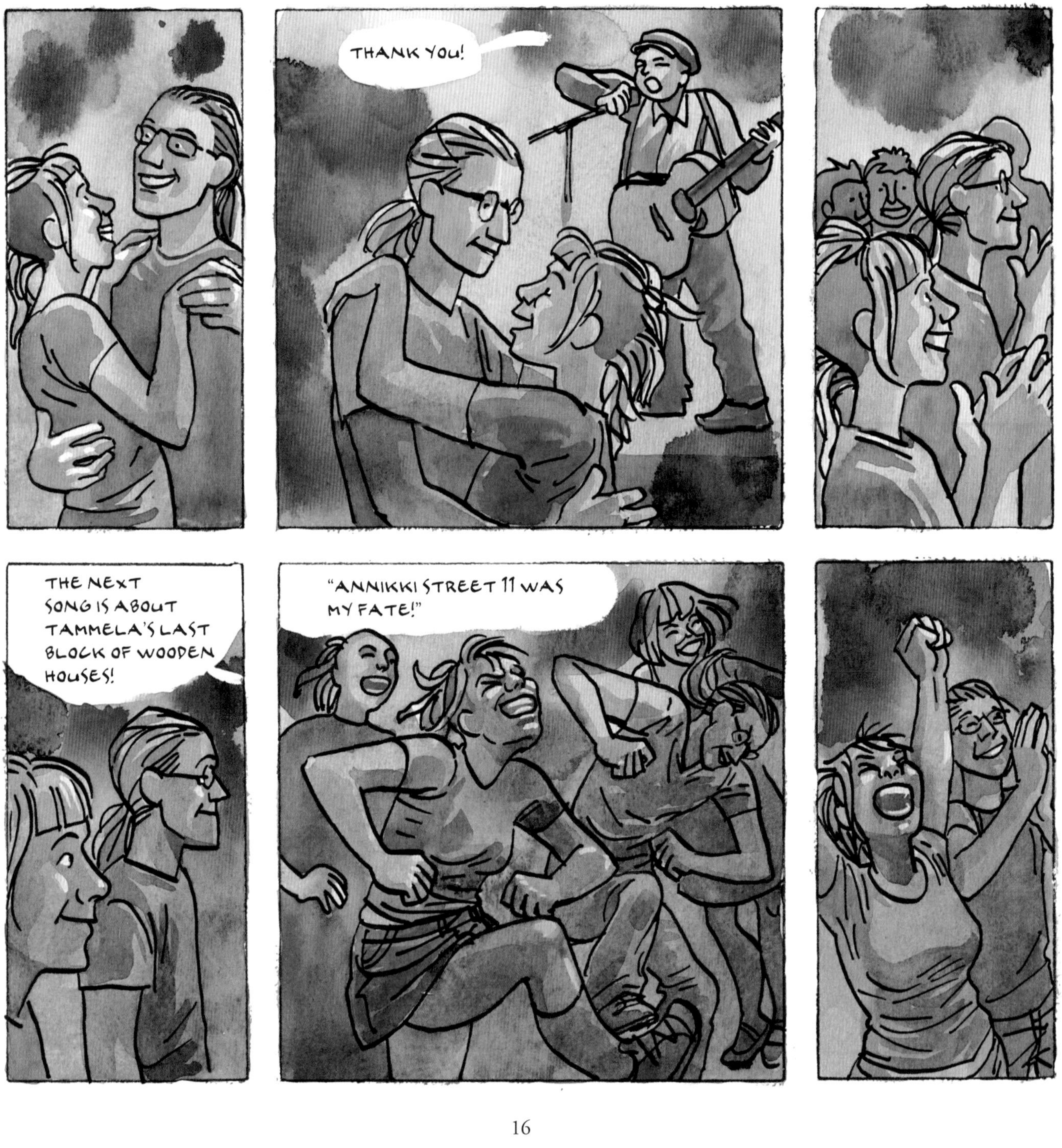
THANK YOU!
THE NEXT SONG IS ABOUT TAMMELA'S LAST BLOCK OF WOODEN HOUSES!
"ANNIKKI STREET 11 WAS MY FATE!"

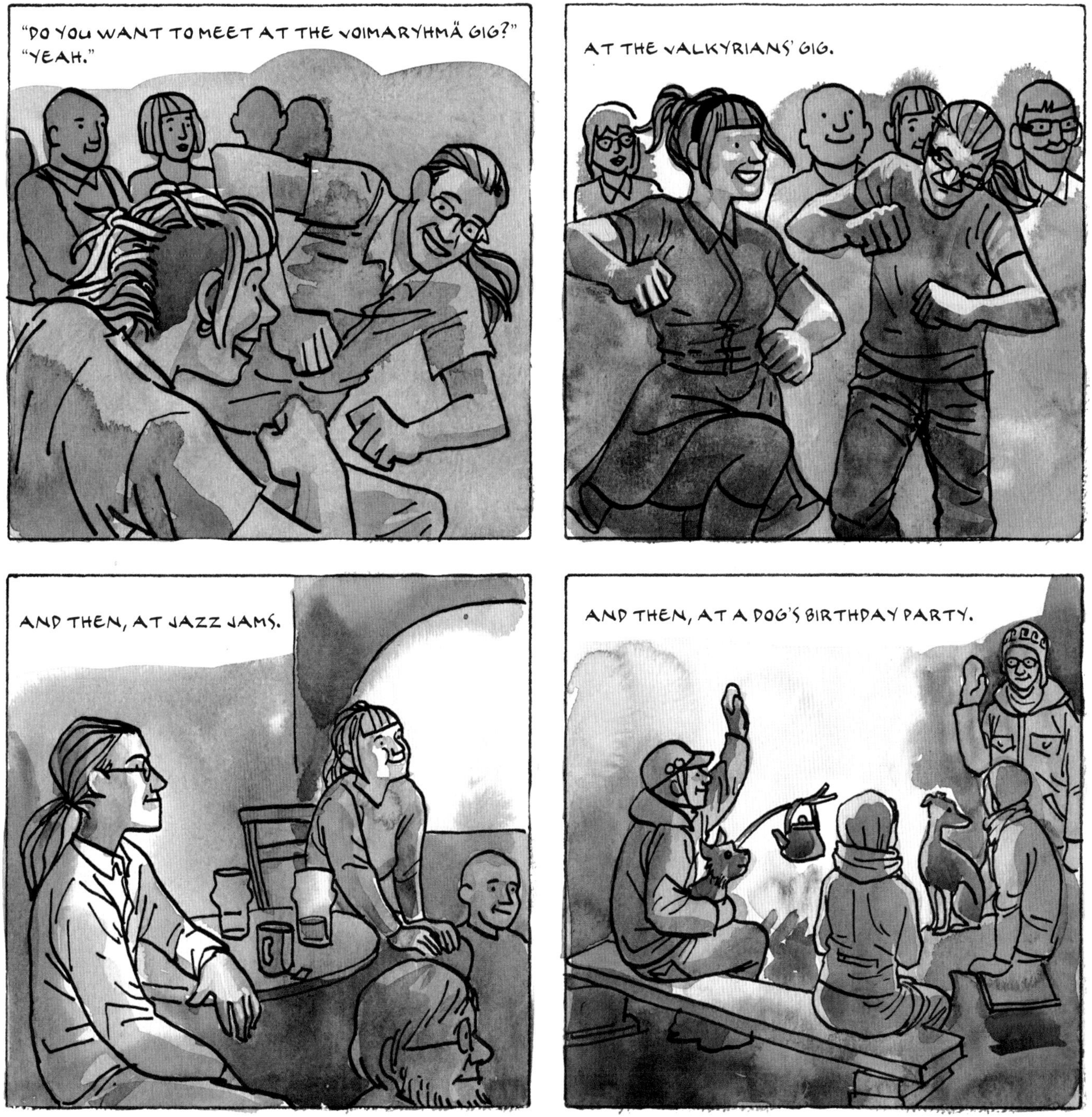
"DO YOU WANT TO MEET AT THE VOIMARYHMÄ GIG?"
"YEAH."
AT THE VALKYRIANS' GIG.
AND THEN, AT JAZZ JAMS.
AND THEN, AT A DOG'S BIRTHDAY PARTY.

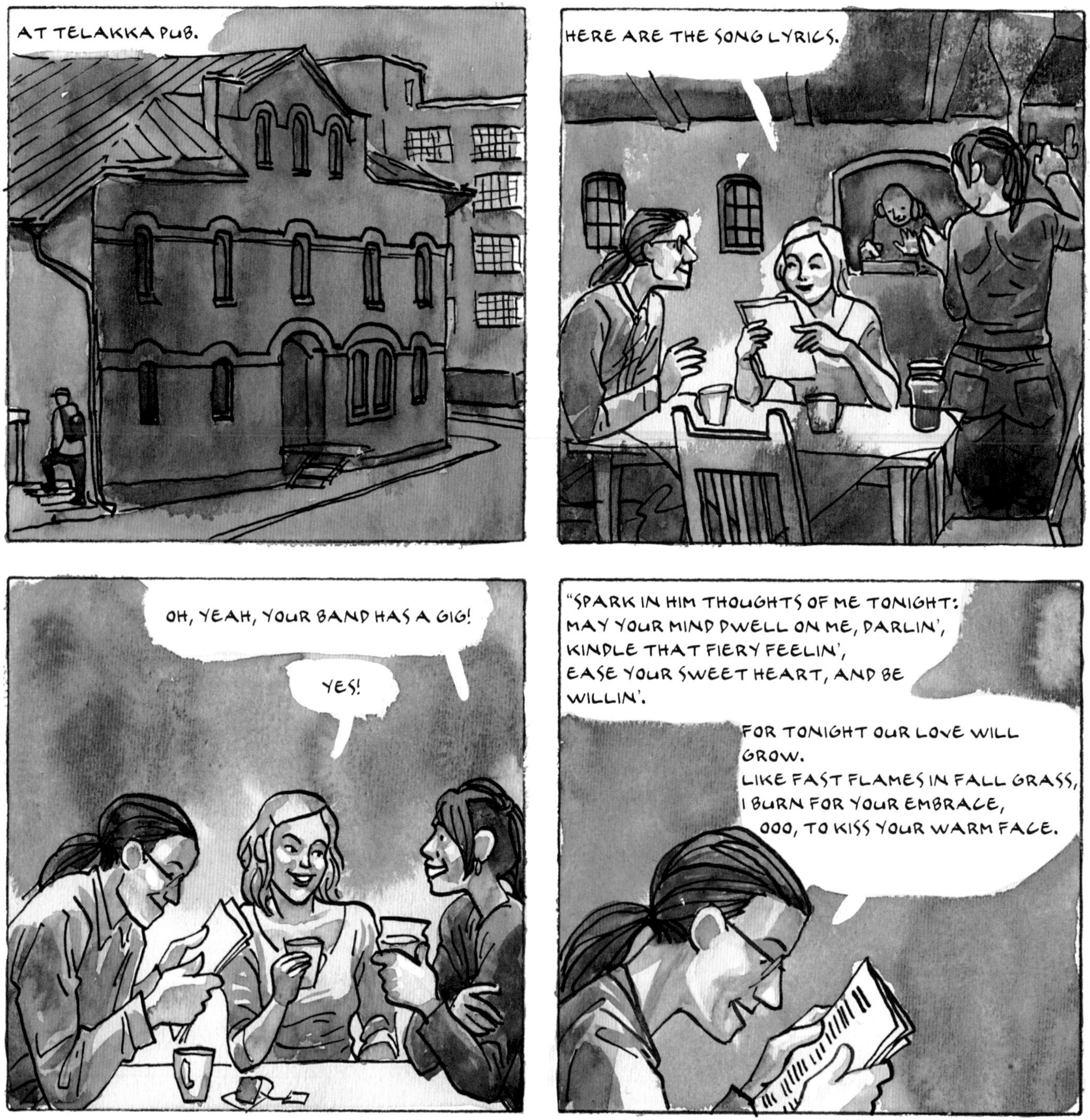
AT TELAKKA PUB.
HERE ARE THE SONG LYRICS.
OH, YEAH, YOUR BAND HAS A GIG!
YES!
"SPARK IN HIM THOUGHTS OF ME TONIGHT:
MAY YOUR MIND DWELL ON ME, DARLIN',
KINDLE THAT FIERY FEELIN',
EASE YOUR SWEET HEART, AND BE
WILLIN'.
FOR TONIGHT OUR LOVE WILL
GROW.
LIKE FAST FLAMES IN FALL GRASS,
I BURN FOR YOUR EMBRACE,
OOO, TO KISS YOUR WARM FACE.

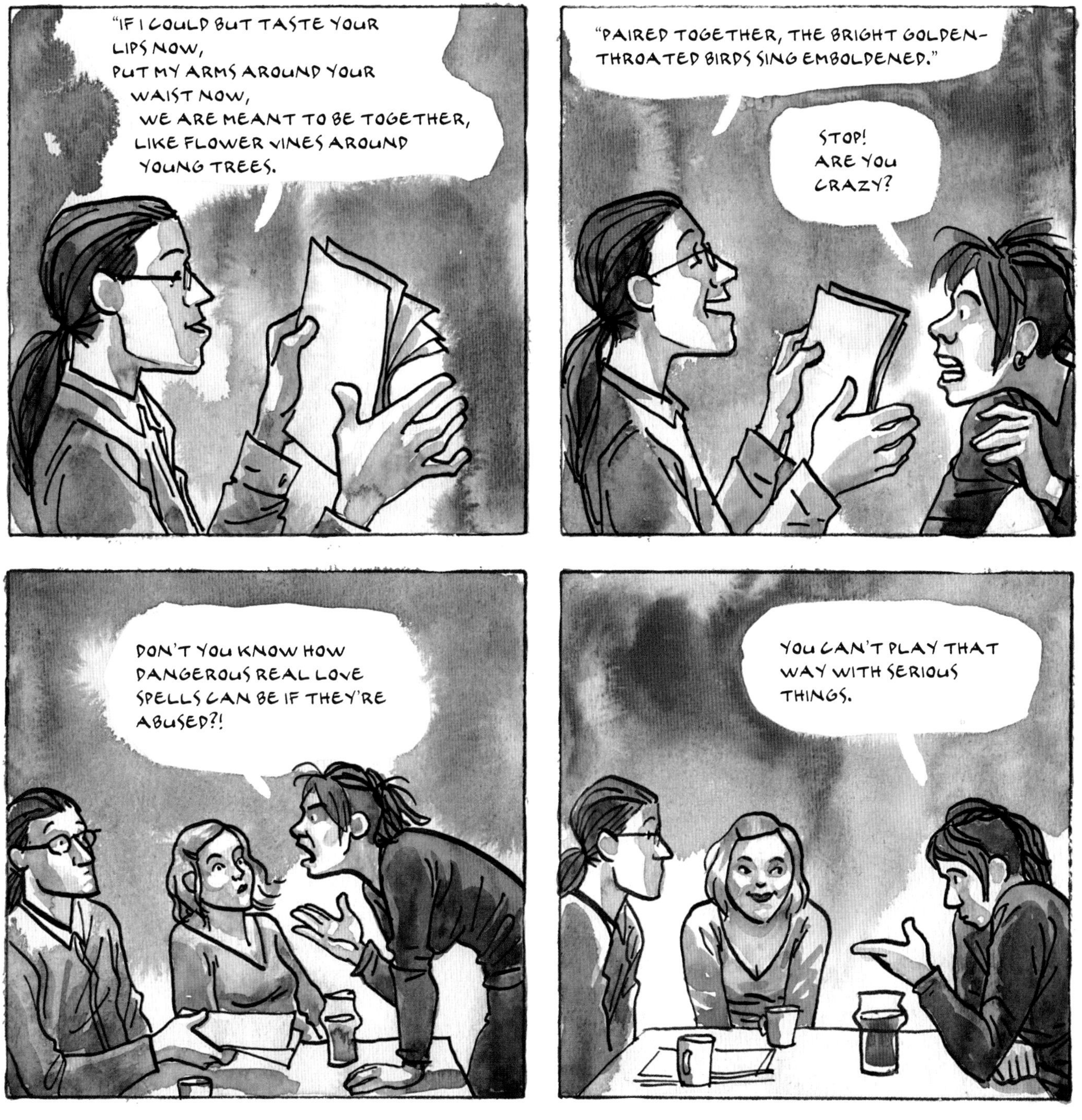
"IF I COULD BUT TASTE YOUR LIPS NOW, PUT MY ARMS AROUND YOUR WAIST NOW, WE ARE MEANT TO BE TOGETHER, LIKE FLOWER VINES AROUND YOUNG TREES.
"PAIRED TOGETHER, THE BRIGHT GOLDEN-THROATED BIRDS SING EMBOLDENED."
STOP! ARE YOU CRAZY?
DON'T YOU KNOW HOW DANGEROUS REAL LOVE SPELLS CAN BE IF THEY'RE ABUSED?!
YOU CAN'T PLAY THAT WAY WITH SERIOUS THINGS.

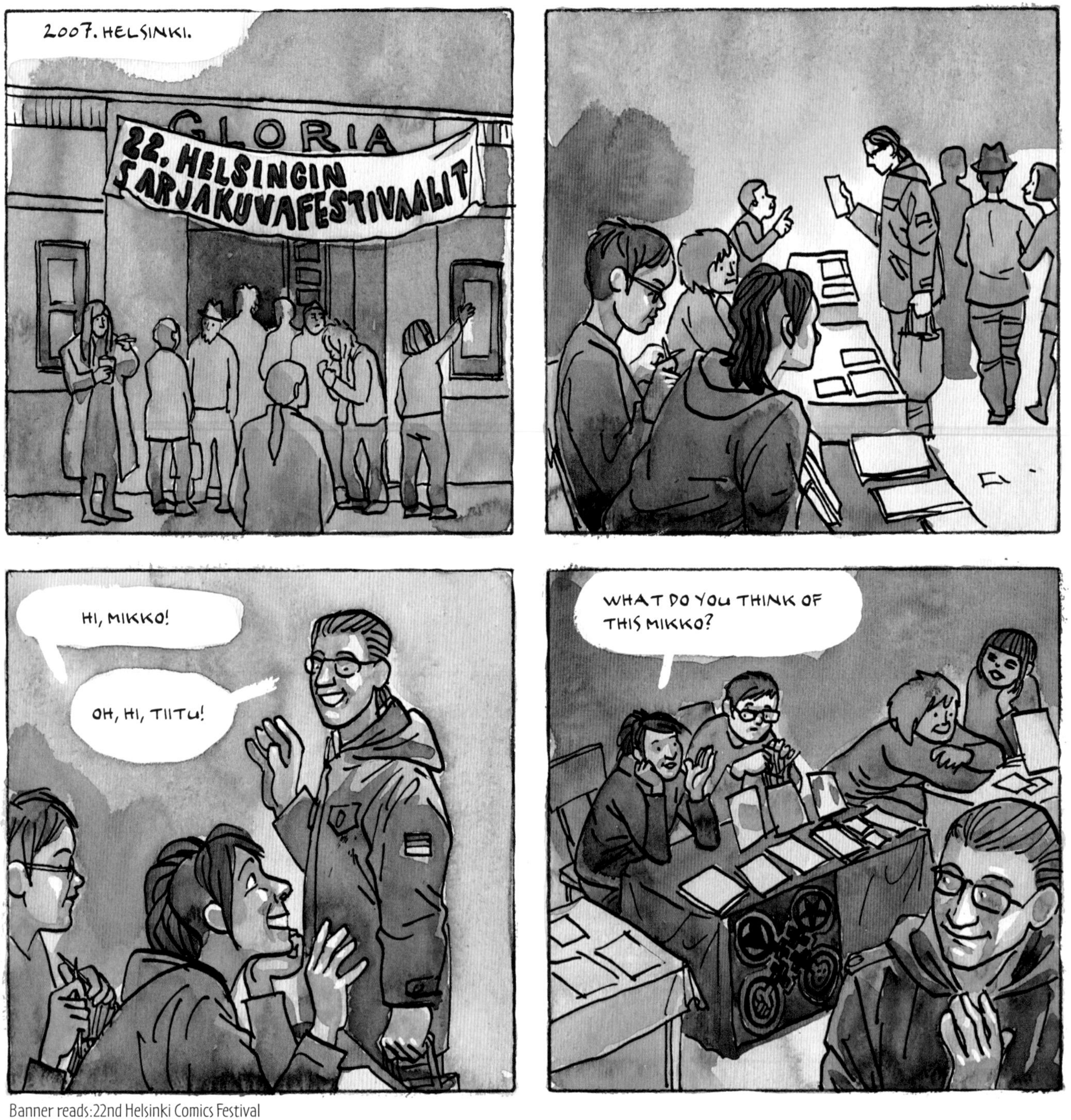
2007. HELSINKI.
GLORIA
22. HELSINGIN SARJAKUVAFESTIVAALIT
HI, MIKKO!
OH, HI, TIITU!
WHAT DO YOU THINK OF THIS MIKKO?

Banner reads:22nd Helsinki Comics Festival

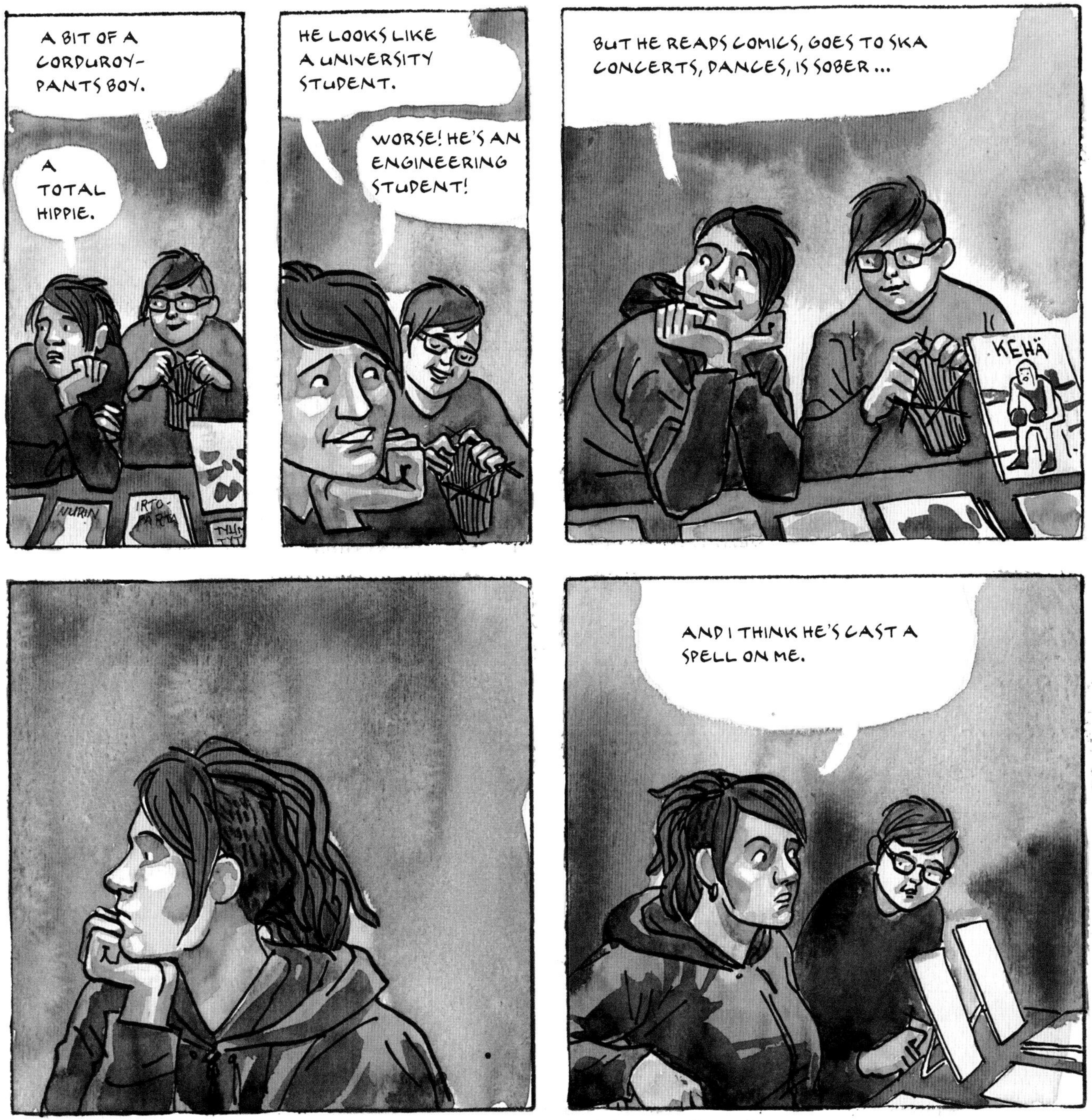
A BIT OF A CORDUROY-PANTS BOY.
A TOTAL HIPPIE.
HE LOOKS LIKE A UNIVERSITY STUDENT.
WORSE! HE'S AN ENGINEERING STUDENT!
BUT HE READS COMICS, GOES TO SKA CONCERTS, DANCES, IS SOBER ...
KEHÄ
AND I THINK HE'S CAST A SPELL ON ME.

On the book cover: Ring

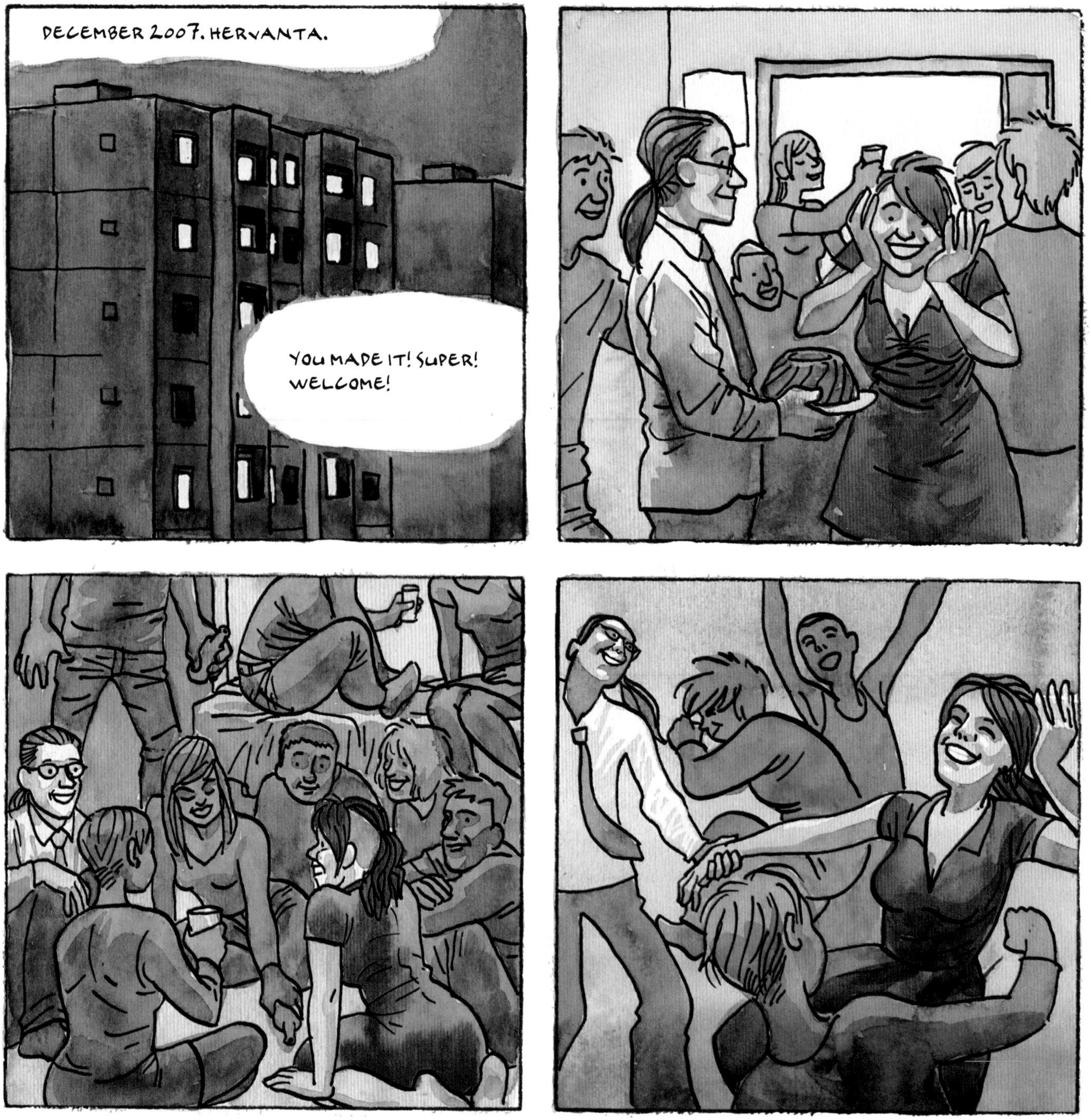
DECEMBER 2007. HERVANTA.
YOU MADE IT! SUPER! WELCOME!

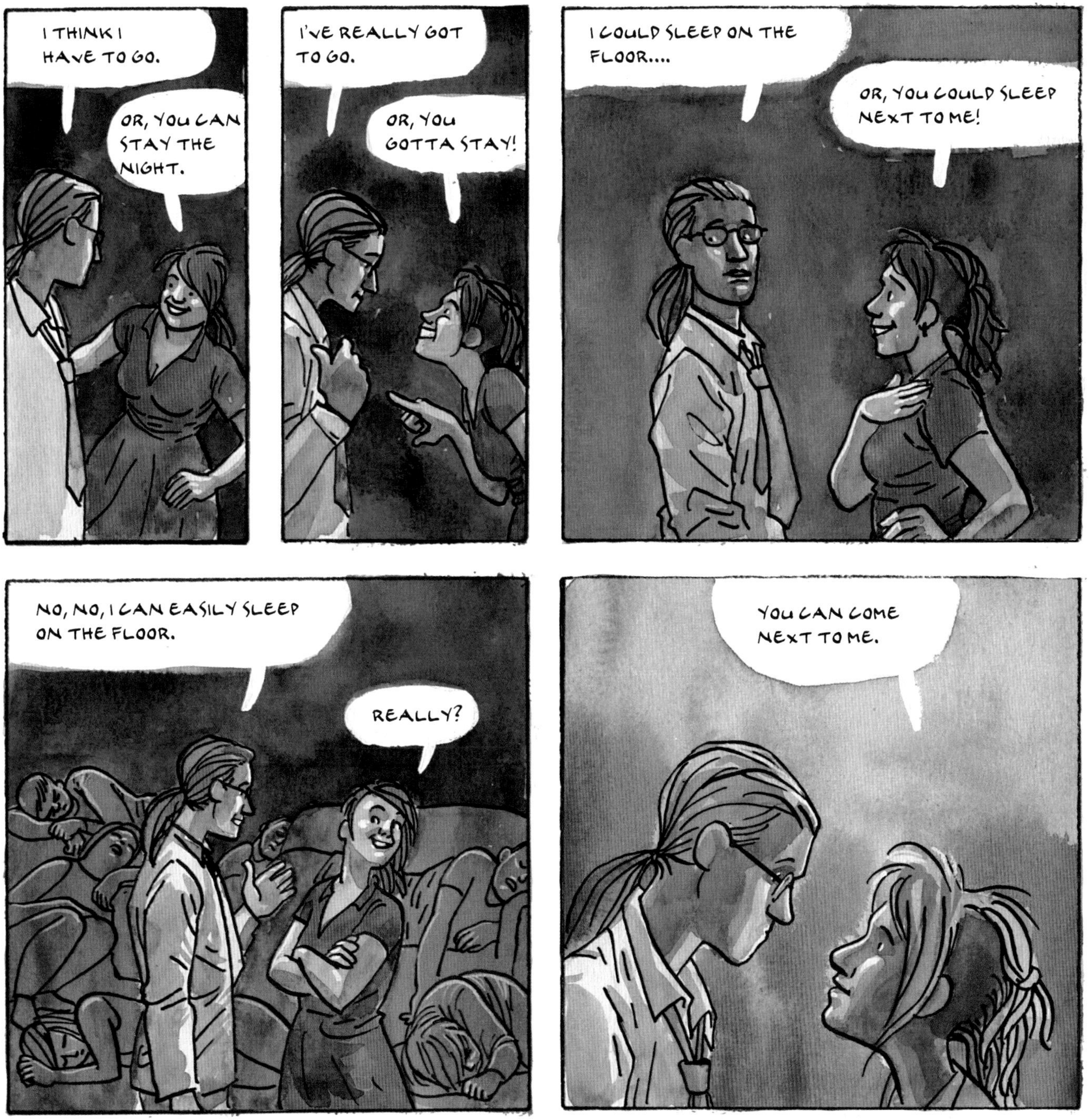
I THINK I HAVE TO GO.
OR, YOU CAN STAY THE NIGHT.
I'VE REALLY GOT TO GO.
OR, YOU GOTTA STAY!
I COULD SLEEP ON THE FLOOR....
OR, YOU COULD SLEEP NEXT TO ME!
NO, NO, I CAN EASILY SLEEP ON THE FLOOR.
REALLY?
YOU CAN COME NEXT TO ME.

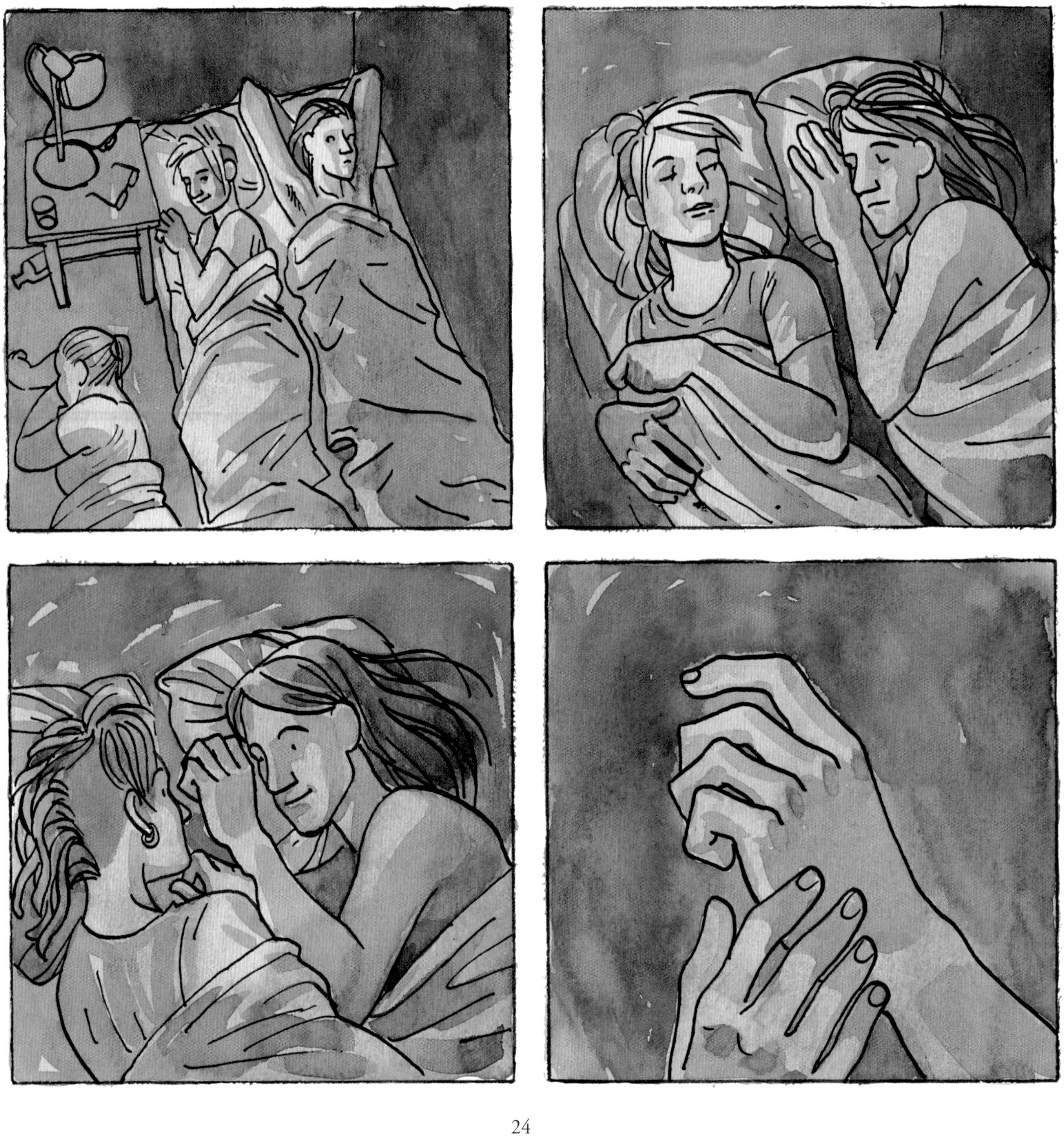

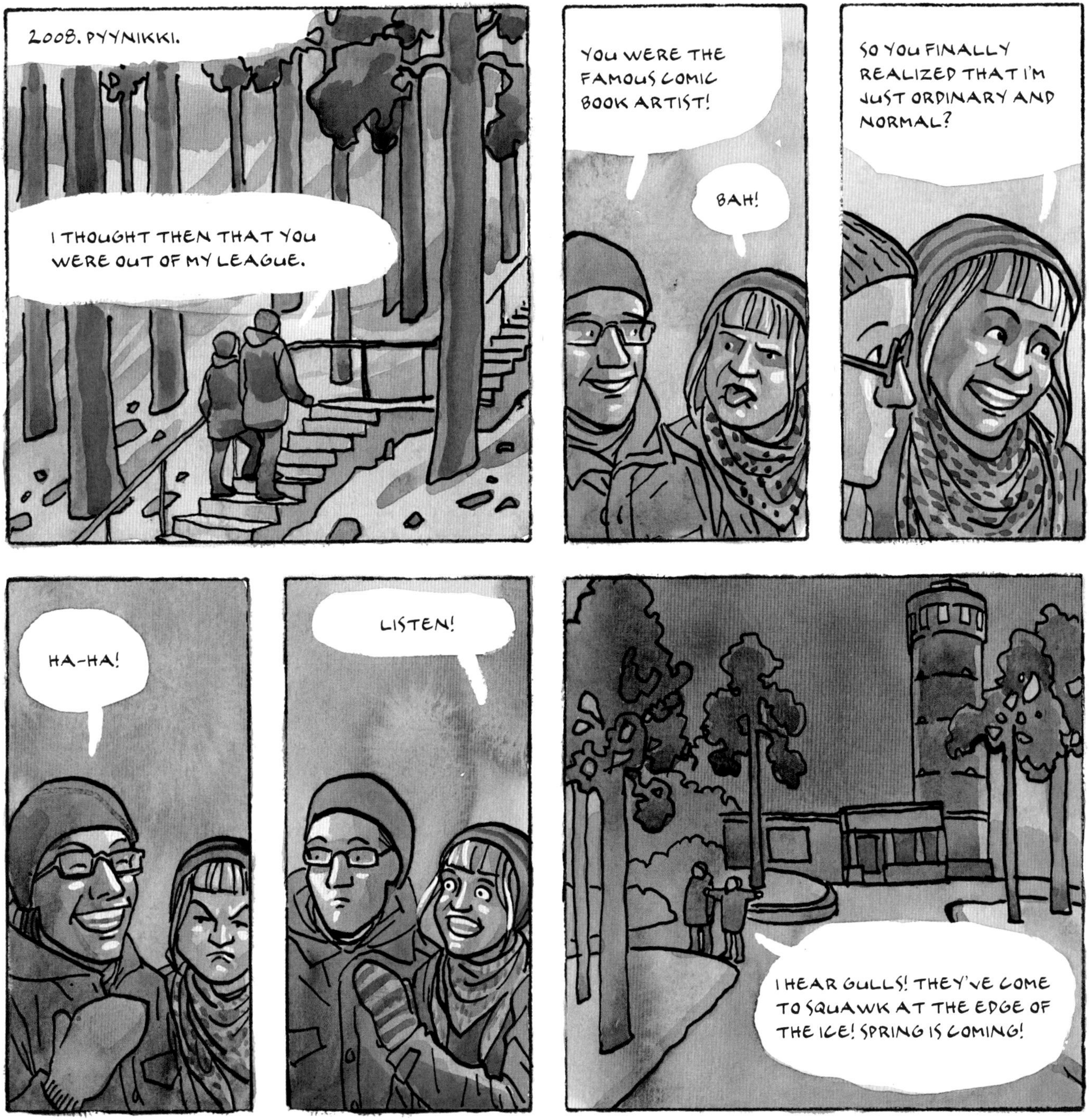
2008. PYYNIKKI.
I THOUGHT THEN THAT YOU WERE OUT OF MY LEAGUE.
YOU WERE THE FAMOUS COMIC BOOK ARTIST!
BAH!
SO YOU FINALLY REALIZED THAT I'M JUST ORDINARY AND NORMAL?
HA-HA!
LISTEN!
I HEAR GULLS! THEY'VE COME TO SQUAWK AT THE EDGE OF THE ICE! SPRING IS COMING!

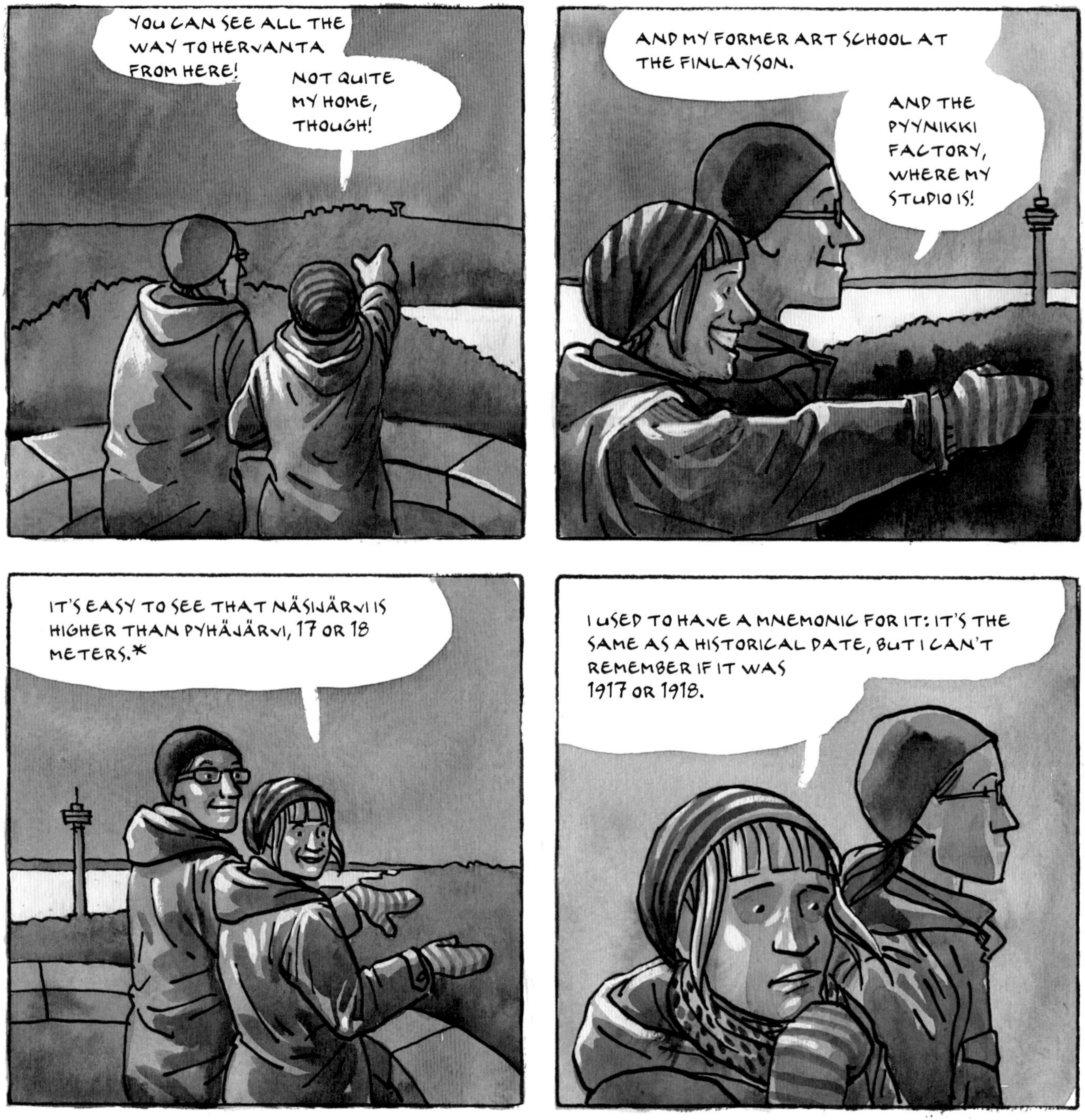
YOU CAN SEE ALL THE WAY TO HERVANTA FROM HERE!
NOT QUITE MY HOME, THOUGH!
AND MY FORMER ART SCHOOL AT THE FINLAYSON.
AND THE PYYNIKKI FACTORY, WHERE MY STUDIO IS!
IT'S EASY TO SEE THAT NÄSIJÄRVI IS HIGHER THAN PYHÄJÄRVI, 17 OR 18 METERS.*
I USED TO HAVE A MNEMONIC FOR IT: IT'S THE SAME AS A HISTORICAL DATE, BUT I CAN'T REMEMBER IF IT WAS 1917 OR 1918.

*56 or 59 feet

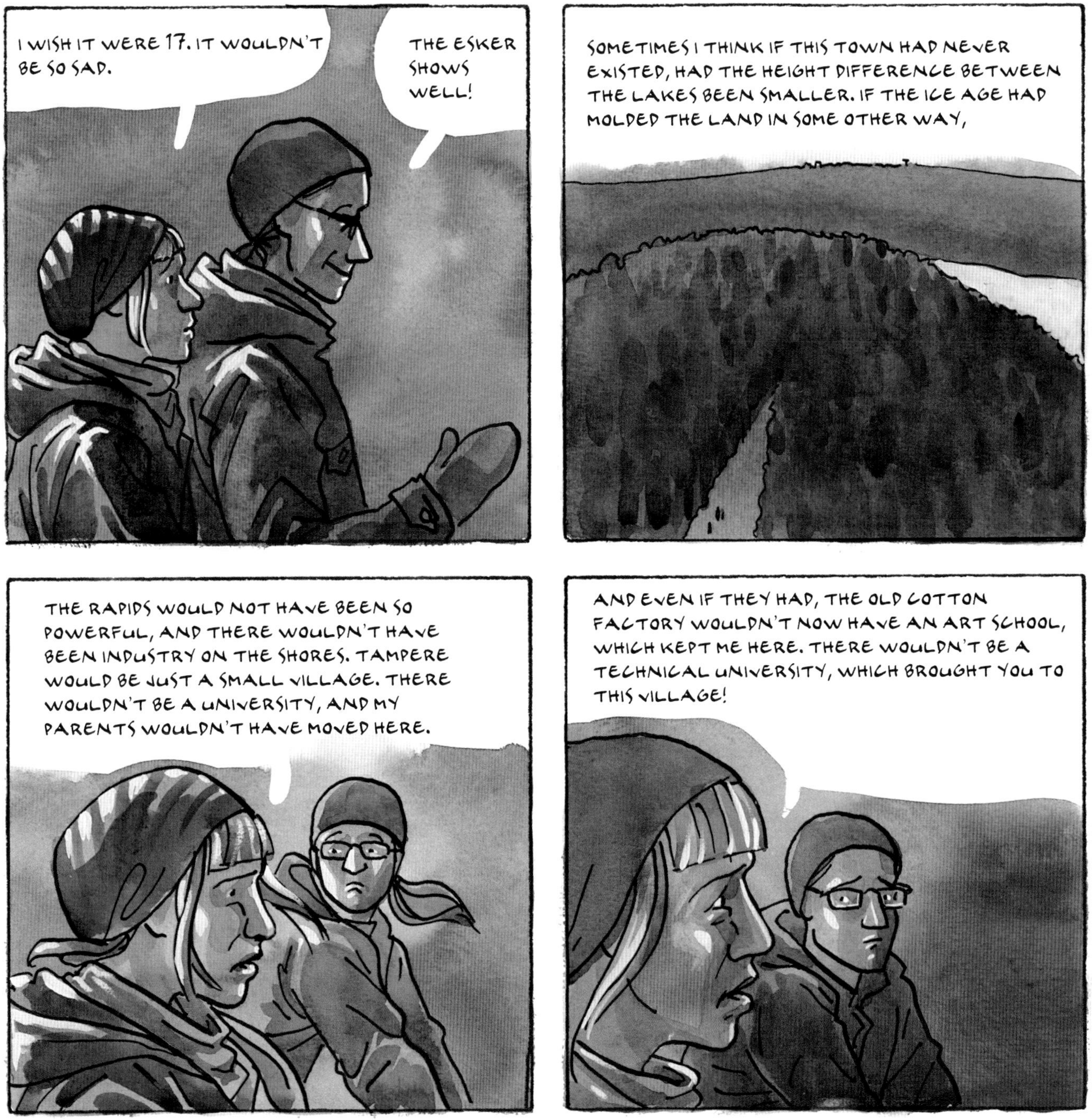
I WISH IT WERE 17. IT WOULDN'T BE SO SAD.
THE ESKER SHOWS WELL!
SOMETIMES I THINK IF THIS TOWN HAD NEVER EXISTED, HAD THE HEIGHT DIFFERENCE BETWEEN THE LAKES BEEN SMALLER. IF THE ICE AGE HAD MOLDED THE LAND IN SOME OTHER WAY,
THE RAPIDS WOULD NOT HAVE BEEN SO POWERFUL, AND THERE WOULDN'T HAVE BEEN INDUSTRY ON THE SHORES. TAMPERE WOULD BE JUST A SMALL VILLAGE. THERE WOULDN'T BE A UNIVERSITY, AND MY PARENTS WOULDN'T HAVE MOVED HERE.
AND EVEN IF THEY HAD, THE OLD COTTON FACTORY WOULDN'T NOW HAVE AN ART SCHOOL, WHICH KEPT ME HERE. THERE WOULDN'T BE A TECHNICAL UNIVERSITY, WHICH BROUGHT YOU TO THIS VILLAGE!

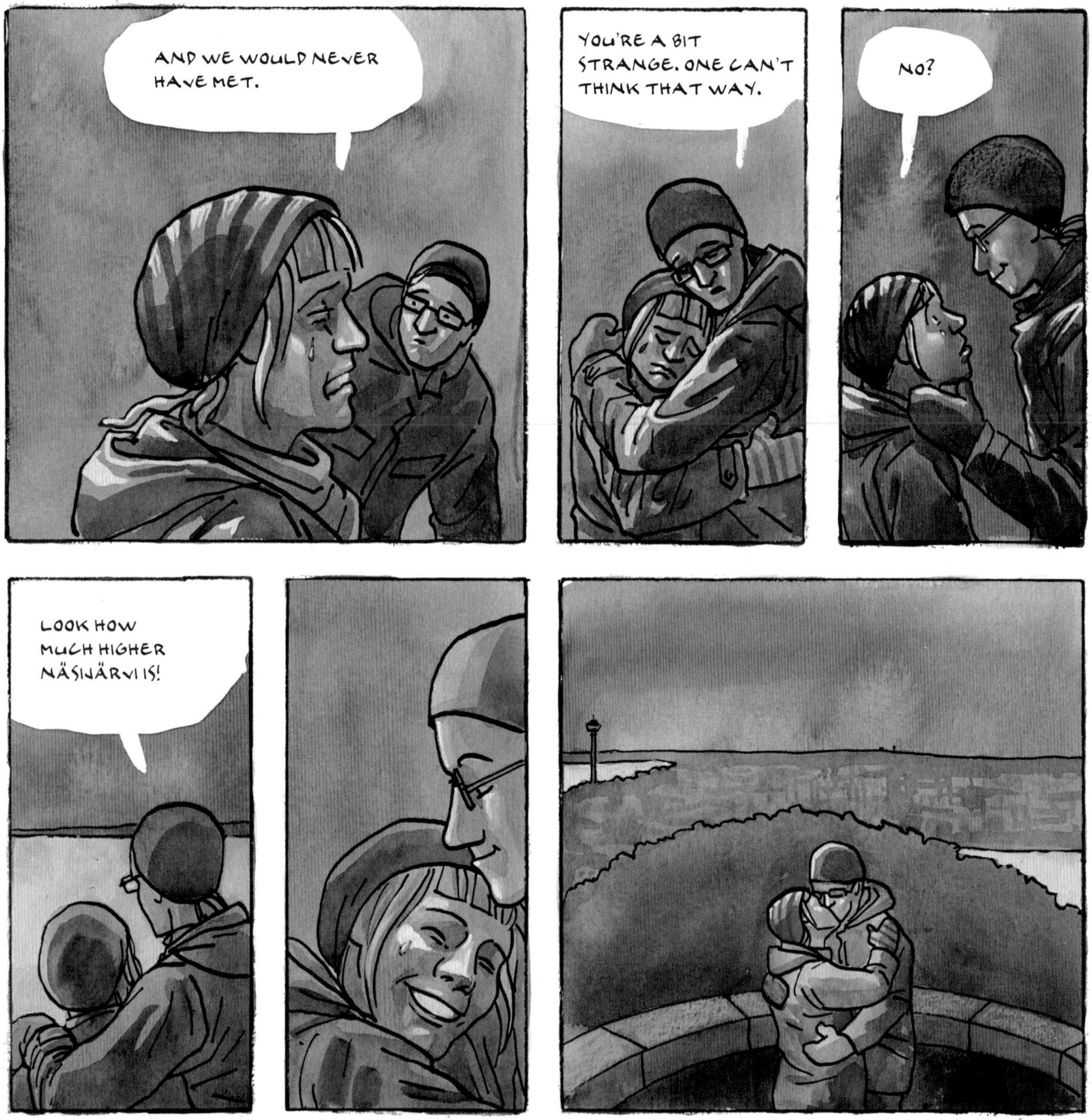
AND WE WOULD NEVER HAVE MET.
YOU'RE A BIT STRANGE. ONE CAN'T THINK THAT WAY.
NO?
LOOK HOW MUCH HIGHER NÄSIJÄRVI IS!

FACTORY, TOWN

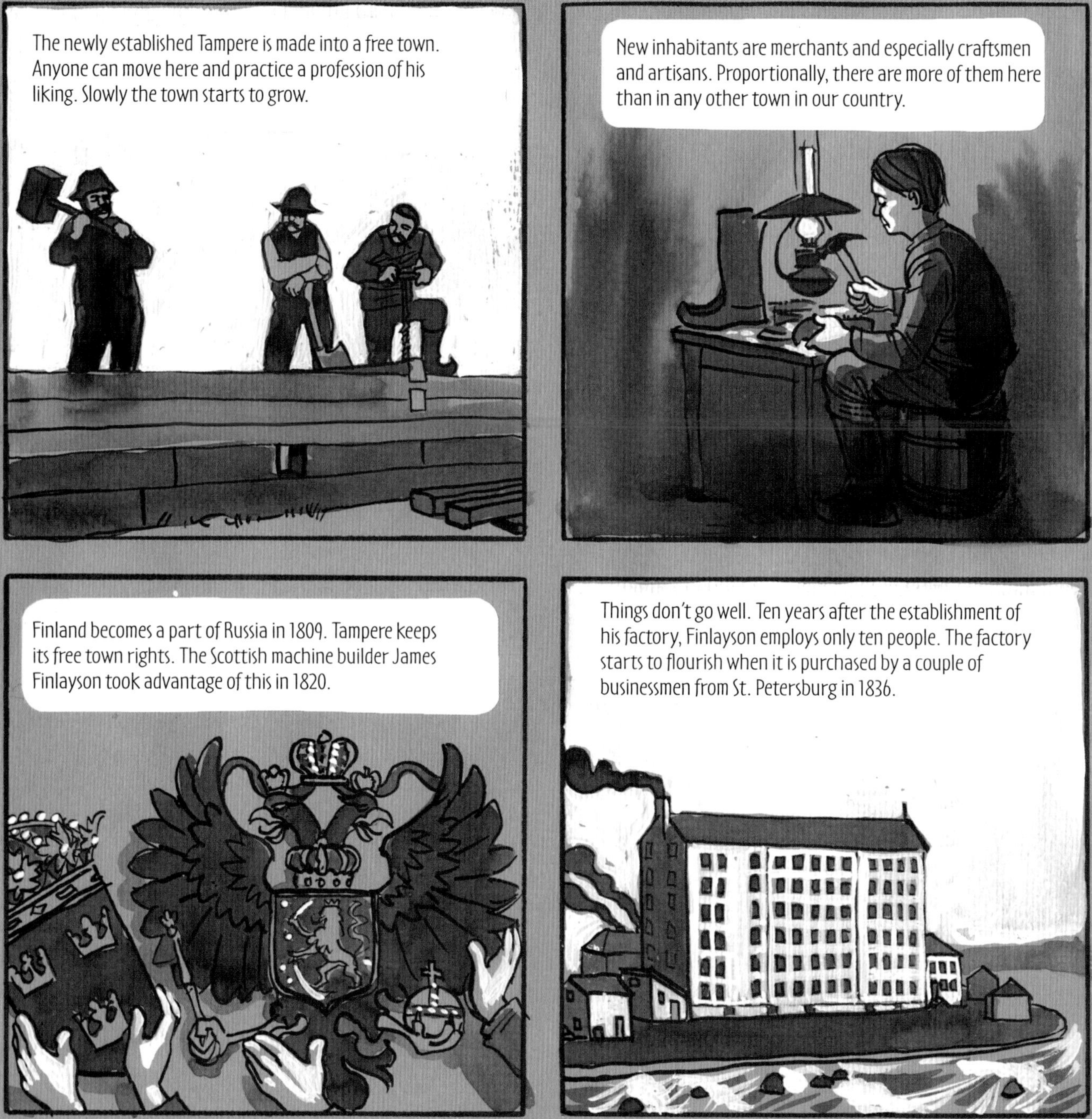
The newly established Tampere is made into a free town. Anyone can move here and practice a profession of his liking. Slowly the town starts to grow.
New inhabitants are merchants and especially craftsmen and artisans. Proportionally, there are more of them here than in any other town in our country.
Finland becomes a part of Russia in 1809. Tampere keeps its free town rights. The Scottish machine builder James Finlayson took advantage of this in 1820.
Things don't go well. Ten years after the establishment of his factory, Finlayson employs only ten people. The factory starts to flourish when it is purchased by a couple of businessmen from St. Petersburg in 1836.

In the 1850s, there are three times more factory workers in the town than craftsmen. Finlayson becomes Finland's biggest industrial complex.

At the turn of the century, Finlayson already has 3,000 employees.

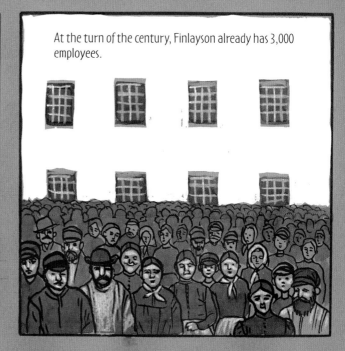

In addition, five other factories rise on the side of the rapids. Almost half of Finland's industrial workers are employed on the shores of the Tammerkoski.

Even though industrialization came slowly to Finland, Tampere industrialized at the same pace as the rest of Europe.

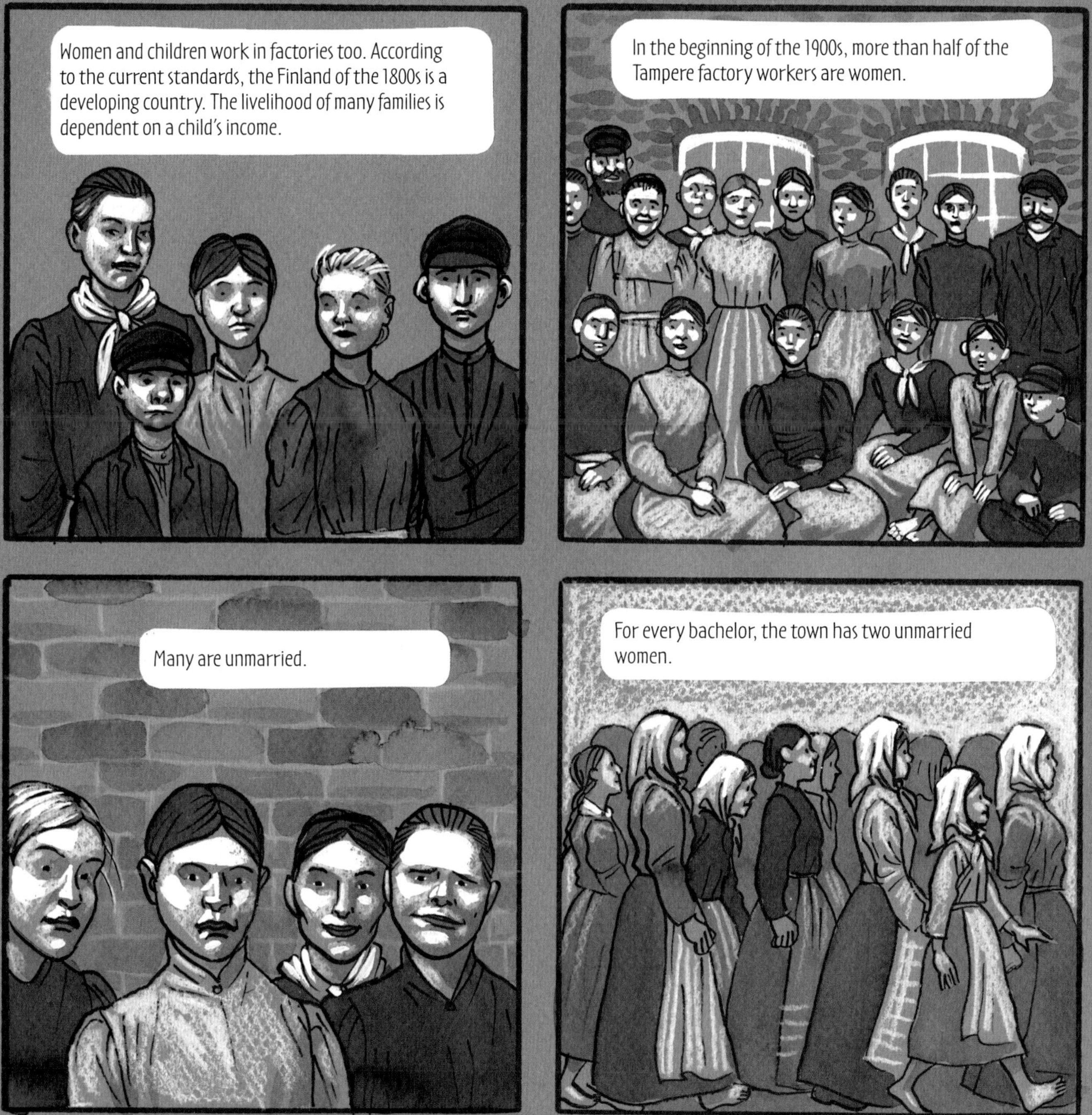
Women and children work in factories too. According to the current standards, the Finland of the 1800s is a developing country. The livelihood of many families is dependent on a child's income.
In the beginning of the 1900s, more than half of the Tampere factory workers are women.
Many are unmarried.
For every bachelor, the town has two unmarried women.

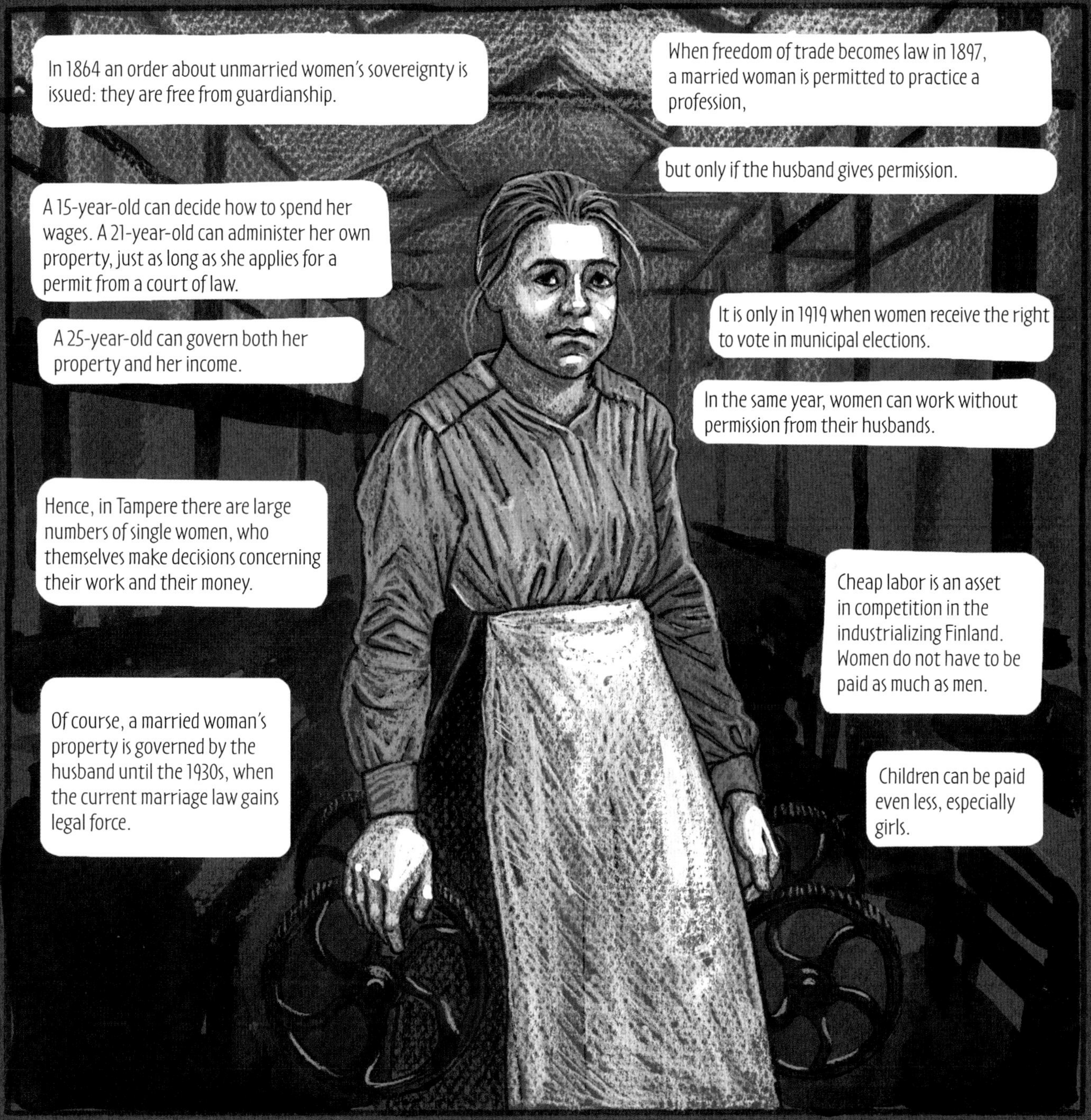
In 1864 an order about unmarried women's sovereignty is issued: they are free from guardianship.
When freedom of trade becomes law in 1897, a married woman is permitted to practice a profession,
but only if the husband gives permission.
A 15-year-old can decide how to spend her wages. A 21-year-old can administer her own property, just as long as she applies for a permit from a court of law.
A 25-year-old can govern both her property and her income.
It is only in 1919 when women receive the right to vote in municipal elections.
In the same year, women can work without permission from their husbands.
Hence, in Tampere there are large numbers of single women, who themselves make decisions concerning their work and their money.
Cheap labor is an asset in competition in the industrializing Finland. Women do not have to be paid as much as men.
Of course, a married woman's property is governed by the husband until the 1930s, when the current marriage law gains legal force.
Children can be paid even less, especially girls.

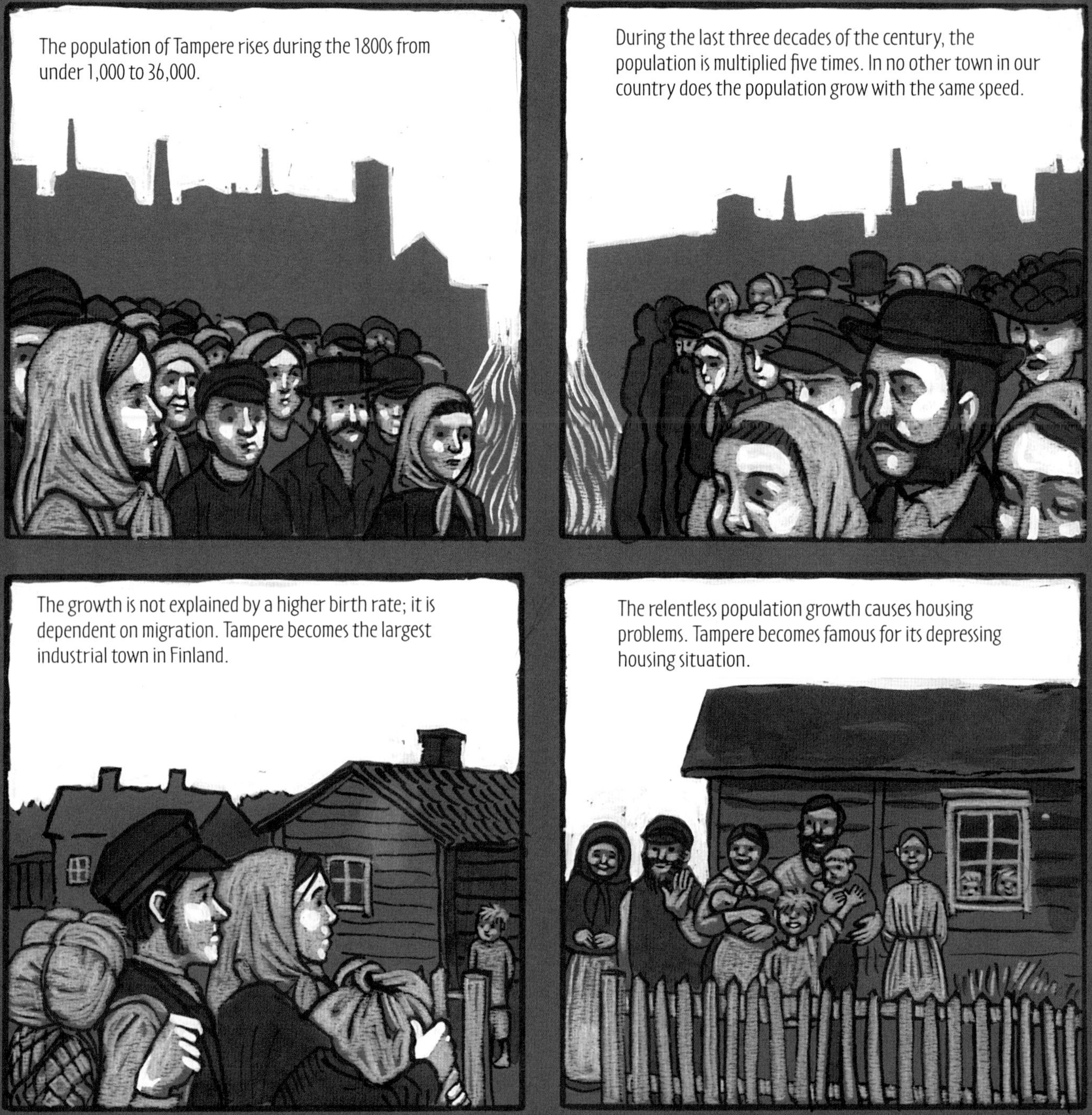
The population of Tampere rises during the 1800s from under 1,000 to 36,000.
During the last three decades of the century, the population is multiplied five times. In no other town in our country does the population grow with the same speed.
The growth is not explained by a higher birth rate; it is dependent on migration. Tampere becomes the largest industrial town in Finland.
The relentless population growth causes housing problems. Tampere becomes famous for its depressing housing situation.

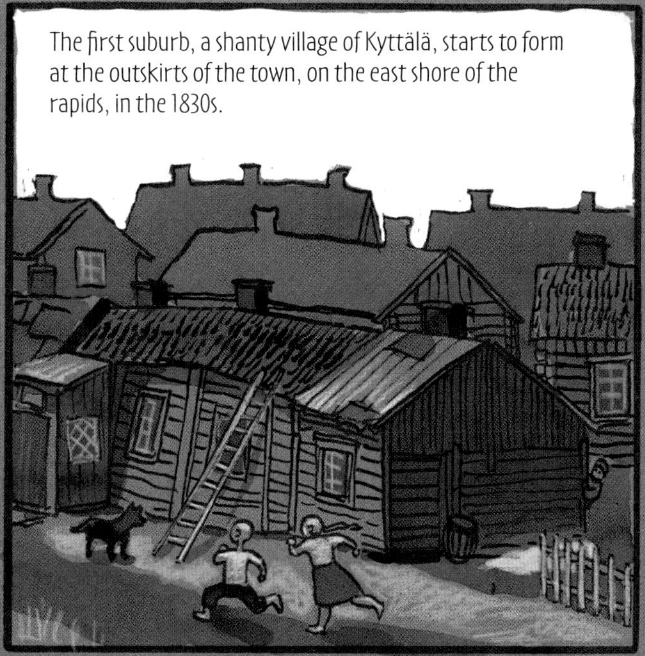
The first suburb, a shanty village of Kyttälä, starts to form at the outskirts of the town, on the east shore of the rapids, in the 1830s.

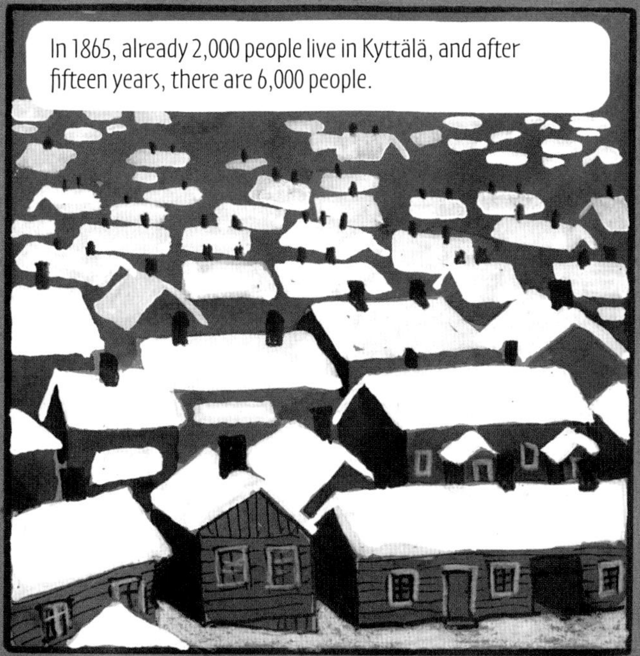
In 1865, already 2,000 people live in Kyttälä, and after fifteen years, there are 6,000 people.

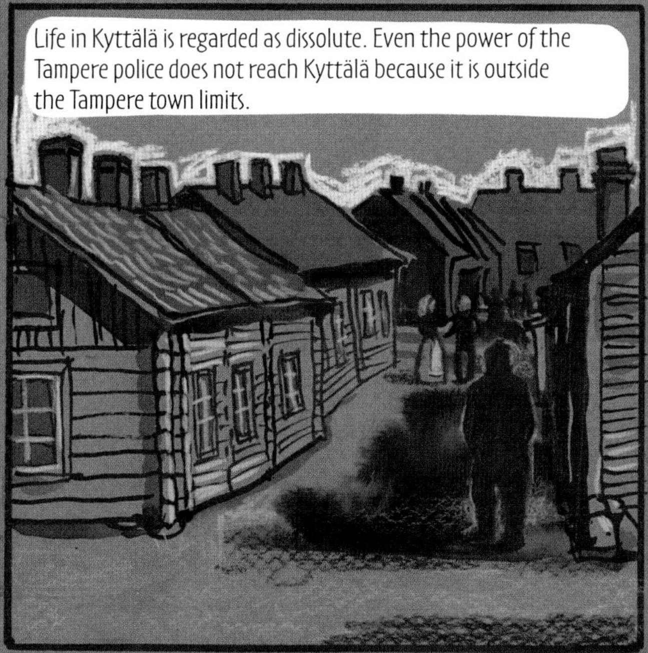
Life in Kyttälä is regarded as dissolute. Even the power of the Tampere police does not reach Kyttälä because it is outside the Tampere town limits.

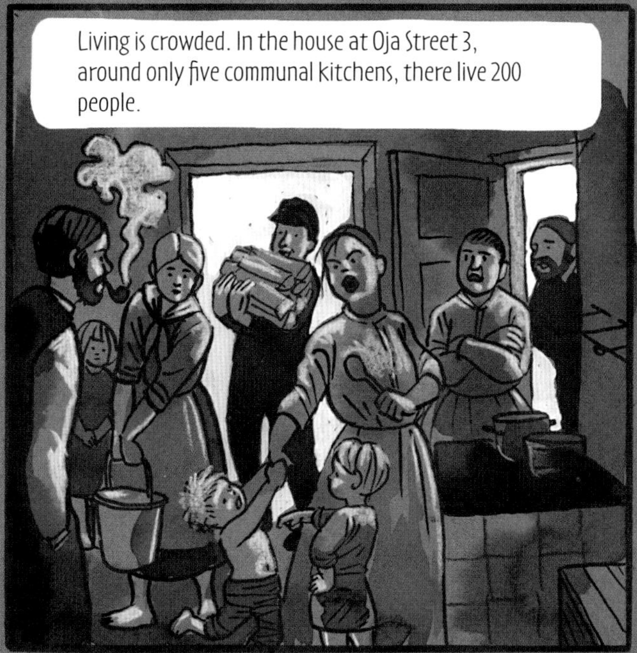
Living is crowded. In the house at Oja Street 3, around only five communal kitchens, there live 200 people.

In 1876, Tampere buys the lands of Kyttälä, which receives a new urban plan. It does not include poor people's hovels. Rental agreements are canceled.

Those evicted are pointed toward plots at Armonkallio.* The area is built up fast. In 1900 there are already over 2,000 inhabitants.

People from Kyttälä move also to the side of Pirkkala, to the Pispala esker.

There is no town plan in Pispala, and people build their cottages however they please and how they can. Lots are on a steep slope; the ice age had done its best when it was forming this hill.

*Armonkallio translates into English literally as "mercy rock." For the first five years the people would not have to pay rent for the lots, and these "years of mercy" gave the name for this part of Tampere: Armonkallio.

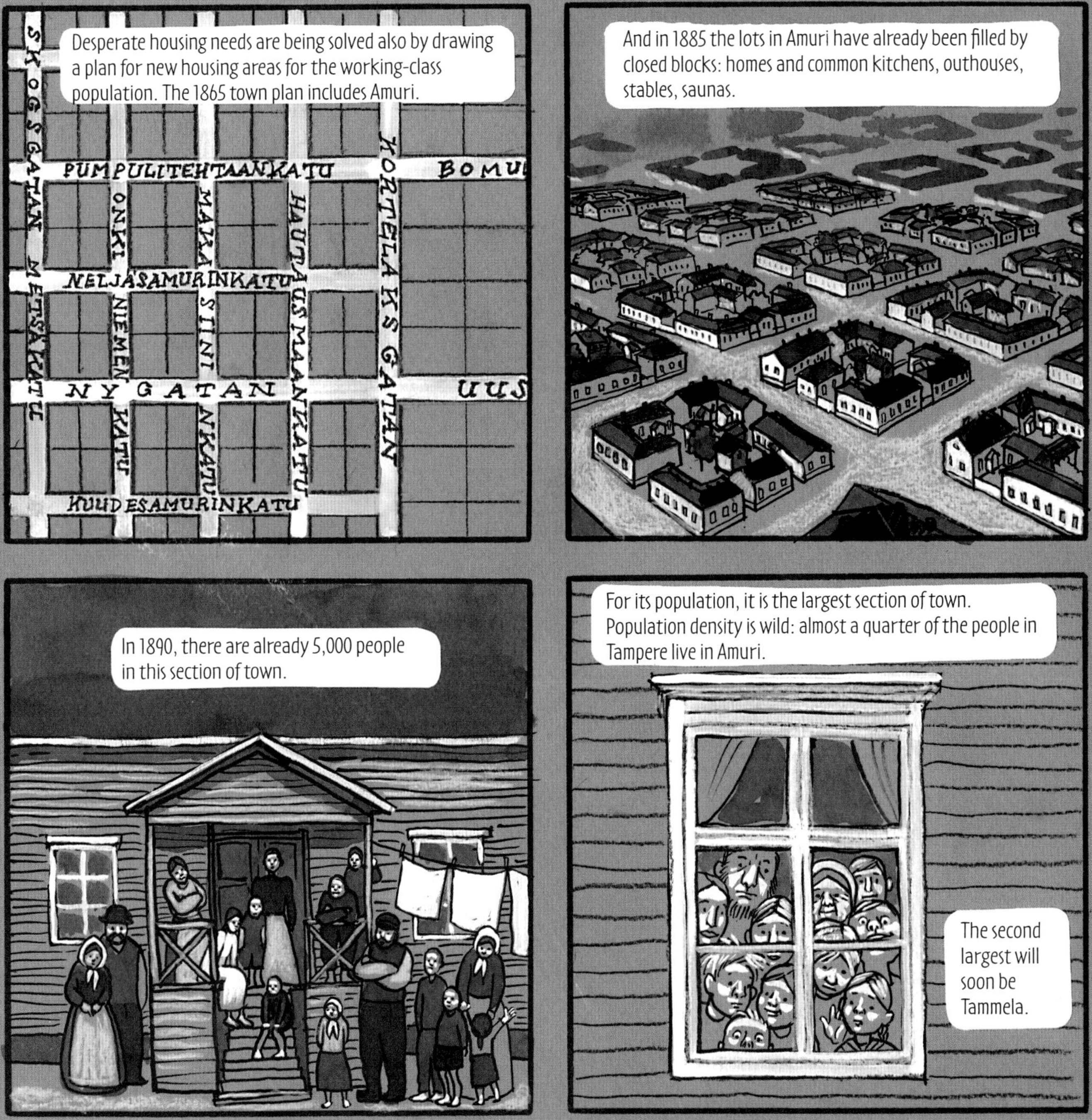
Desperate housing needs are being solved also by drawing a plan for new housing areas for the working-class population. The 1865 town plan includes Amuri.
PUMPULITEHTAANKATU
BOMU
NELJÄSAMURINKATU
NY GATAN
UUS
KUUDESAMURINKATU
KORTELAKS GATAN
HAUTAUSMAANKATU
And in 1885 the lots in Amuri have already been filled by closed blocks: homes and common kitchens, outhouses, stables, saunas.
In 1890, there are already 5,000 people in this section of town.
For its population, it is the largest section of town. Population density is wild: almost a quarter of the people in Tampere live in Amuri.
The second largest will soon be Tammela.

XIV SECTION OF TOWN

BLOCK 247, LOTS 85 AND 86

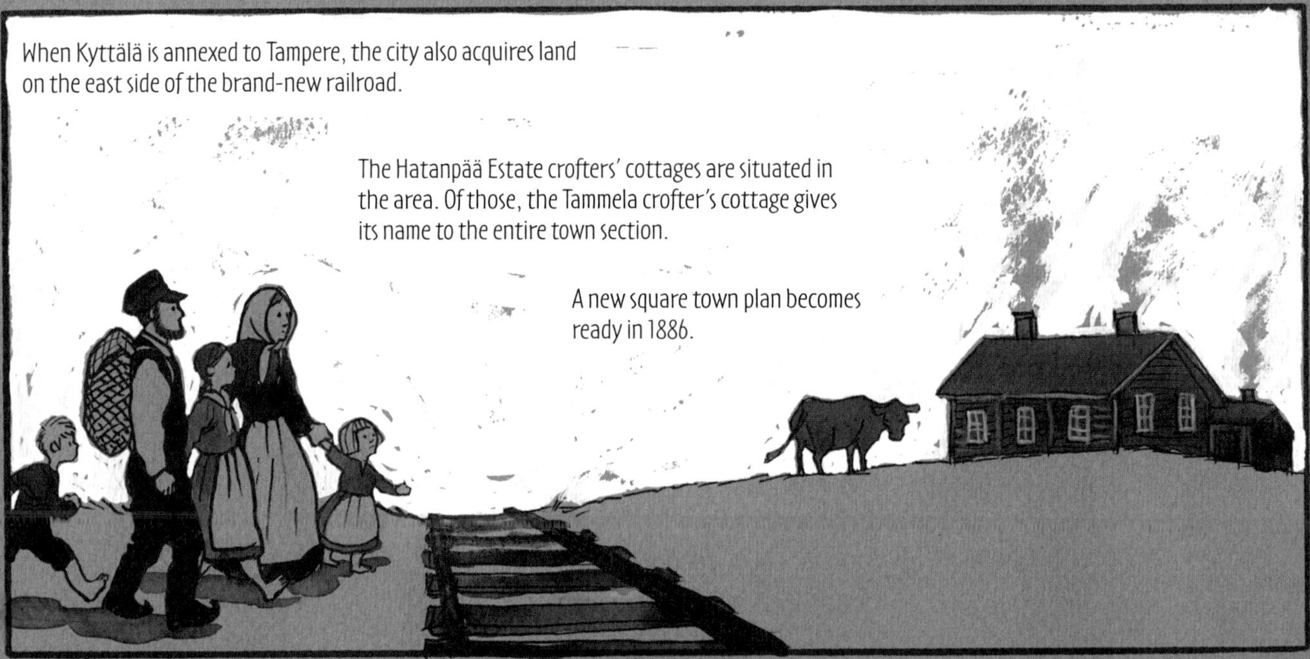
When Kyttälä is annexed to Tampere, the city also acquires land on the east side of the brand-new railroad.
The Hatanpää Estate crofters' cottages are situated in the area. Of those, the Tammela crofter's cottage gives its name to the entire town section.
A new square town plan becomes ready in 1886.

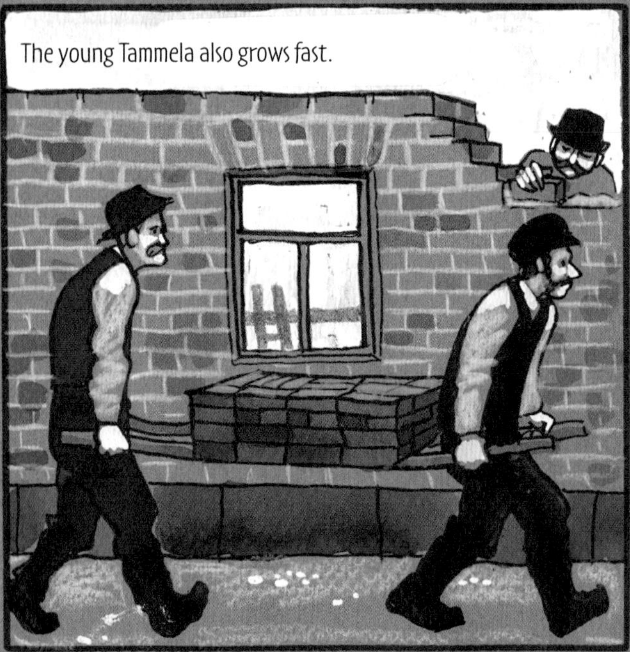
The young Tammela also grows fast.

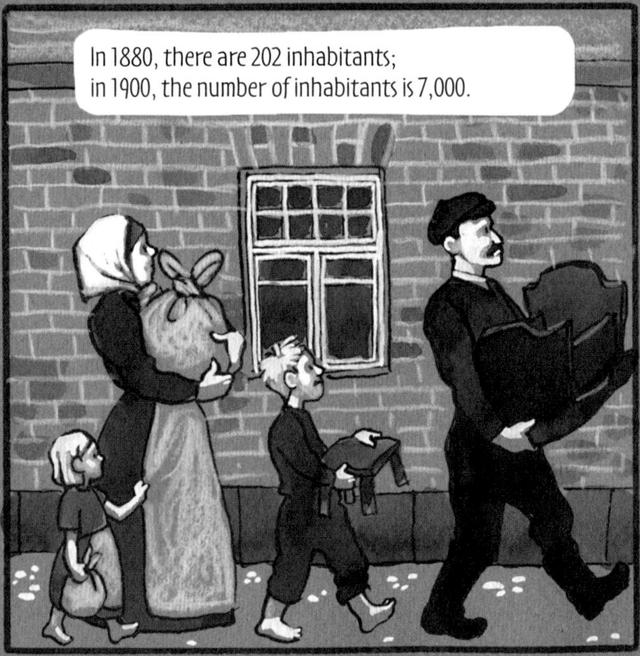
In 1880, there are 202 inhabitants; in 1900, the number of inhabitants is 7,000.

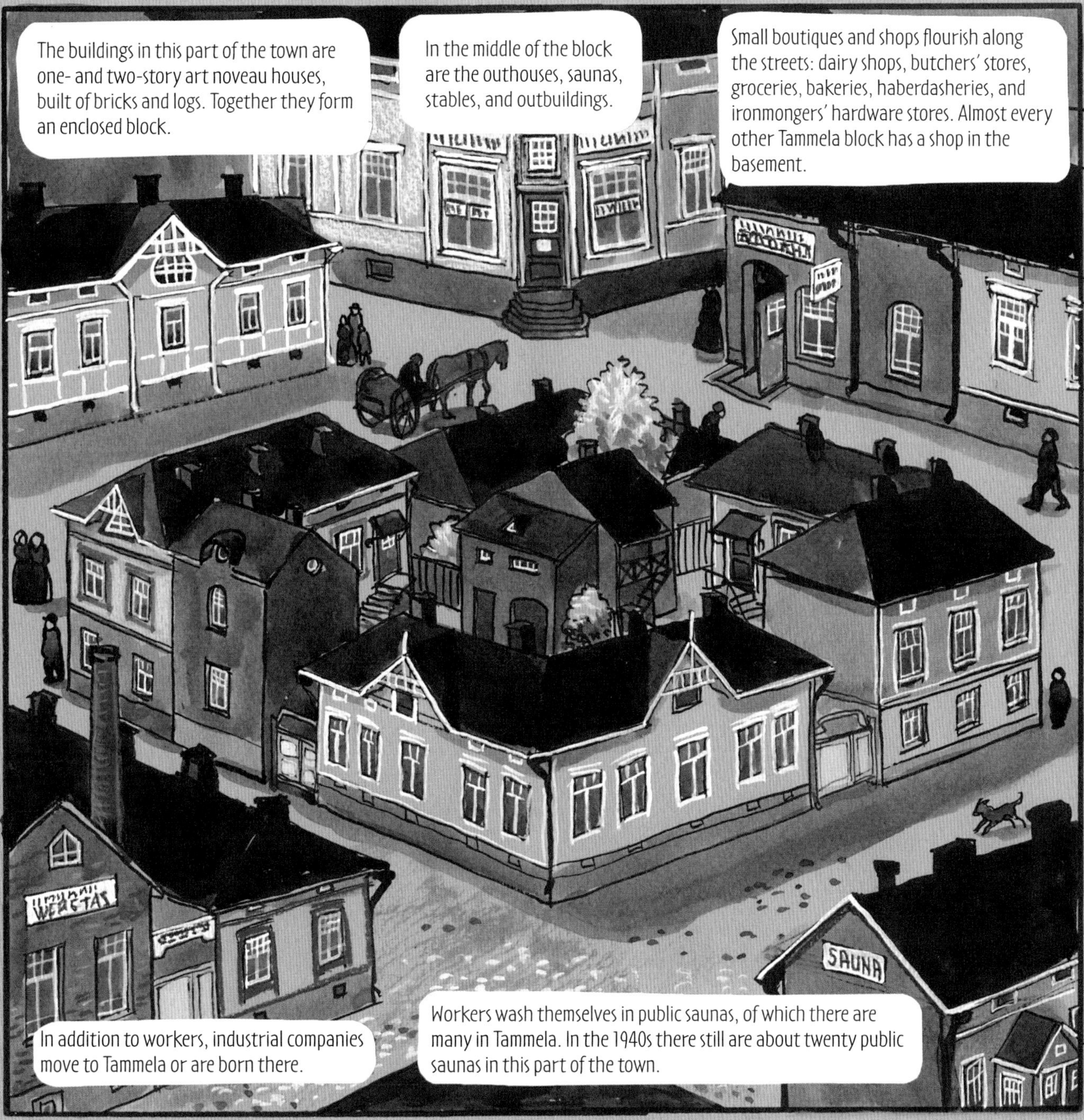
The buildings in this part of the town are one- and two-story art noveau houses, built of bricks and logs. Together they form an enclosed block.
In the middle of the block are the outhouses, saunas, stables, and outbuildings.
Small boutiques and shops flourish along the streets: dairy shops, butchers' stores, groceries, bakeries, haberdasheries, and ironmongers' hardware stores. Almost every other Tammela block has a shop in the basement.
SAUNA
In addition to workers, industrial companies move to Tammela or are born there.
Workers wash themselves in public saunas, of which there are many in Tammela. In the 1940s there still are about twenty public saunas in this part of the town.

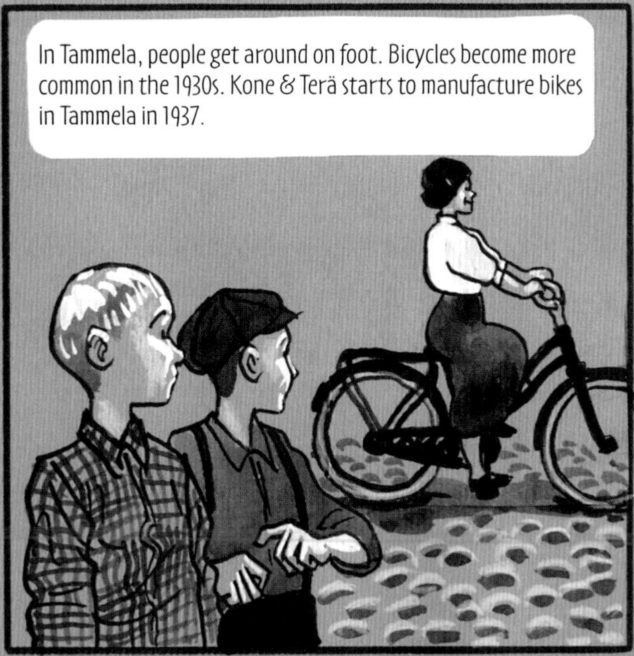
In Tammela, people get around on foot. Bicycles become more common in the 1930s. Kone & Terä starts to manufacture bikes in Tammela in 1937.

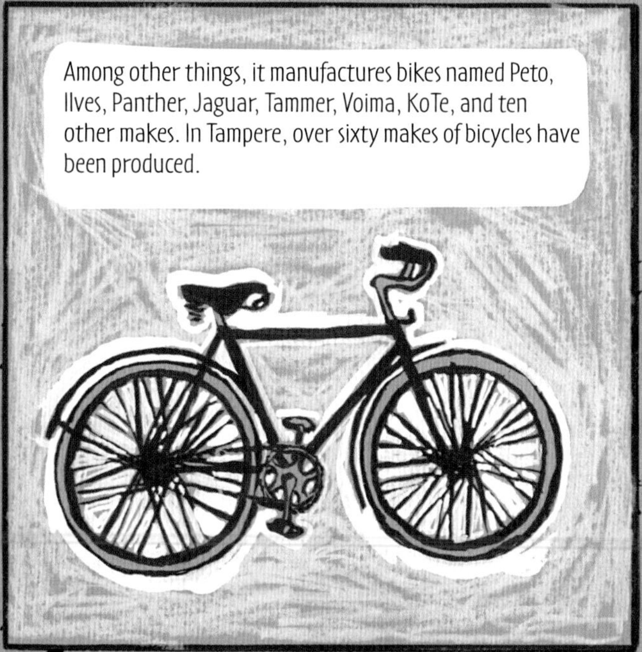
Among other things, it manufactures bikes named Peto, Ilves, Panther, Jaguar, Tammer, Voima, KoTe, and ten other makes. In Tampere, over sixty makes of bicycles have been produced.

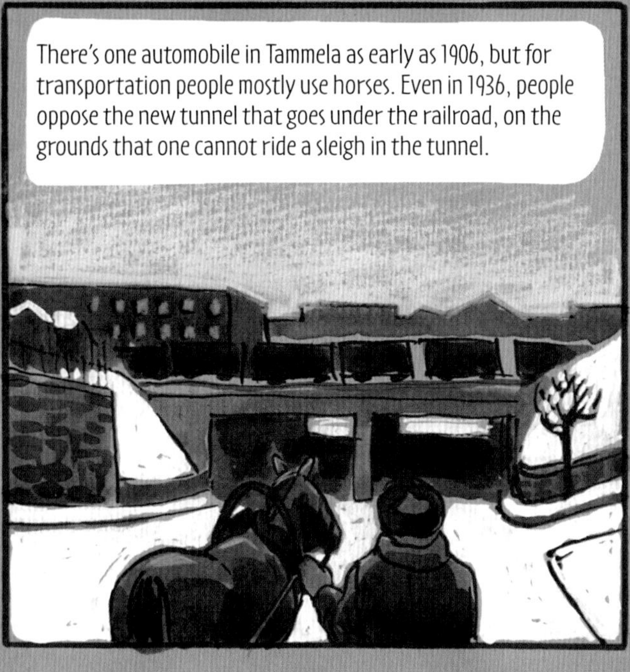
There's one automobile in Tammela as early as 1906, but for transportation people mostly use horses. Even in 1936, people oppose the new tunnel that goes under the railroad, on the grounds that one cannot ride a sleigh in the tunnel.

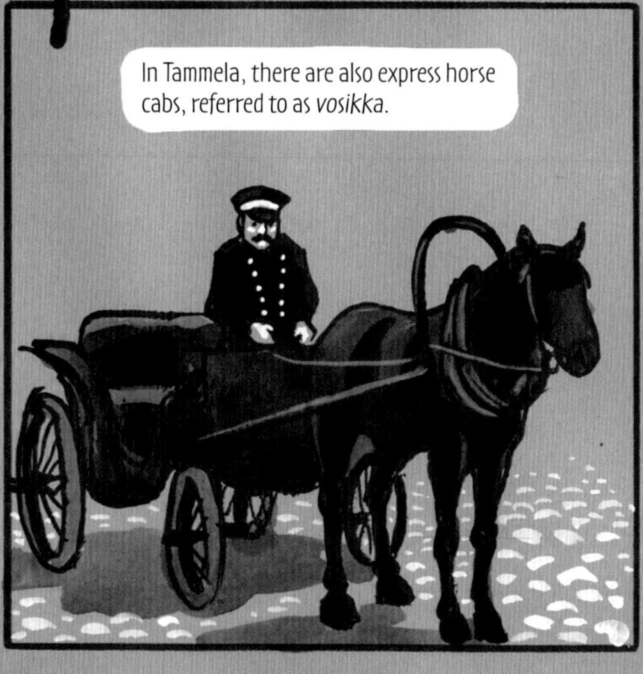
In Tammela, there are also express horse cabs, referred to as *vosikka*.

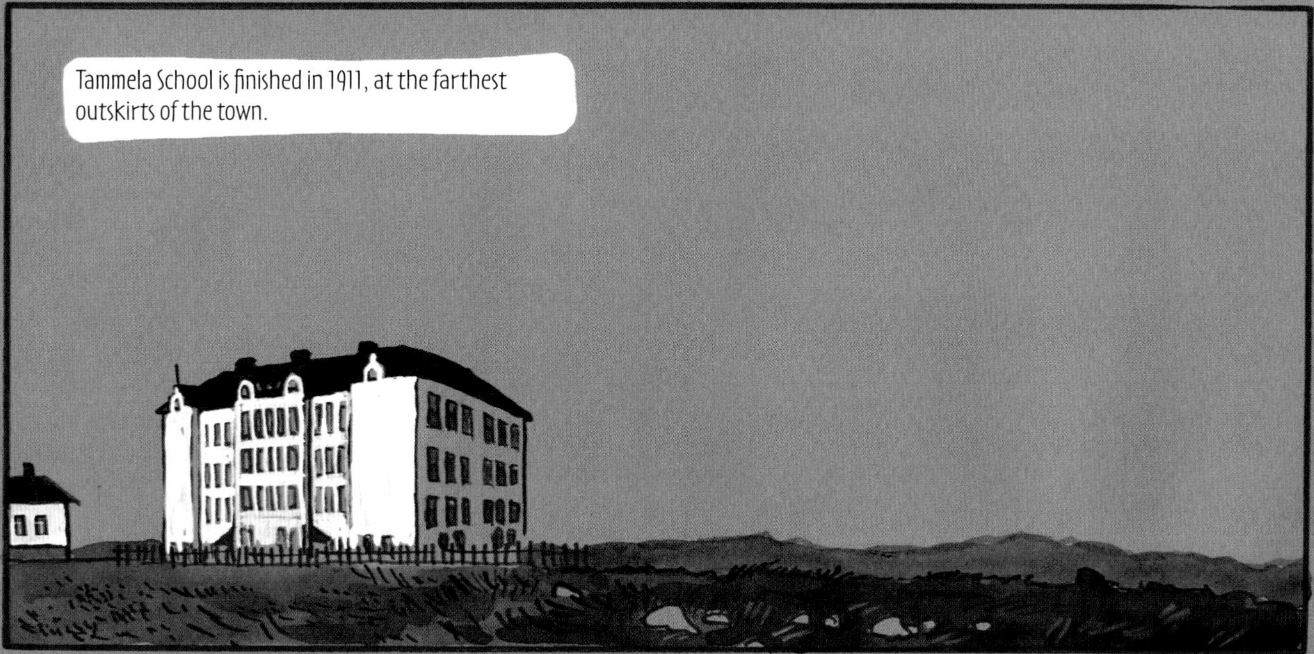
Tammela School is finished in 1911, at the farthest outskirts of the town.

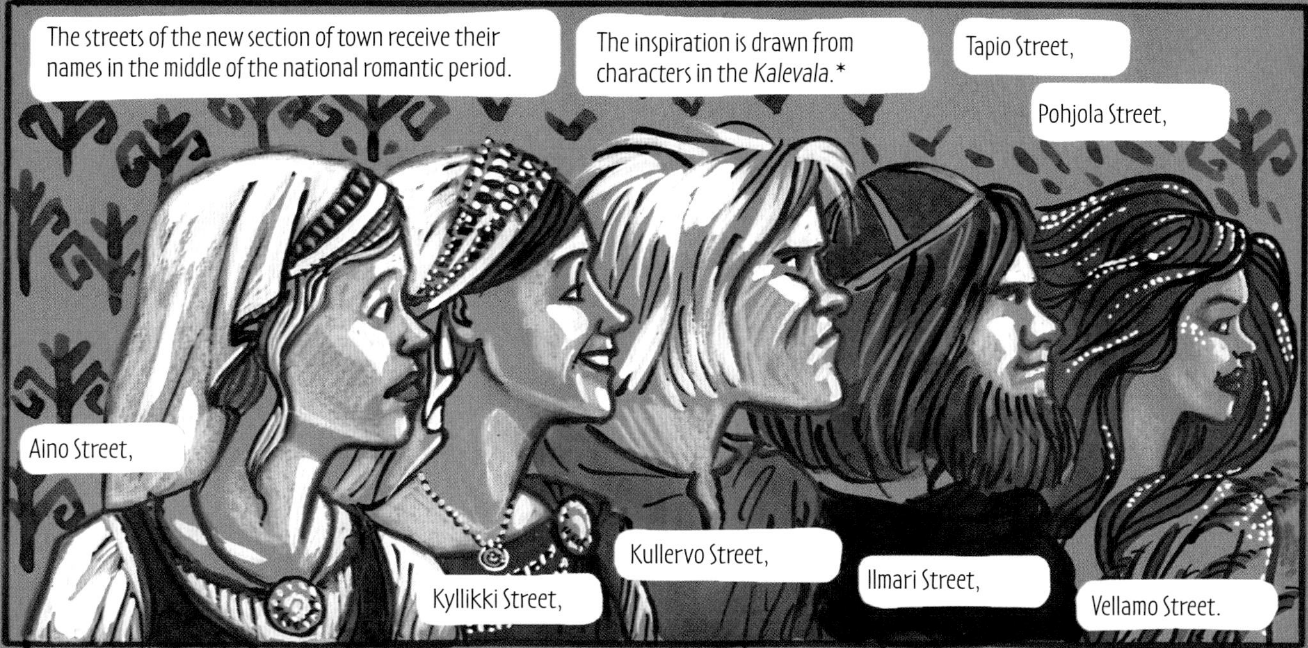
The streets of the new section of town receive their names in the middle of the national romantic period.
The inspiration is drawn from characters in the *Kalevala*.*
Tapio Street,
Pohjola Street,
Aino Street,
Kyllikki Street,
Kullervo Street,
Ilmari Street,
Vellamo Street.

*Finland's national epic.

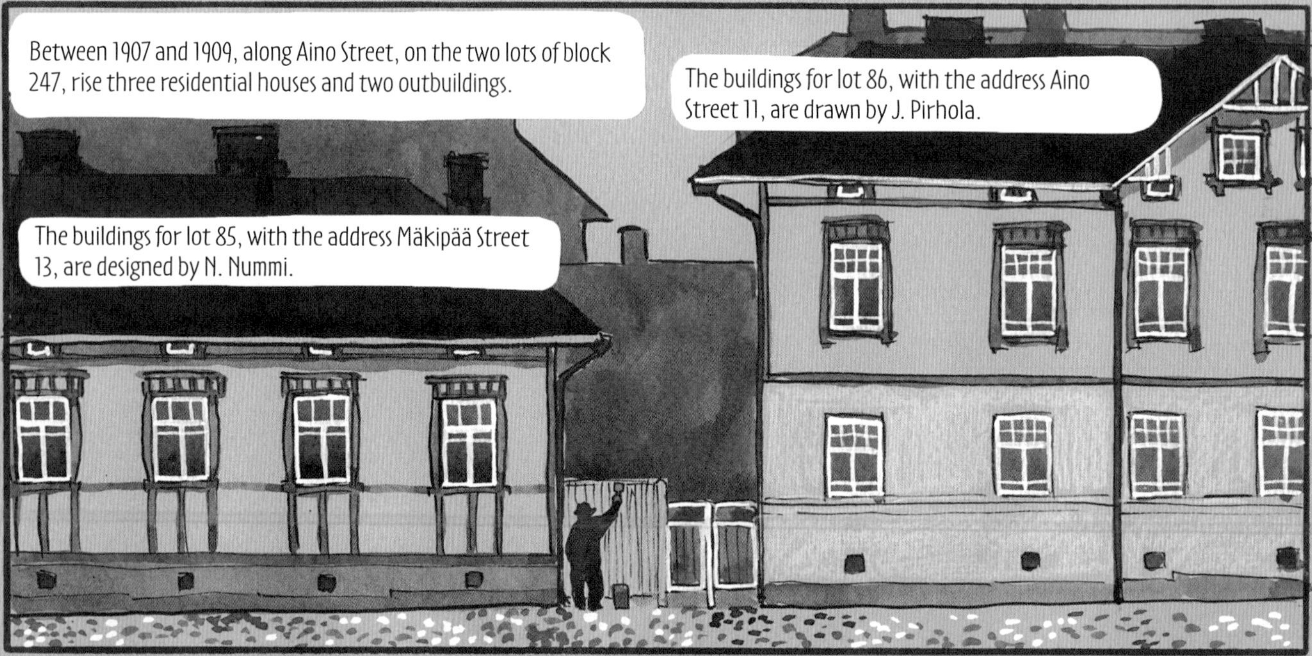
Between 1907 and 1909, along Aino Street, on the two lots of block 247, rise three residential houses and two outbuildings.
The buildings for lot 86, with the address Aino Street 11, are drawn by J. Pirhola.
The buildings for lot 85, with the address Mäkipää Street 13, are designed by N. Nummi.

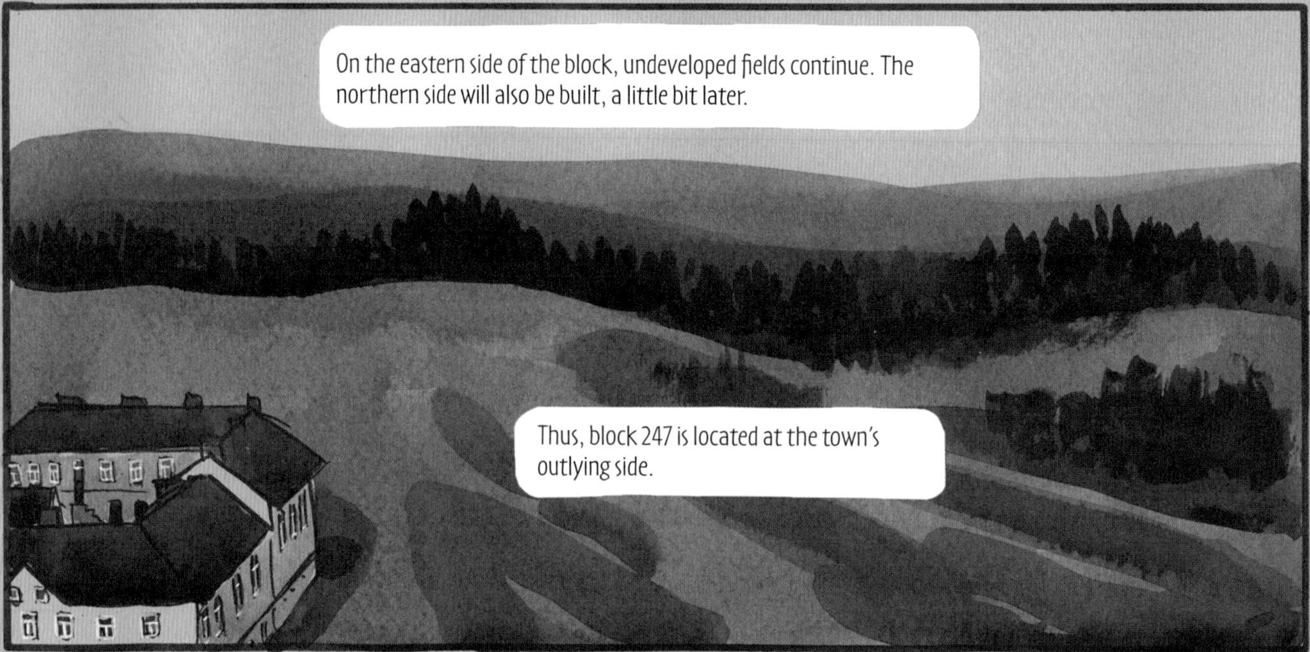
On the eastern side of the block, undeveloped fields continue. The northern side will also be built, a little bit later.
Thus, block 247 is located at the town's outlying side.

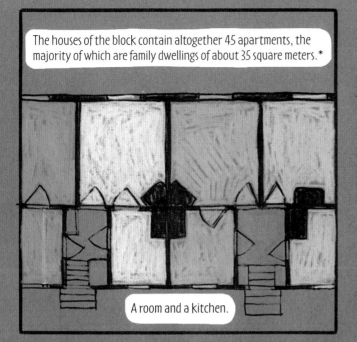

The houses of the block contain altogether 45 apartments, the majority of which are family dwellings of about 35 square meters.*

A room and a kitchen.

The houses represent modern working-class living. Every home has its own kitchen, not shared kitchens like in Kyttälä and in Amuri. Soon there is electricity, running water, and sewage.

Water comes in and goes out on its own, without anyone having to carry it.

In the building outside, the apartments have their own outhouse closets. Earlier, people used outhouses shared by everyone.

Progress is also shown by the fact that the homes have windows that open.

Inhabitants are mostly renters. The owners of the houses live in bigger dwellings, usually in corner apartments.

*377 square feet

45

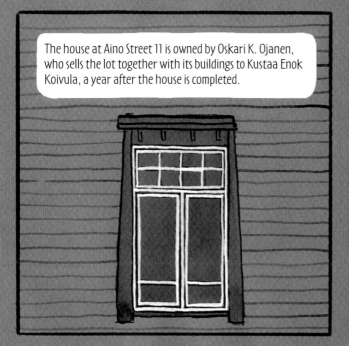

The house at Aino Street 11 is owned by Oskari K. Ojanen, who sells the lot together with its buildings to Kustaa Enok Koivula, a year after the house is completed.

Koivula changes part of the apartments into a shoe factory.

Shoe factories start to concentrate in Tammela. The factories Attila and Aaltonen grow to be the biggest.

At least twenty shoe factories have been in operation in Tammela. In the beginning of the 1900s, most of Finland's shoes are manufactured in Tampere

The most famous shoe manufacturer, Emil Aaltonen, establishes his first shoe factory in Tammela in 1905. In 1909, he buys new space and a lot for his factory from manufacturer Rudolf Winter.

In the same year, the owner of Mäkipää Street 13, Nestor E. Tuliniemi, sells his house to this Rudolf Winter.

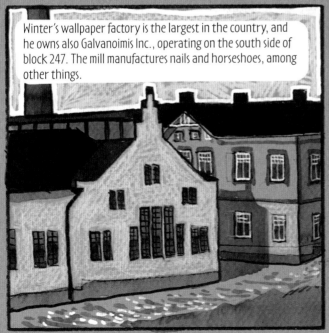

Winter's wallpaper factory is the largest in the country, and he owns also Galvanoimis Inc., operating on the south side of block 247. The mill manufactures nails and horseshoes, among other things.

The apartments in the house owned by Winter are rented by the nail and wallpaper factories' workers.

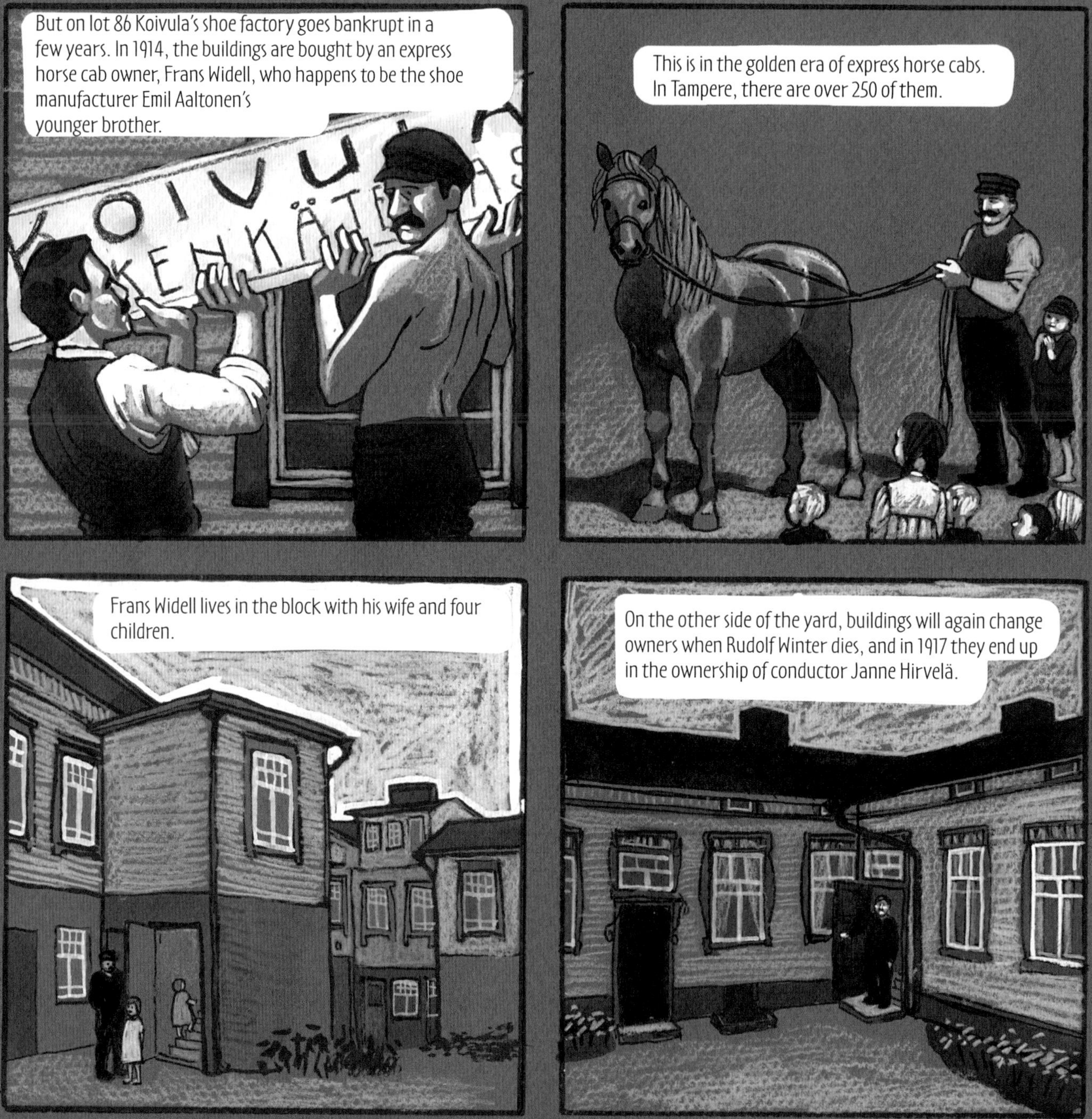
But on lot 86 Koivula's shoe factory goes bankrupt in a few years. In 1914, the buildings are bought by an express horse cab owner, Frans Widell, who happens to be the shoe manufacturer Emil Aaltonen's younger brother.
This is in the golden era of express horse cabs. In Tampere, there are over 250 of them.
Frans Widell lives in the block with his wife and four children.
On the other side of the yard, buildings will again change owners when Rudolf Winter dies, and in 1917 they end up in the ownership of conductor Janne Hirvelä.

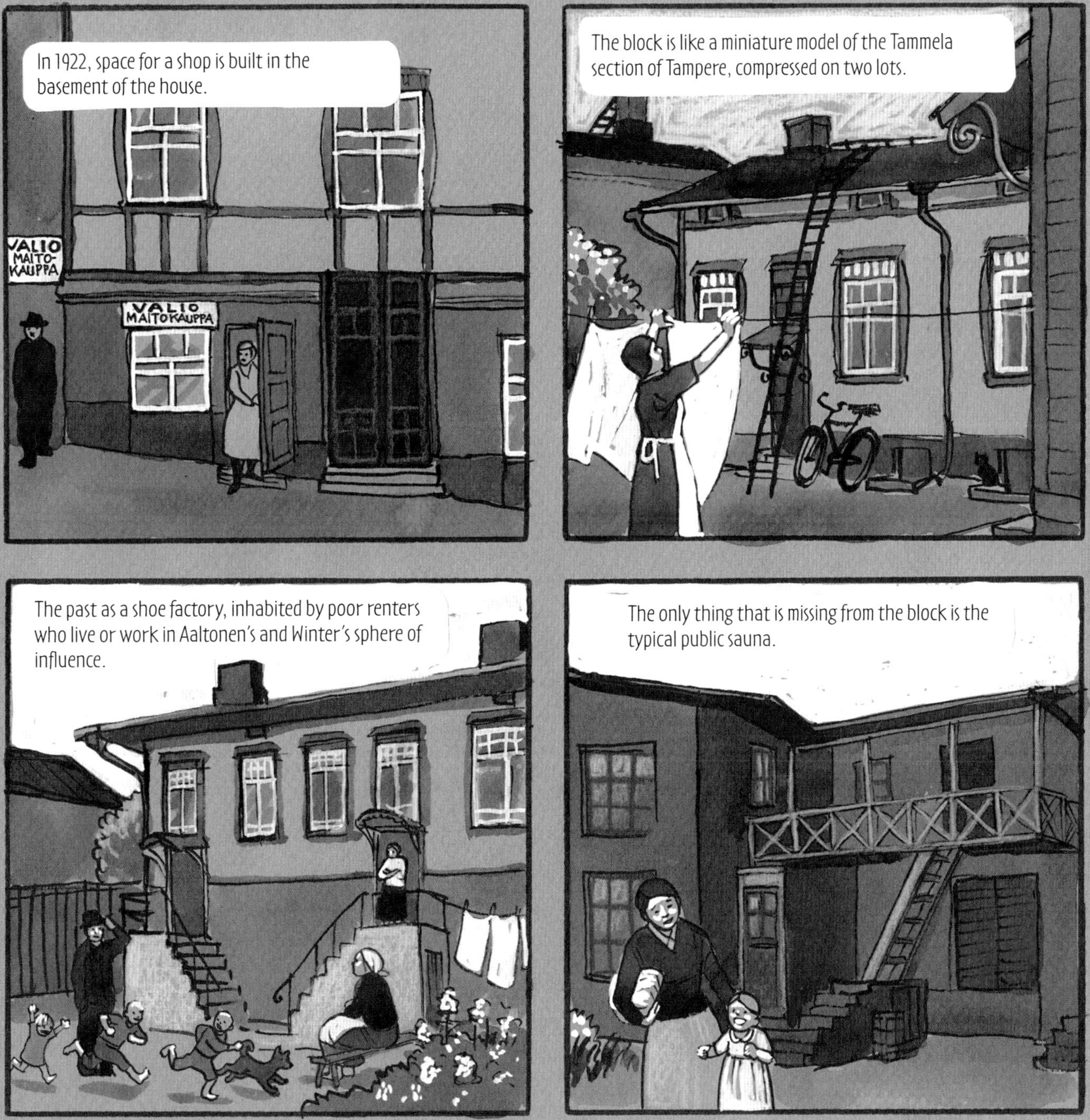
In 1922, space for a shop is built in the basement of the house.
VALIO MAITO-KAUPPA
VALIO MAITOKAUPPA
The block is like a miniature model of the Tammela section of Tampere, compressed on two lots.
The past as a shoe factory, inhabited by poor renters who live or work in Aaltonen's and Winter's sphere of influence.
The only thing that is missing from the block is the typical public sauna.

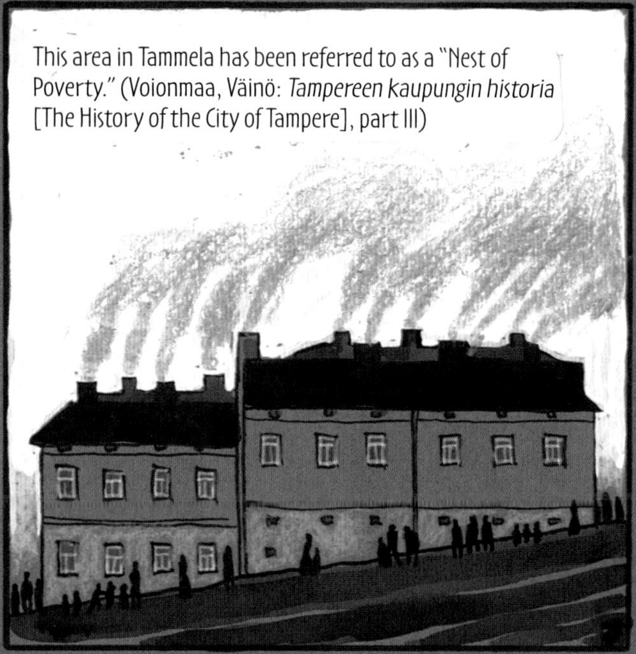
This area in Tammela has been referred to as a "Nest of Poverty." (Voionmaa, Väinö: *Tampereen kaupungin historia* [The History of the City of Tampere], part III)

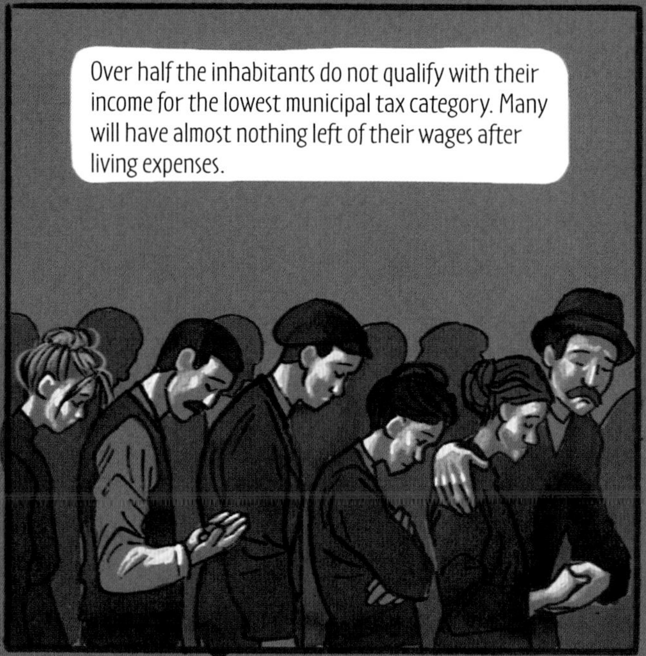
Over half the inhabitants do not qualify with their income for the lowest municipal tax category. Many will have almost nothing left of their wages after living expenses.

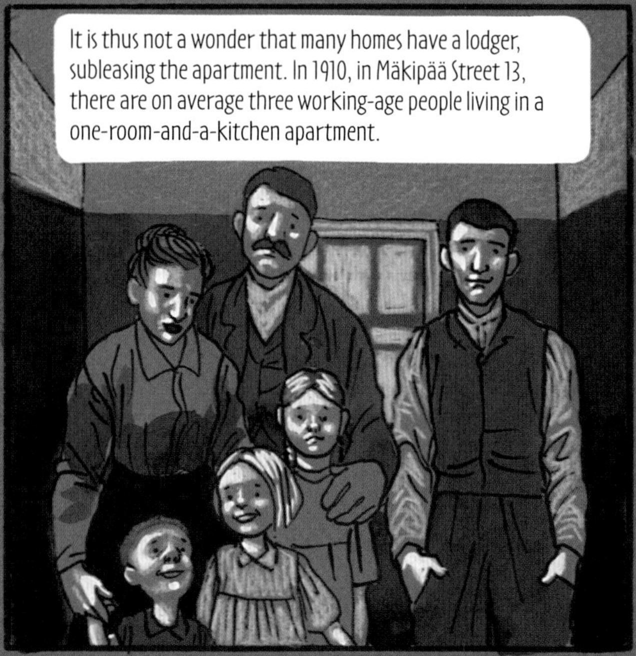
It is thus not a wonder that many homes have a lodger, subleasing the apartment. In 1910, in Mäkipää Street 13, there are on average three working-age people living in a one-room-and-a-kitchen apartment.

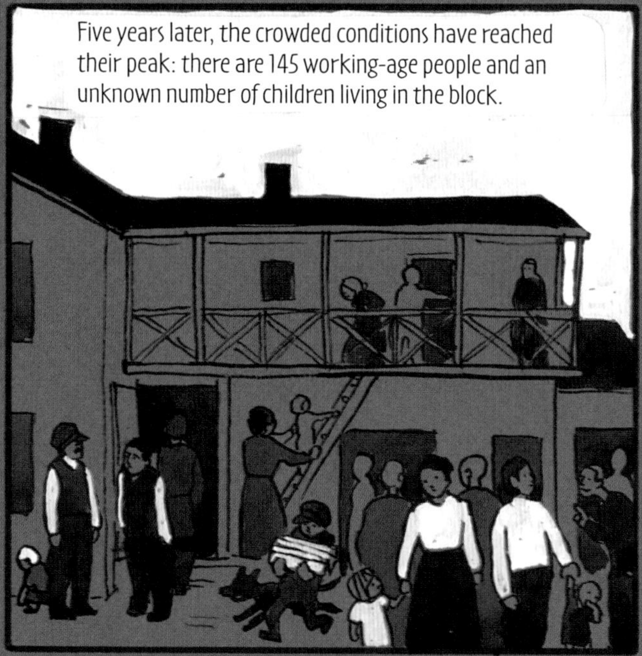
Five years later, the crowded conditions have reached their peak: there are 145 working-age people and an unknown number of children living in the block.

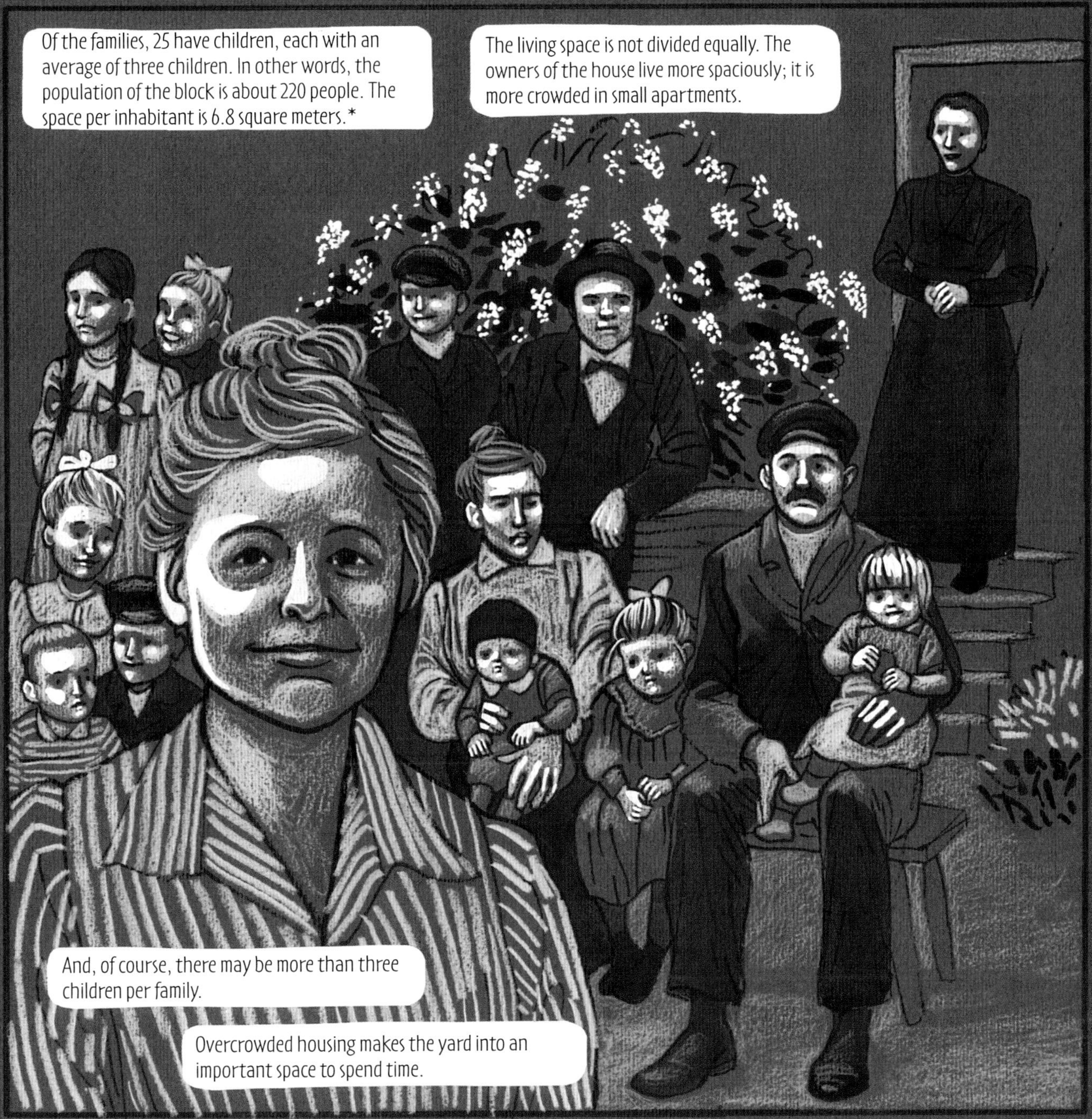
Of the families, 25 have children, each with an average of three children. In other words, the population of the block is about 220 people. The space per inhabitant is 6.8 square meters.*
The living space is not divided equally. The owners of the house live more spaciously; it is more crowded in small apartments.
And, of course, there may be more than three children per family.
Overcrowded housing makes the yard into an important space to spend time.

*73 square feet

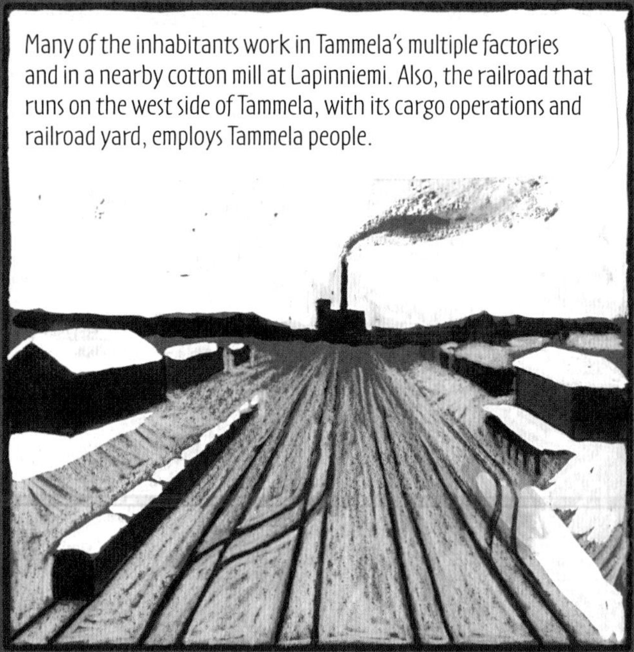
Many of the inhabitants work in Tammela's multiple factories and in a nearby cotton mill at Lapinniemi. Also, the railroad that runs on the west side of Tammela, with its cargo operations and railroad yard, employs Tammela people.

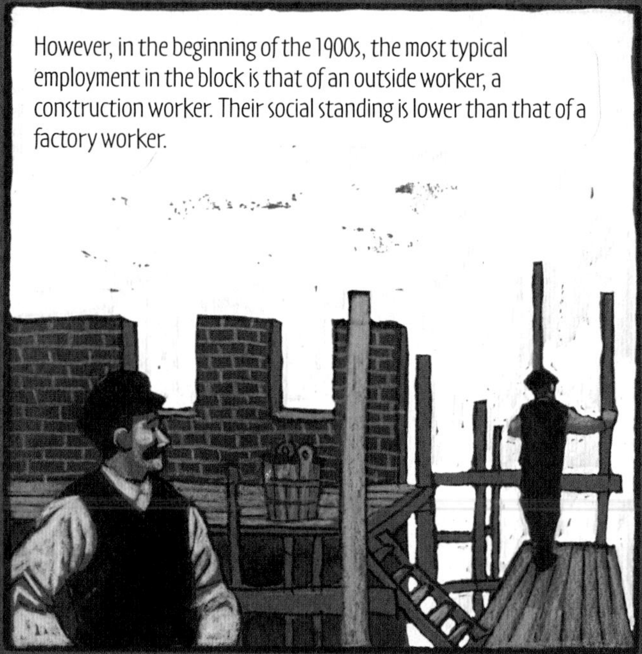
However, in the beginning of the 1900s, the most typical employment in the block is that of an outside worker, a construction worker. Their social standing is lower than that of a factory worker.

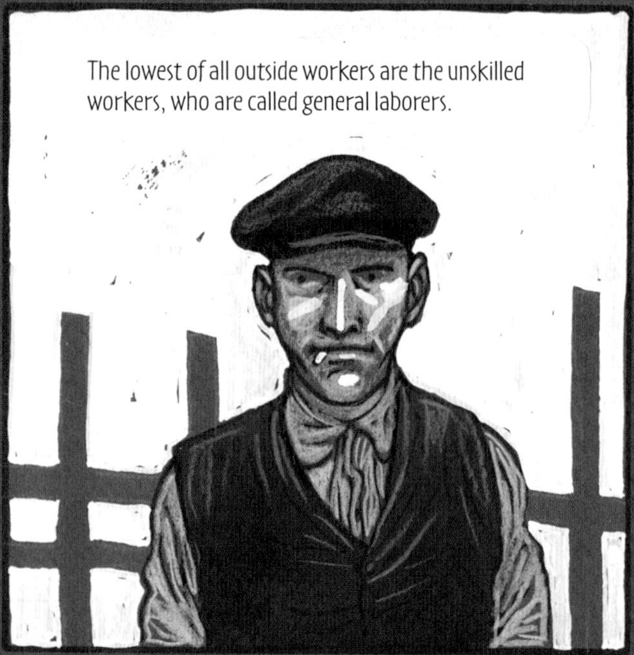
The lowest of all outside workers are the unskilled workers, who are called general laborers.

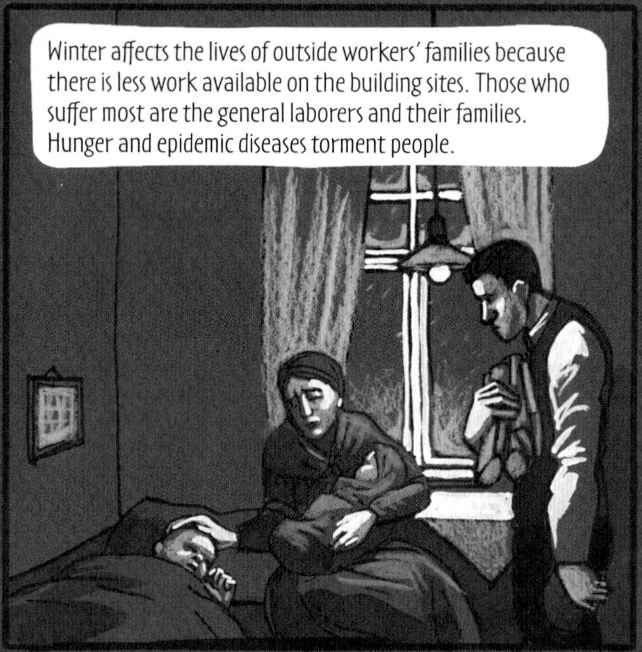
Winter affects the lives of outside workers' families because there is less work available on the building sites. Those who suffer most are the general laborers and their families. Hunger and epidemic diseases torment people.

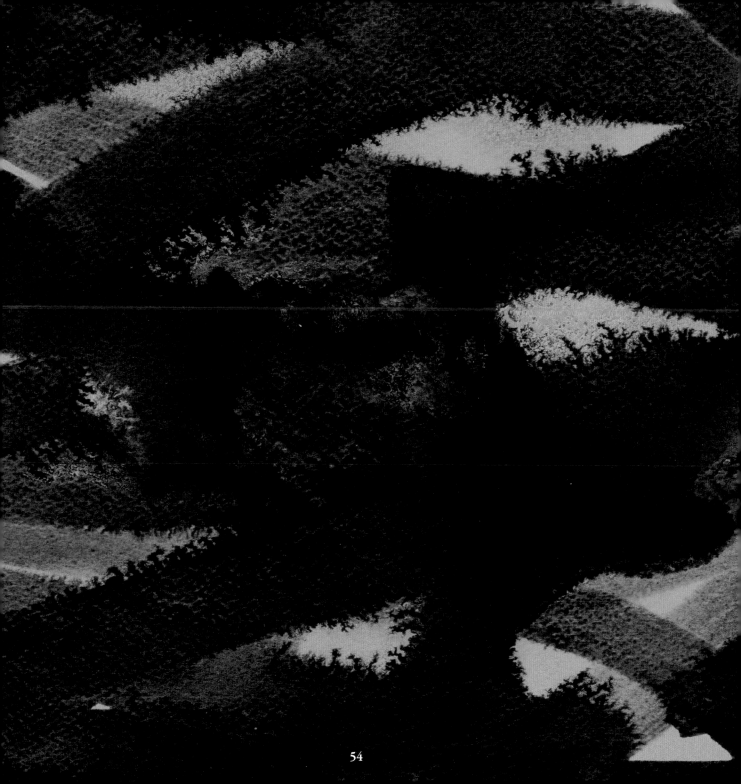

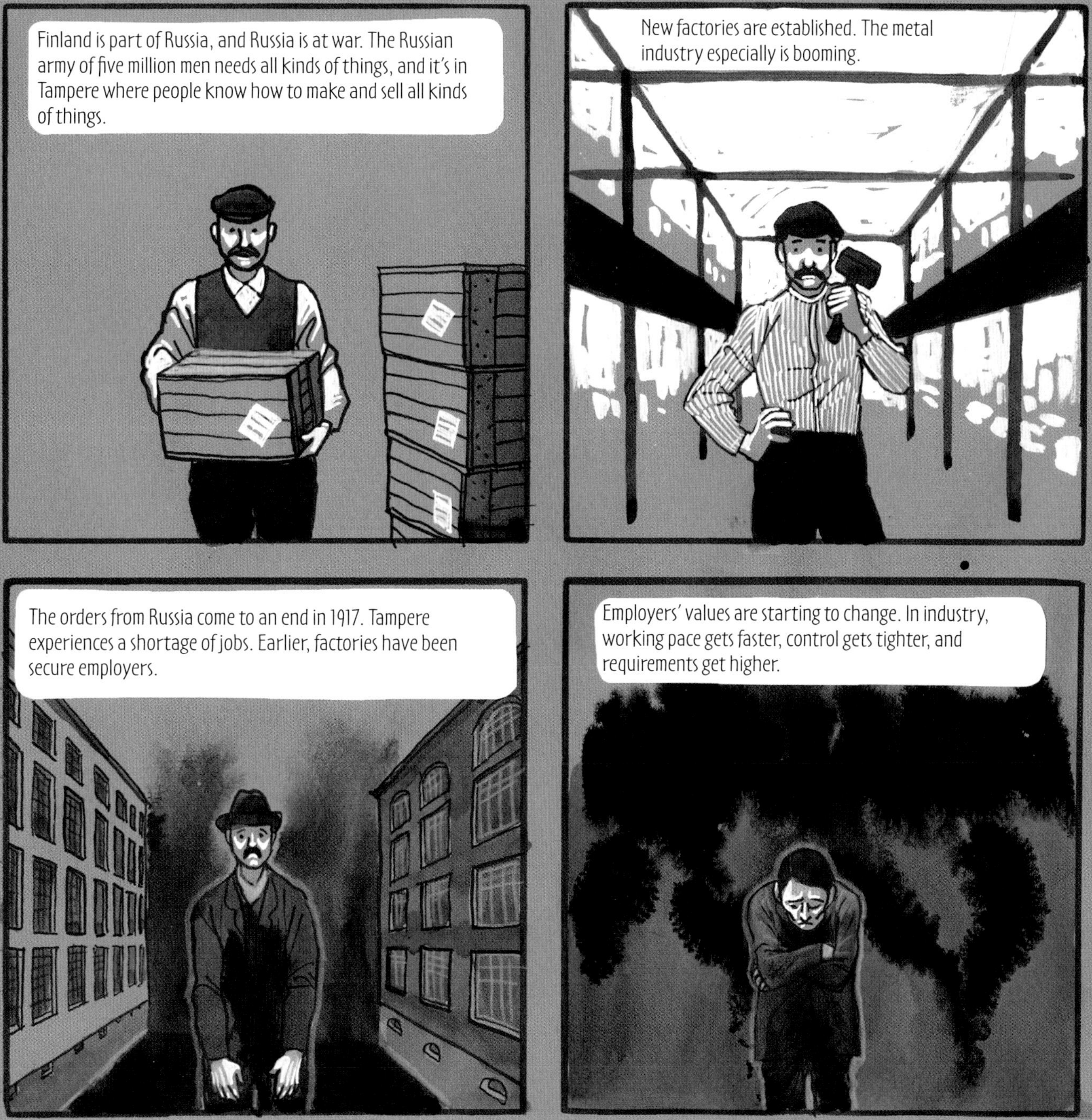
Finland is part of Russia, and Russia is at war. The Russian army of five million men needs all kinds of things, and it's in Tampere where people know how to make and sell all kinds of things.
New factories are established. The metal industry especially is booming.
The orders from Russia come to an end in 1917. Tampere experiences a shortage of jobs. Earlier, factories have been secure employers.
Employers' values are starting to change. In industry, working pace gets faster, control gets tighter, and requirements get higher.

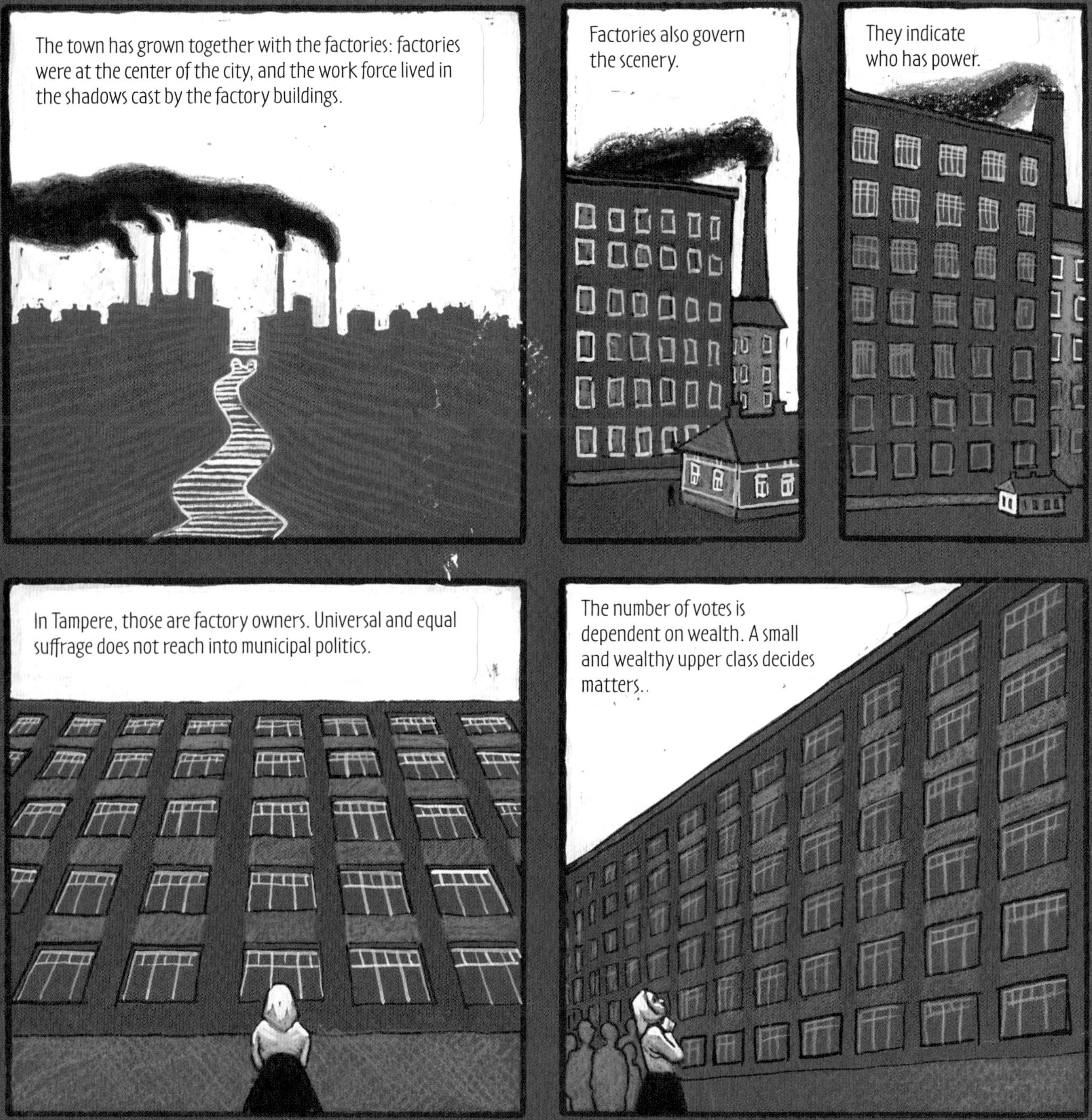
The town has grown together with the factories: factories were at the center of the city, and the work force lived in the shadows cast by the factory buildings.
Factories also govern the scenery.
They indicate who has power.
In Tampere, those are factory owners. Universal and equal suffrage does not reach into municipal politics.
The number of votes is dependent on wealth. A small and wealthy upper class decides matters..

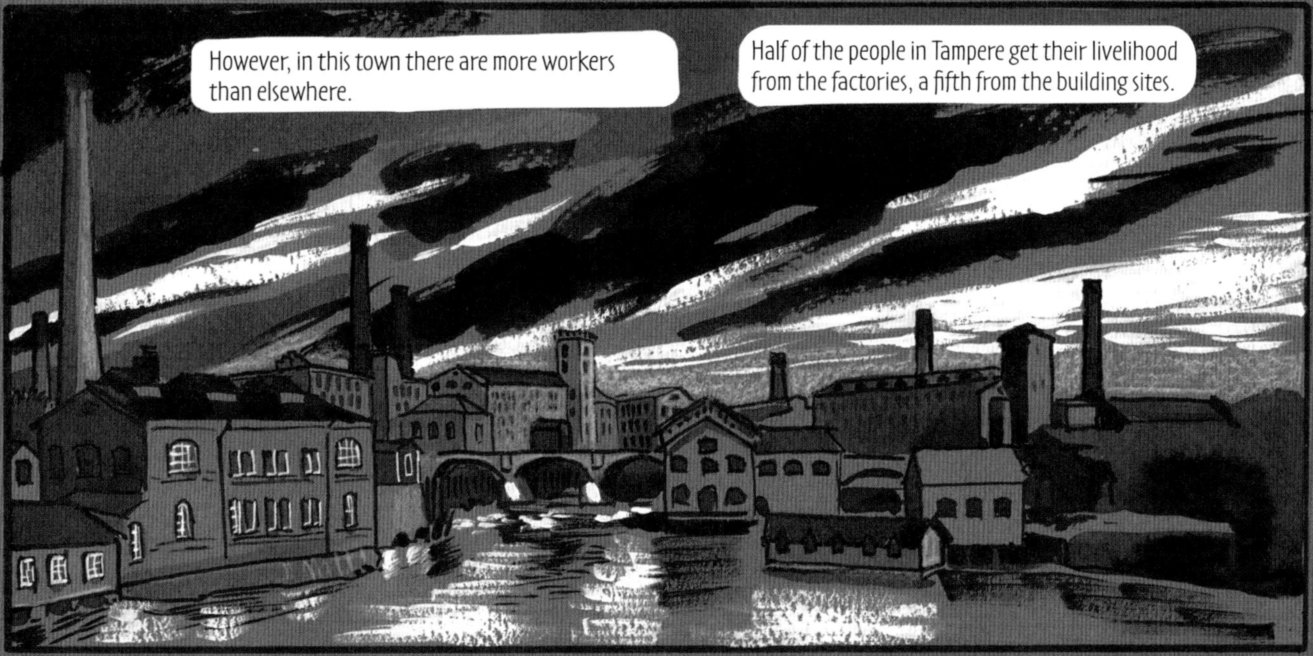
However, in this town there are more workers than elsewhere.
Half of the people in Tampere get their livelihood from the factories, a fifth from the building sites.

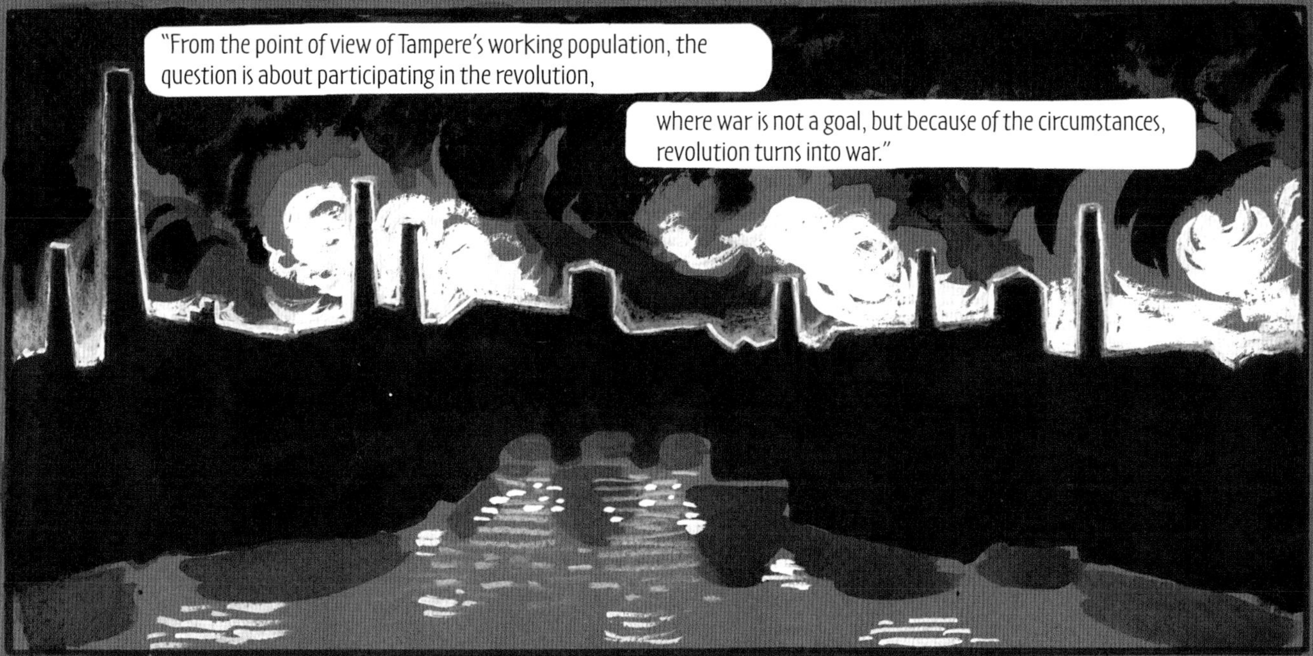
"From the point of view of Tampere's working population, the question is about participating in the revolution,
where war is not a goal, but because of the circumstances, revolution turns into war."

(Haapala: *Tehtaan valossa* [In the light of the factory], 1986)

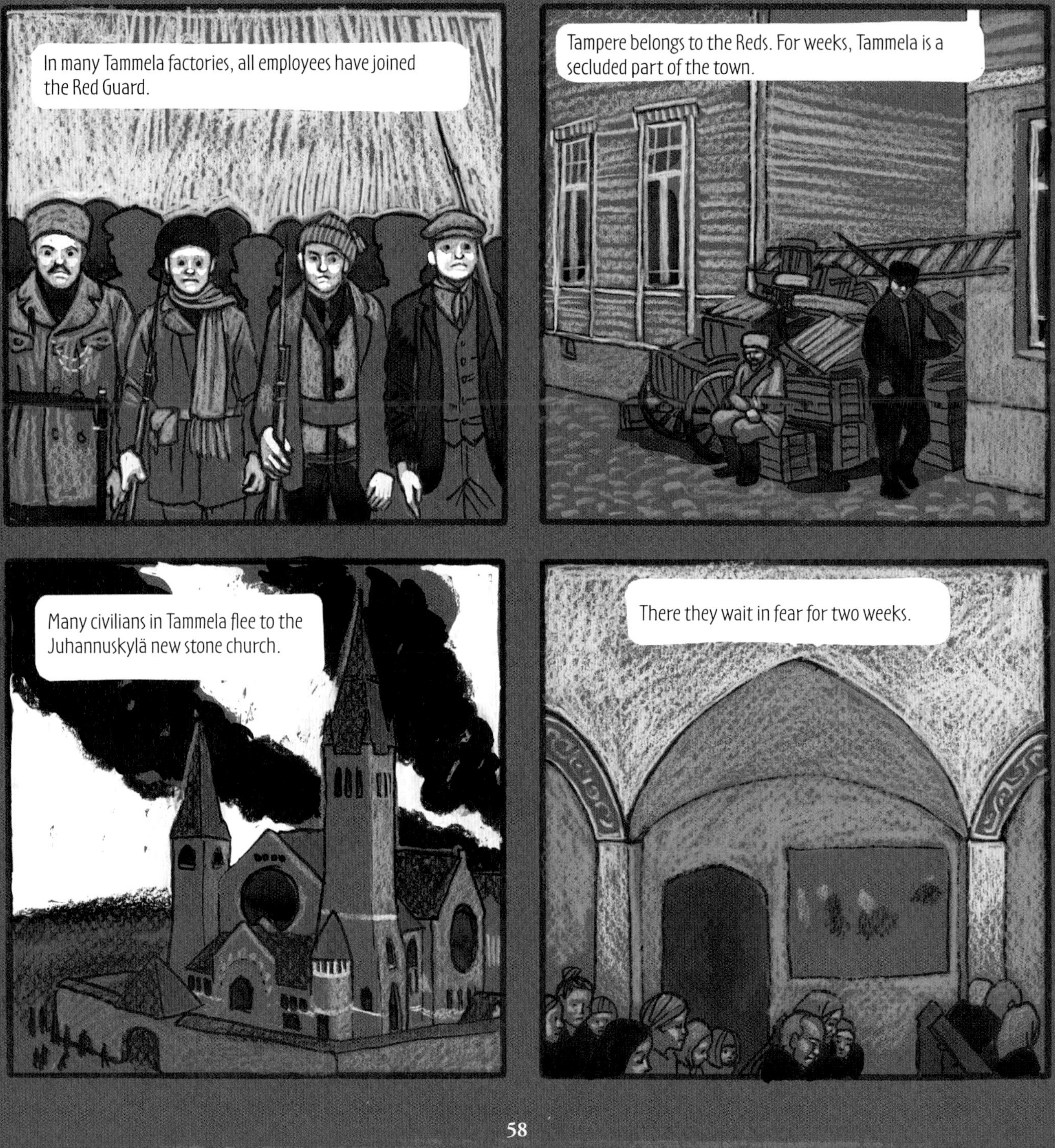
In many Tammela factories, all employees have joined the Red Guard.
Tampere belongs to the Reds. For weeks, Tammela is a secluded part of the town.
Many civilians in Tammela flee to the Juhannuskylä new stone church.
There they wait in fear for two weeks.

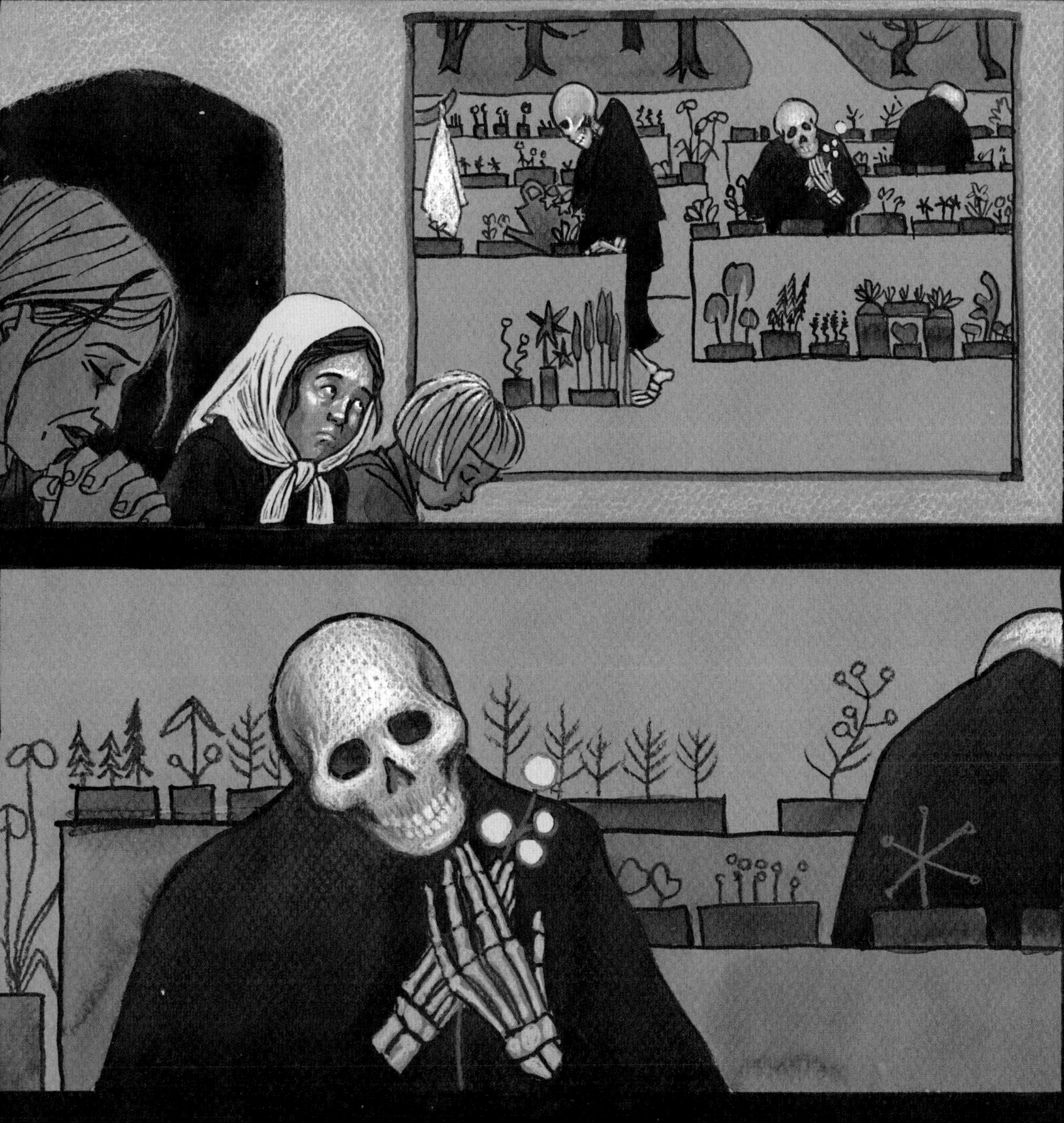

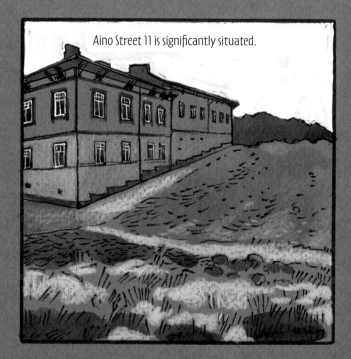

Aino Street 11 is significantly situated.

Especially the Widells' parlor.

Even though the table is too high.

On the evening of April 2, 1918, the machine gun is moved to the Tammela School.

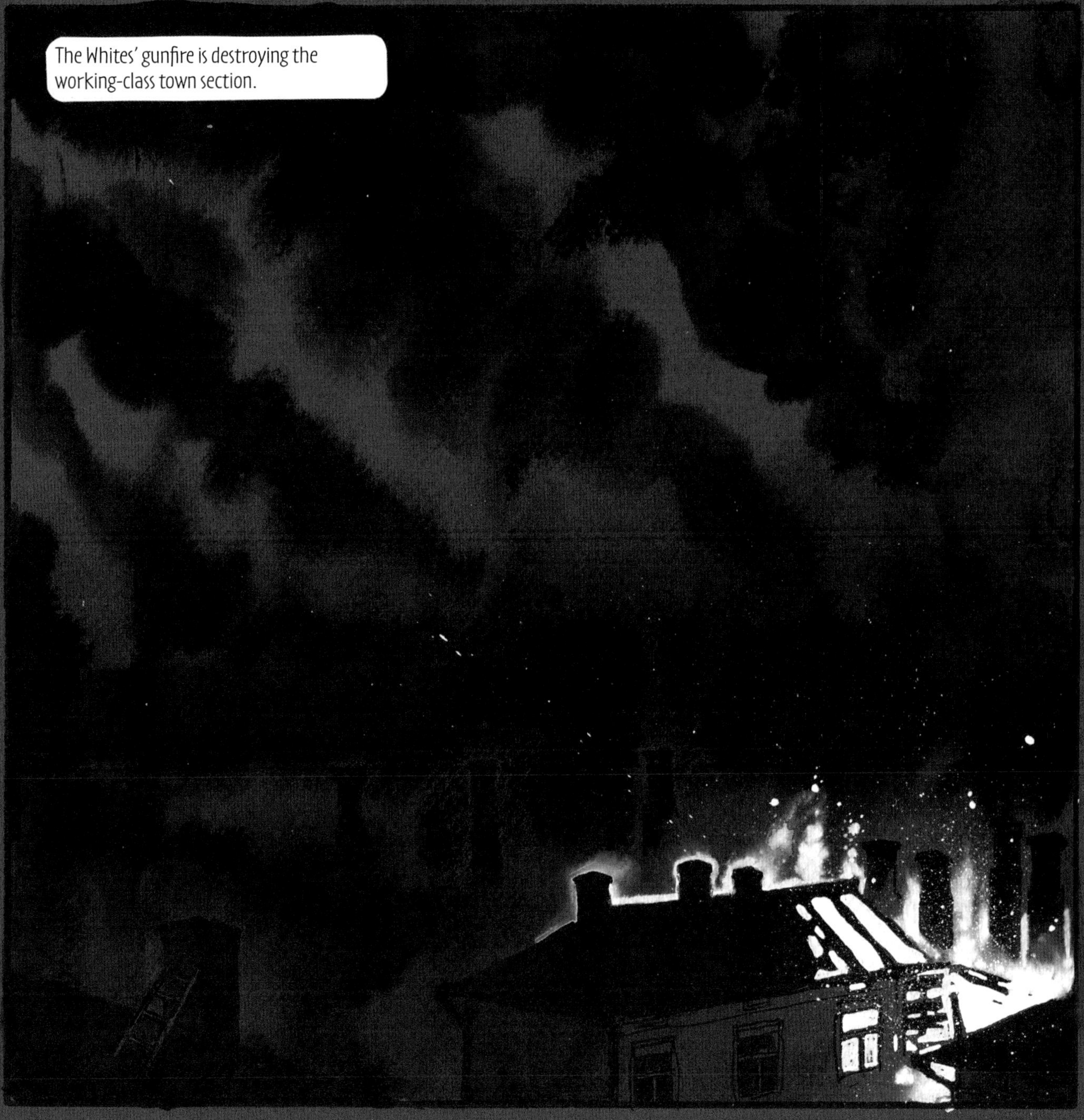
The Whites' gunfire is destroying the working-class town section.

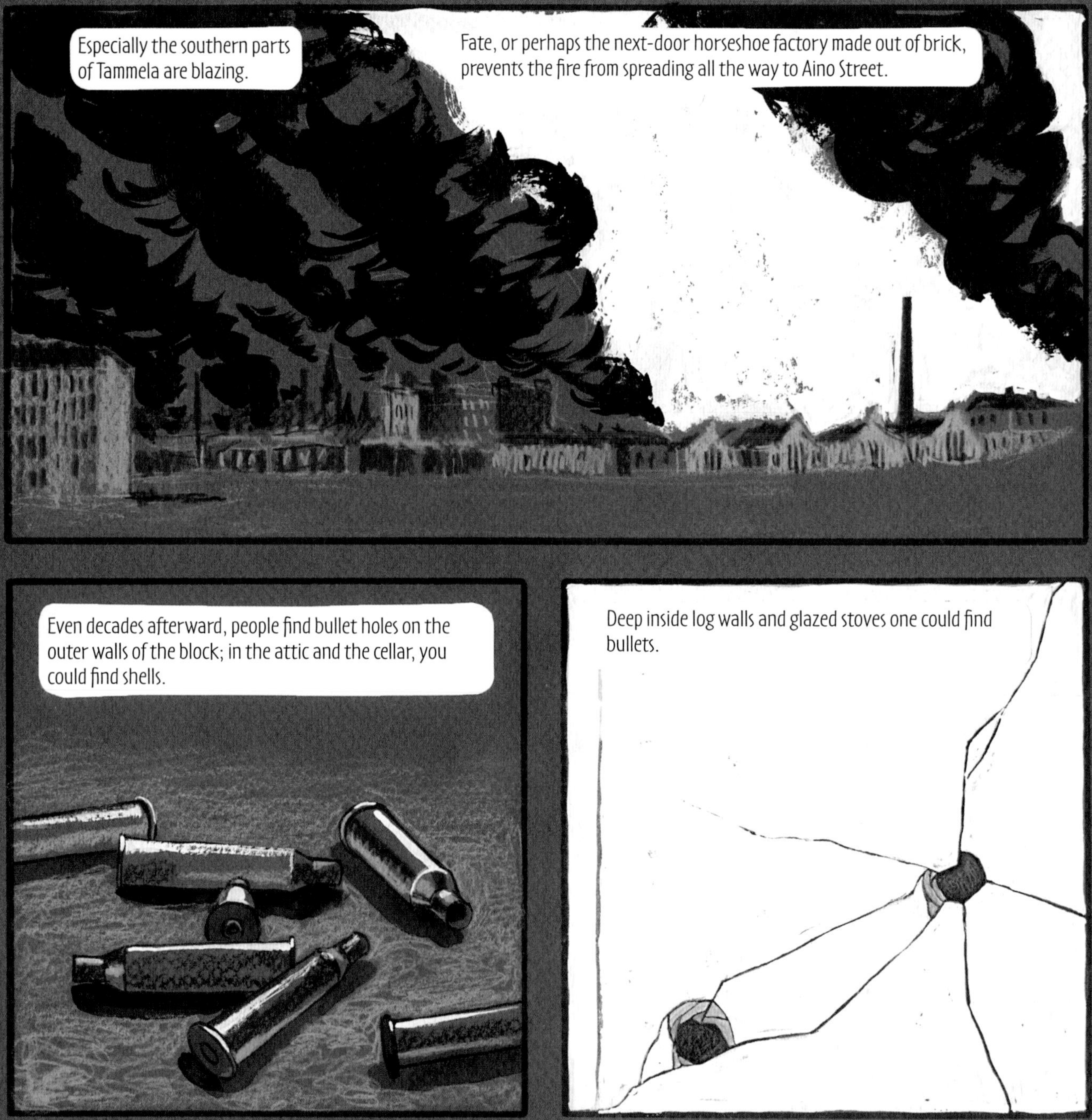
Especially the southern parts of Tammela are blazing.
Fate, or perhaps the next-door horseshoe factory made out of brick, prevents the fire from spreading all the way to Aino Street.
Even decades afterward, people find bullet holes on the outer walls of the block; in the attic and the cellar, you could find shells.
Deep inside log walls and glazed stoves one could find bullets.

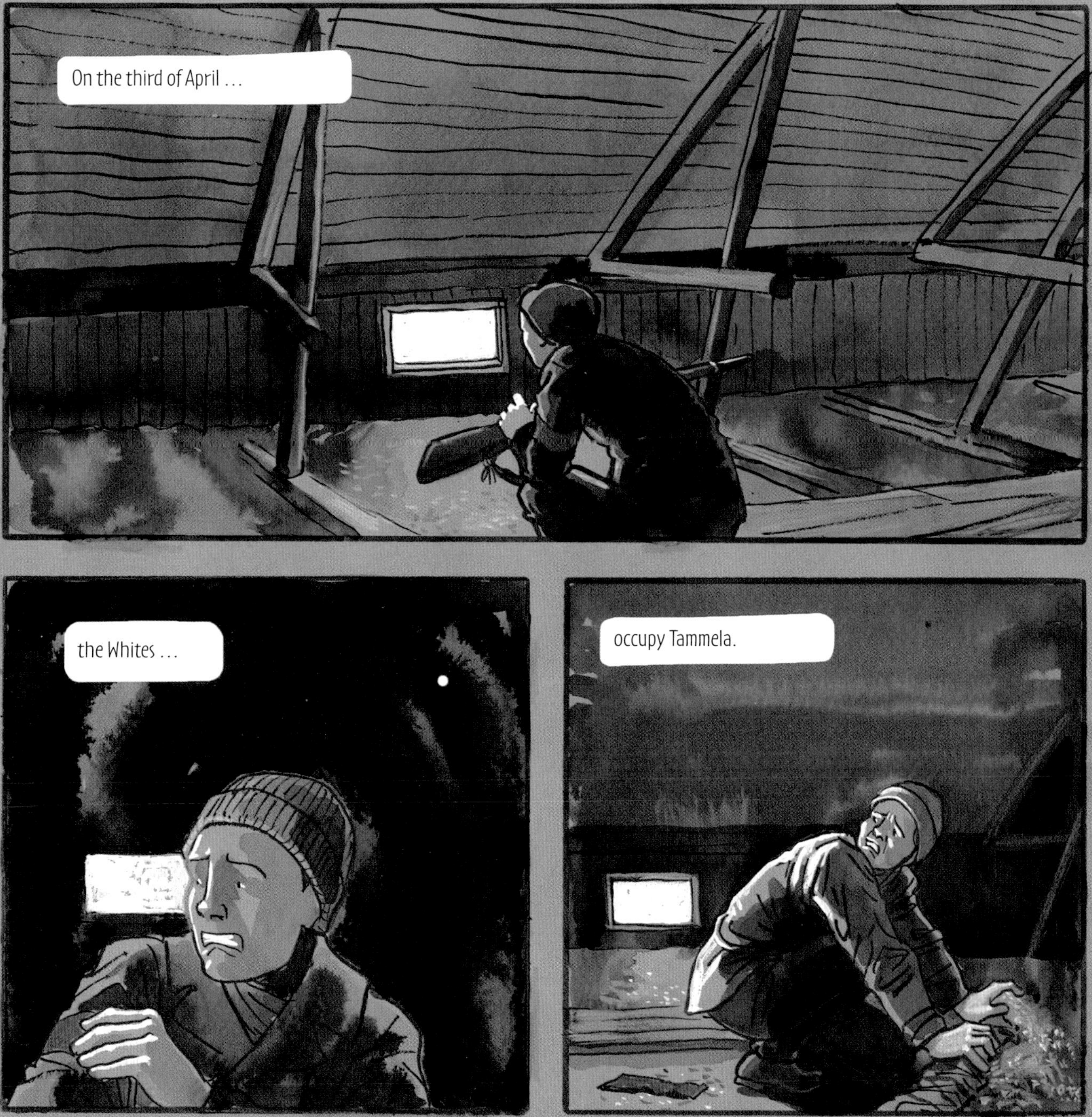
On the third of April . . .
the Whites . . .
occupy Tammela.

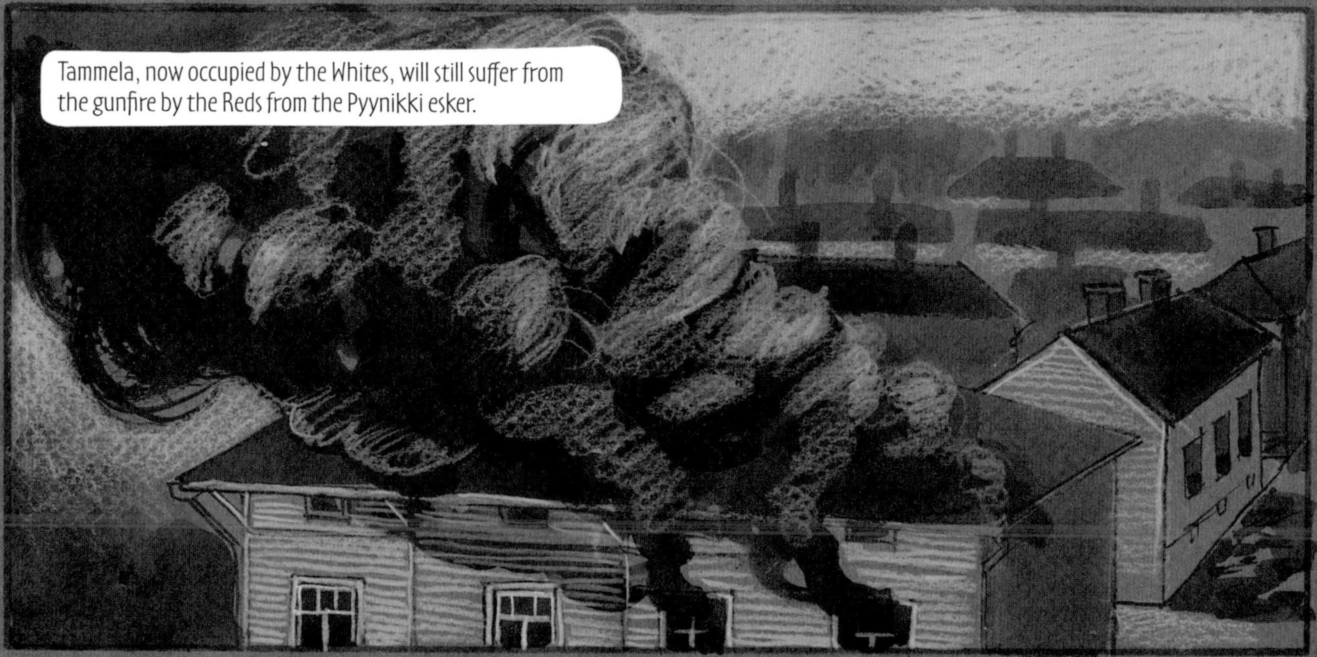
Tammela, now occupied by the Whites, will still suffer from the gunfire by the Reds from the Pyynikki esker.

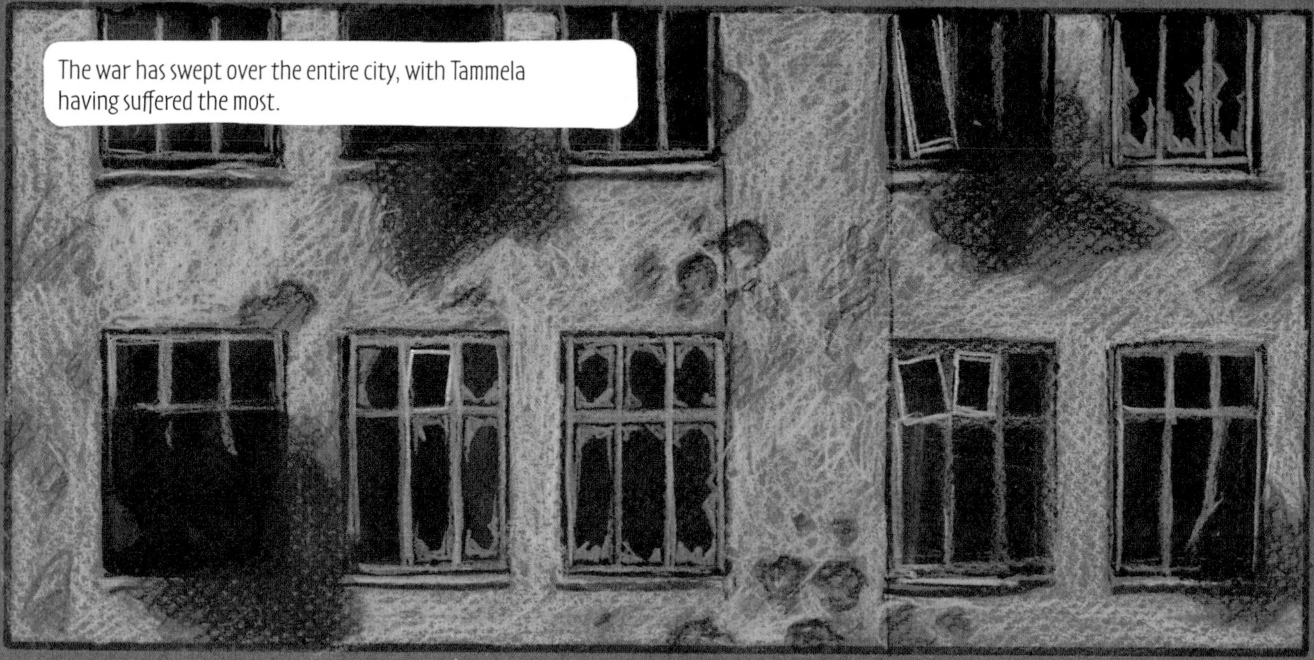
The war has swept over the entire city, with Tammela having suffered the most.

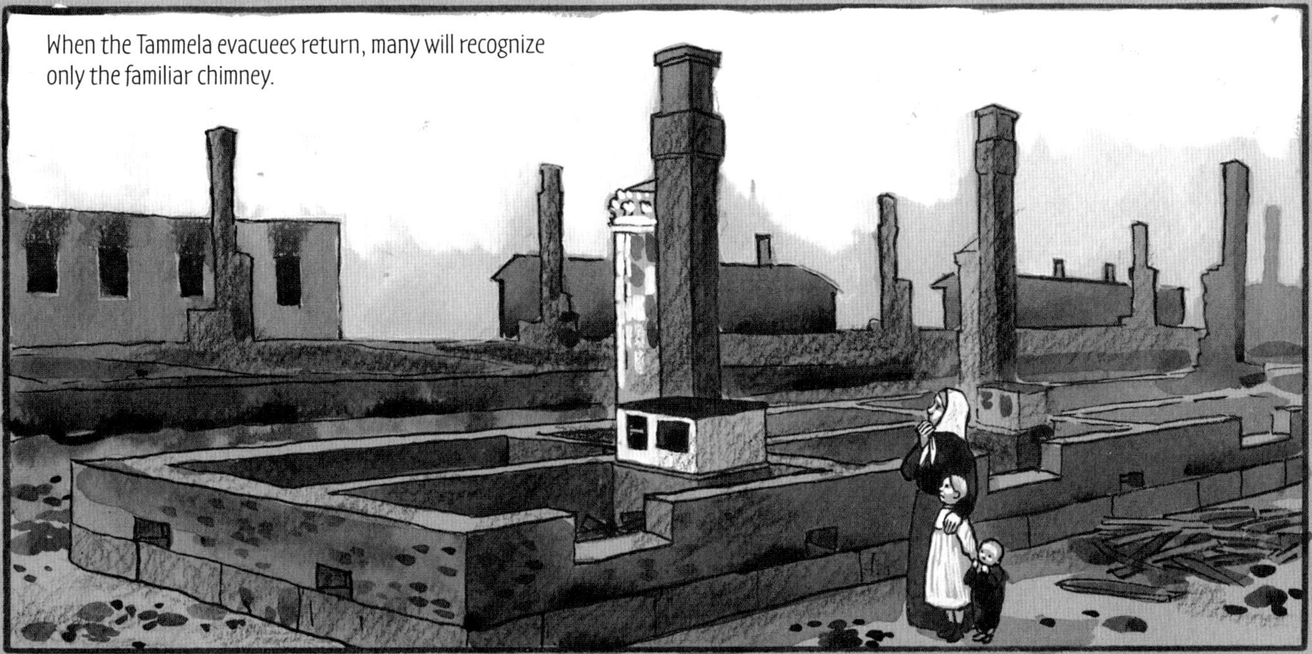
When the Tammela evacuees return, many will recognize only the familiar chimney.

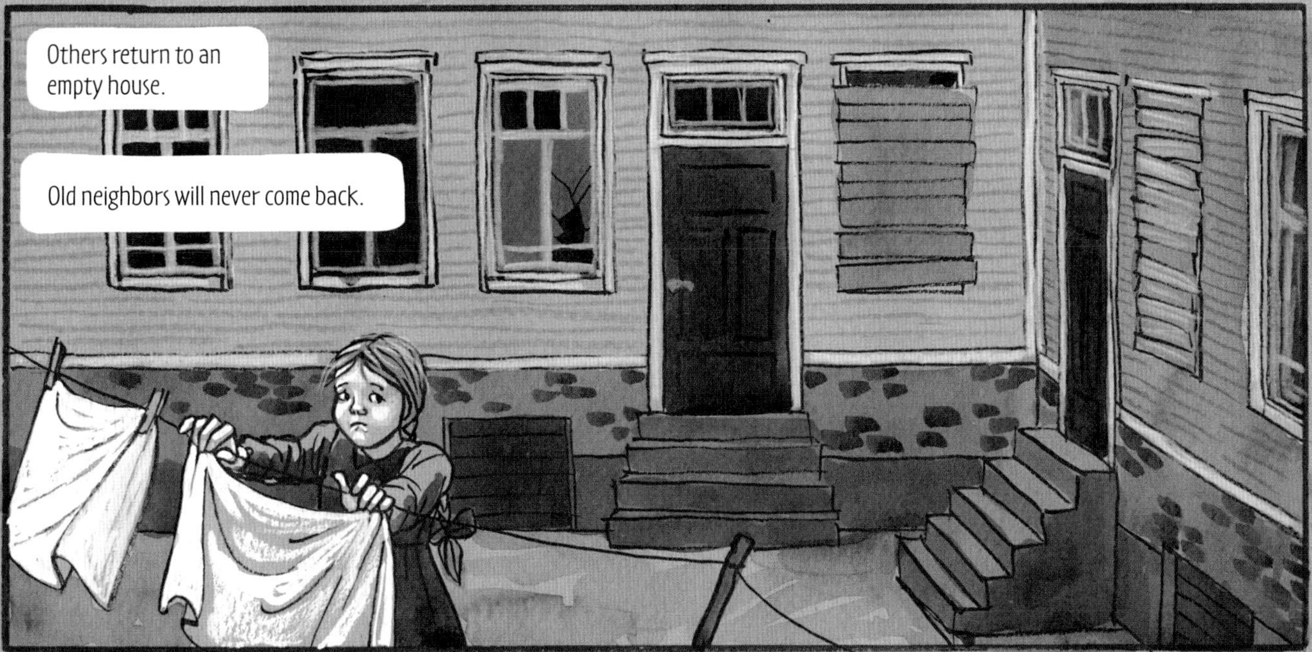
Others return to an empty house.
Old neighbors will never come back.

Specifically in Tampere, the war of 1918 with its aftermath …

… is especially sad.

Measured in human lives, and in relation to population, it is darker than the next war,

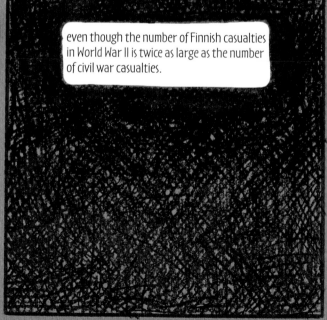

even though the number of Finnish casualties in World War II is twice as large as the number of civil war casualties.

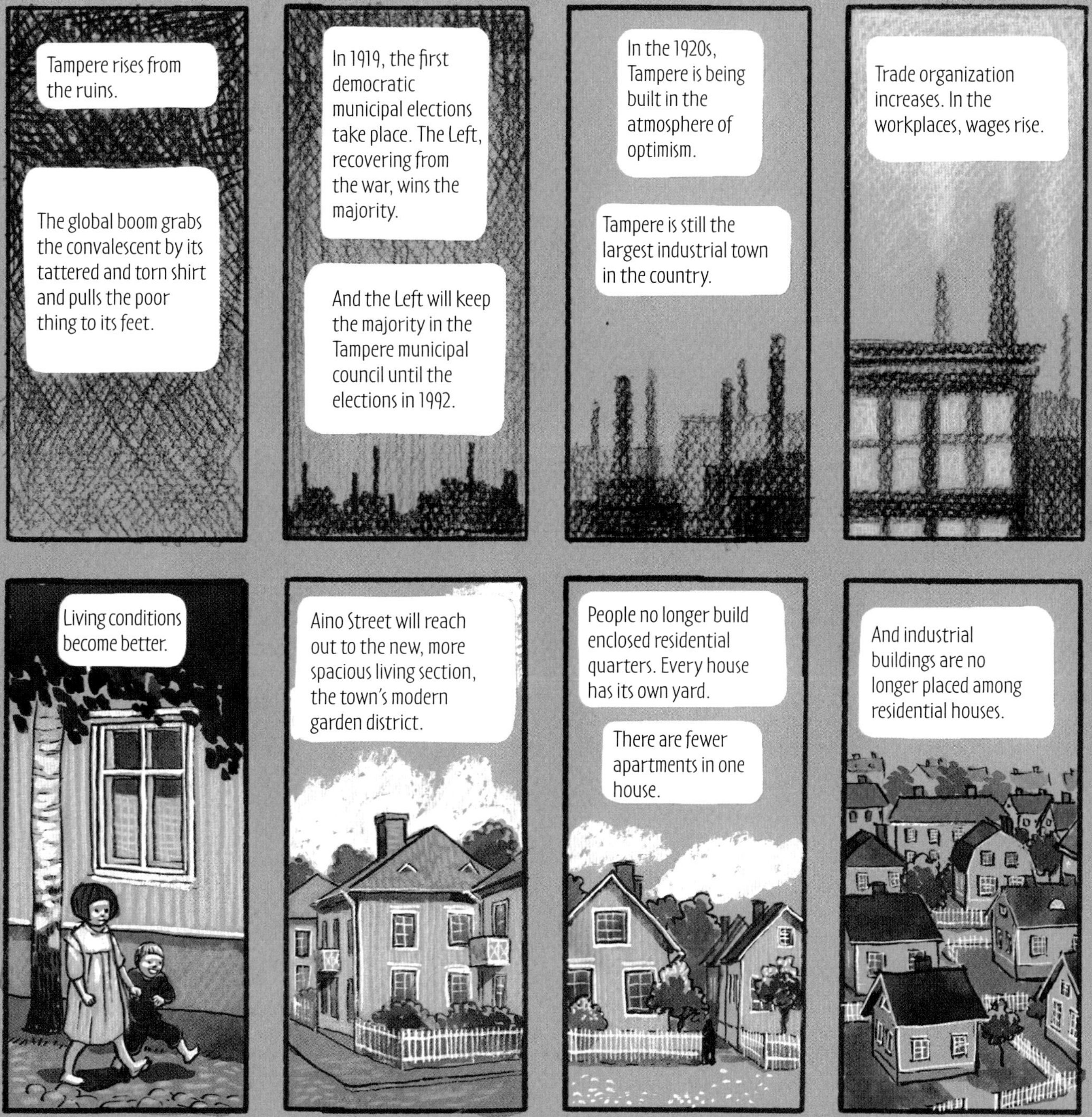
Tampere rises from the ruins.
The global boom grabs the convalescent by its tattered and torn shirt and pulls the poor thing to its feet.
In 1919, the first democratic municipal elections take place. The Left, recovering from the war, wins the majority.
And the Left will keep the majority in the Tampere municipal council until the elections in 1992.
In the 1920s, Tampere is being built in the atmosphere of optimism.
Tampere is still the largest industrial town in the country.
Trade organization increases. In the workplaces, wages rise.
Living conditions become better.
Aino Street will reach out to the new, more spacious living section, the town's modern garden district.
People no longer build enclosed residential quarters. Every house has its own yard.
There are fewer apartments in one house.
And industrial buildings are no longer placed among residential houses.

A downswing follows the upswing.

And an upswing the downswing.

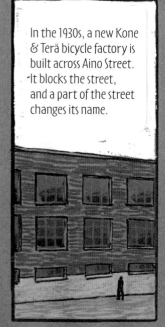

In the 1930s, a new Kone & Terä bicycle factory is built across Aino Street. It blocks the street, and a part of the street changes its name.

Aino Street 11 is now Annikki Street 11.

During the next war, the Tammela factories also manufacture products for war industry. The people of Tammela will feel it in the bombings of the Winter War.

On December 21, 1939, 23 bombs are dropped on Tammela.

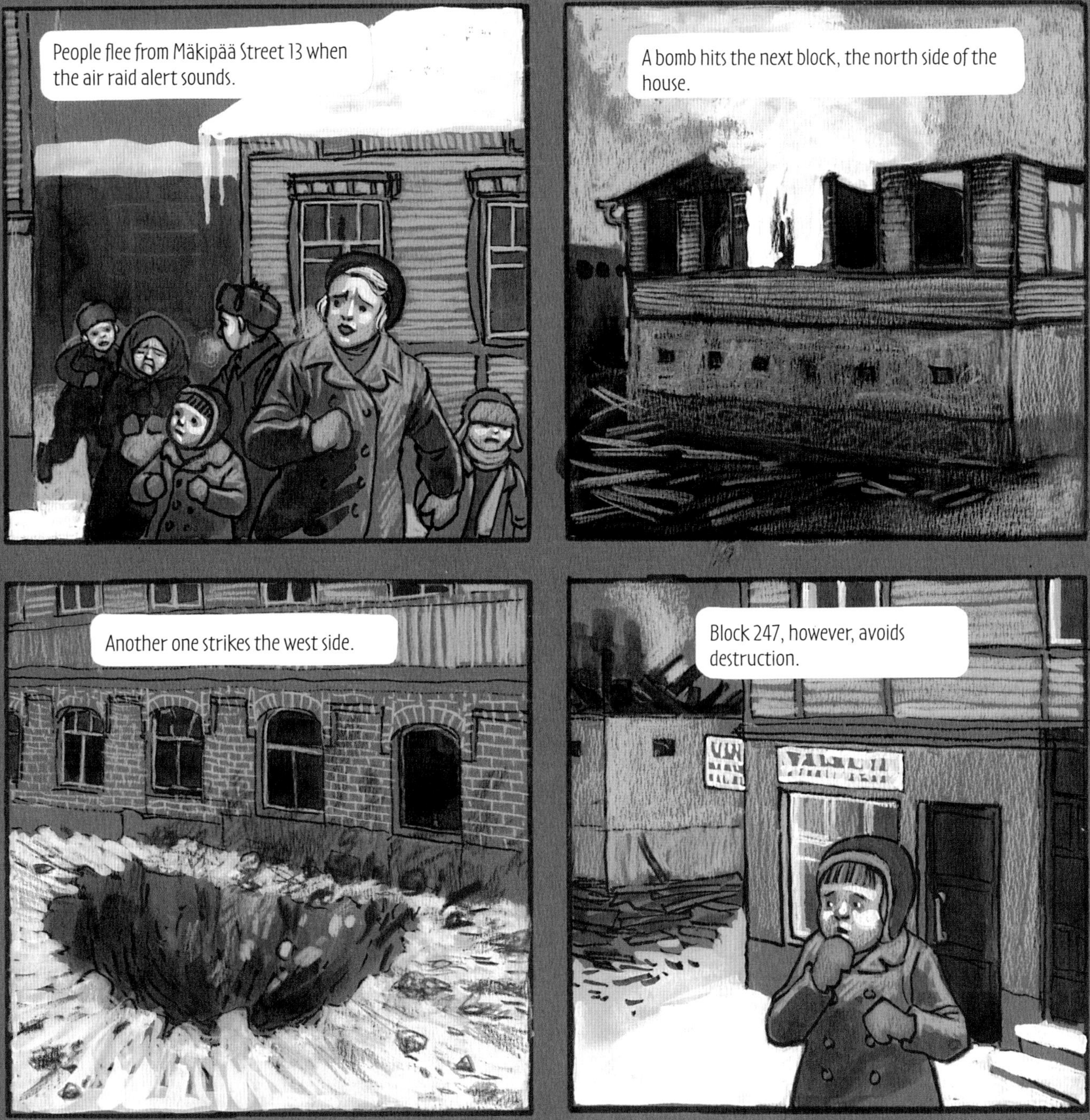
People flee from Mäkipää Street 13 when the air raid alert sounds.
A bomb hits the next block, the north side of the house.
Another one strikes the west side.
Block 247, however, avoids destruction.

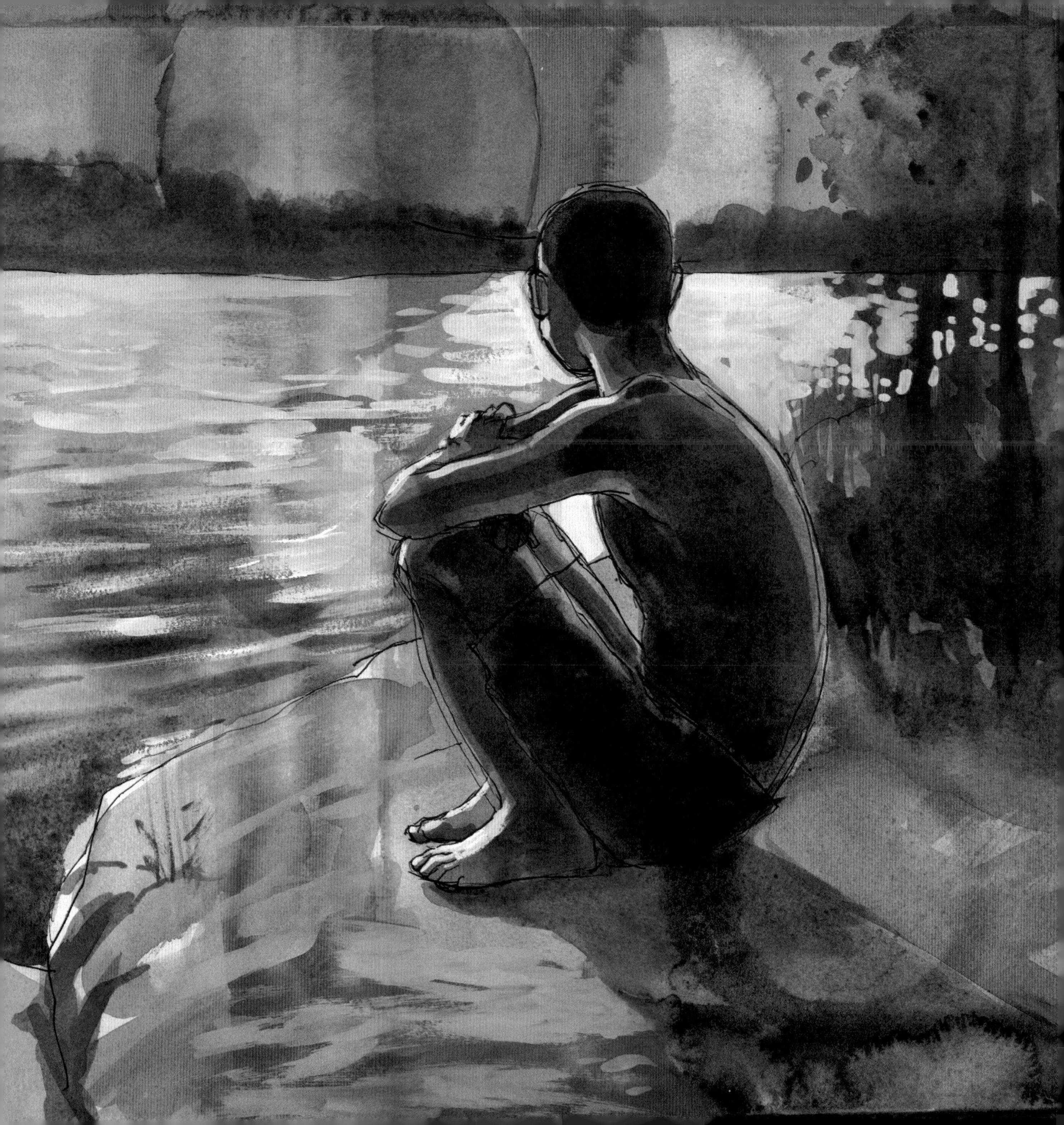

THE THREAT OF A
DREAM ABOUT TO
BE FULFILLED

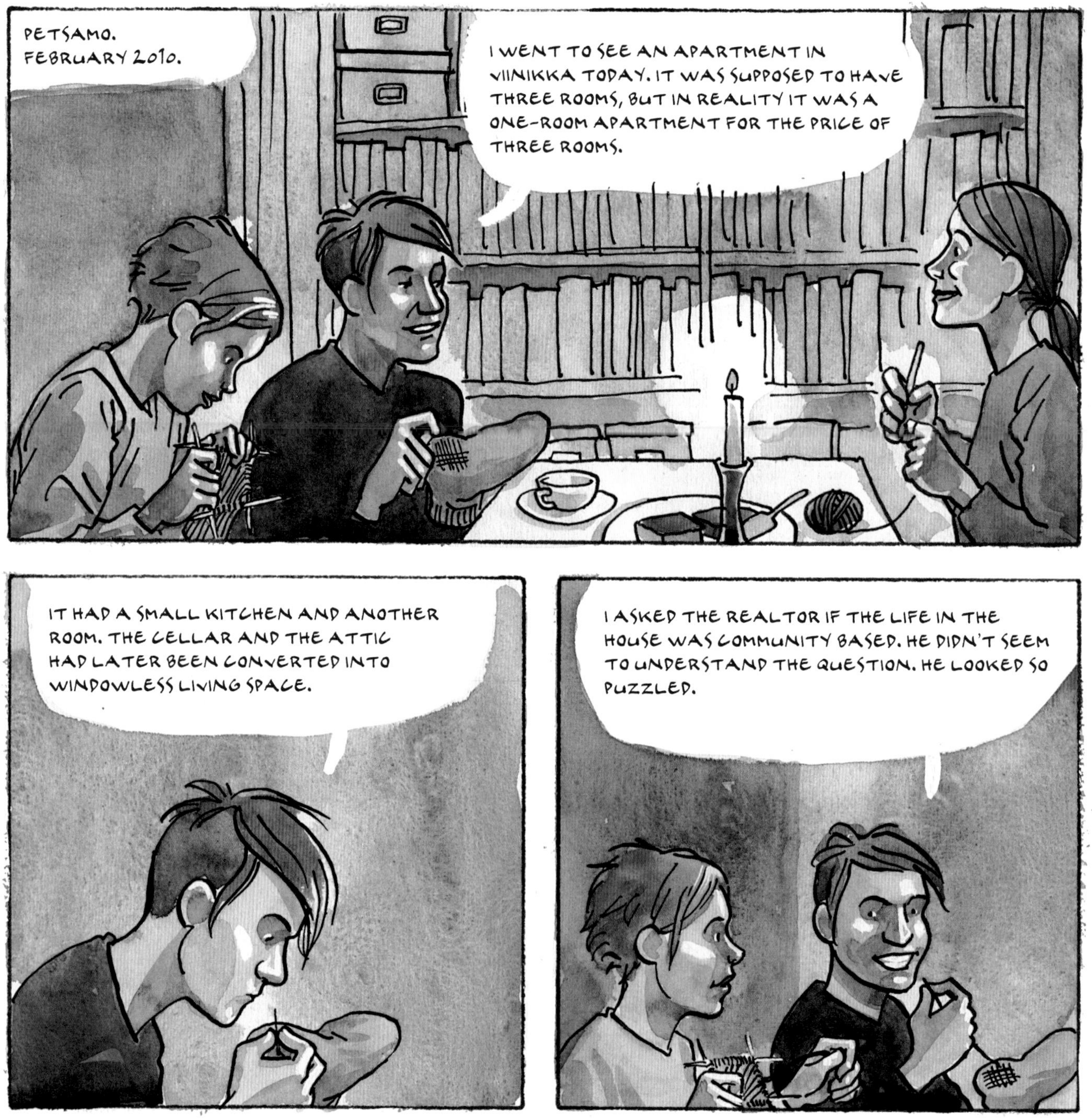
PETSAMO. FEBRUARY 2010.
I WENT TO SEE AN APARTMENT IN VIINIKKA TODAY. IT WAS SUPPOSED TO HAVE THREE ROOMS, BUT IN REALITY IT WAS A ONE-ROOM APARTMENT FOR THE PRICE OF THREE ROOMS.
IT HAD A SMALL KITCHEN AND ANOTHER ROOM. THE CELLAR AND THE ATTIC HAD LATER BEEN CONVERTED INTO WINDOWLESS LIVING SPACE.
I ASKED THE REALTOR IF THE LIFE IN THE HOUSE WAS COMMUNITY BASED. HE DIDN'T SEEM TO UNDERSTAND THE QUESTION. HE LOOKED SO PUZZLED.

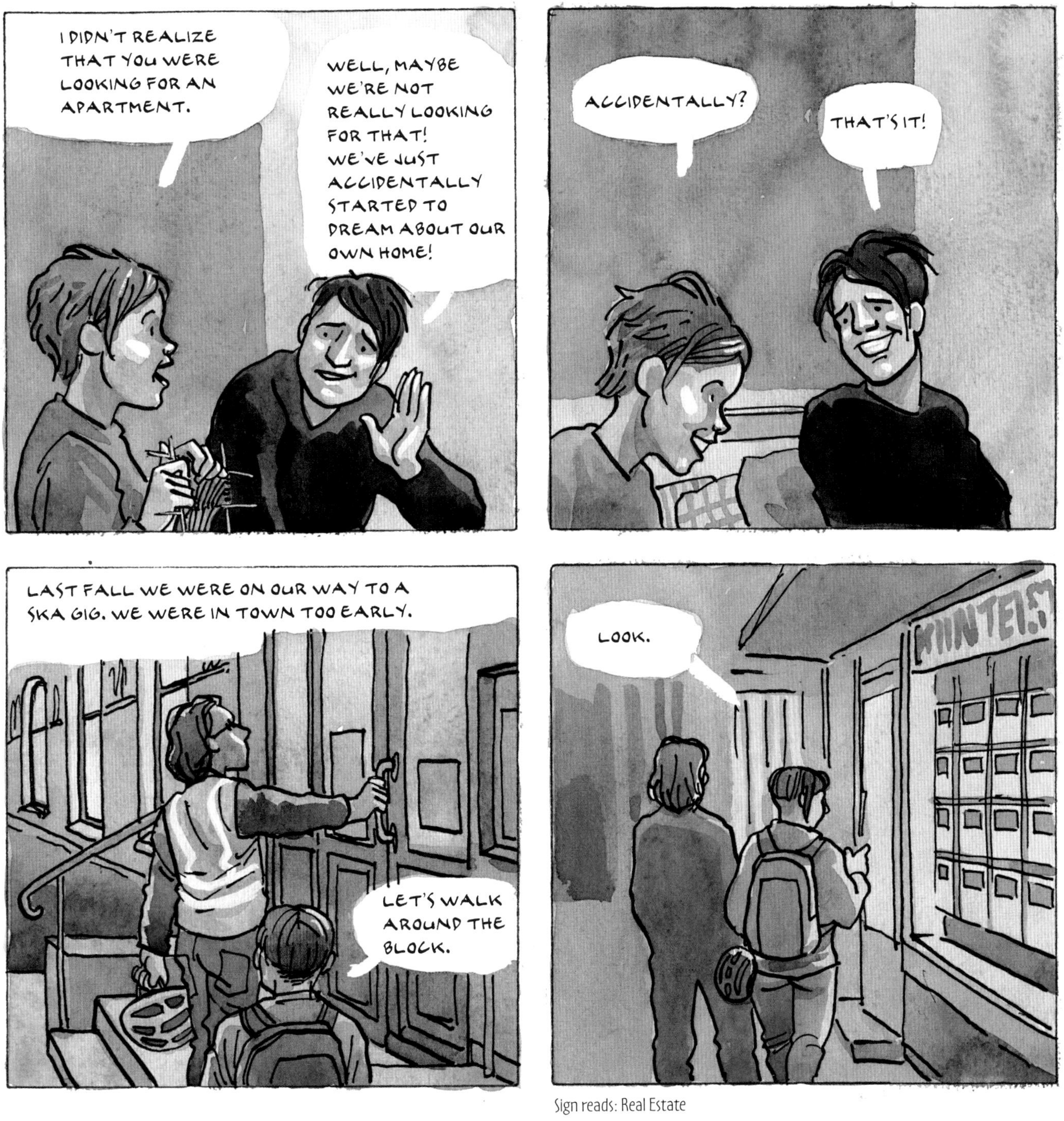
I DIDN'T REALIZE THAT YOU WERE LOOKING FOR AN APARTMENT.
WELL, MAYBE WE'RE NOT REALLY LOOKING FOR THAT! WE'VE JUST ACCIDENTALLY STARTED TO DREAM ABOUT OUR OWN HOME!
ACCIDENTALLY?
THAT'S IT!
LAST FALL WE WERE ON OUR WAY TO A SKA GIG. WE WERE IN TOWN TOO EARLY.
LET'S WALK AROUND THE BLOCK.
LOOK.

Sign reads: Real Estate

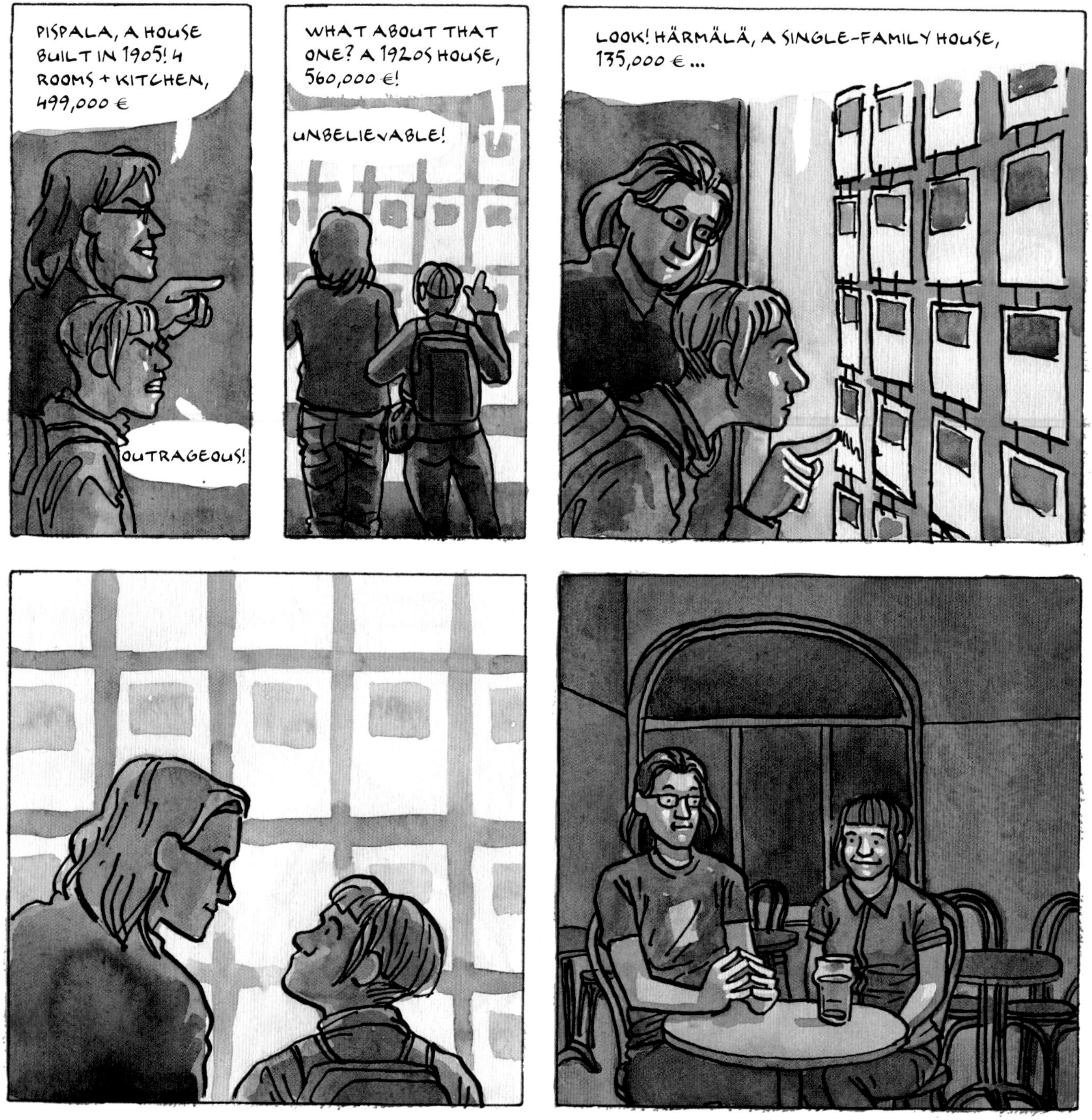
PISPALA, A HOUSE BUILT IN 1905! 4 ROOMS + KITCHEN, 499,000 €
OUTRAGEOUS!
WHAT ABOUT THAT ONE? A 1920S HOUSE, 560,000 €!
UNBELIEVABLE!
LOOK! HÄRMÄLÄ, A SINGLE-FAMILY HOUSE, 135,000 € ...

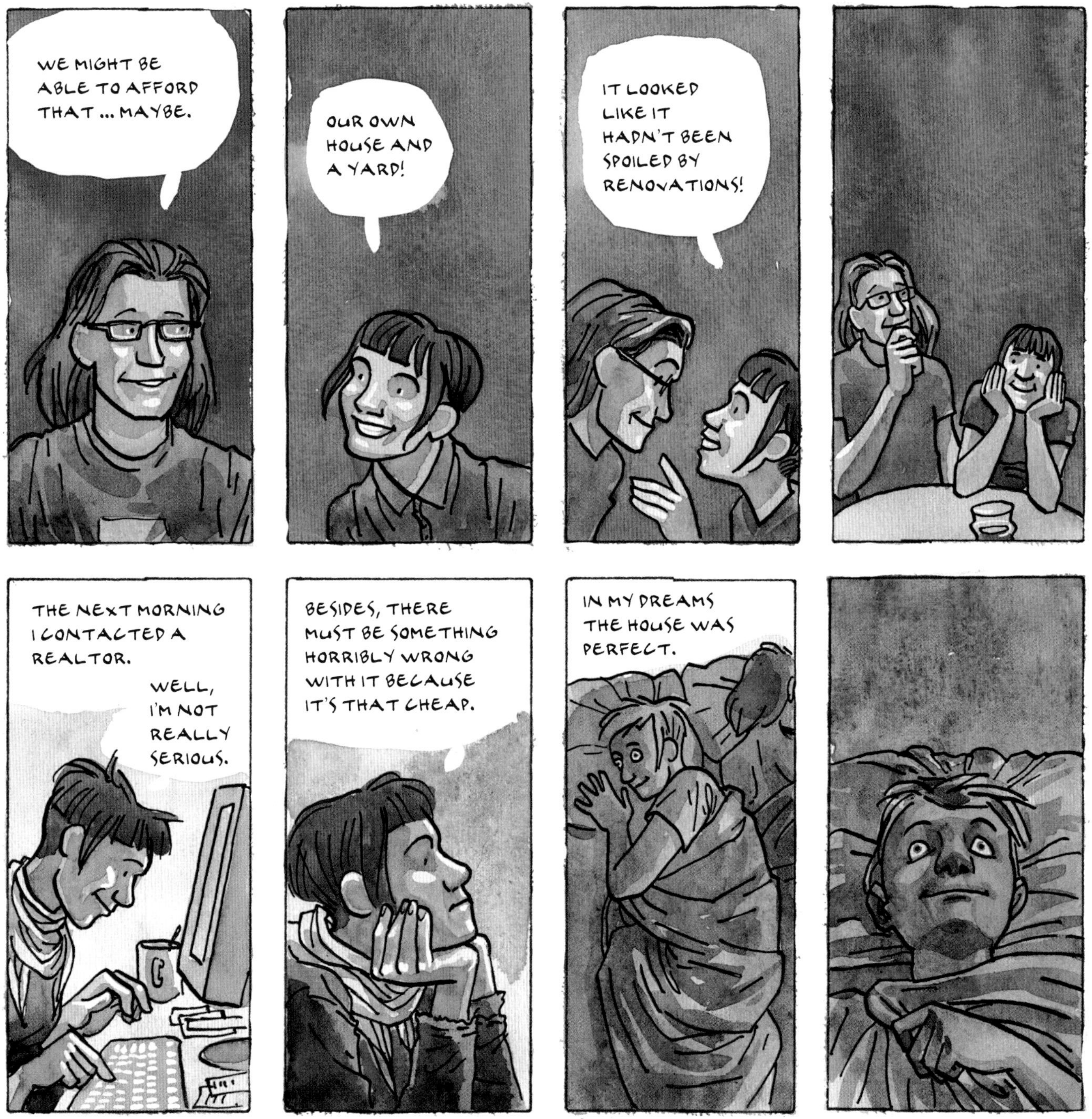
WE MIGHT BE ABLE TO AFFORD THAT ... MAYBE.
OUR OWN HOUSE AND A YARD!
IT LOOKED LIKE IT HADN'T BEEN SPOILED BY RENOVATIONS!
THE NEXT MORNING I CONTACTED A REALTOR.
WELL, I'M NOT REALLY SERIOUS.
BESIDES, THERE MUST BE SOMETHING HORRIBLY WRONG WITH IT BECAUSE IT'S THAT CHEAP.
IN MY DREAMS THE HOUSE WAS PERFECT.

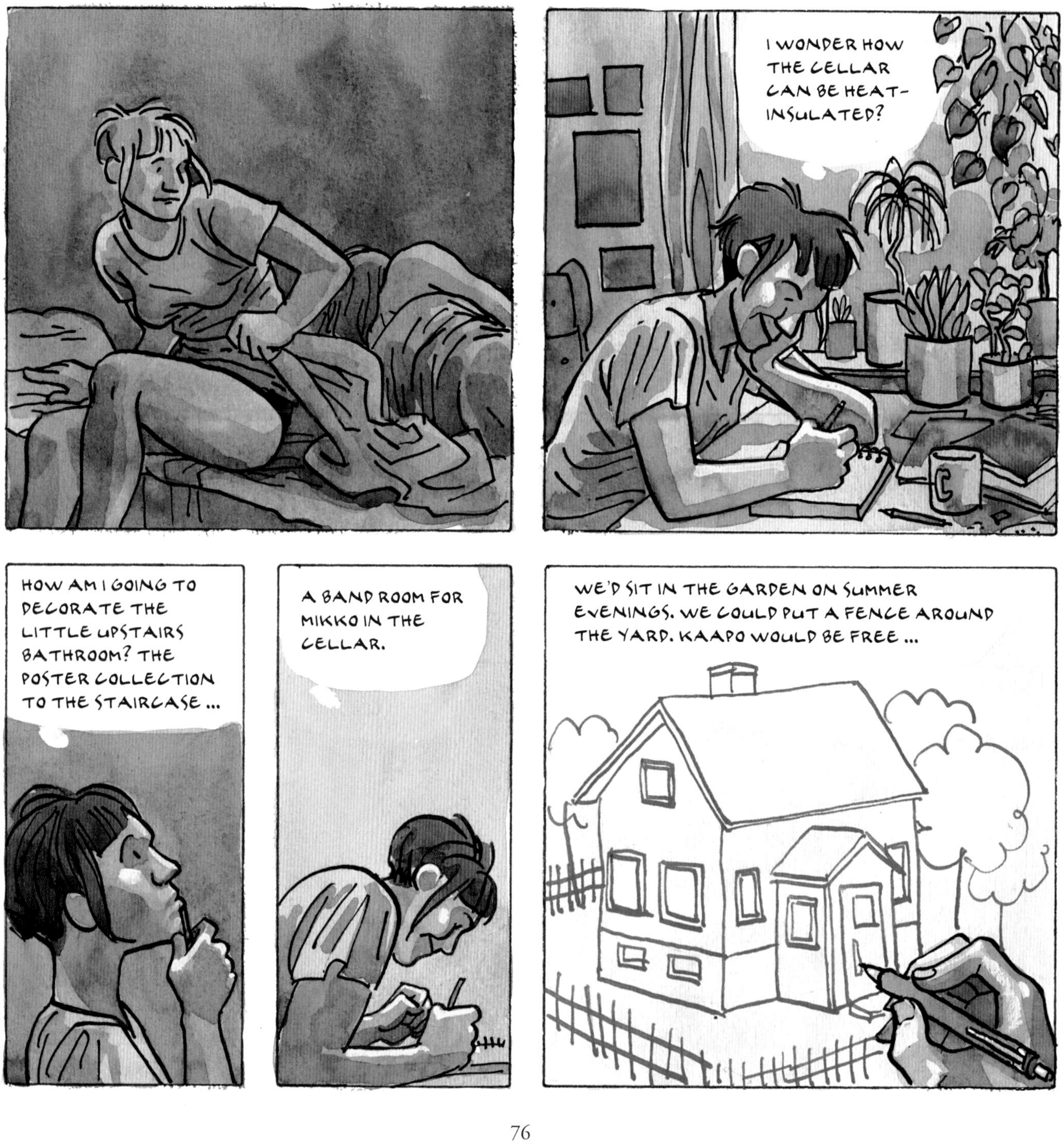
I WONDER HOW THE CELLAR CAN BE HEAT-INSULATED?
HOW AM I GOING TO DECORATE THE LITTLE UPSTAIRS BATHROOM? THE POSTER COLLECTION TO THE STAIRCASE ...
A BAND ROOM FOR MIKKO IN THE CELLAR.
WE'D SIT IN THE GARDEN ON SUMMER EVENINGS. WE COULD PUT A FENCE AROUND THE YARD. KAAPO WOULD BE FREE ...

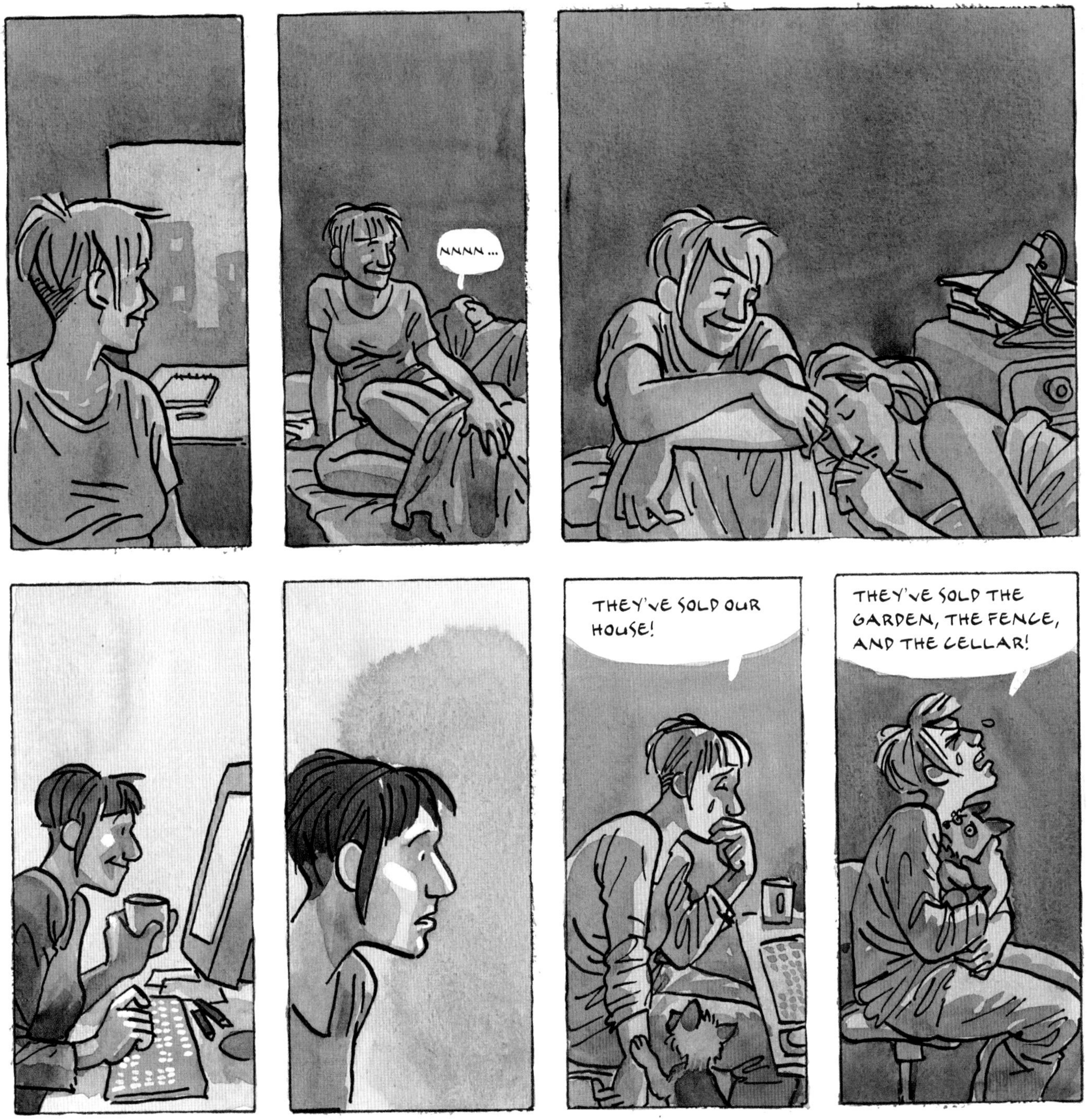
NNNN...
THEY'VE SOLD OUR HOUSE!
THEY'VE SOLD THE GARDEN, THE FENCE, AND THE CELLAR!

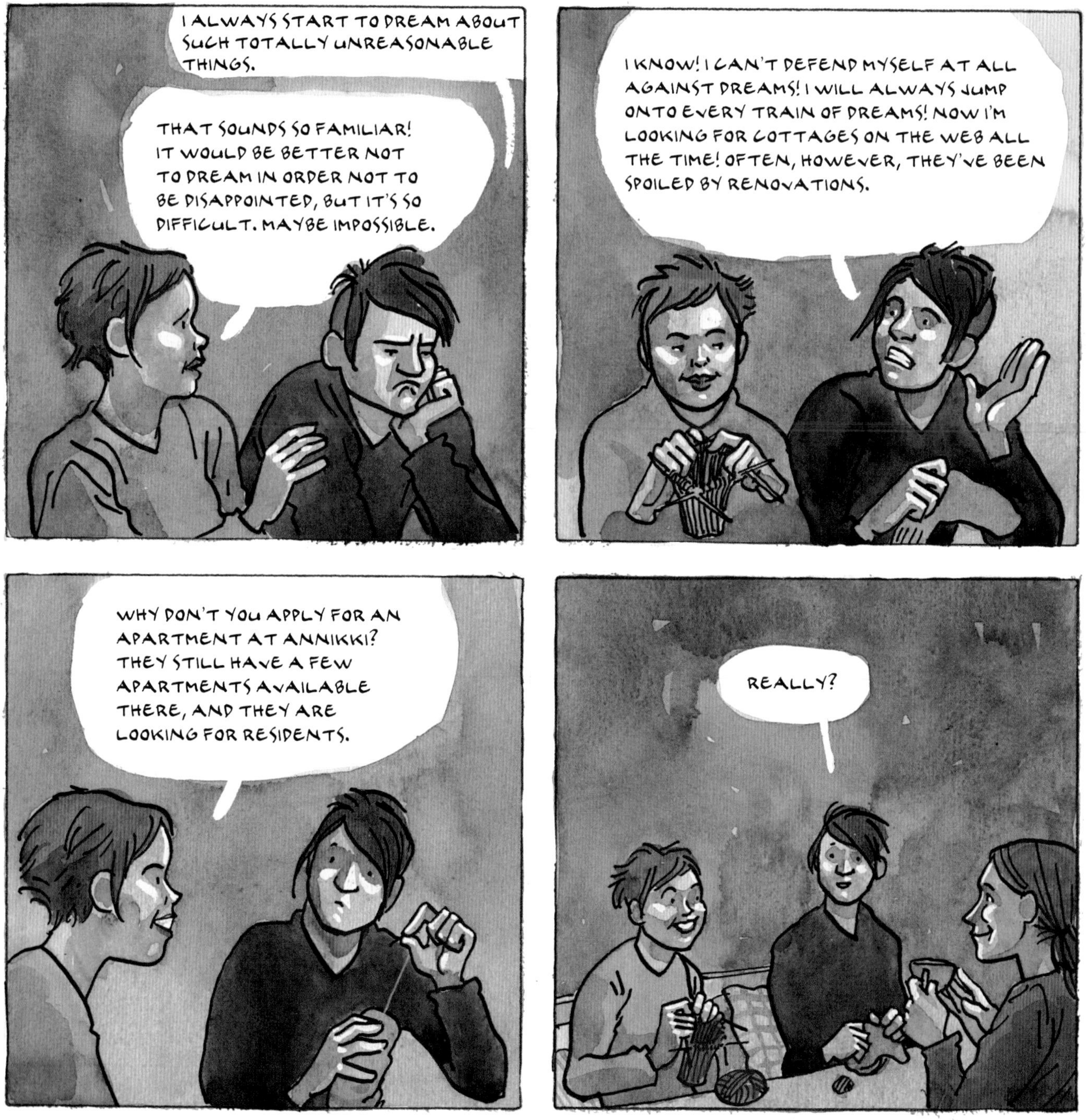
I ALWAYS START TO DREAM ABOUT SUCH TOTALLY UNREASONABLE THINGS.
THAT SOUNDS SO FAMILIAR! IT WOULD BE BETTER NOT TO DREAM IN ORDER NOT TO BE DISAPPOINTED, BUT IT'S SO DIFFICULT. MAYBE IMPOSSIBLE.
I KNOW! I CAN'T DEFEND MYSELF AT ALL AGAINST DREAMS! I WILL ALWAYS JUMP ONTO EVERY TRAIN OF DREAMS! NOW I'M LOOKING FOR COTTAGES ON THE WEB ALL THE TIME! OFTEN, HOWEVER, THEY'VE BEEN SPOILED BY RENOVATIONS.
WHY DON'T YOU APPLY FOR AN APARTMENT AT ANNIKKI? THEY STILL HAVE A FEW APARTMENTS AVAILABLE THERE, AND THEY ARE LOOKING FOR RESIDENTS.
REALLY?

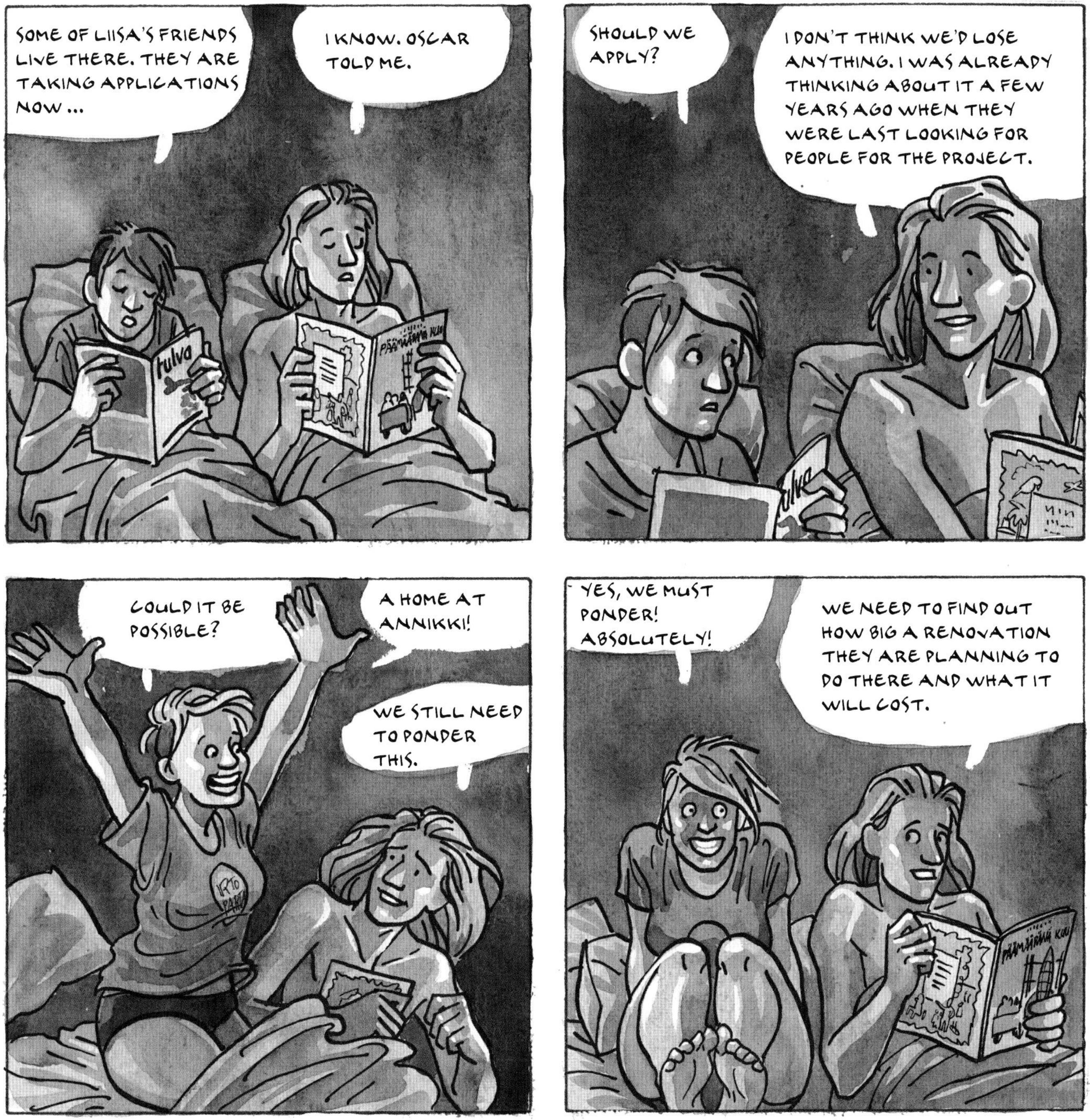
SOME OF LIISA'S FRIENDS LIVE THERE. THEY ARE TAKING APPLICATIONS NOW ...
I KNOW. OSCAR TOLD ME.
SHOULD WE APPLY?
I DON'T THINK WE'D LOSE ANYTHING. I WAS ALREADY THINKING ABOUT IT A FEW YEARS AGO WHEN THEY WERE LAST LOOKING FOR PEOPLE FOR THE PROJECT.
COULD IT BE POSSIBLE?
A HOME AT ANNIKKI!
WE STILL NEED TO PONDER THIS.
YES, WE MUST PONDER! ABSOLUTELY!
WE NEED TO FIND OUT HOW BIG A RENOVATION THEY ARE PLANNING TO DO THERE AND WHAT IT WILL COST.

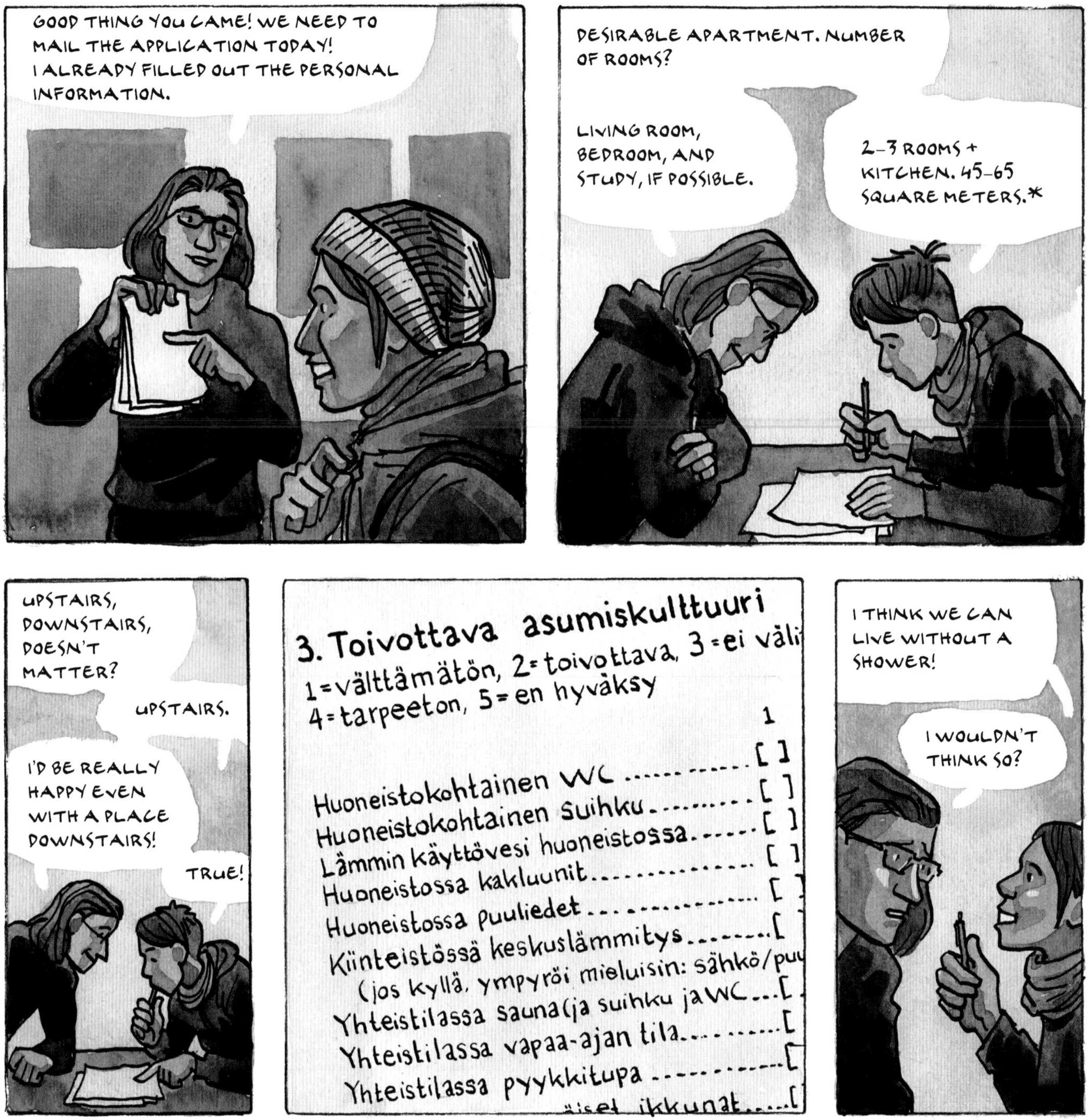
GOOD THING YOU CAME! WE NEED TO MAIL THE APPLICATION TODAY! I ALREADY FILLED OUT THE PERSONAL INFORMATION.
DESIRABLE APARTMENT. NUMBER OF ROOMS?
LIVING ROOM, BEDROOM, AND STUDY, IF POSSIBLE.
2–3 ROOMS + KITCHEN. 45–65 SQUARE METERS.*
UPSTAIRS, DOWNSTAIRS, DOESN'T MATTER?
UPSTAIRS.
I'D BE REALLY HAPPY EVEN WITH A PLACE DOWNSTAIRS!
TRUE!
3. Toivottava asumiskulttuuri
1 = välttämätön, 2 = toivottava, 3 = ei väli
4 = tarpeeton, 5 = en hyväksy
1
[ ]
Huoneistokohtainen WC .... [ ]
Huoneistokohtainen suihku .... [ ]
Lämmin käyttövesi huoneistossa .... [ ]
Huoneistossa kakluunit .... [ ]
Huoneistossa puuliedet .... [
Kiinteistössä keskuslämmitys .... [
(jos kyllä, ympyröi mieluisin: sähkö/puu
Yhteistilassa sauna (ja suihku ja WC ... [
Yhteistilassa vapaa-ajan tila .... [
Yhteistilassa pyykkitupa .... [
ikkunat ..... [
I THINK WE CAN LIVE WITHOUT A SHOWER!
I WOULDN'T THINK SO?

*500–700 square feet

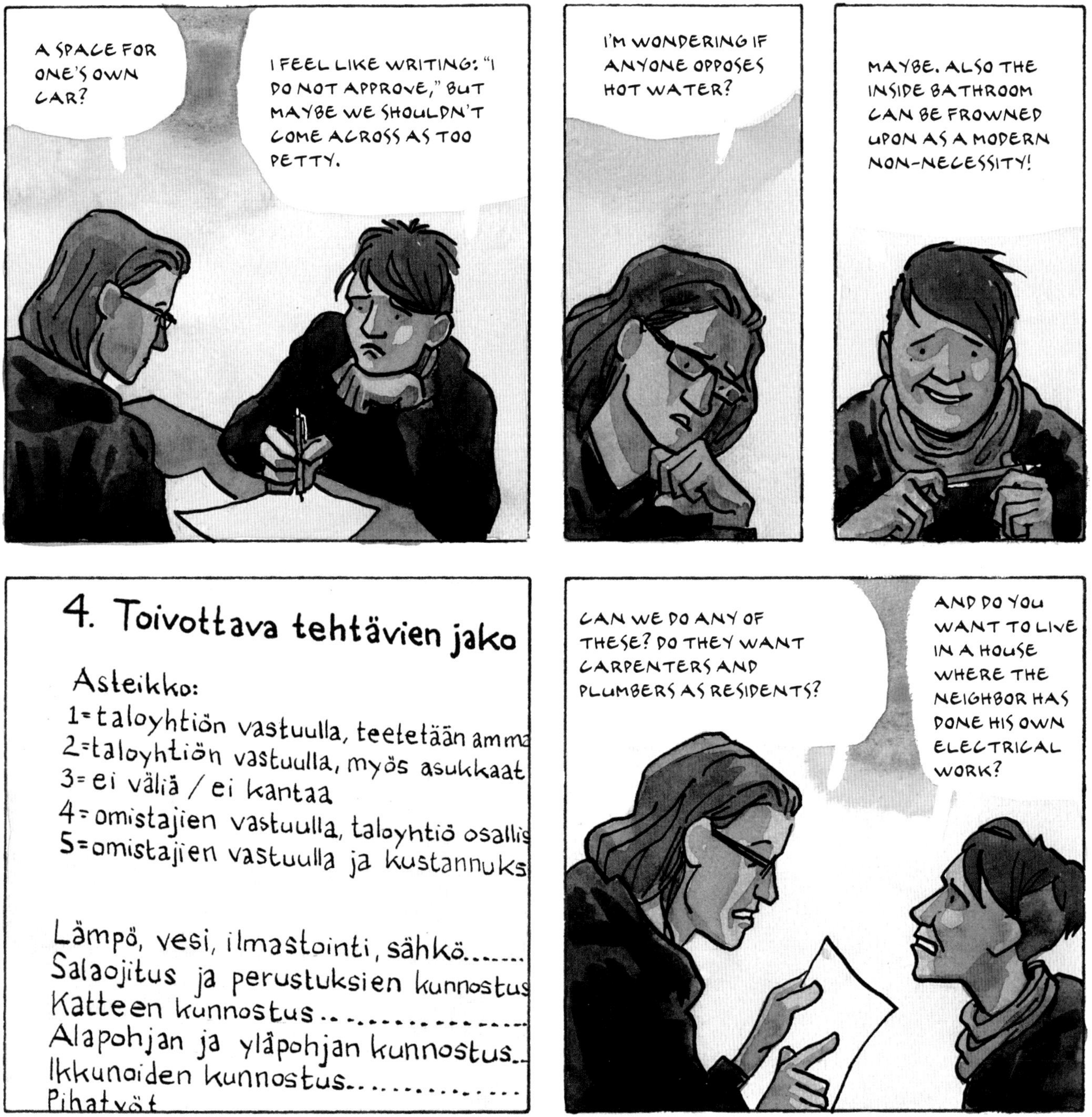
A SPACE FOR ONE'S OWN CAR?
I FEEL LIKE WRITING: "I DO NOT APPROVE," BUT MAYBE WE SHOULDN'T COME ACROSS AS TOO PETTY.
I'M WONDERING IF ANYONE OPPOSES HOT WATER?
MAYBE. ALSO THE INSIDE BATHROOM CAN BE FROWNED UPON AS A MODERN NON-NECESSITY!
4. Toivottava tehtävien jako
Asteikko:
1=taloyhtiön vastuulla, teetetään amm
2=taloyhtiön vastuulla, myös asukkaat
3=ei väliä / ei kantaa
4=omistajien vastuulla, taloyhtiö osallis
5=omistajien vastuulla ja kustannuks
Lämpö, vesi, ilmastointi, sähkö......
Salaojitus ja perustuksien kunnostus
Katteen kunnostus..............
Alapohjan ja yläpohjan kunnostus..
Ikkunoiden kunnostus..............
Pihatyöt
CAN WE DO ANY OF THESE? DO THEY WANT CARPENTERS AND PLUMBERS AS RESIDENTS?
AND DO YOU WANT TO LIVE IN A HOUSE WHERE THE NEIGHBOR HAS DONE HIS OWN ELECTRICAL WORK?

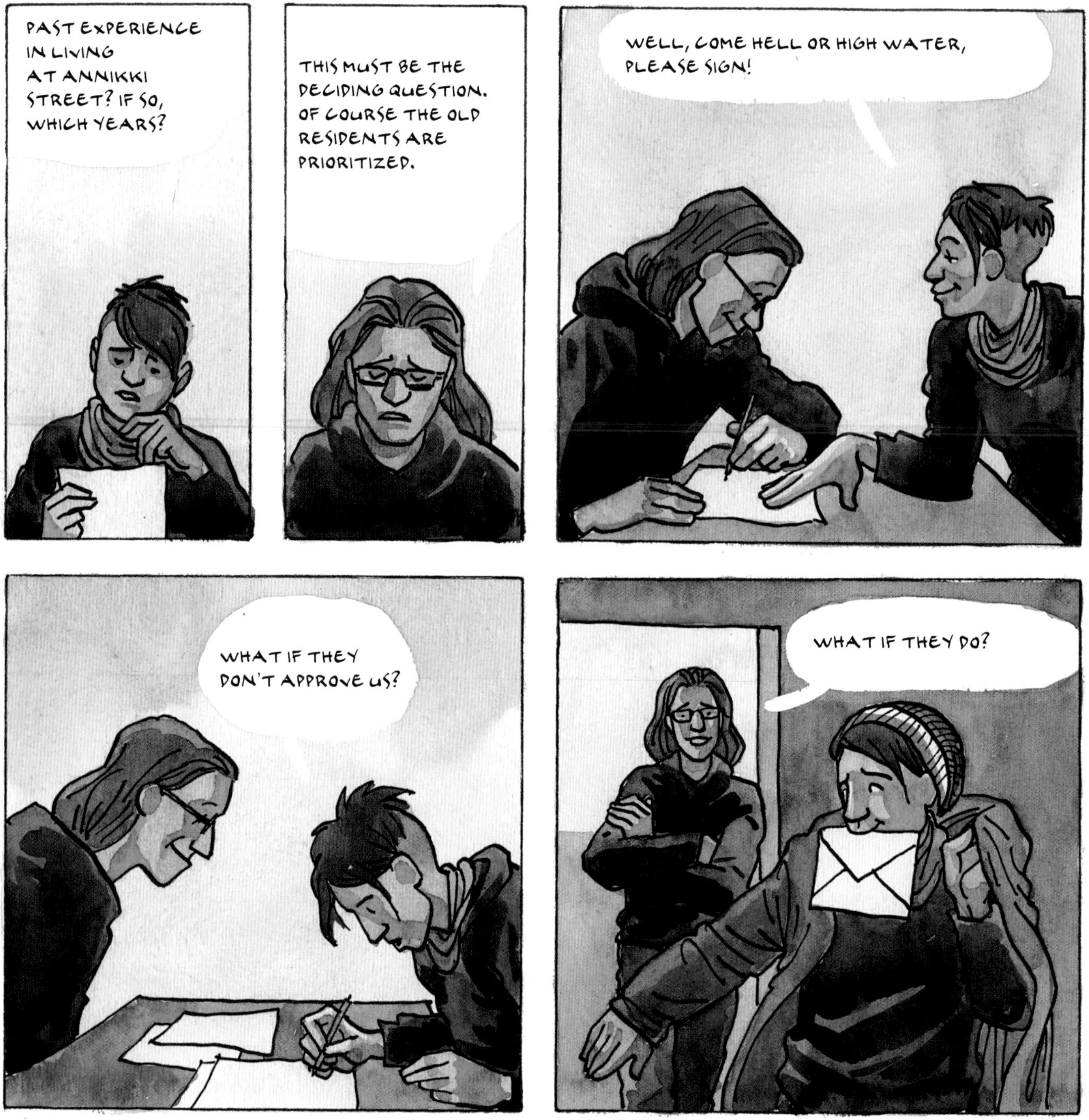
PAST EXPERIENCE IN LIVING AT ANNIKKI STREET? IF SO, WHICH YEARS?
THIS MUST BE THE DECIDING QUESTION. OF COURSE THE OLD RESIDENTS ARE PRIORITIZED.
WELL, COME HELL OR HIGH WATER, PLEASE SIGN!
WHAT IF THEY DON'T APPROVE US?
WHAT IF THEY DO?

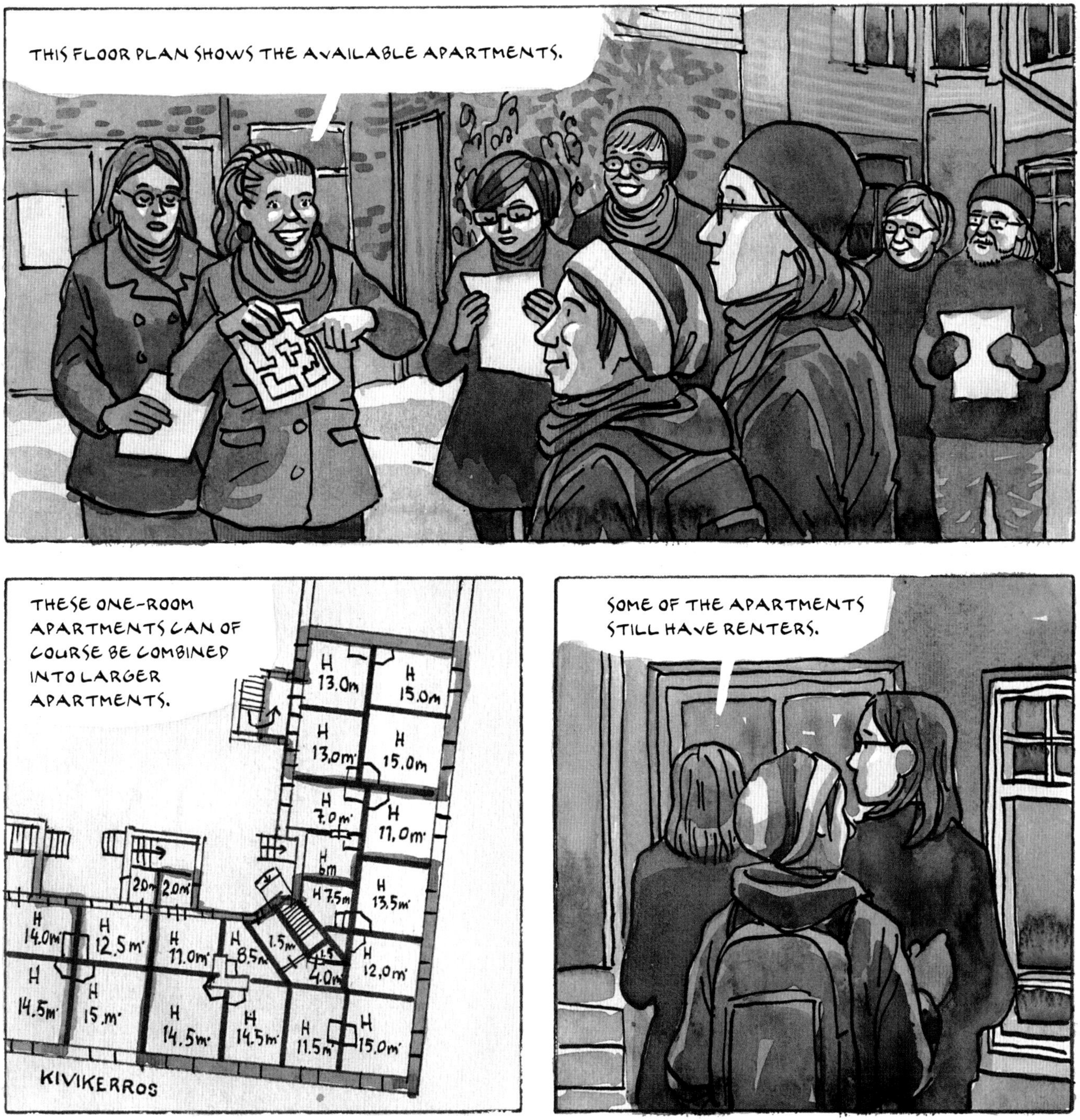
THIS FLOOR PLAN SHOWS THE AVAILABLE APARTMENTS.
THESE ONE-ROOM APARTMENTS CAN OF COURSE BE COMBINED INTO LARGER APARTMENTS.
H 13.0m
H 15.0m
H 13,0m
H 15.0m
H 7.0m
H 11,0m
H 6m
H 7.5m
H 13.5m
2.0m
2.0m
H 14.0m
H 12.5m
H 11.0m
H 8.5m
1.5m
1.5
4.0m
H 12,0m
H 14.5m
H 15.m
H 14.5m
H 14.5m
H 11.5m
H 15.0m
KIVIKERROS
SOME OF THE APARTMENTS STILL HAVE RENTERS.

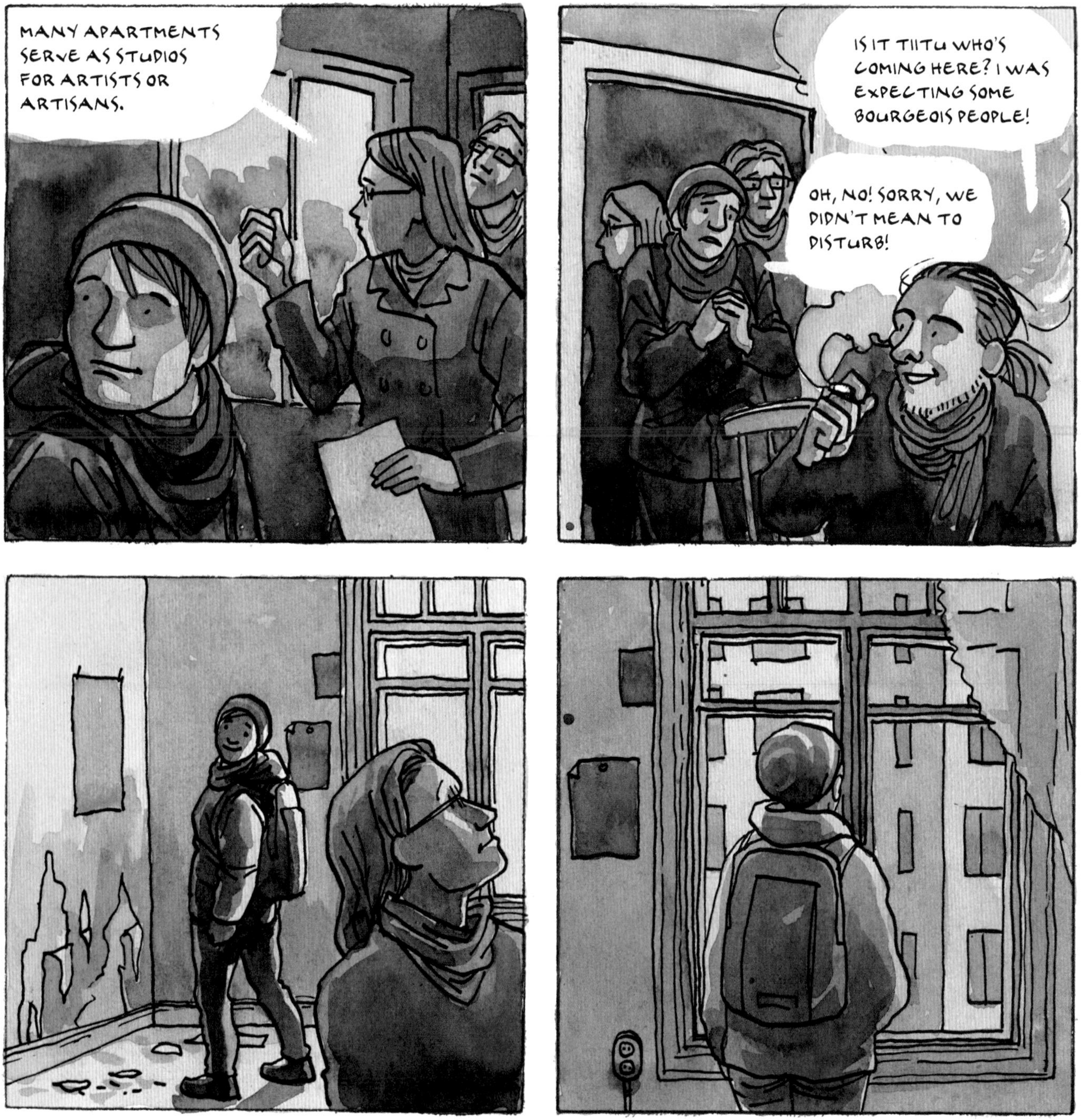
MANY APARTMENTS SERVE AS STUDIOS FOR ARTISTS OR ARTISANS.
IS IT TIITU WHO'S COMING HERE? I WAS EXPECTING SOME BOURGEOIS PEOPLE!
OH, NO! SORRY, WE DIDN'T MEAN TO DISTURB!

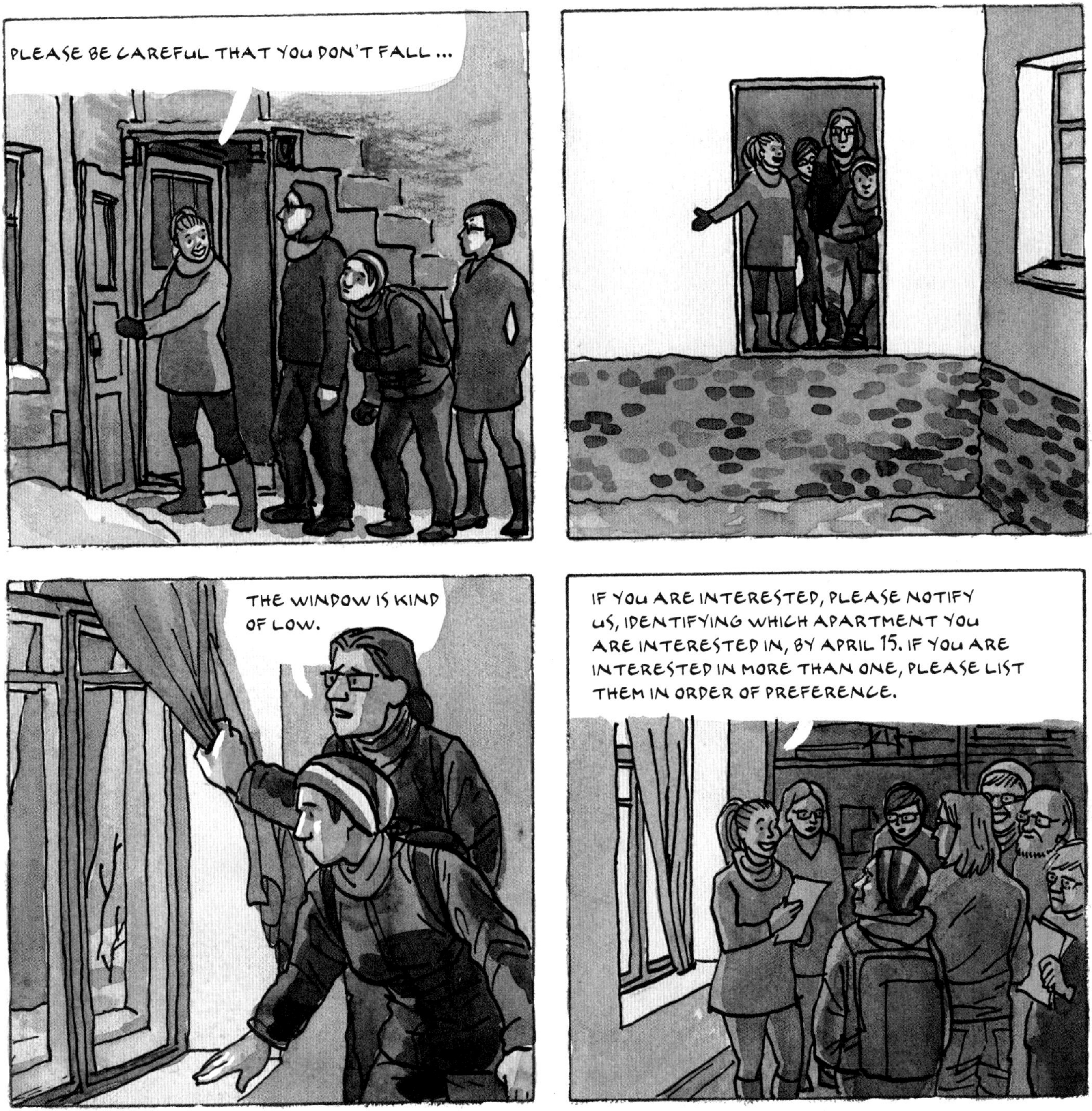
PLEASE BE CAREFUL THAT YOU DON'T FALL ...
THE WINDOW IS KIND OF LOW.
IF YOU ARE INTERESTED, PLEASE NOTIFY US, IDENTIFYING WHICH APARTMENT YOU ARE INTERESTED IN, BY APRIL 15. IF YOU ARE INTERESTED IN MORE THAN ONE, PLEASE LIST THEM IN ORDER OF PREFERENCE.

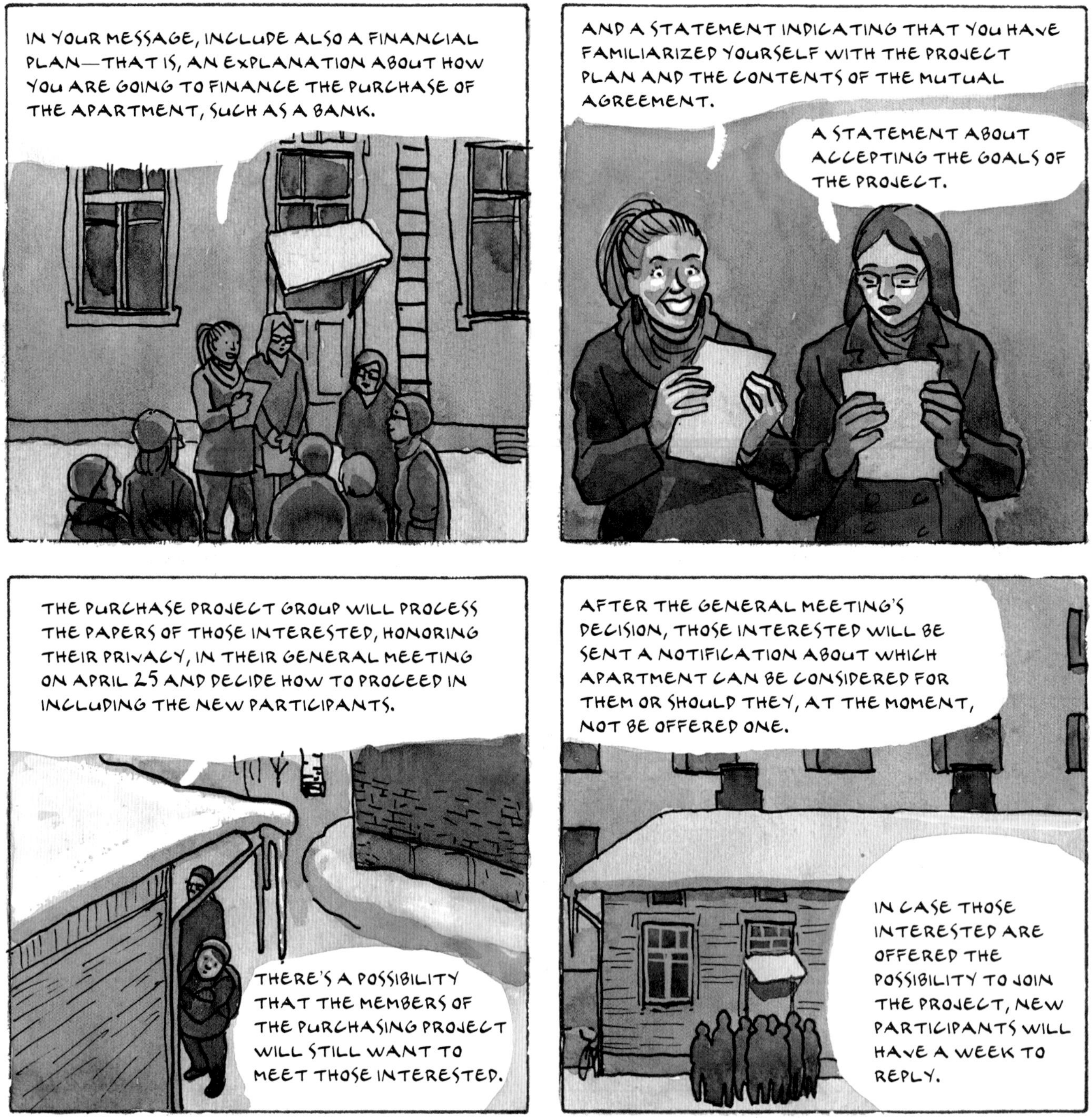
IN YOUR MESSAGE, INCLUDE ALSO A FINANCIAL PLAN—THAT IS, AN EXPLANATION ABOUT HOW YOU ARE GOING TO FINANCE THE PURCHASE OF THE APARTMENT, SUCH AS A BANK.
AND A STATEMENT INDICATING THAT YOU HAVE FAMILIARIZED YOURSELF WITH THE PROJECT PLAN AND THE CONTENTS OF THE MUTUAL AGREEMENT.
A STATEMENT ABOUT ACCEPTING THE GOALS OF THE PROJECT.
THE PURCHASE PROJECT GROUP WILL PROCESS THE PAPERS OF THOSE INTERESTED, HONORING THEIR PRIVACY, IN THEIR GENERAL MEETING ON APRIL 25 AND DECIDE HOW TO PROCEED IN INCLUDING THE NEW PARTICIPANTS.
THERE'S A POSSIBILITY THAT THE MEMBERS OF THE PURCHASING PROJECT WILL STILL WANT TO MEET THOSE INTERESTED.
AFTER THE GENERAL MEETING'S DECISION, THOSE INTERESTED WILL BE SENT A NOTIFICATION ABOUT WHICH APARTMENT CAN BE CONSIDERED FOR THEM OR SHOULD THEY, AT THE MOMENT, NOT BE OFFERED ONE.
IN CASE THOSE INTERESTED ARE OFFERED THE POSSIBILITY TO JOIN THE PROJECT, NEW PARTICIPANTS WILL HAVE A WEEK TO REPLY.

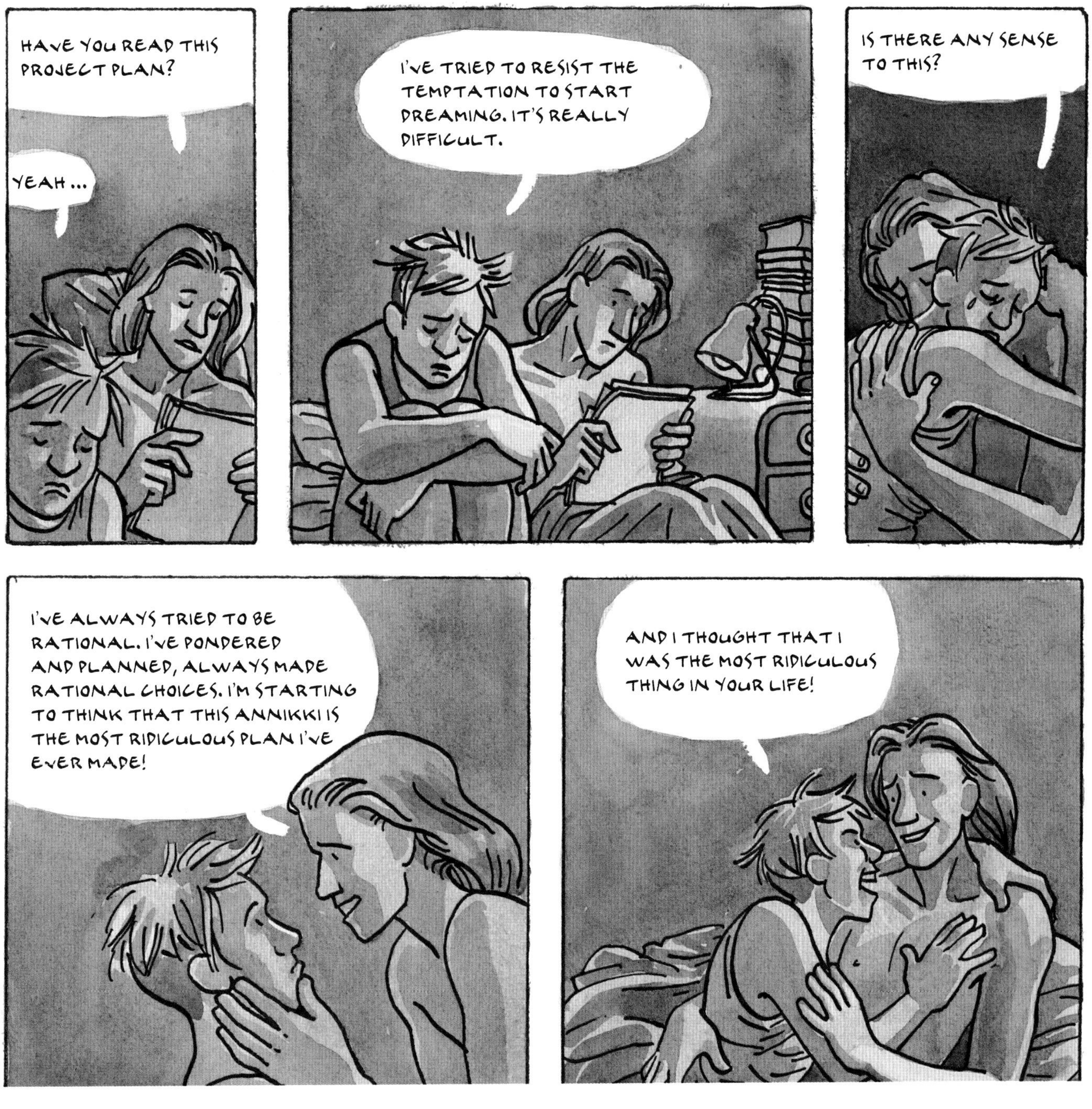
HAVE YOU READ THIS PROJECT PLAN?
YEAH ...
I'VE TRIED TO RESIST THE TEMPTATION TO START DREAMING. IT'S REALLY DIFFICULT.
IS THERE ANY SENSE TO THIS?
I'VE ALWAYS TRIED TO BE RATIONAL. I'VE PONDERED AND PLANNED, ALWAYS MADE RATIONAL CHOICES. I'M STARTING TO THINK THAT THIS ANNIKKI IS THE MOST RIDICULOUS PLAN I'VE EVER MADE!
AND I THOUGHT THAT I WAS THE MOST RIDICULOUS THING IN YOUR LIFE!

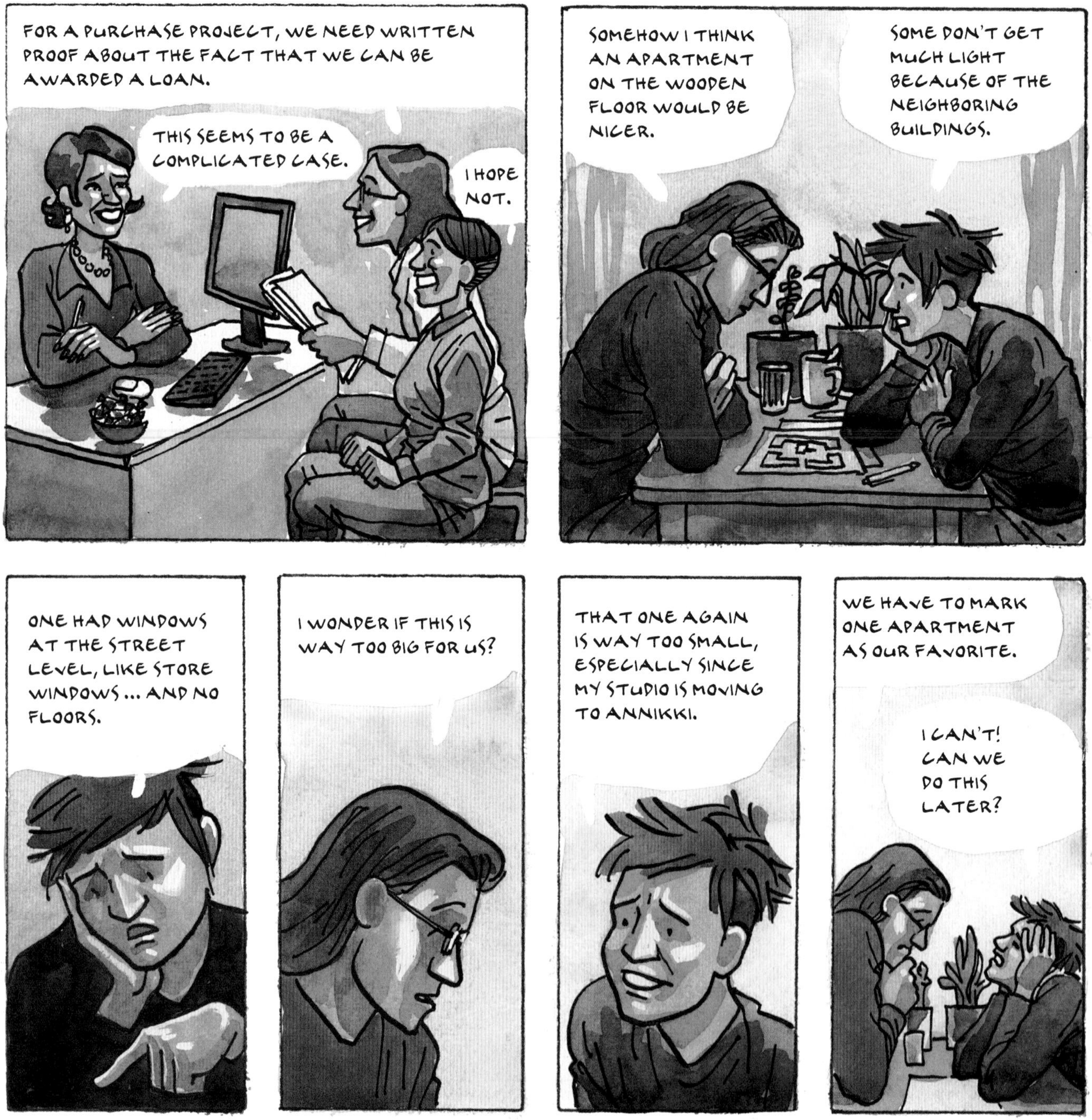
FOR A PURCHASE PROJECT, WE NEED WRITTEN PROOF ABOUT THE FACT THAT WE CAN BE AWARDED A LOAN.
THIS SEEMS TO BE A COMPLICATED CASE.
I HOPE NOT.
SOMEHOW I THINK AN APARTMENT ON THE WOODEN FLOOR WOULD BE NICER.
SOME DON'T GET MUCH LIGHT BECAUSE OF THE NEIGHBORING BUILDINGS.
ONE HAD WINDOWS AT THE STREET LEVEL, LIKE STORE WINDOWS ... AND NO FLOORS.
I WONDER IF THIS IS WAY TOO BIG FOR US?
THAT ONE AGAIN IS WAY TOO SMALL, ESPECIALLY SINCE MY STUDIO IS MOVING TO ANNIKKI.
WE HAVE TO MARK ONE APARTMENT AS OUR FAVORITE.
I CAN'T! CAN WE DO THIS LATER?

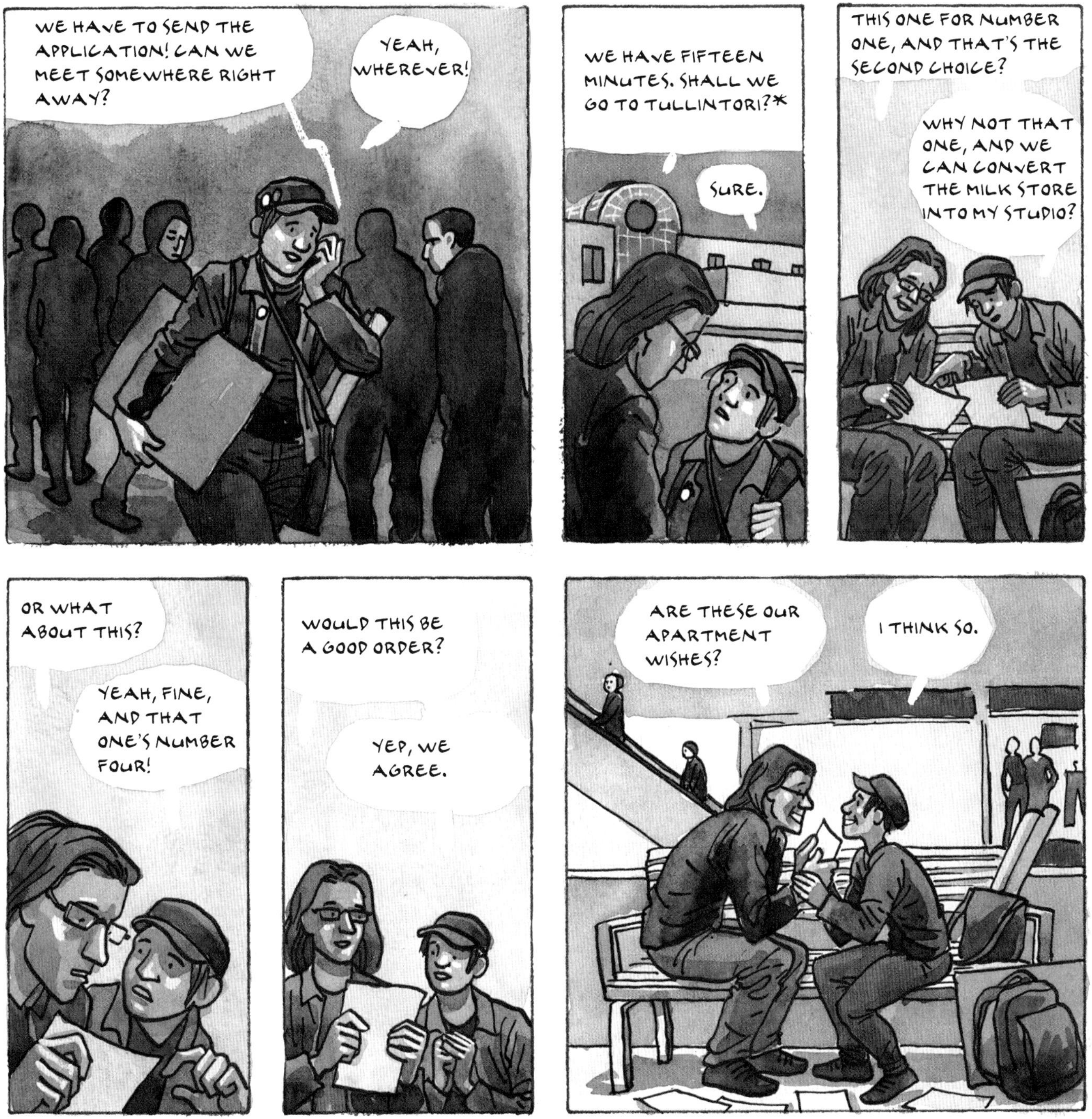
WE HAVE TO SEND THE APPLICATION! CAN WE MEET SOMEWHERE RIGHT AWAY?
YEAH, WHEREVER!
WE HAVE FIFTEEN MINUTES. SHALL WE GO TO TULLINTORI?*
SURE.
THIS ONE FOR NUMBER ONE, AND THAT'S THE SECOND CHOICE?
WHY NOT THAT ONE, AND WE CAN CONVERT THE MILK STORE INTO MY STUDIO?
OR WHAT ABOUT THIS?
YEAH, FINE, AND THAT ONE'S NUMBER FOUR!
WOULD THIS BE A GOOD ORDER?
YEP, WE AGREE.
ARE THESE OUR APARTMENT WISHES?
I THINK SO.

*A shopping center in Tampere.

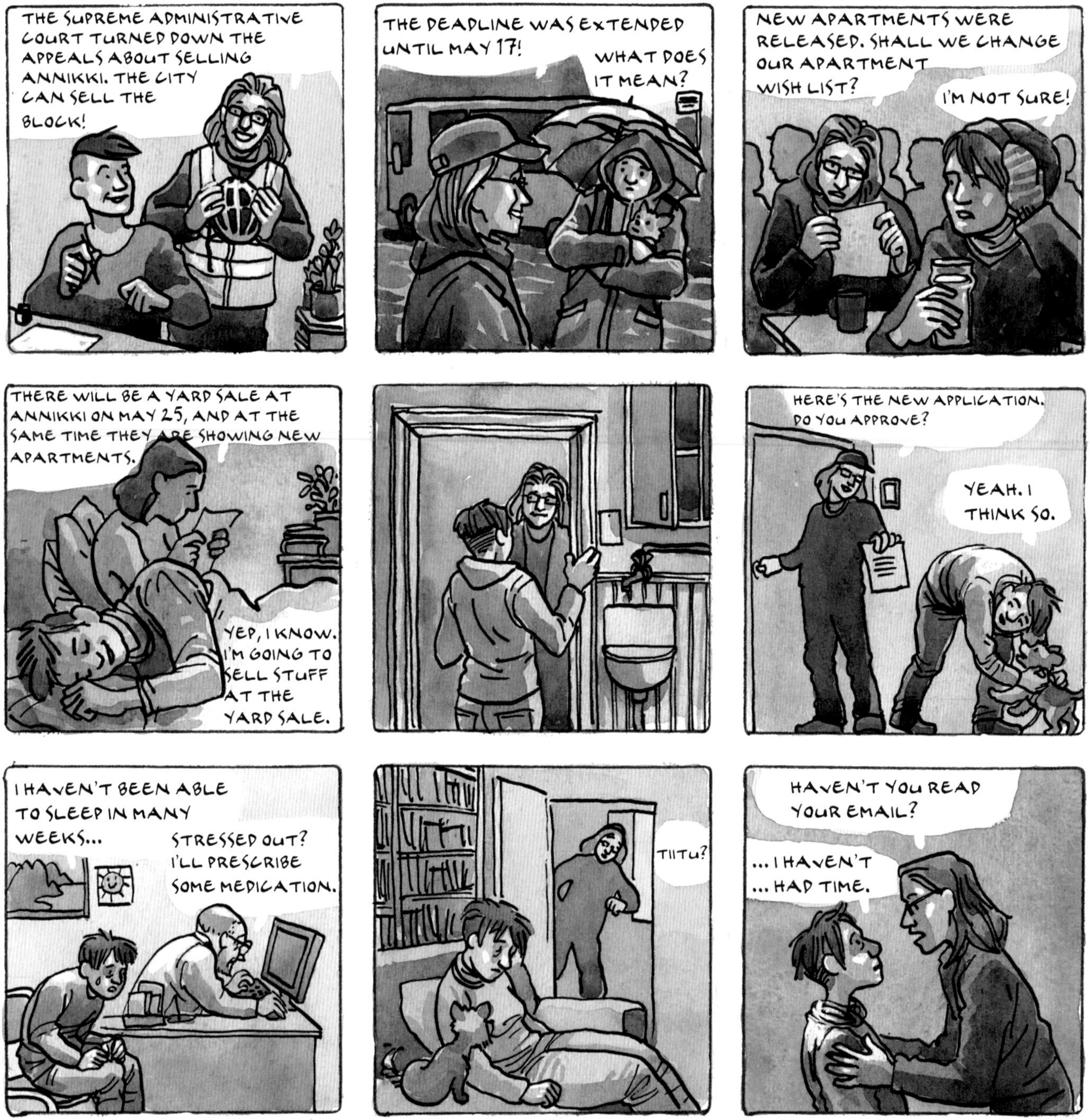
THE SUPREME ADMINISTRATIVE COURT TURNED DOWN THE APPEALS ABOUT SELLING ANNIKKI. THE CITY CAN SELL THE BLOCK!
THE DEADLINE WAS EXTENDED UNTIL MAY 17!
WHAT DOES IT MEAN?
NEW APARTMENTS WERE RELEASED. SHALL WE CHANGE OUR APARTMENT WISH LIST?
I'M NOT SURE!
THERE WILL BE A YARD SALE AT ANNIKKI ON MAY 25, AND AT THE SAME TIME THEY ARE SHOWING NEW APARTMENTS.
YEP, I KNOW. I'M GOING TO SELL STUFF AT THE YARD SALE.
HERE'S THE NEW APPLICATION. DO YOU APPROVE?
YEAH. I THINK SO.
I HAVEN'T BEEN ABLE TO SLEEP IN MANY WEEKS...
STRESSED OUT? I'LL PRESCRIBE SOME MEDICATION.
TIITU?
HAVEN'T YOU READ YOUR EMAIL?
... I HAVEN'T ... HAD TIME.

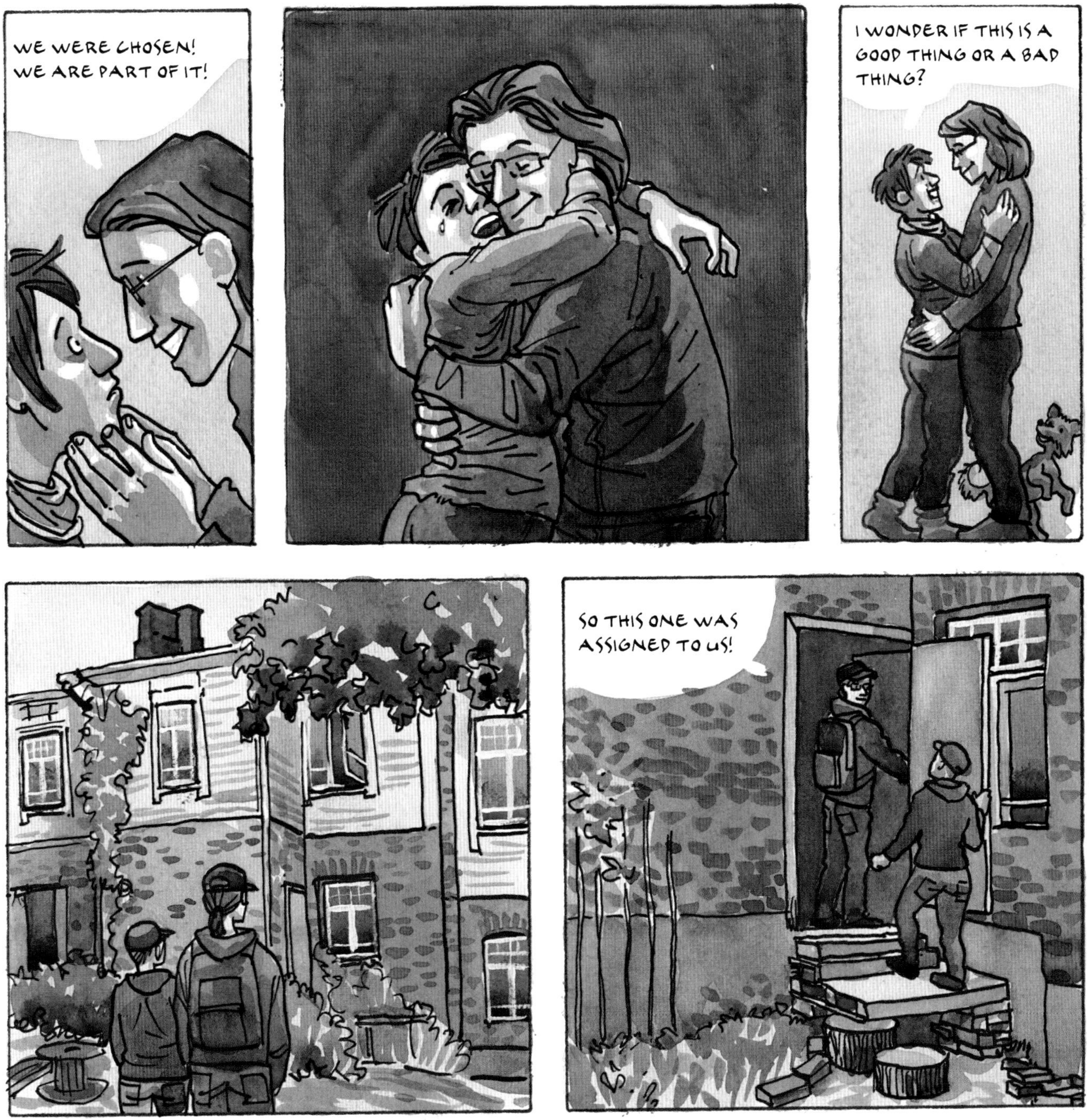
WE WERE CHOSEN! WE ARE PART OF IT!
I WONDER IF THIS IS A GOOD THING OR A BAD THING?
SO THIS ONE WAS ASSIGNED TO US!

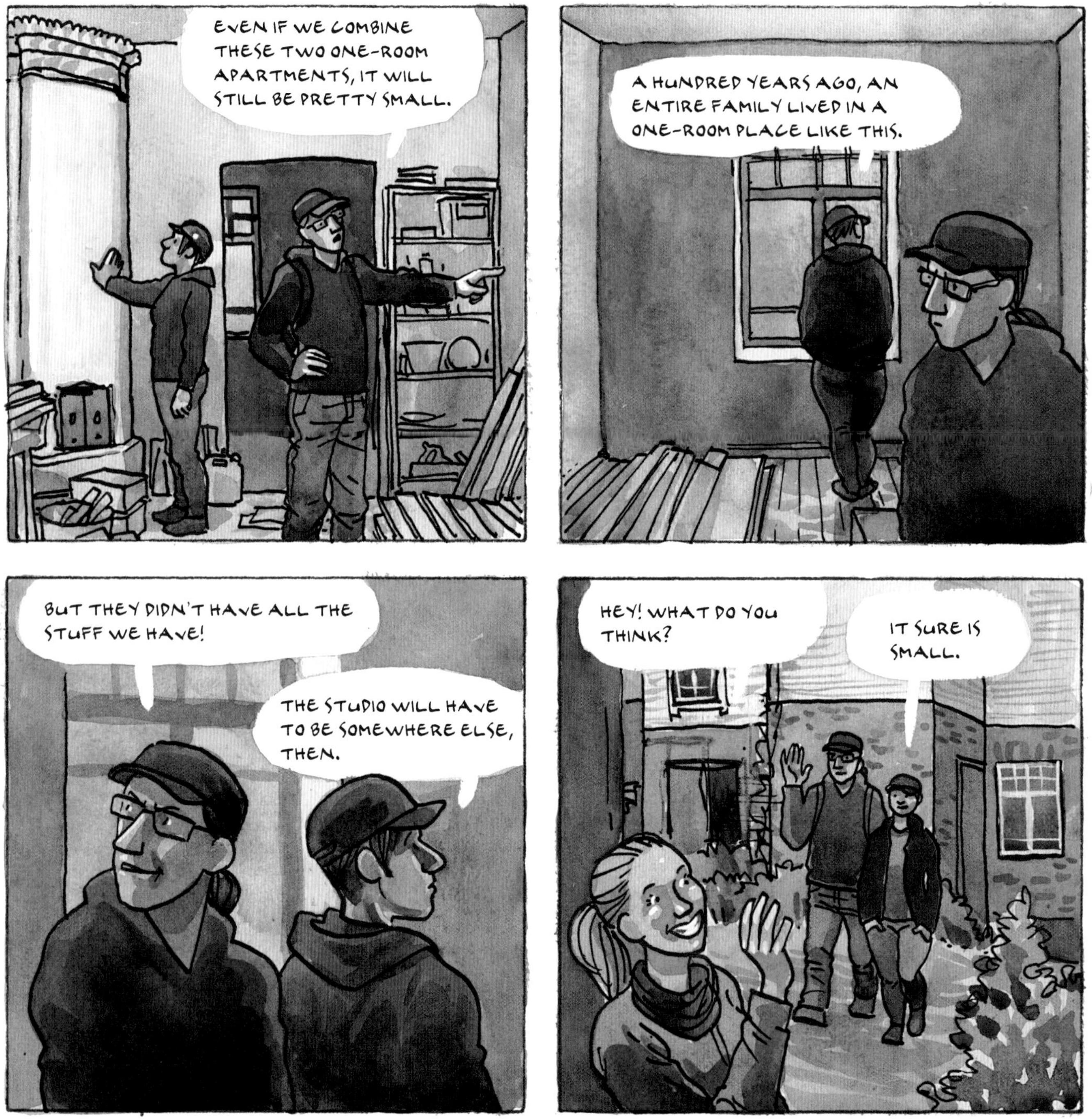
EVEN IF WE COMBINE THESE TWO ONE-ROOM APARTMENTS, IT WILL STILL BE PRETTY SMALL.
A HUNDRED YEARS AGO, AN ENTIRE FAMILY LIVED IN A ONE-ROOM PLACE LIKE THIS.
BUT THEY DIDN'T HAVE ALL THE STUFF WE HAVE!
THE STUDIO WILL HAVE TO BE SOMEWHERE ELSE, THEN.
HEY! WHAT DO YOU THINK?
IT SURE IS SMALL.

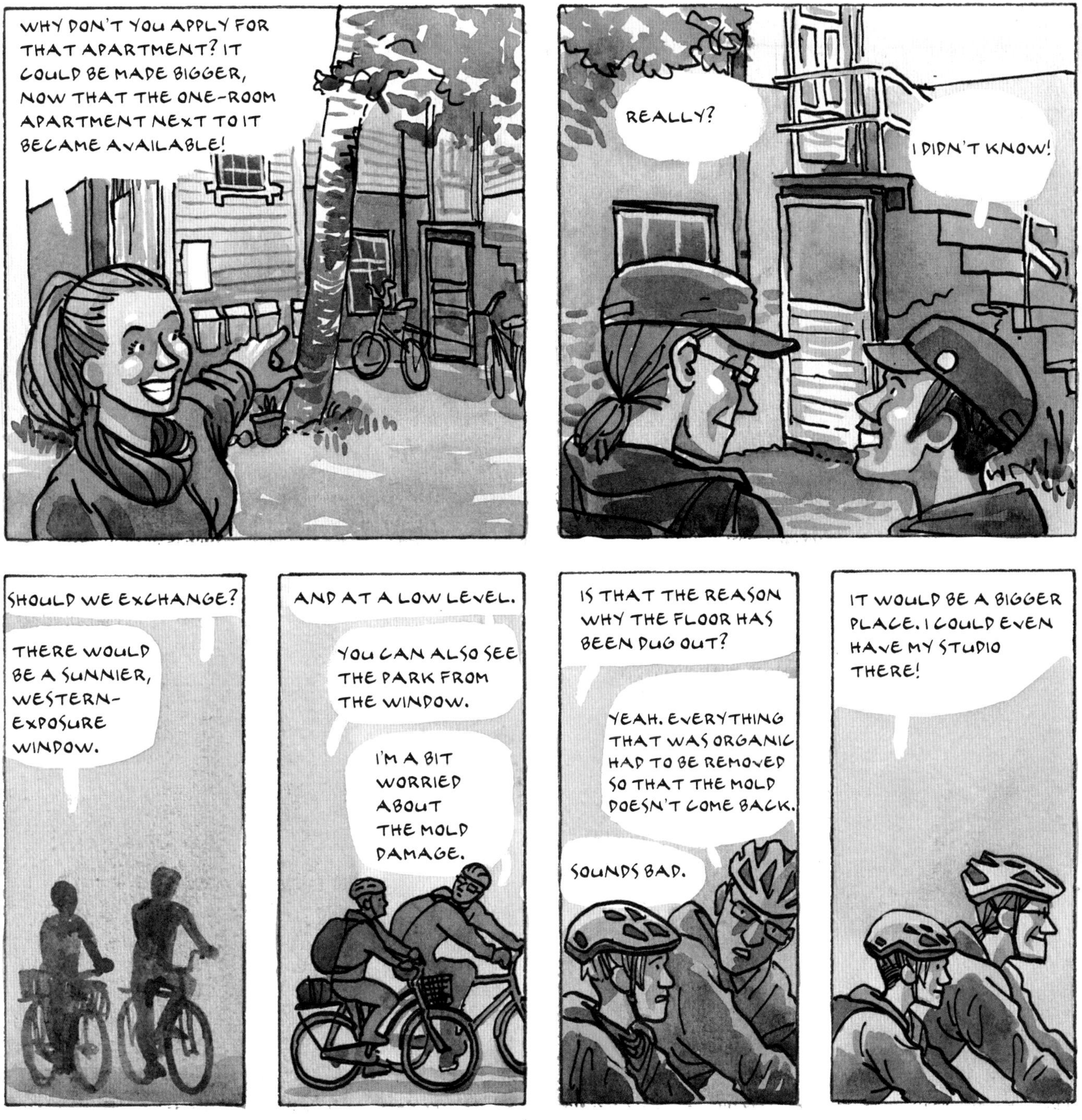
WHY DON'T YOU APPLY FOR THAT APARTMENT? IT COULD BE MADE BIGGER, NOW THAT THE ONE-ROOM APARTMENT NEXT TO IT BECAME AVAILABLE!
REALLY?
I DIDN'T KNOW!
SHOULD WE EXCHANGE?
THERE WOULD BE A SUNNIER, WESTERN-EXPOSURE WINDOW.
AND AT A LOW LEVEL.
YOU CAN ALSO SEE THE PARK FROM THE WINDOW.
I'M A BIT WORRIED ABOUT THE MOLD DAMAGE.
IS THAT THE REASON WHY THE FLOOR HAS BEEN DUG OUT?
YEAH. EVERYTHING THAT WAS ORGANIC HAD TO BE REMOVED SO THAT THE MOLD DOESN'T COME BACK.
SOUNDS BAD.
IT WOULD BE A BIGGER PLACE. I COULD EVEN HAVE MY STUDIO THERE!

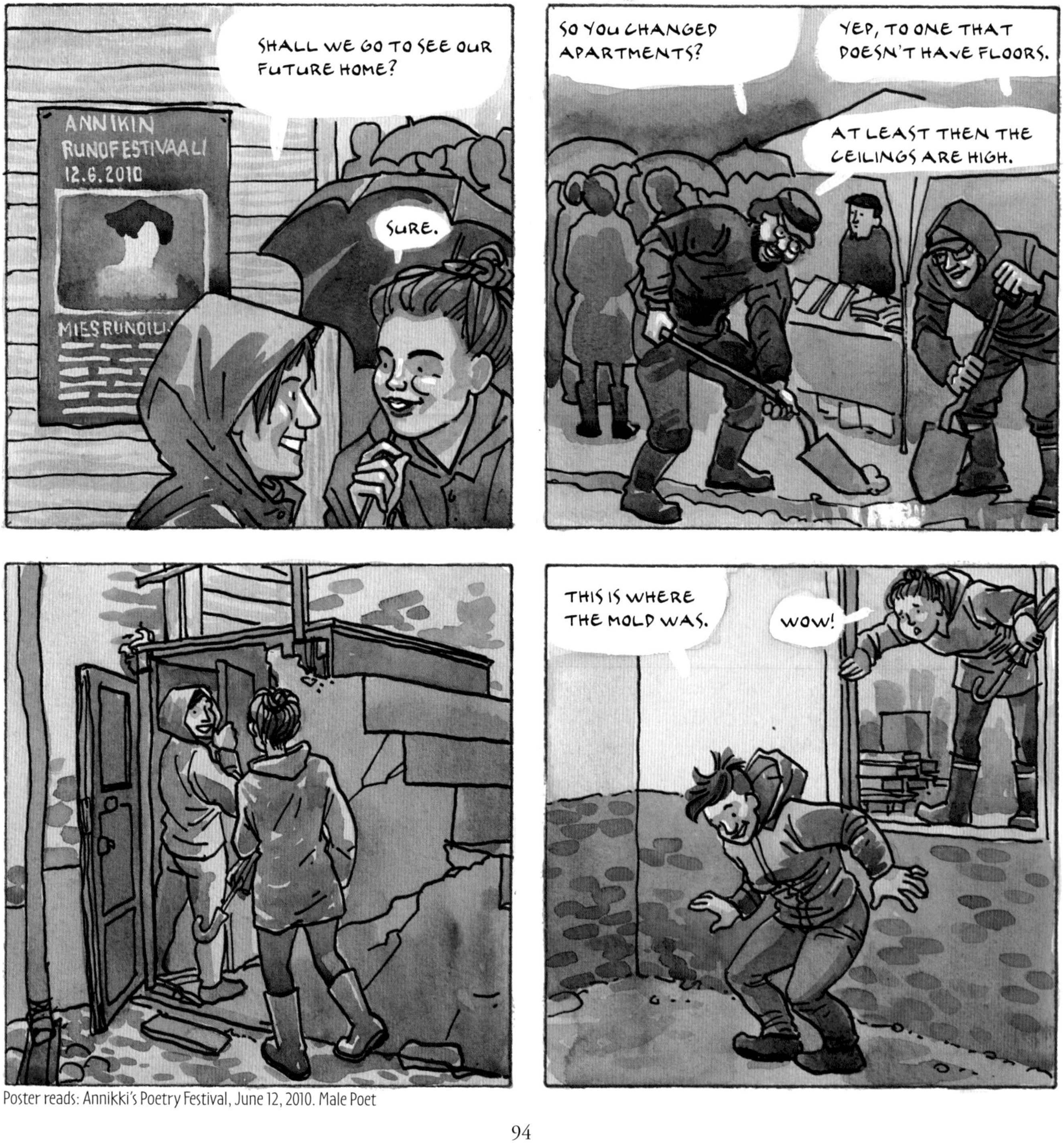
SHALL WE GO TO SEE OUR FUTURE HOME?
ANNIKIN RUNOFESTIVAALI 12.6.2010
MIESRUNOILIJ
SURE.
SO YOU CHANGED APARTMENTS?
YEP, TO ONE THAT DOESN'T HAVE FLOORS.
AT LEAST THEN THE CEILINGS ARE HIGH.
THIS IS WHERE THE MOLD WAS.
WOW!

Poster reads: Annikki's Poetry Festival, June 12, 2010. Male Poet

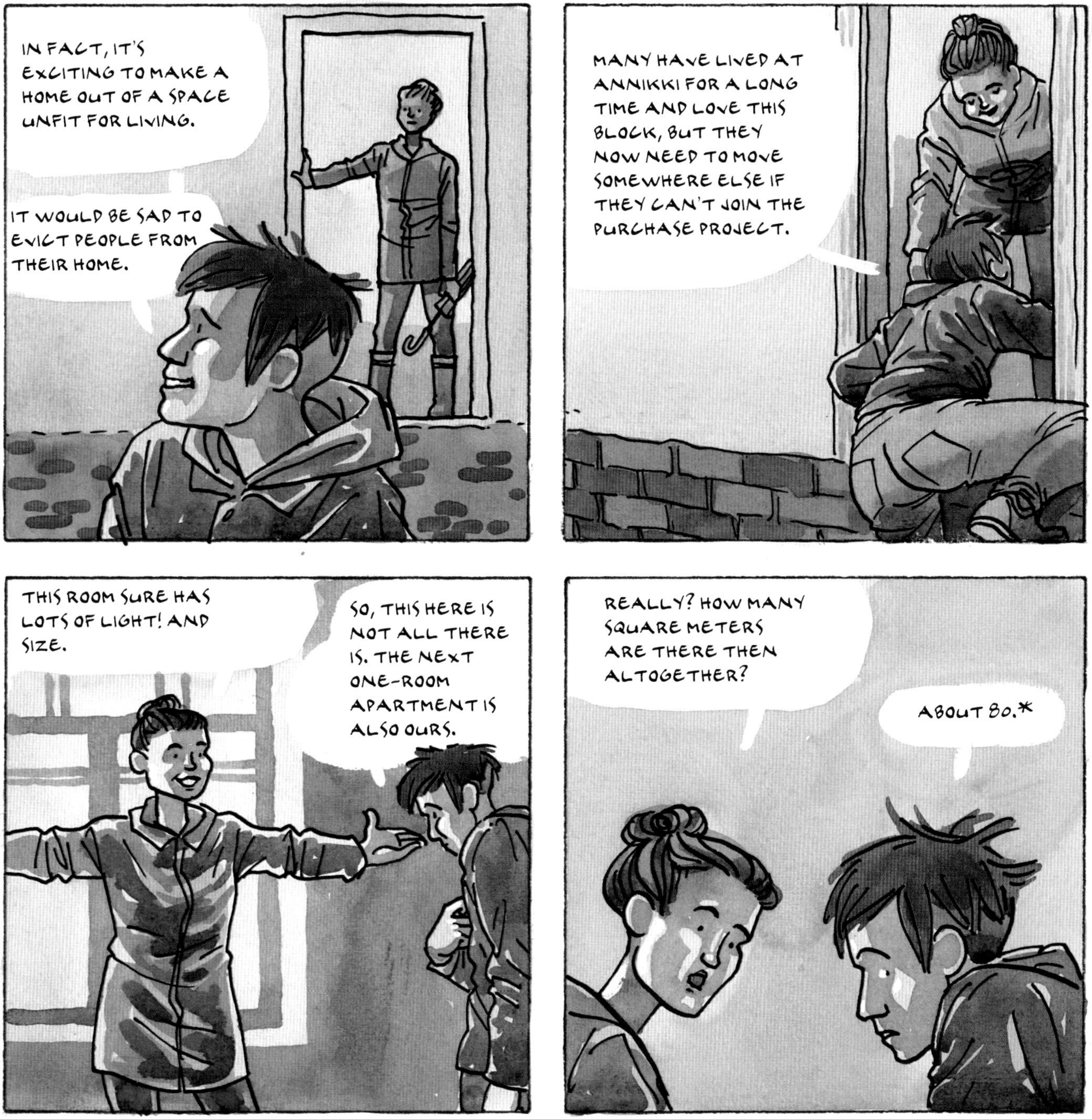
IN FACT, IT'S EXCITING TO MAKE A HOME OUT OF A SPACE UNFIT FOR LIVING.
IT WOULD BE SAD TO EVICT PEOPLE FROM THEIR HOME.
MANY HAVE LIVED AT ANNIKKI FOR A LONG TIME AND LOVE THIS BLOCK, BUT THEY NOW NEED TO MOVE SOMEWHERE ELSE IF THEY CAN'T JOIN THE PURCHASE PROJECT.
THIS ROOM SURE HAS LOTS OF LIGHT! AND SIZE.
SO, THIS HERE IS NOT ALL THERE IS. THE NEXT ONE-ROOM APARTMENT IS ALSO OURS.
REALLY? HOW MANY SQUARE METERS ARE THERE THEN ALTOGETHER?
ABOUT 80.*

*860 square feet

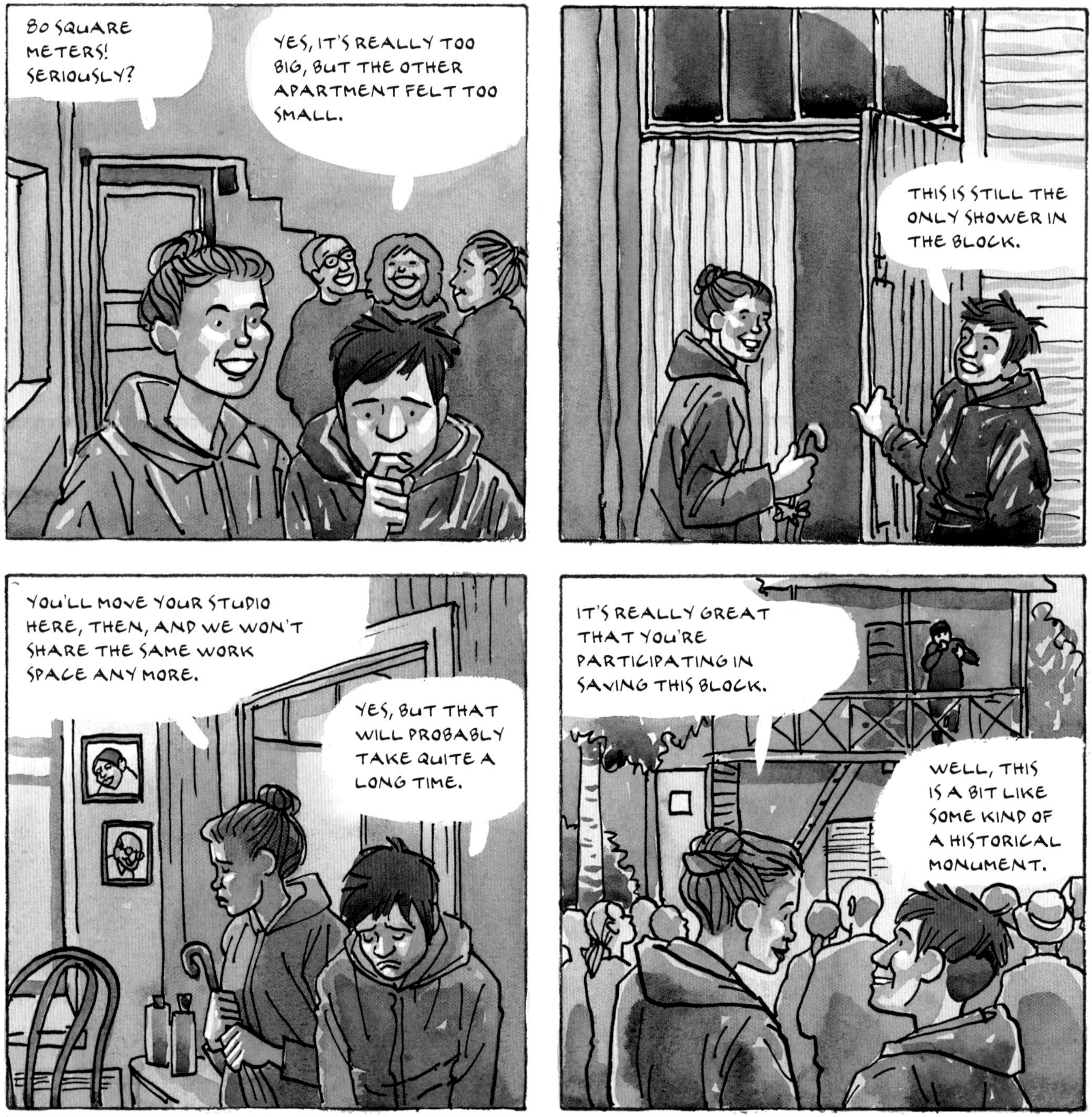
80 SQUARE METERS! SERIOUSLY?
YES, IT'S REALLY TOO BIG, BUT THE OTHER APARTMENT FELT TOO SMALL.
THIS IS STILL THE ONLY SHOWER IN THE BLOCK.
YOU'LL MOVE YOUR STUDIO HERE, THEN, AND WE WON'T SHARE THE SAME WORK SPACE ANY MORE.
YES, BUT THAT WILL PROBABLY TAKE QUITE A LONG TIME.
IT'S REALLY GREAT THAT YOU'RE PARTICIPATING IN SAVING THIS BLOCK.
WELL, THIS IS A BIT LIKE SOME KIND OF A HISTORICAL MONUMENT.

THE CITY GROWS CONCRETE

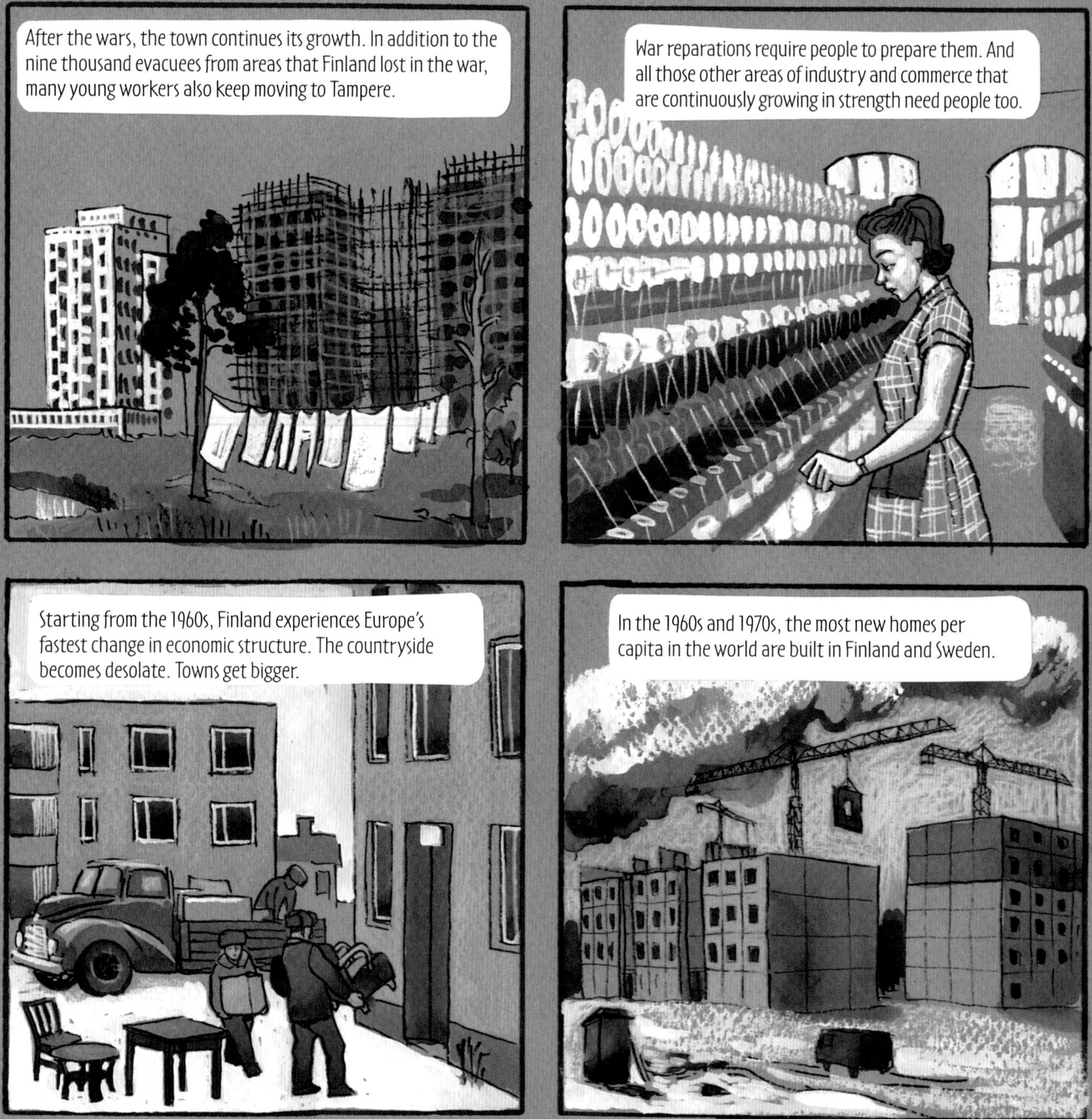
After the wars, the town continues its growth. In addition to the nine thousand evacuees from areas that Finland lost in the war, many young workers also keep moving to Tampere.
War reparations require people to prepare them. And all those other areas of industry and commerce that are continuously growing in strength need people too.
Starting from the 1960s, Finland experiences Europe's fastest change in economic structure. The countryside becomes desolate. Towns get bigger.
In the 1960s and 1970s, the most new homes per capita in the world are built in Finland and Sweden.

Tammela lies no longer at the far end of the town. The borders move farther, at the same pace as the growth of factory production and the number of jobs offered in industry.

But that is not enough. No way. While in 1940 the town's population is 70,000, in 1960 it is 125,500. And the following decade it grows again by 30,000.

People's attention turns from the outer parts of the town to its center, and earlier outskirts suddenly become central.

Tammela receives a new town plan in 1966. The plan changes Tammela into an area of six- and seven-story concrete houses.

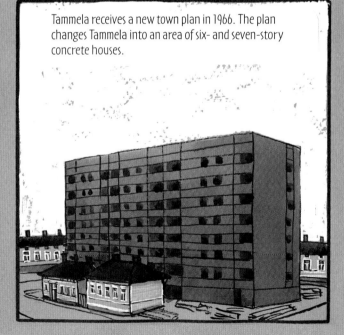

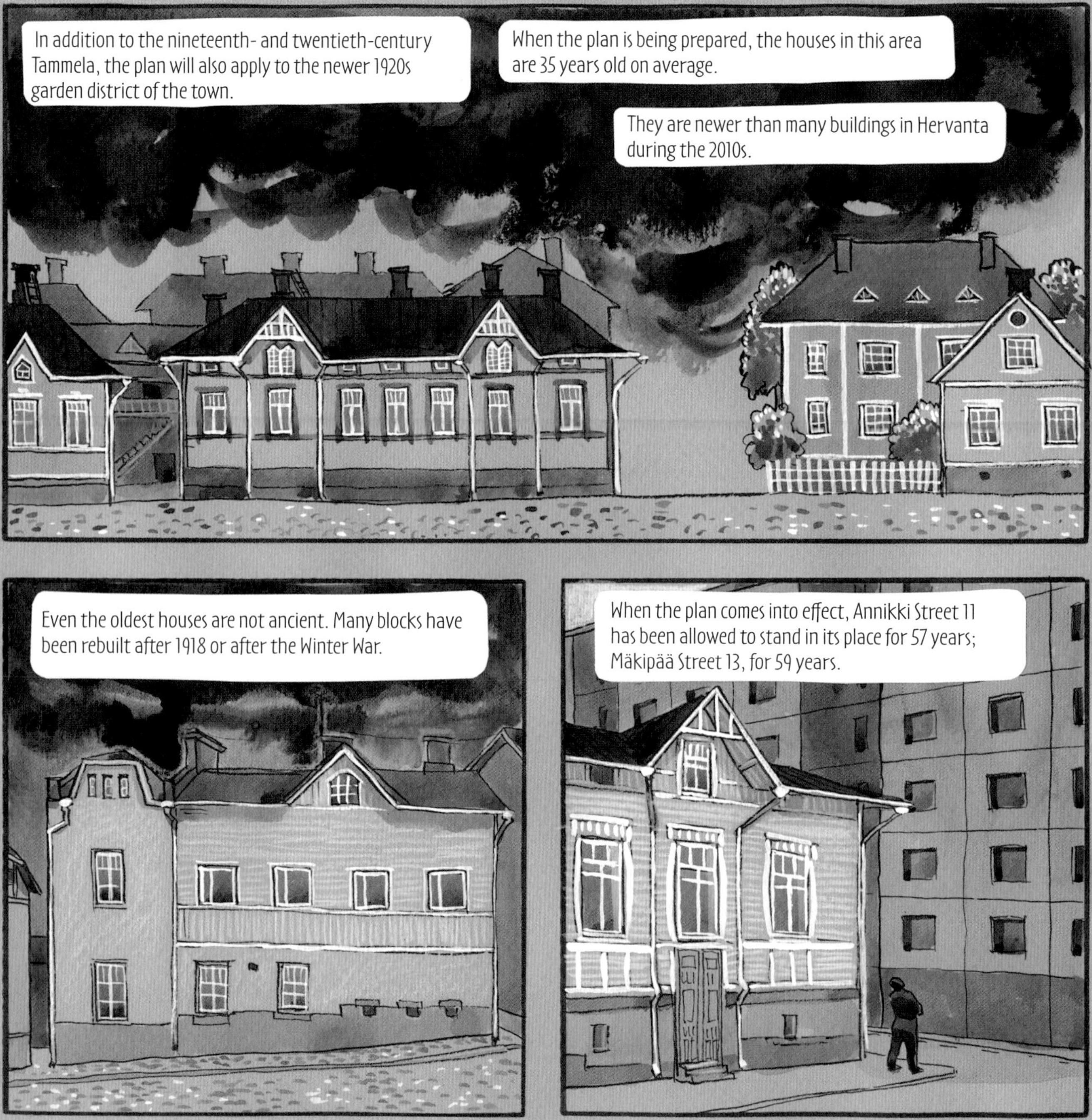
In addition to the nineteenth- and twentieth-century Tammela, the plan will also apply to the newer 1920s garden district of the town.
When the plan is being prepared, the houses in this area are 35 years old on average.
They are newer than many buildings in Hervanta during the 2010s.
Even the oldest houses are not ancient. Many blocks have been rebuilt after 1918 or after the Winter War.
When the plan comes into effect, Annikki Street 11 has been allowed to stand in its place for 57 years; Mäkipää Street 13, for 59 years.

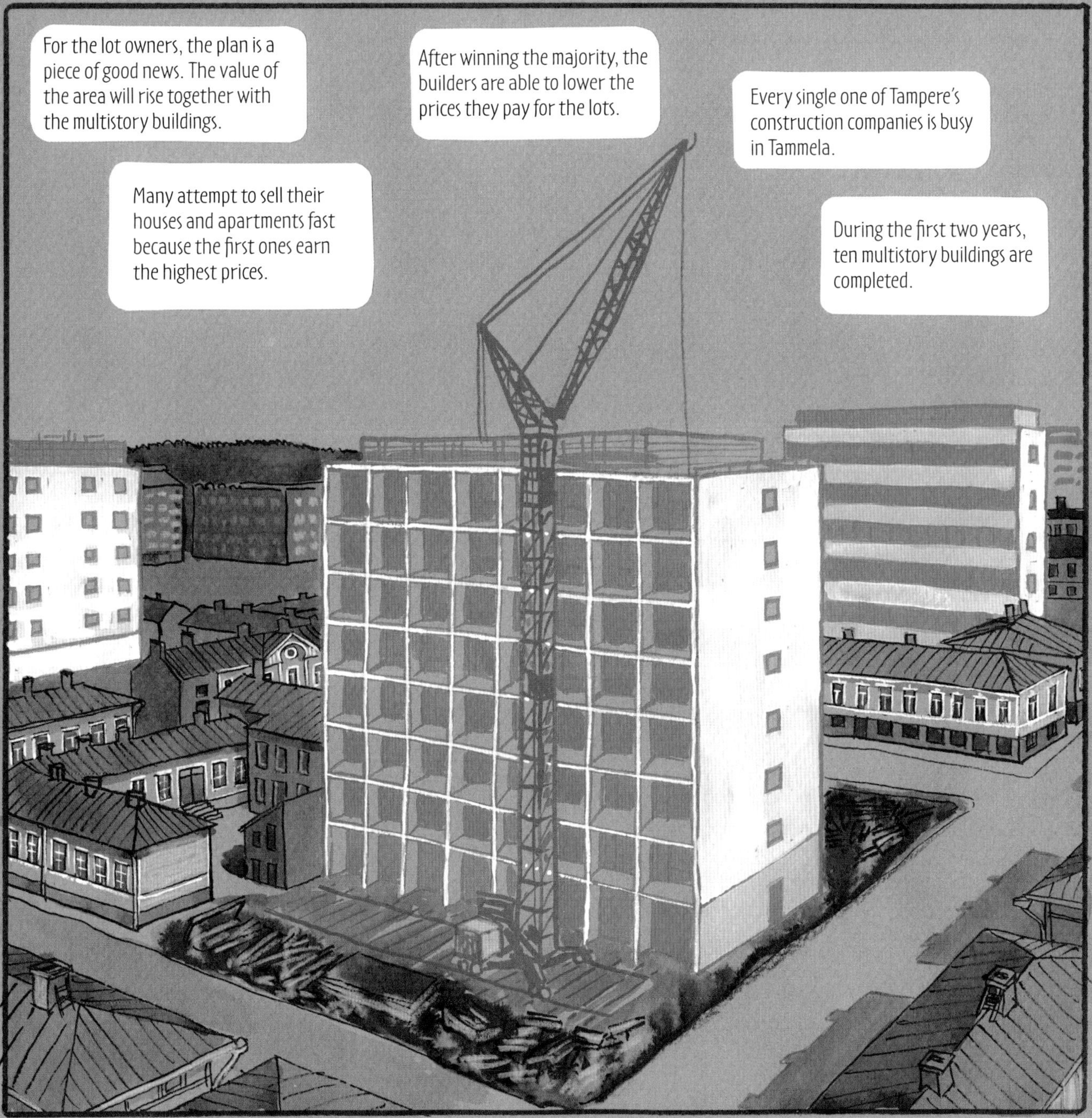
For the lot owners, the plan is a piece of good news. The value of the area will rise together with the multistory buildings.
Many attempt to sell their houses and apartments fast because the first ones earn the highest prices.
After winning the majority, the builders are able to lower the prices they pay for the lots.
Every single one of Tampere's construction companies is busy in Tammela.
During the first two years, ten multistory buildings are completed.

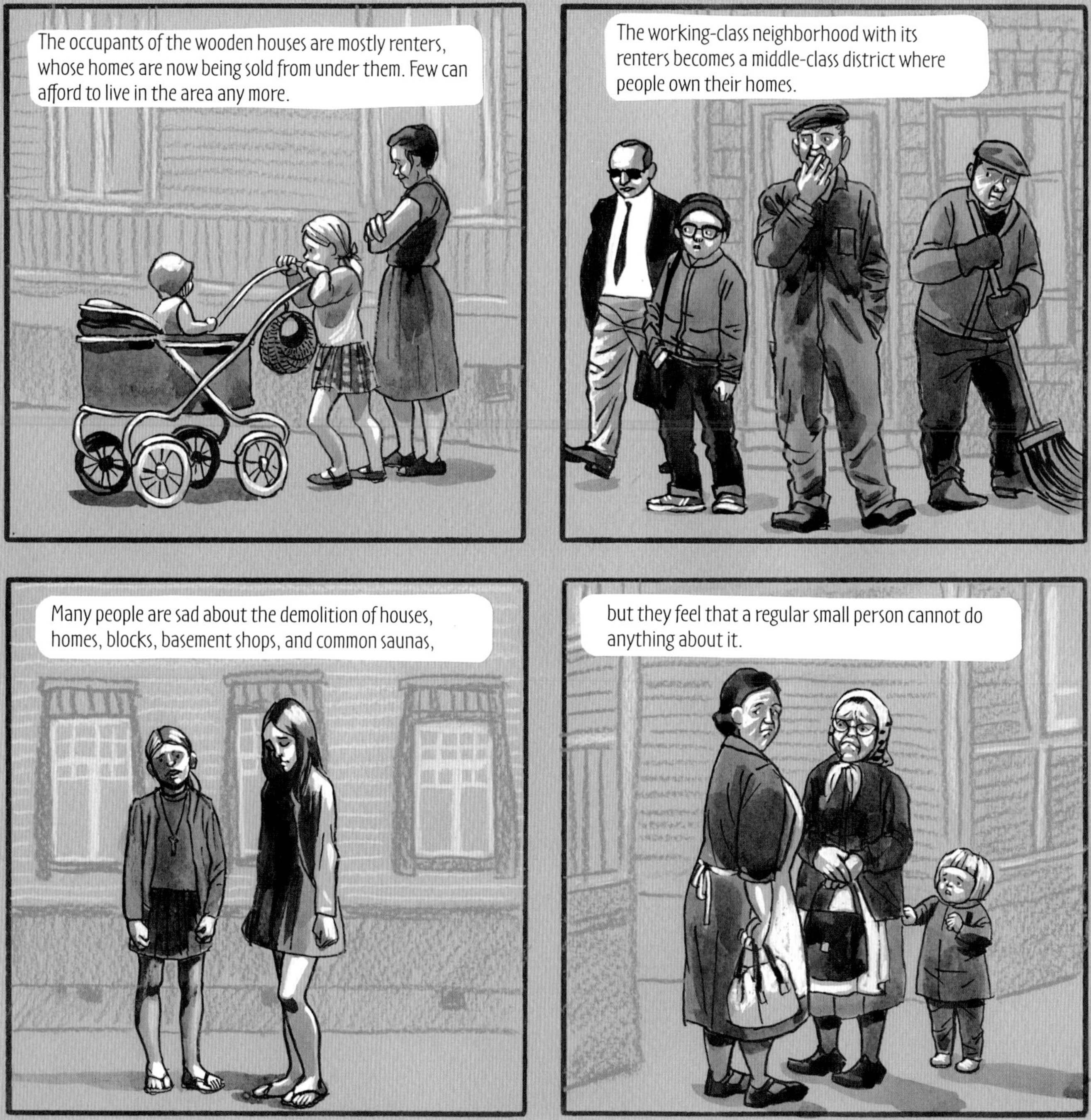
The occupants of the wooden houses are mostly renters, whose homes are now being sold from under them. Few can afford to live in the area any more.
The working-class neighborhood with its renters becomes a middle-class district where people own their homes.
Many people are sad about the demolition of houses, homes, blocks, basement shops, and common saunas,
but they feel that a regular small person cannot do anything about it.

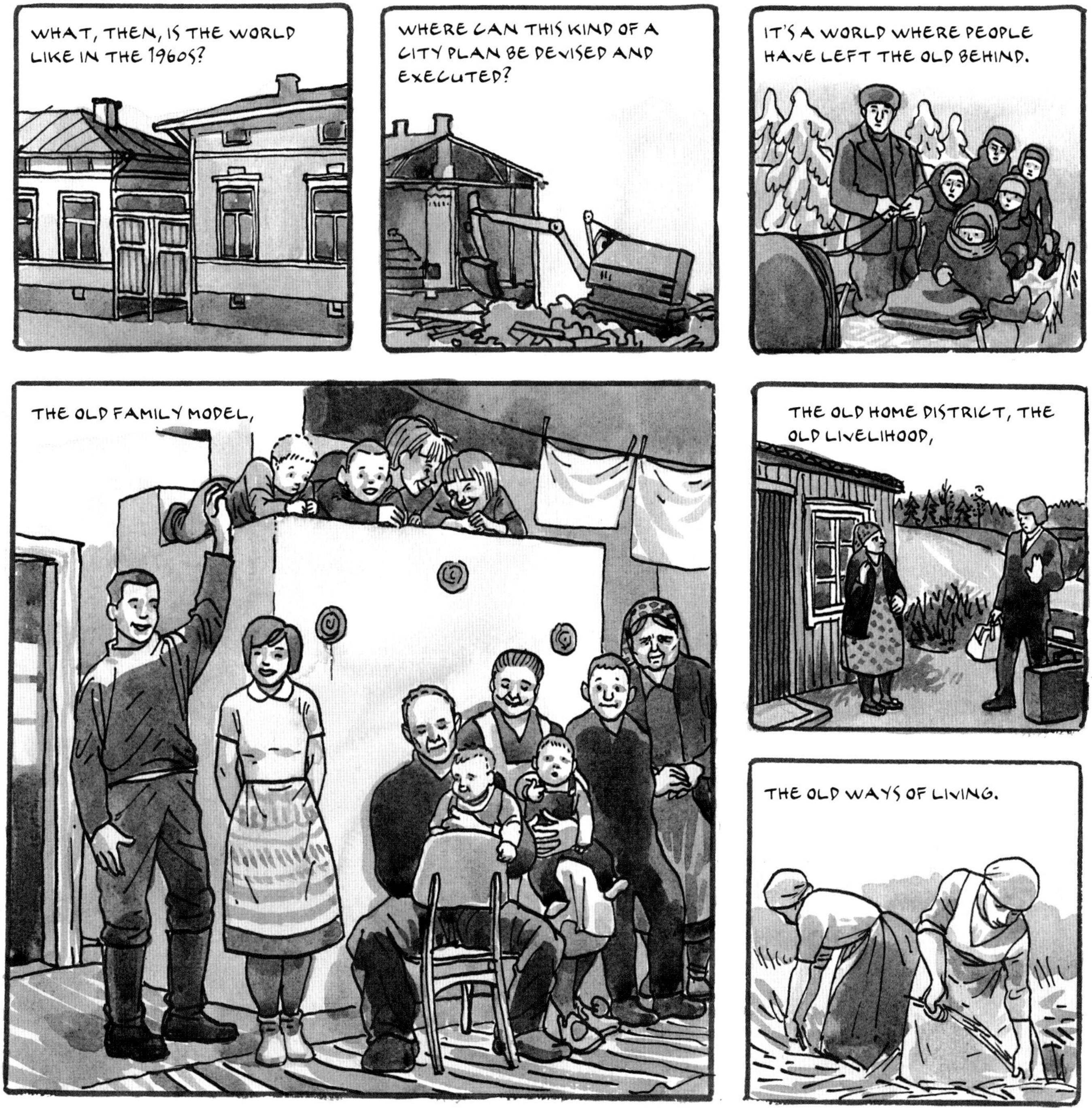
WHAT, THEN, IS THE WORLD LIKE IN THE 1960S?
WHERE CAN THIS KIND OF A CITY PLAN BE DEVISED AND EXECUTED?
IT'S A WORLD WHERE PEOPLE HAVE LEFT THE OLD BEHIND.
THE OLD FAMILY MODEL,
THE OLD HOME DISTRICT, THE OLD LIVELIHOOD,
THE OLD WAYS OF LIVING.

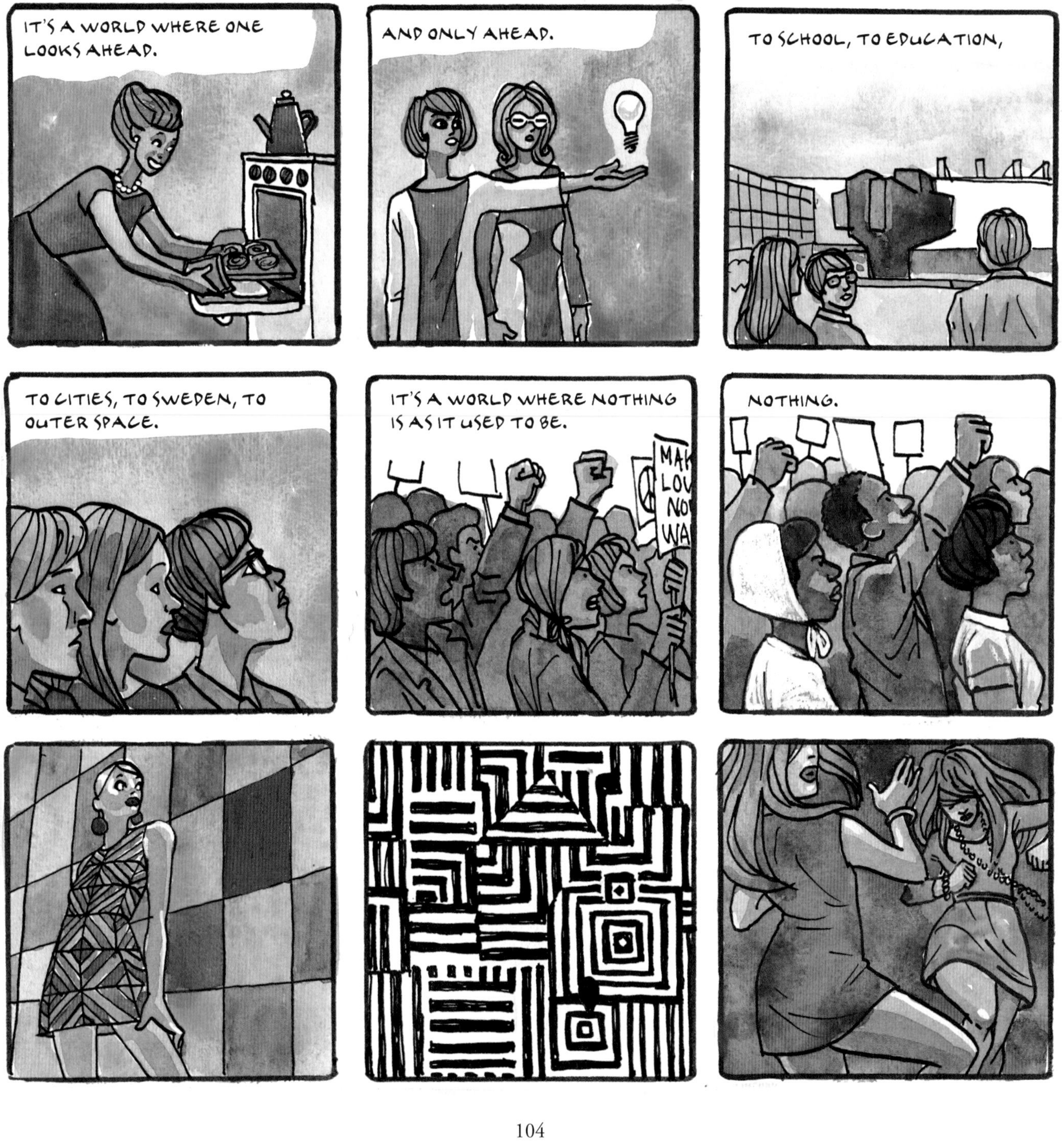
IT'S A WORLD WHERE ONE LOOKS AHEAD.
AND ONLY AHEAD.
TO SCHOOL, TO EDUCATION,
TO CITIES, TO SWEDEN, TO OUTER SPACE.
IT'S A WORLD WHERE NOTHING IS AS IT USED TO BE.
NOTHING.

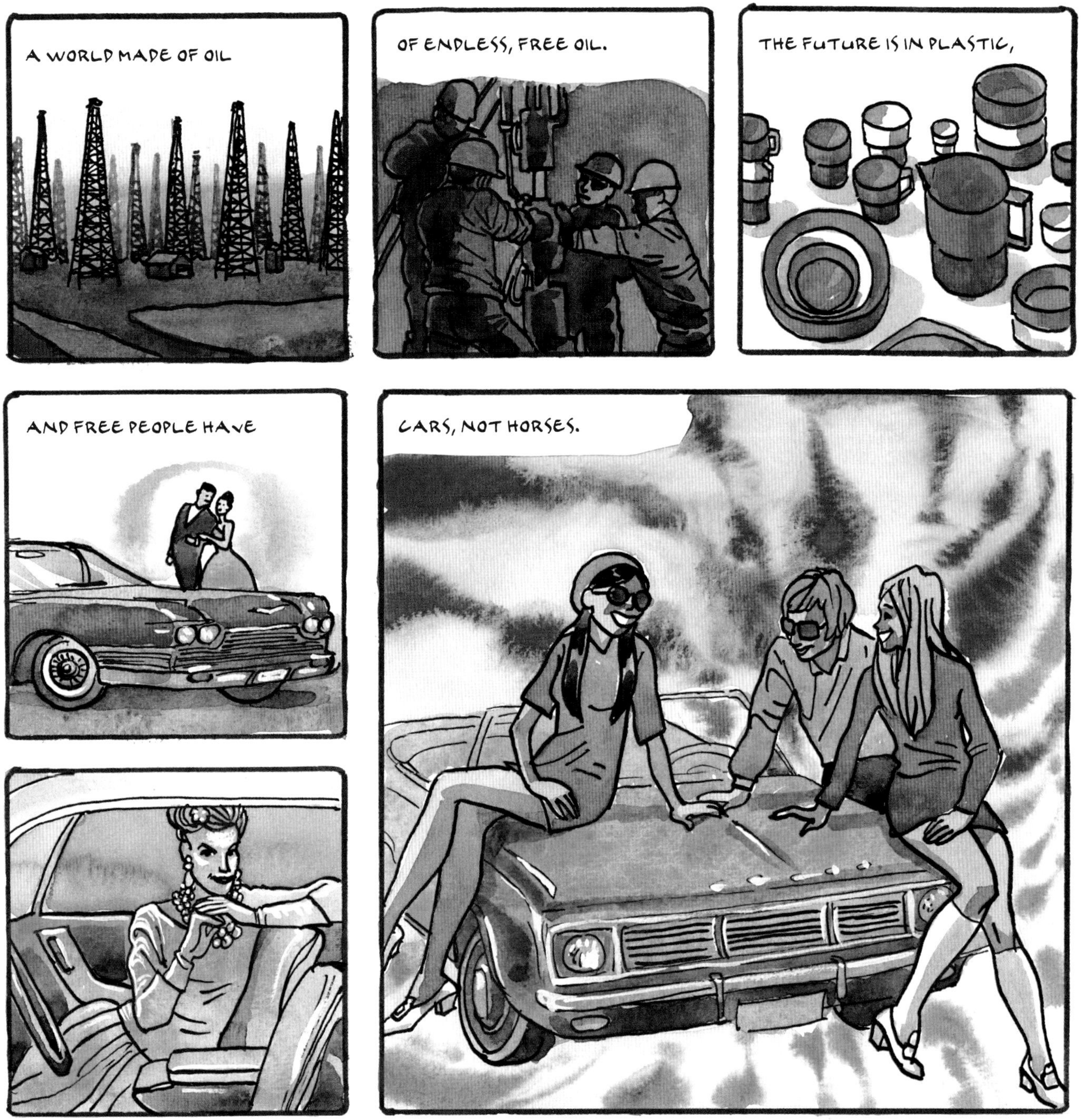
A WORLD MADE OF OIL
OF ENDLESS, FREE OIL.
THE FUTURE IS IN PLASTIC,
AND FREE PEOPLE HAVE
CARS, NOT HORSES.

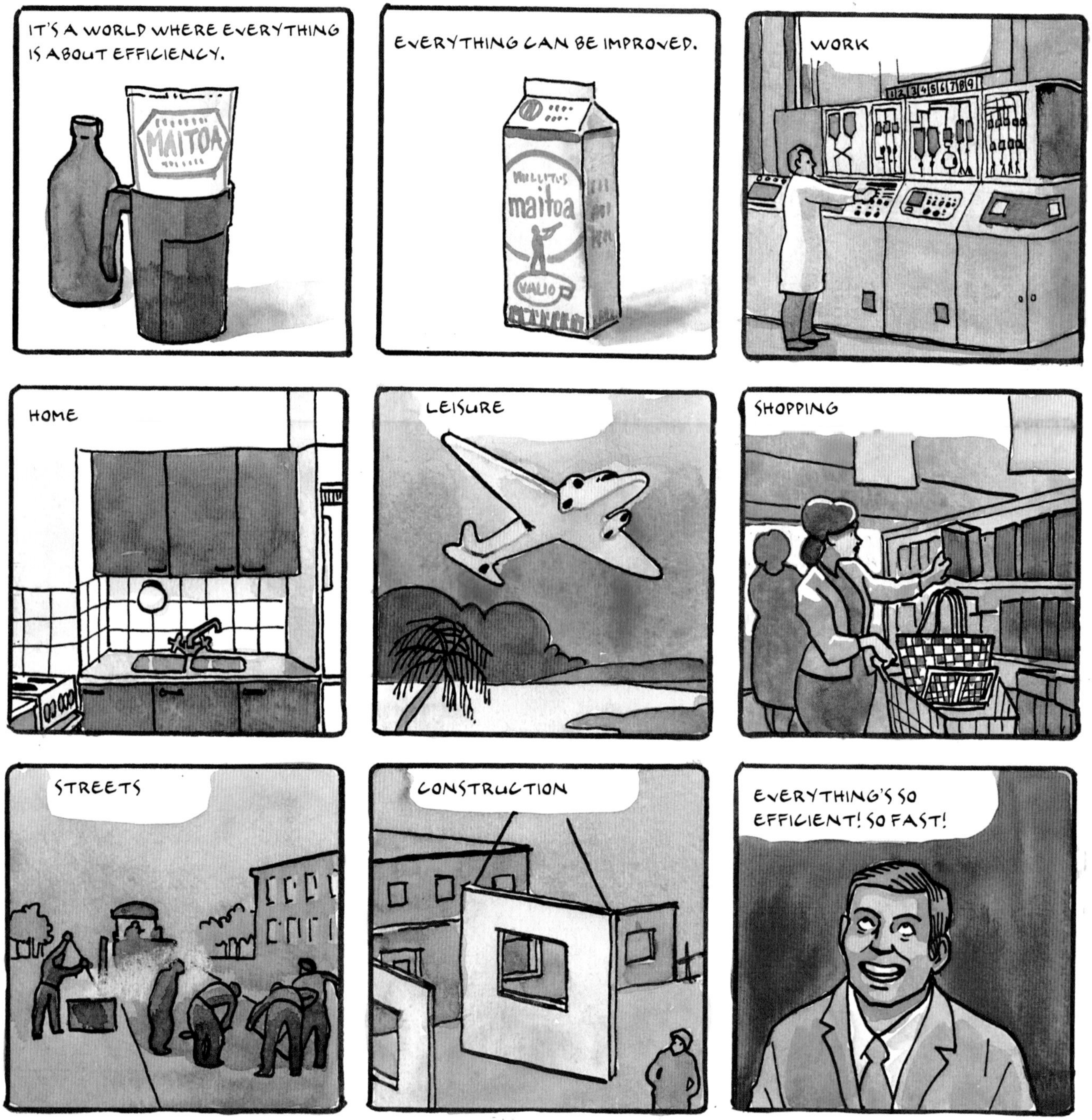
IT'S A WORLD WHERE EVERYTHING IS ABOUT EFFICIENCY.
MAITOA
EVERYTHING CAN BE IMPROVED.
maitoa
VALIO
WORK
HOME
LEISURE
SHOPPING
STREETS
CONSTRUCTION
EVERYTHING'S SO EFFICIENT! SO FAST!

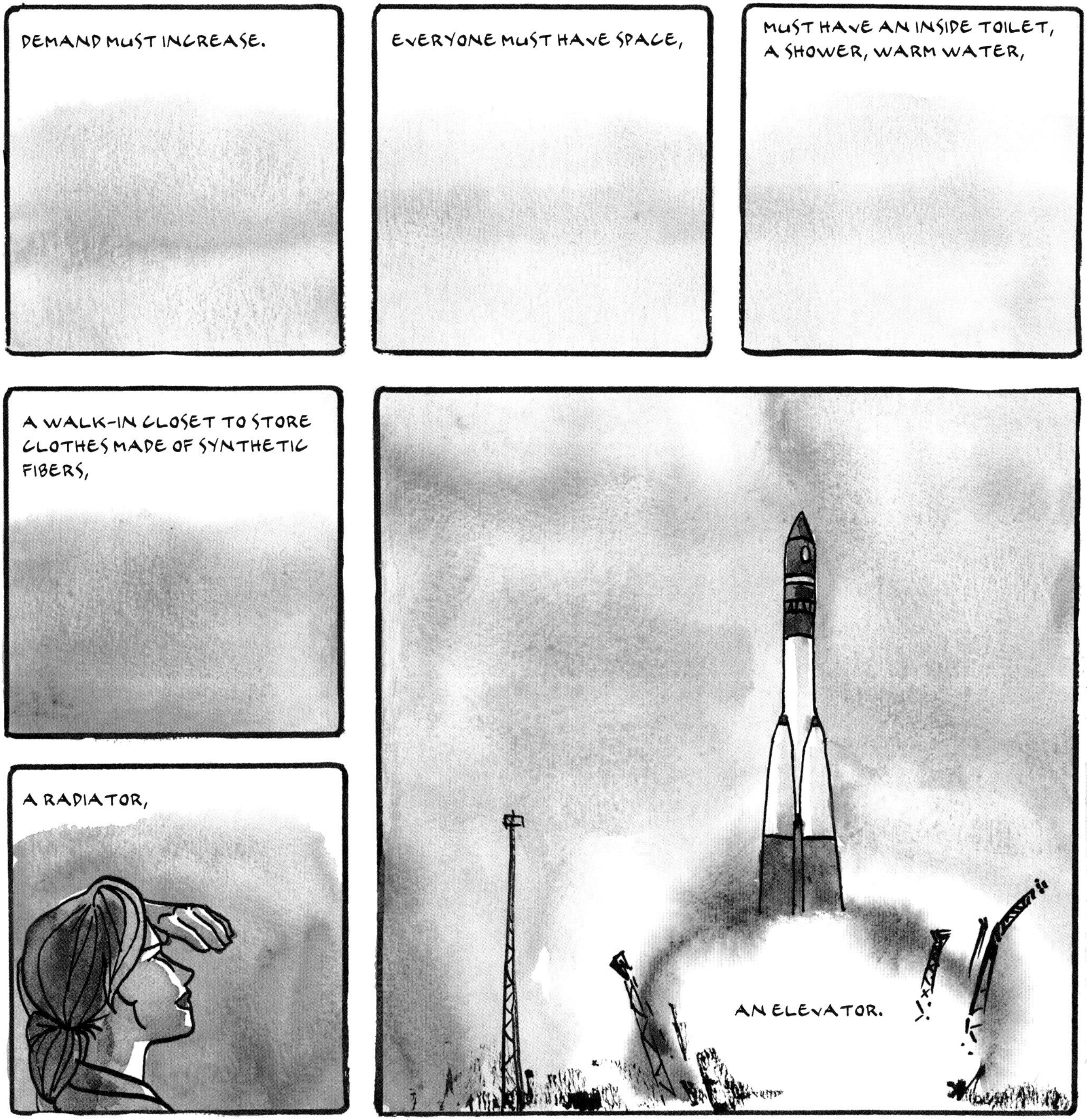
DEMAND MUST INCREASE.
EVERYONE MUST HAVE SPACE,
MUST HAVE AN INSIDE TOILET, A SHOWER, WARM WATER,
A WALK-IN CLOSET TO STORE CLOTHES MADE OF SYNTHETIC FIBERS,
A RADIATOR,
AN ELEVATOR.

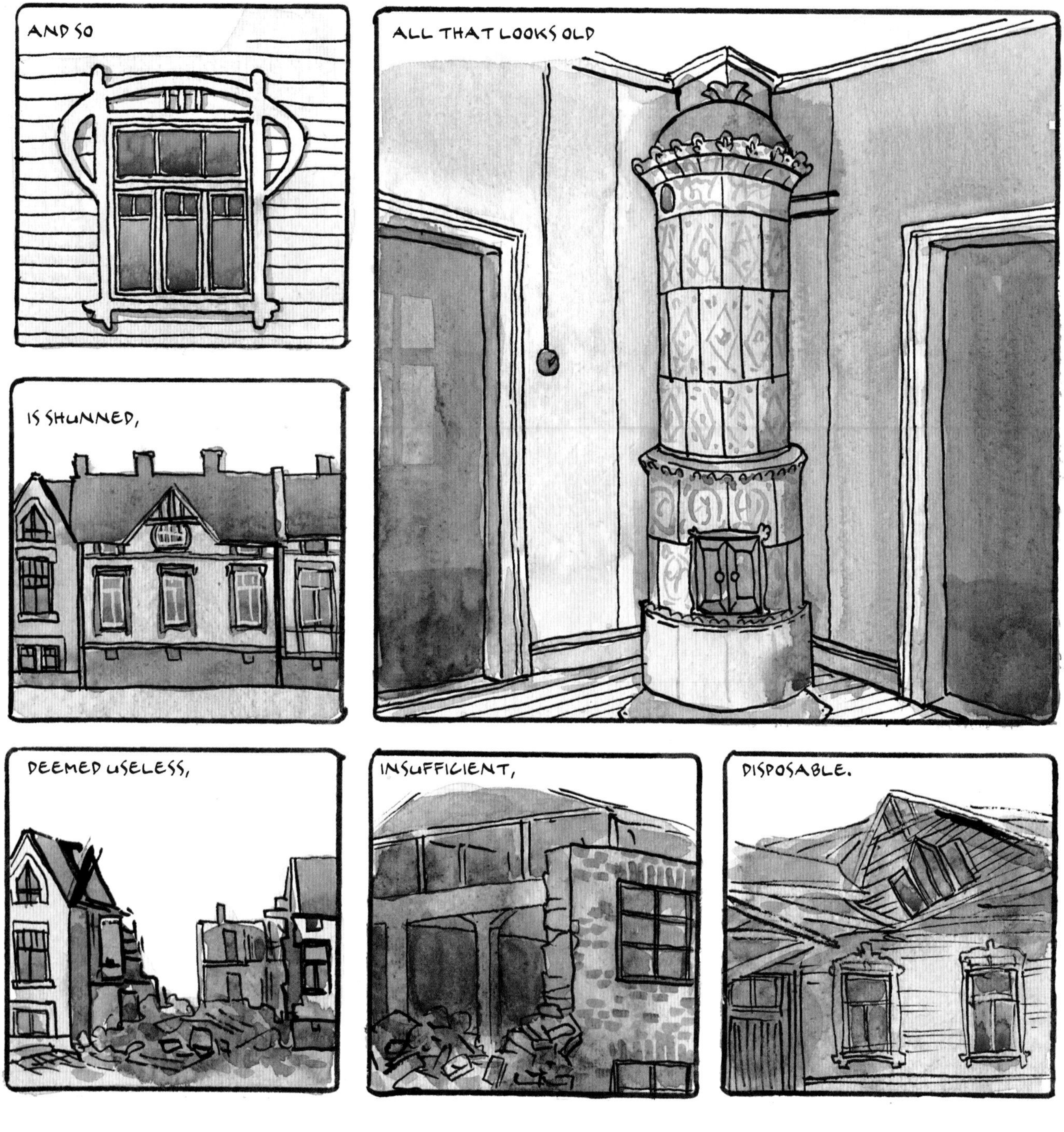
AND SO
ALL THAT LOOKS OLD
IS SHUNNED,
DEEMED USELESS,
INSUFFICIENT,
DISPOSABLE.

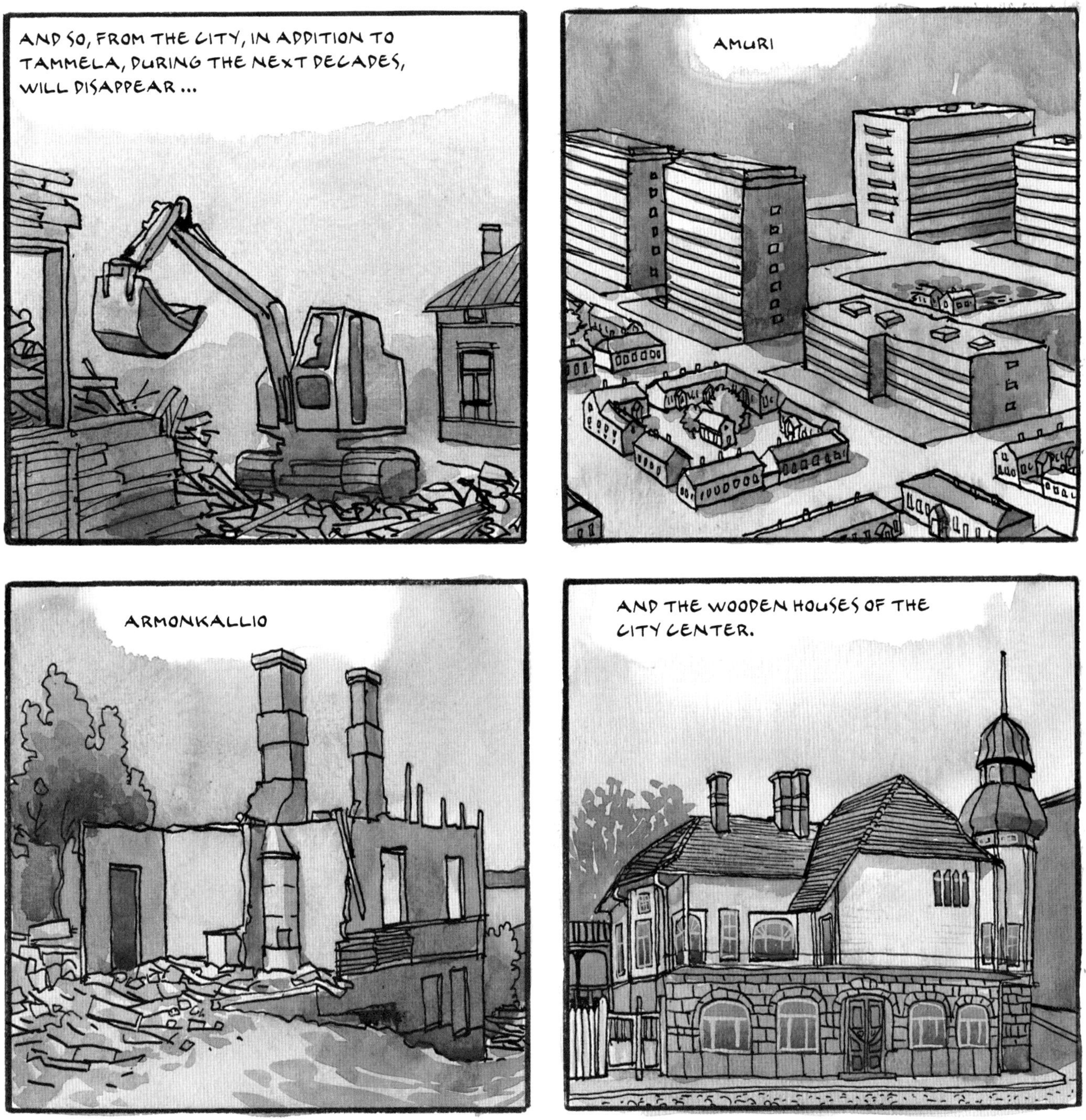
AND SO, FROM THE CITY, IN ADDITION TO TAMMELA, DURING THE NEXT DECADES, WILL DISAPPEAR ...
AMURI
ARMONKALLIO
AND THE WOODEN HOUSES OF THE CITY CENTER.

THE TAMMELA OF WOOD AND STONE

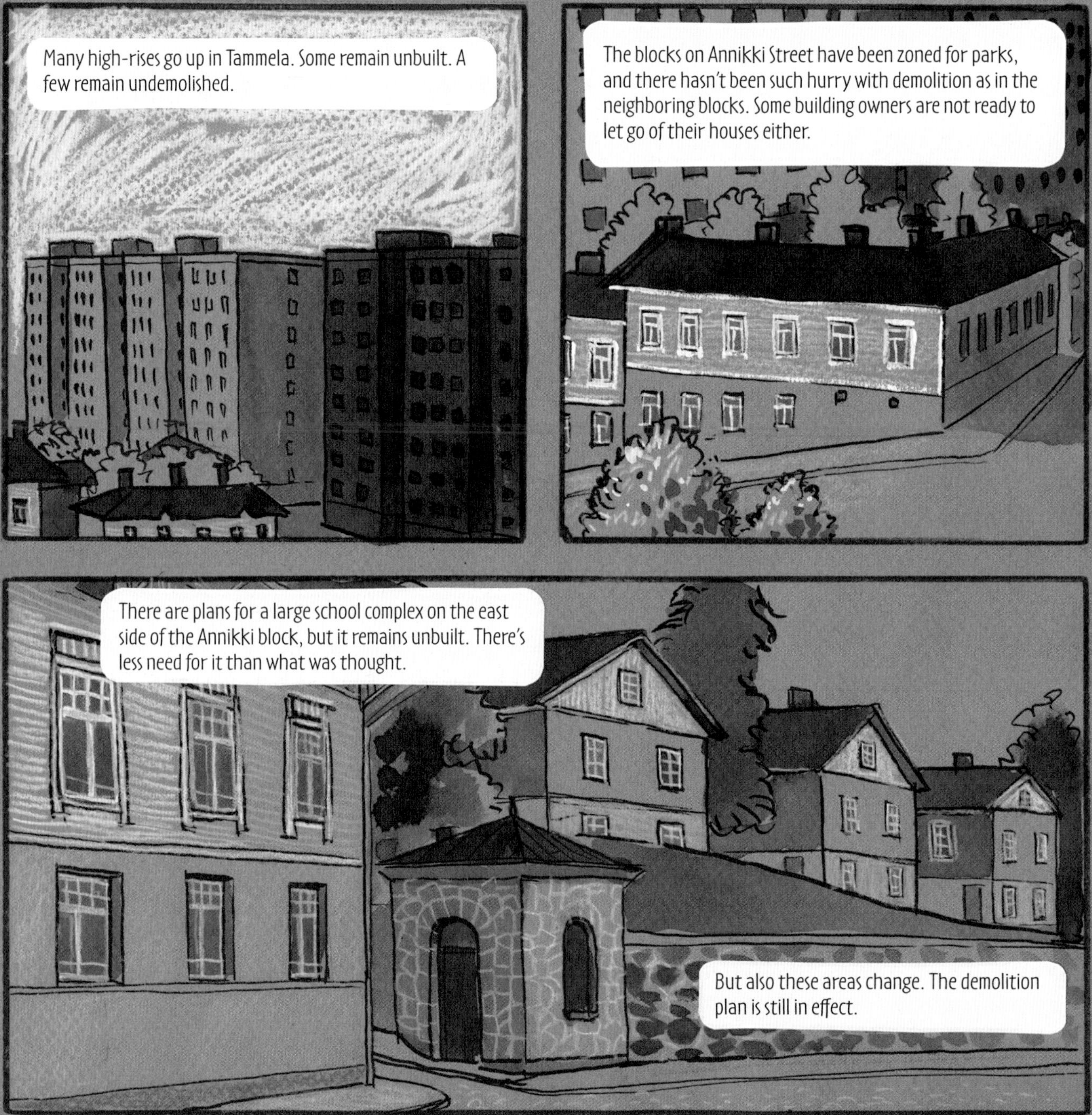
Many high-rises go up in Tammela. Some remain unbuilt. A few remain undemolished.
The blocks on Annikki Street have been zoned for parks, and there hasn't been such hurry with demolition as in the neighboring blocks. Some building owners are not ready to let go of their houses either.
There are plans for a large school complex on the east side of the Annikki block, but it remains unbuilt. There's less need for it than what was thought.
But also these areas change. The demolition plan is still in effect.

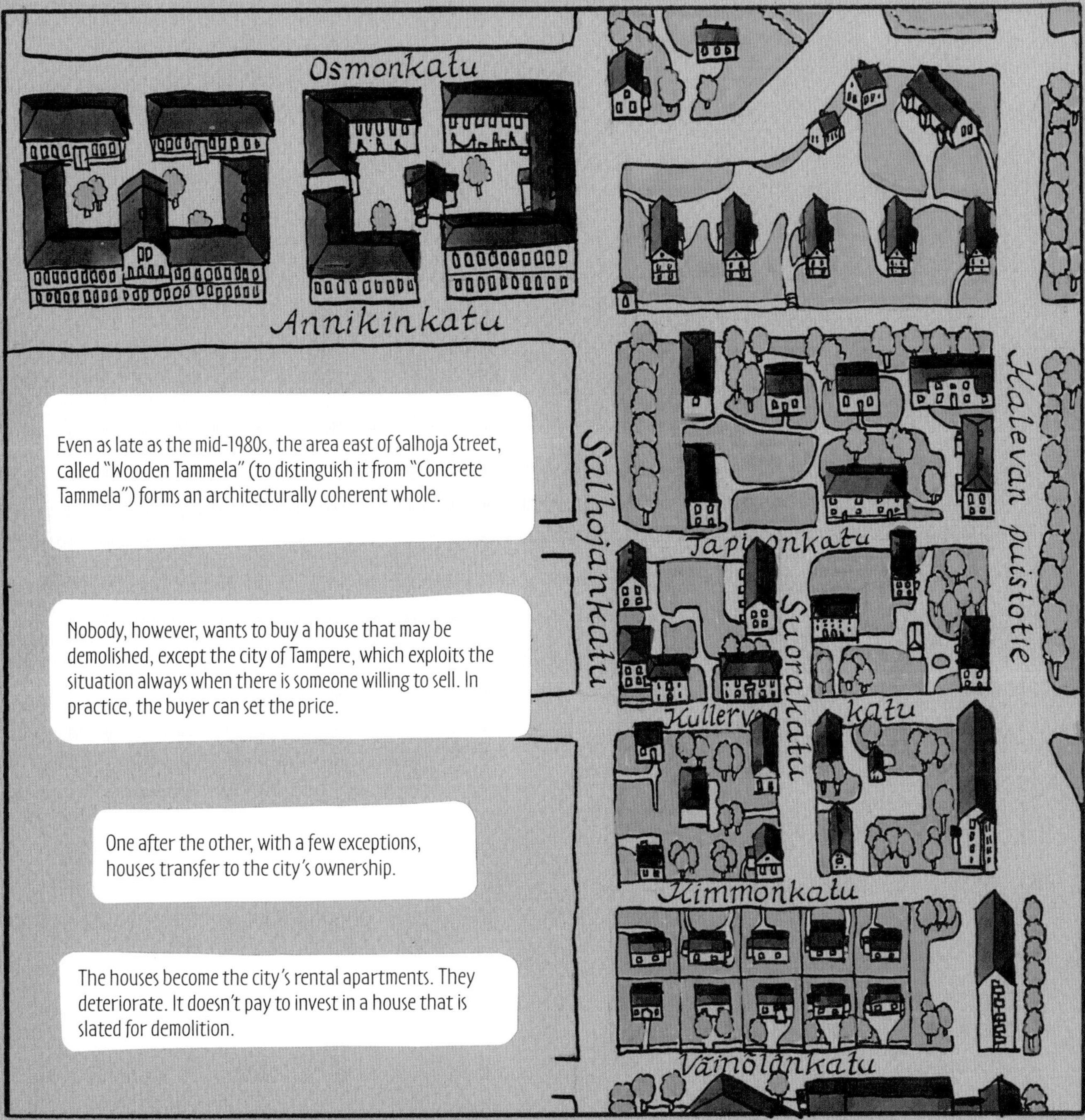
Osmonkatu
Annikinkatu
Even as late as the mid-1980s, the area east of Salhoja Street, called "Wooden Tammela" (to distinguish it from "Concrete Tammela") forms an architecturally coherent whole.
Salhojankatu
Kalevan puistotie
Suorakatu
Nobody, however, wants to buy a house that may be demolished, except the city of Tampere, which exploits the situation always when there is someone willing to sell. In practice, the buyer can set the price.
One after the other, with a few exceptions, houses transfer to the city's ownership.
Himmonkatu
The houses become the city's rental apartments. They deteriorate. It doesn't pay to invest in a house that is slated for demolition.
Väinölänkatu

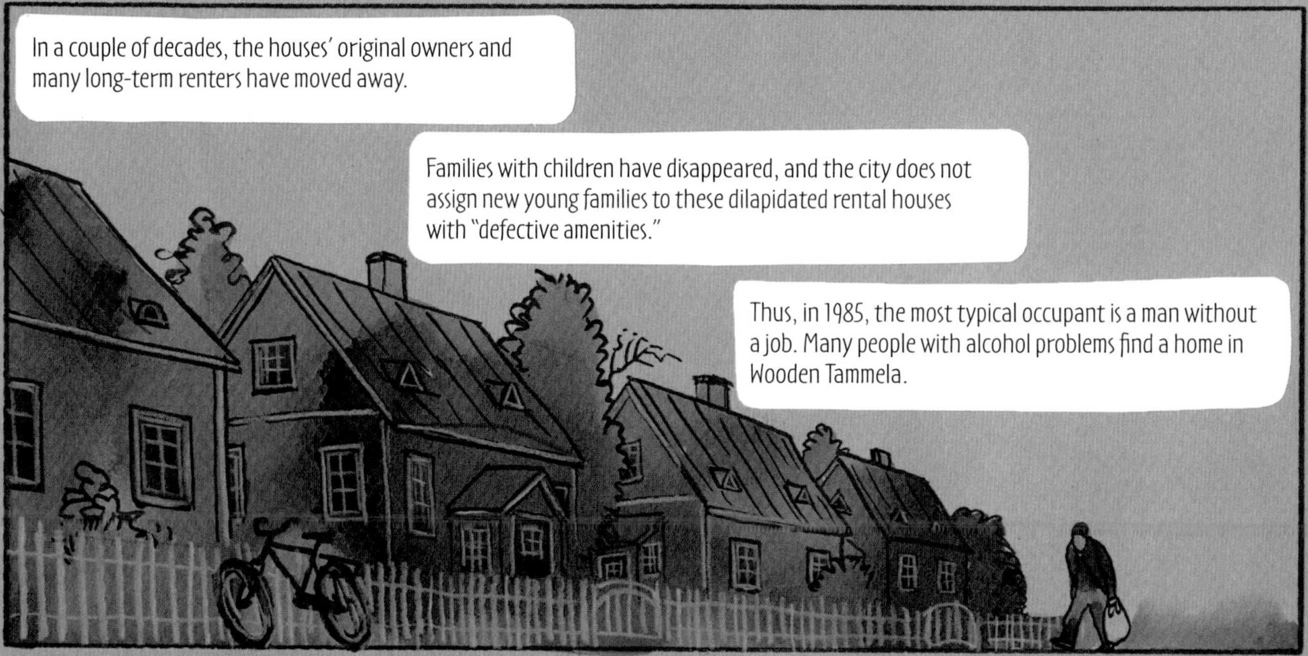
In a couple of decades, the houses' original owners and many long-term renters have moved away.
Families with children have disappeared, and the city does not assign new young families to these dilapidated rental houses with "defective amenities."
Thus, in 1985, the most typical occupant is a man without a job. Many people with alcohol problems find a home in Wooden Tammela.

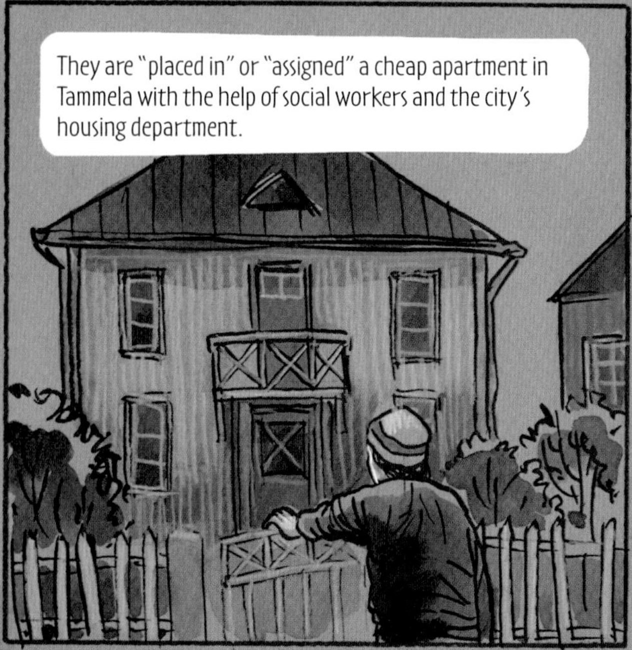
They are "placed in" or "assigned" a cheap apartment in Tammela with the help of social workers and the city's housing department.

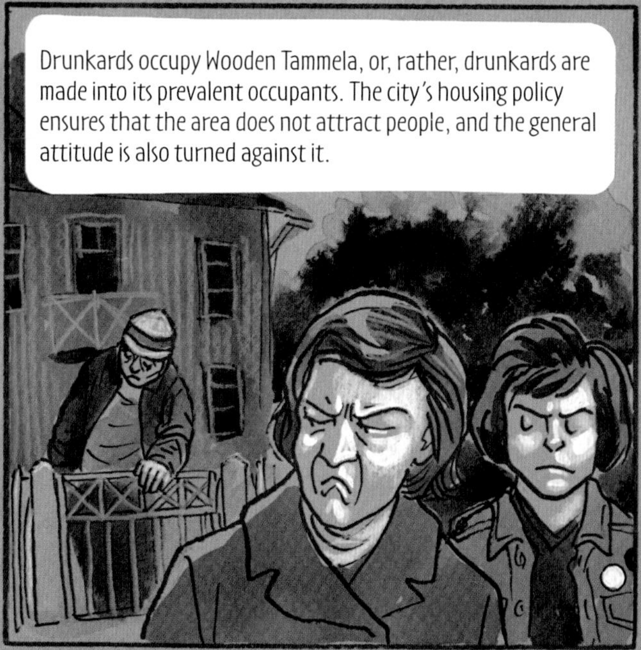
Drunkards occupy Wooden Tammela, or, rather, drunkards are made into its prevalent occupants. The city's housing policy ensures that the area does not attract people, and the general attitude is also turned against it.

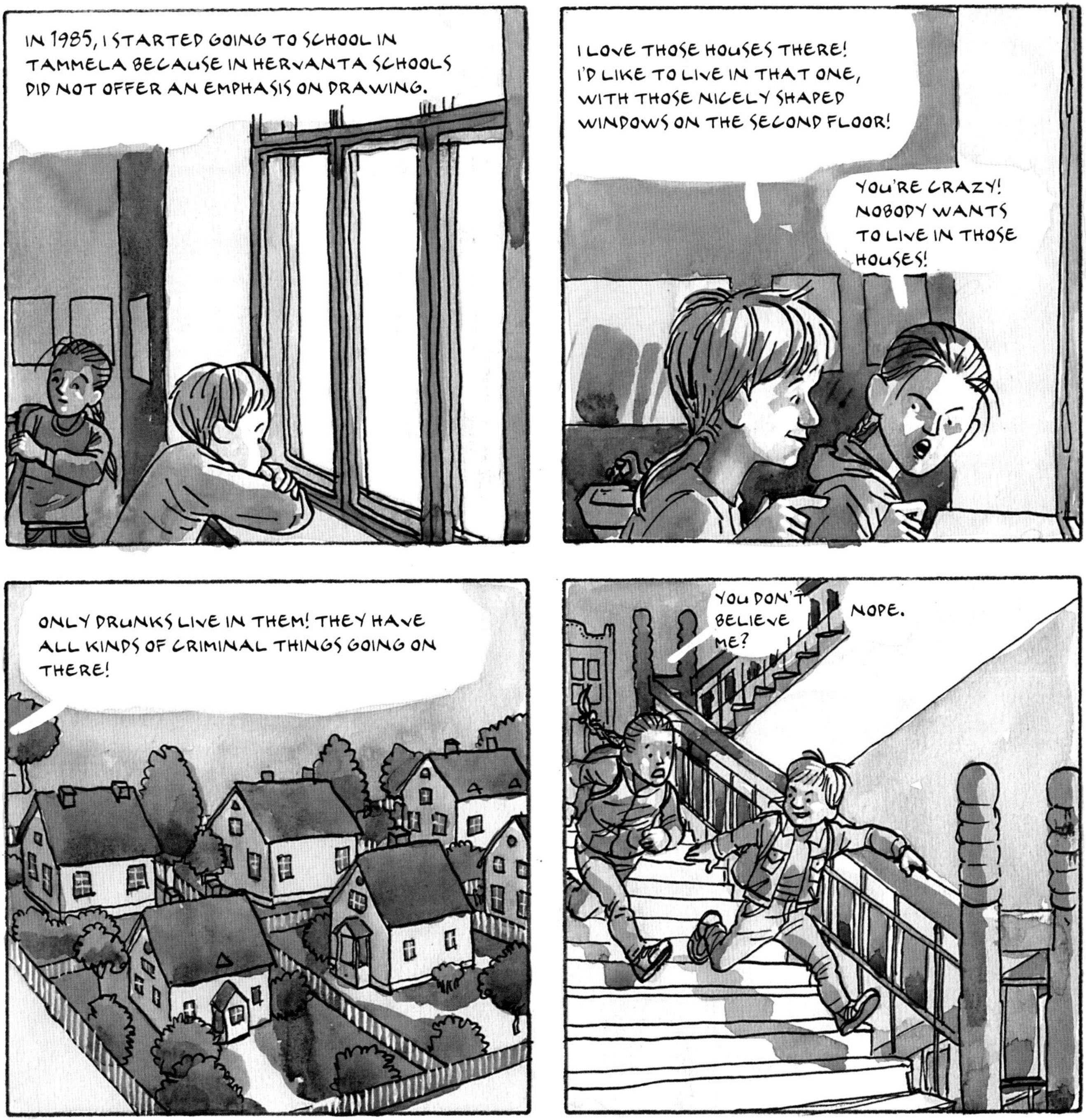
IN 1985, I STARTED GOING TO SCHOOL IN TAMMELA BECAUSE IN HERVANTA SCHOOLS DID NOT OFFER AN EMPHASIS ON DRAWING.
I LOVE THOSE HOUSES THERE! I'D LIKE TO LIVE IN THAT ONE, WITH THOSE NICELY SHAPED WINDOWS ON THE SECOND FLOOR!
YOU'RE CRAZY! NOBODY WANTS TO LIVE IN THOSE HOUSES!
ONLY DRUNKS LIVE IN THEM! THEY HAVE ALL KINDS OF CRIMINAL THINGS GOING ON THERE!
YOU DON'T BELIEVE ME?
NOPE.

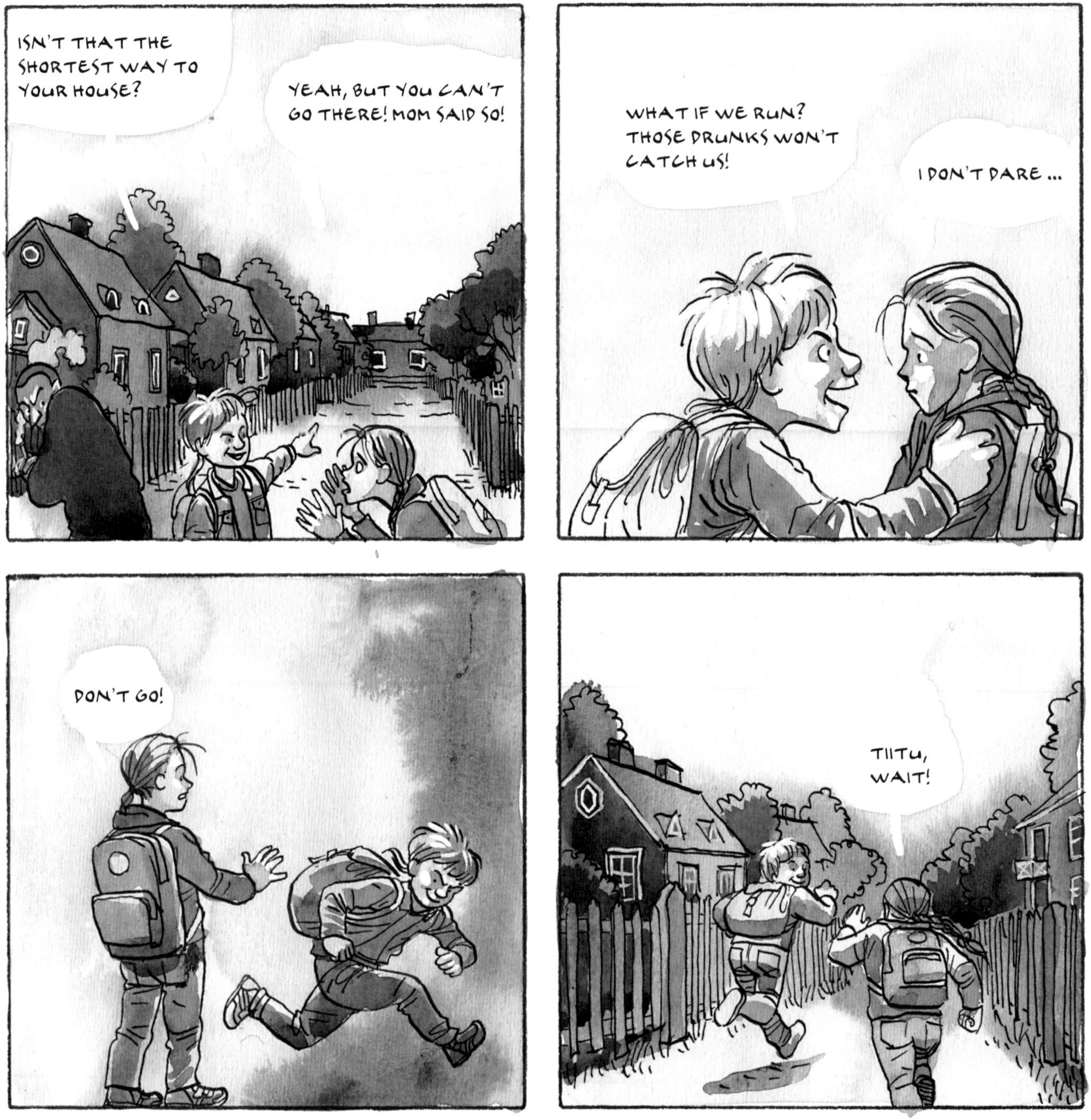
ISN'T THAT THE SHORTEST WAY TO YOUR HOUSE?
YEAH, BUT YOU CAN'T GO THERE! MOM SAID SO!
WHAT IF WE RUN? THOSE DRUNKS WON'T CATCH US!
I DON'T DARE...
DON'T GO!
TIITU, WAIT!

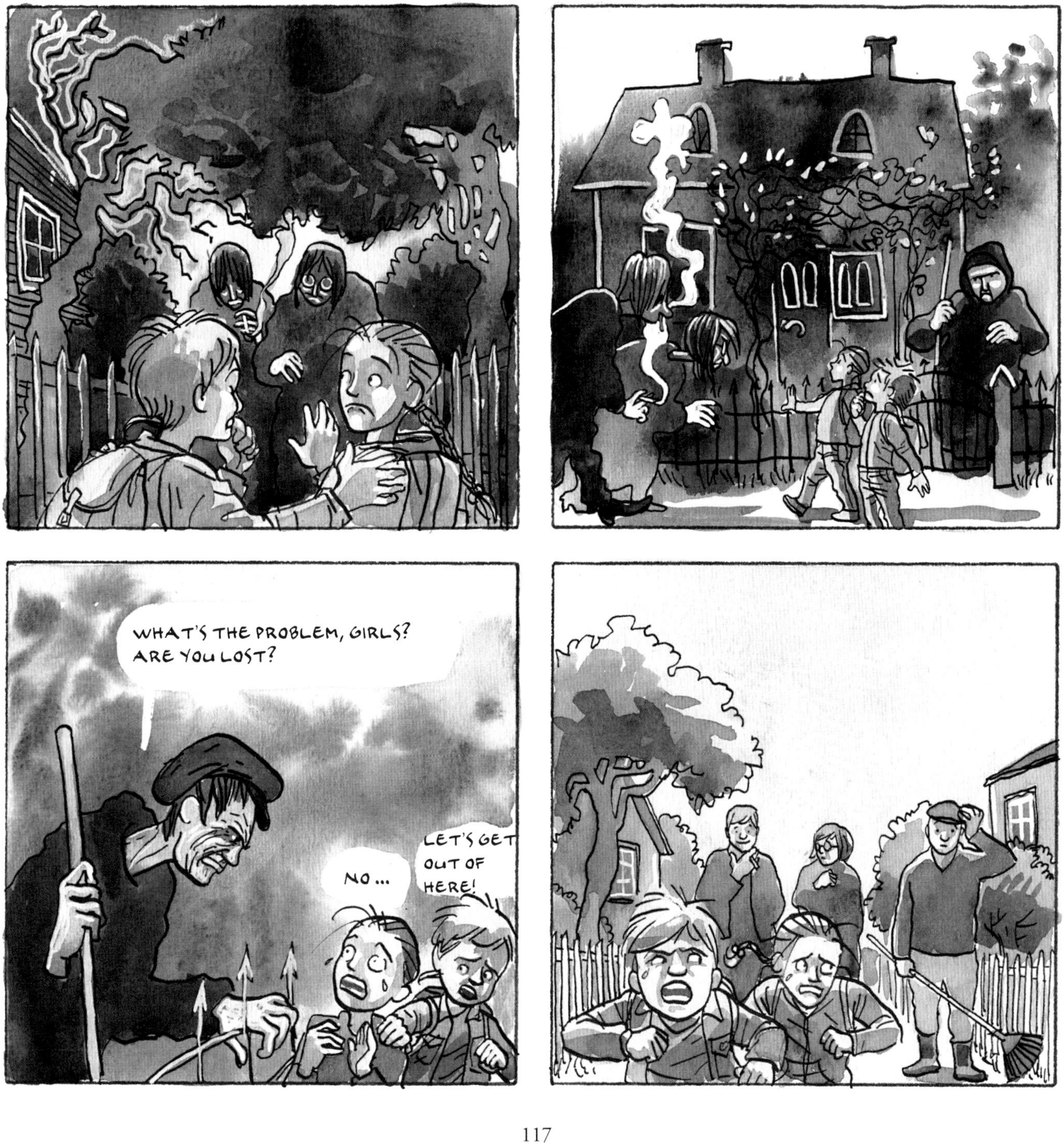
WHAT'S THE PROBLEM, GIRLS? ARE YOU LOST?
NO...
LET'S GET OUT OF HERE!

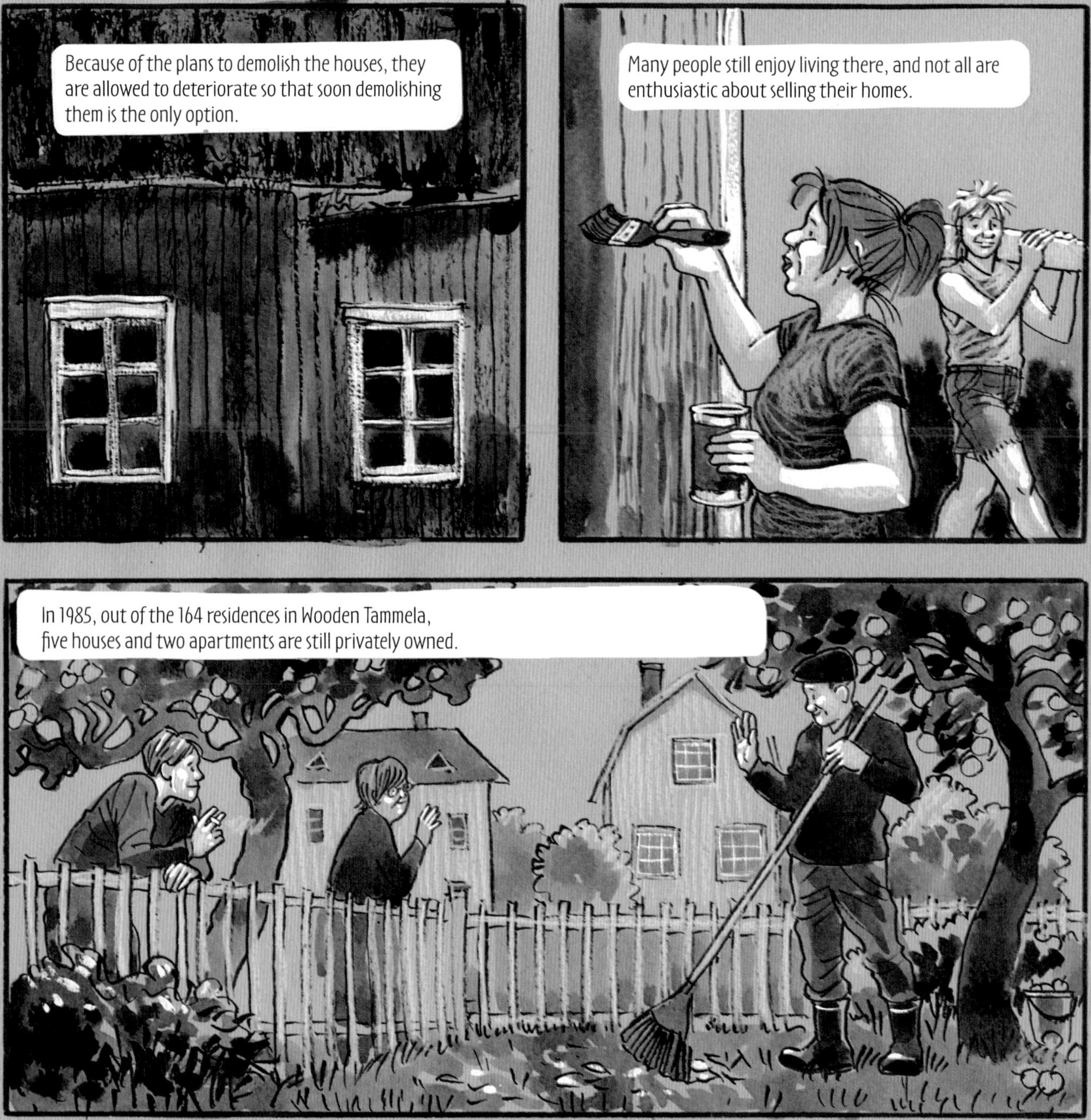
Because of the plans to demolish the houses, they are allowed to deteriorate so that soon demolishing them is the only option.
Many people still enjoy living there, and not all are enthusiastic about selling their homes.
In 1985, out of the 164 residences in Wooden Tammela, five houses and two apartments are still privately owned.

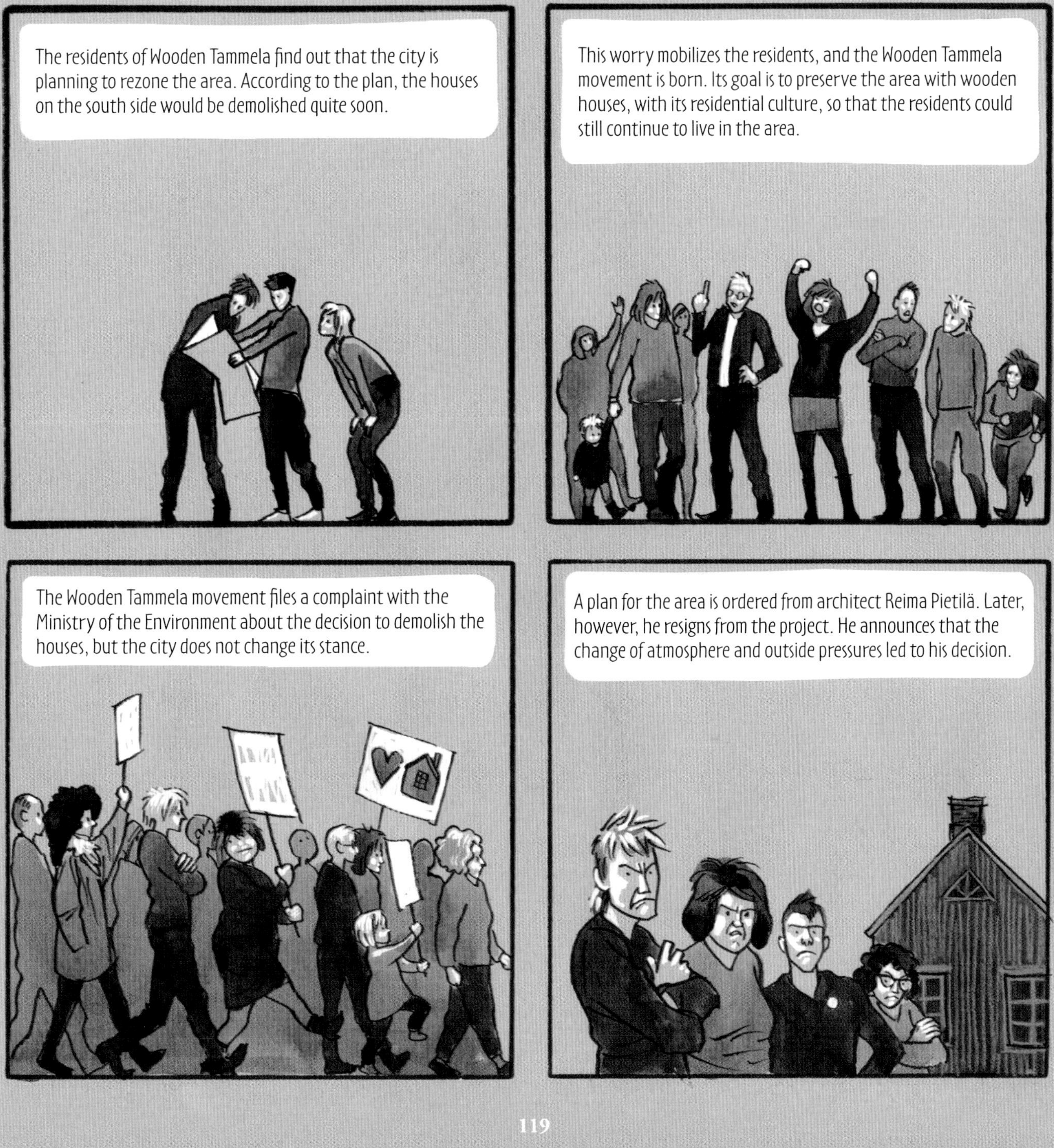
The residents of Wooden Tammela find out that the city is planning to rezone the area. According to the plan, the houses on the south side would be demolished quite soon.
This worry mobilizes the residents, and the Wooden Tammela movement is born. Its goal is to preserve the area with wooden houses, with its residential culture, so that the residents could still continue to live in the area.
The Wooden Tammela movement files a complaint with the Ministry of the Environment about the decision to demolish the houses, but the city does not change its stance.
A plan for the area is ordered from architect Reima Pietilä. Later, however, he resigns from the project. He announces that the change of atmosphere and outside pressures led to his decision.

At the end of 1985, the Ministry of the Environment decides not to ratify the city zoning plan. According to the justifications, the proposal for the plan did not take adequately into consideration the use, preservation, and renovation of the existing buildings. A two-year building ban is announced for the area.

A tumult in Wooden Tammela begins when Tampere hosts the 1990 annual Finnish housing fair.

The theme is renovation and supplementary building. Four old houses are renovated; they also receive criticism for the style in which they are renovated.

Three times that many new houses are built. For every new building, older ones are demolished to make way.

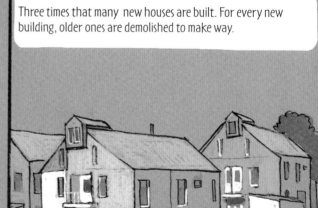

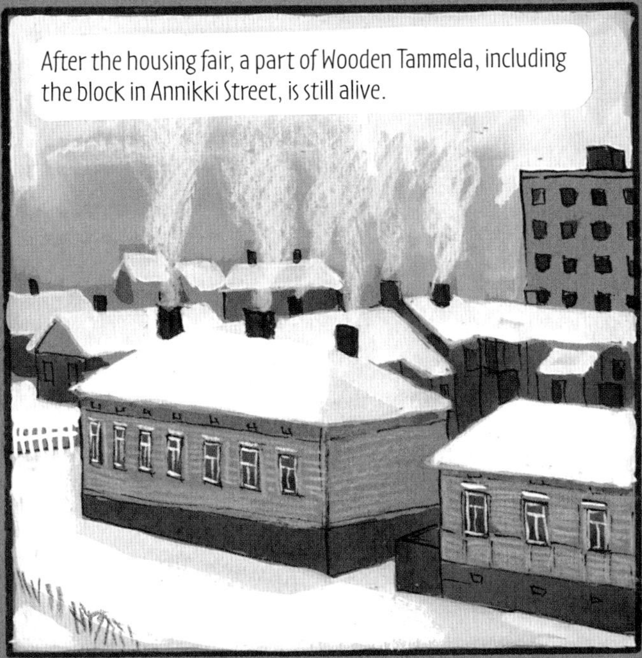
After the housing fair, a part of Wooden Tammela, including the block in Annikki Street, is still alive.

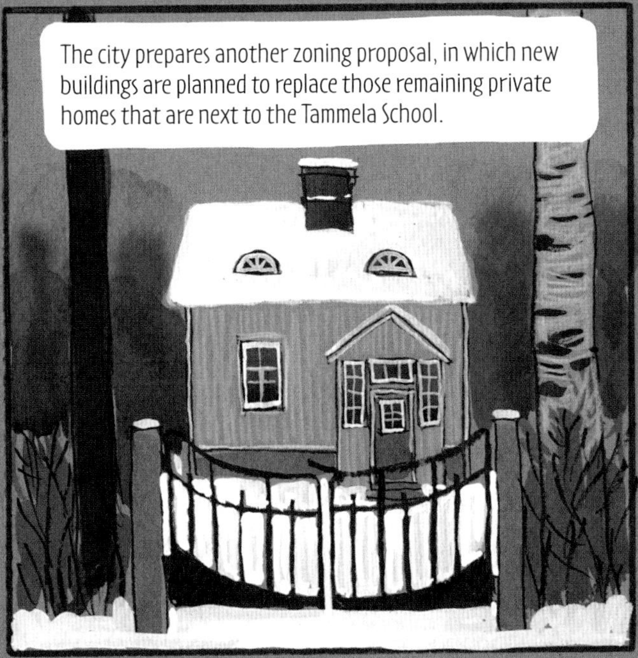
The city prepares another zoning proposal, in which new buildings are planned to replace those remaining private homes that are next to the Tammela School.

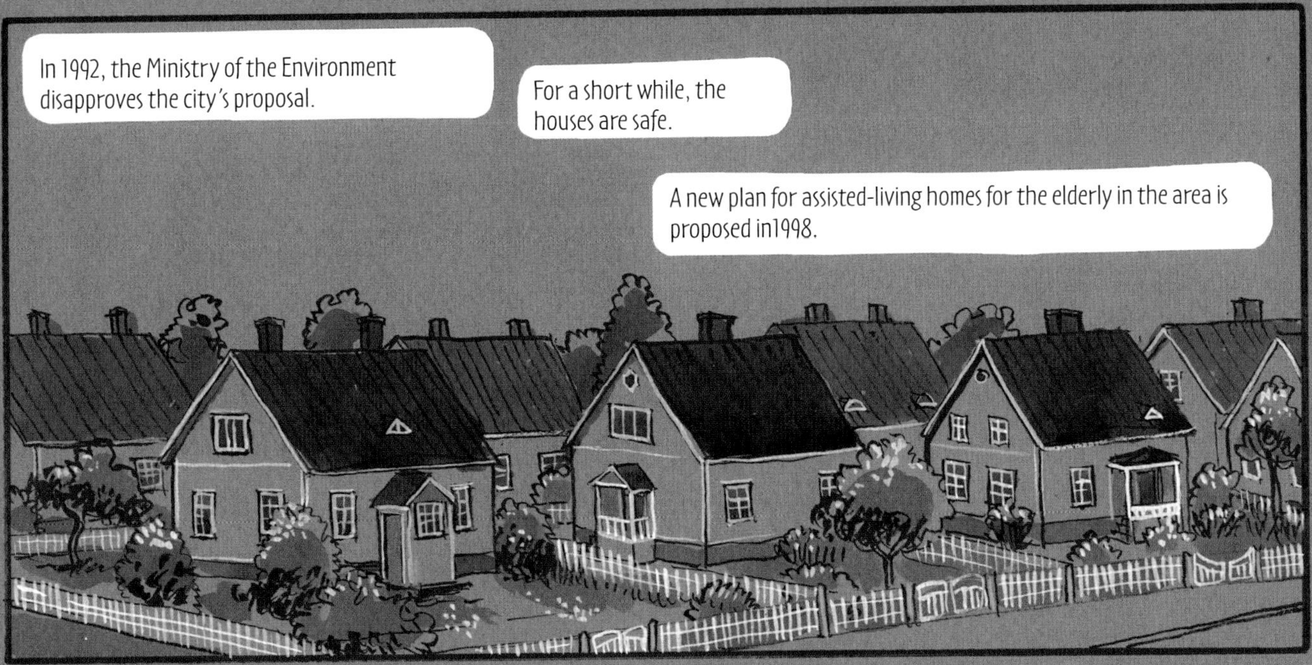
In 1992, the Ministry of the Environment disapproves the city's proposal.
For a short while, the houses are safe.
A new plan for assisted-living homes for the elderly in the area is proposed in1998.

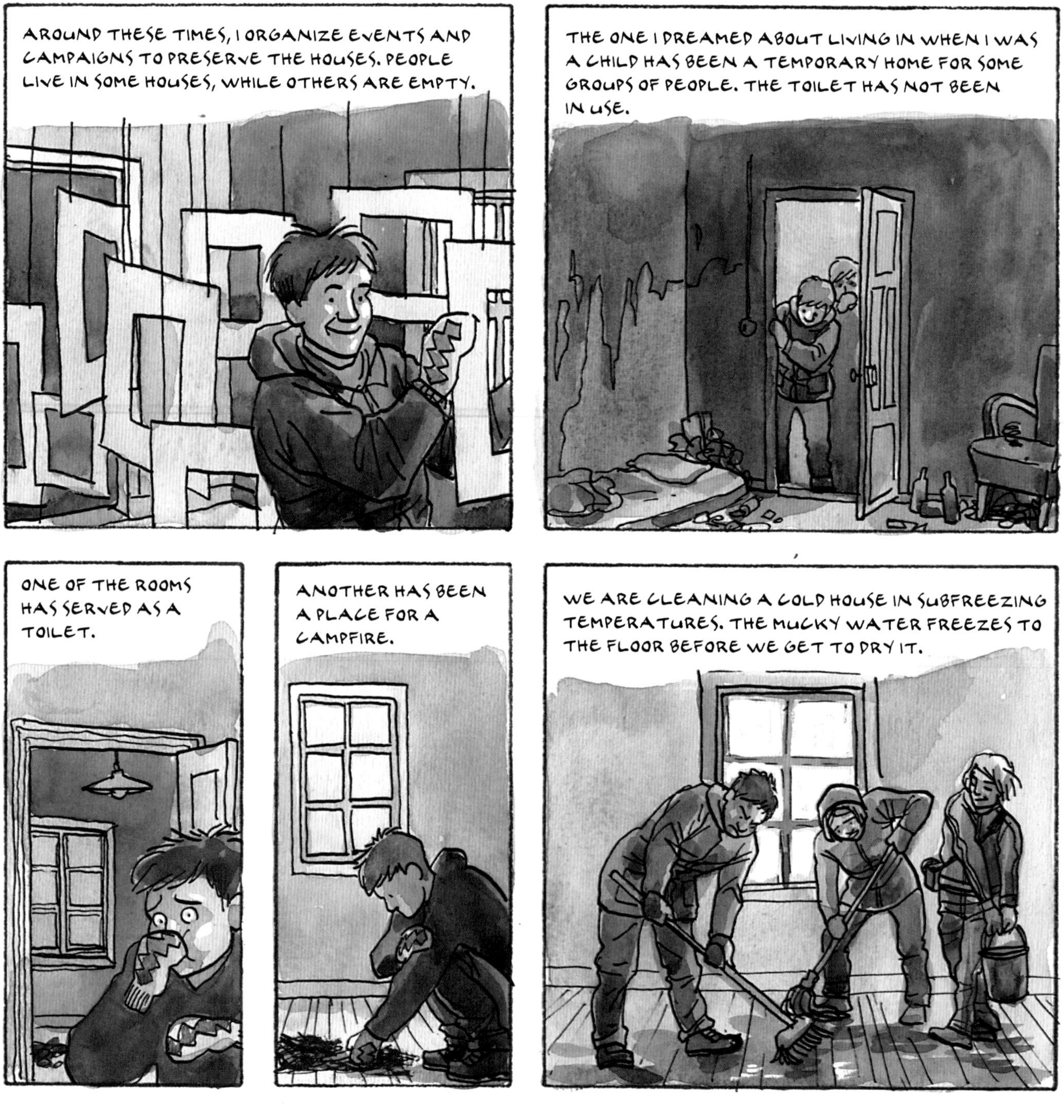
AROUND THESE TIMES, I ORGANIZE EVENTS AND CAMPAIGNS TO PRESERVE THE HOUSES. PEOPLE LIVE IN SOME HOUSES, WHILE OTHERS ARE EMPTY.
THE ONE I DREAMED ABOUT LIVING IN WHEN I WAS A CHILD HAS BEEN A TEMPORARY HOME FOR SOME GROUPS OF PEOPLE. THE TOILET HAS NOT BEEN IN USE.
ONE OF THE ROOMS HAS SERVED AS A TOILET.
ANOTHER HAS BEEN A PLACE FOR A CAMPFIRE.
WE ARE CLEANING A COLD HOUSE IN SUBFREEZING TEMPERATURES. THE MUCKY WATER FREEZES TO THE FLOOR BEFORE WE GET TO DRY IT.

A FRIEND OF MINE WRITES A LETTER TO THE EDITOR OF THE *HELSINGIN SANOMAT* ABOUT THE FATE OF THE HOUSES. THE LETTER IS PUBLISHED, BUT NOT WITH A PICTURE OF THE THREATENED ONES—IT APPEARS WITH A PICTURE OF THE NEARBY ANNIKKI BLOCK YARD.

ON MY SUGGESTION, THE MAGAZINE VOIMA PICKS UP THE TOPIC. THIS TIME, I PROVIDE THE PHOTOS FOR THE STORY MYSELF. HOWEVER, THE REPORTER CHOOSES TO ADD AN INTERVIEW—WITH ANNIKKI'S RESIDENTS.

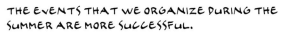

WE HAVE AN OPEN HOUSE IN ORDER TO SHOW THAT THE HOUSES ARE SPLENDID AND OF HIGH VALUE.

NÄYTTÖ

THE SMELL OF HUMAN FECES SPOILS THE ATMOSPHERE A BIT.

WOULD YOU LIKE TO HAVE SOME COFFEE?

NO THANK YOU.

THE EVENTS THAT WE ORGANIZE DURING THE SUMMER ARE MORE SUCCESSFUL.

NÄYTTELY

Sign: Open House

Sign: Exhibition

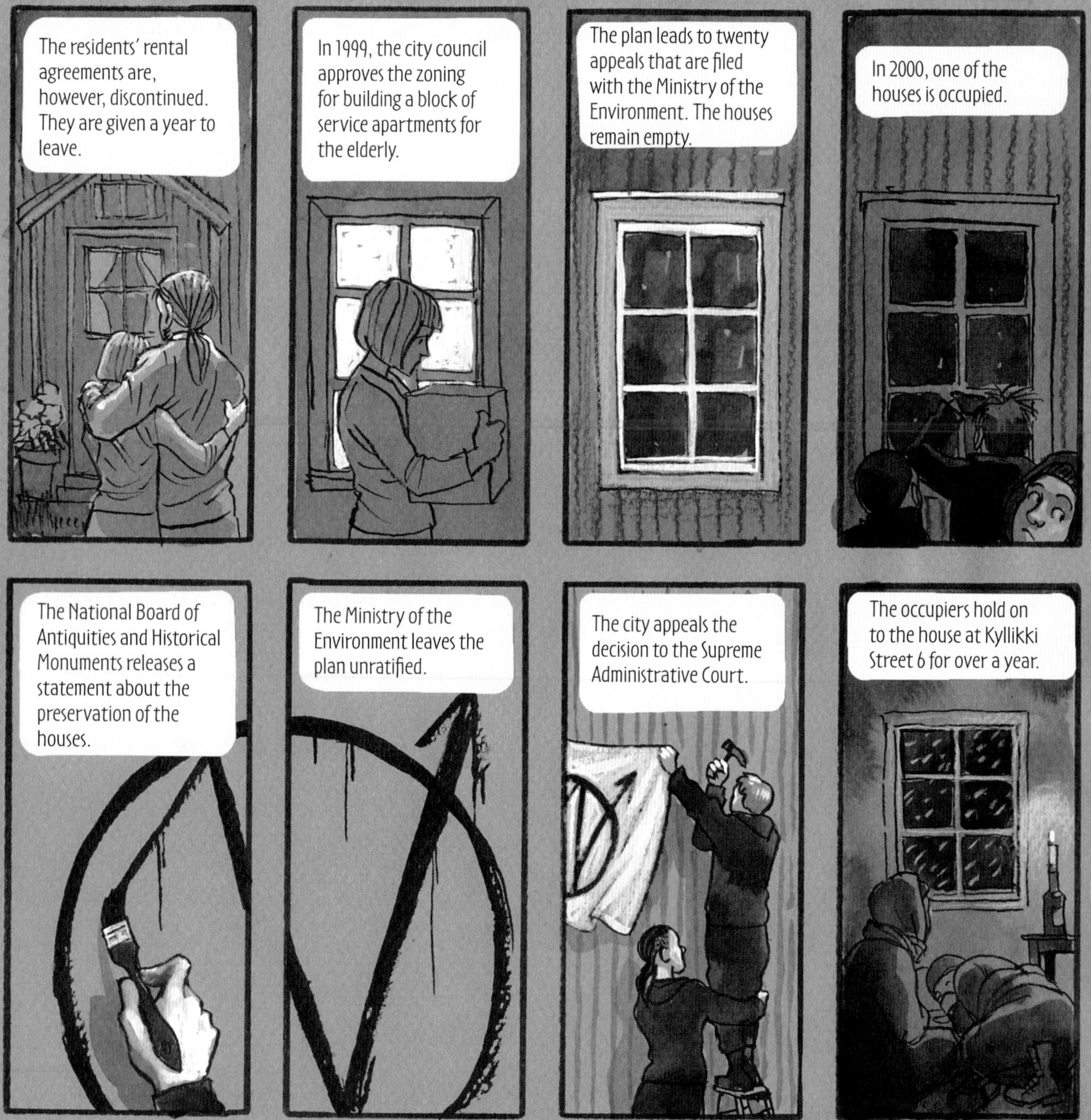
The residents' rental agreements are, however, discontinued. They are given a year to leave.
In 1999, the city council approves the zoning for building a block of service apartments for the elderly.
The plan leads to twenty appeals that are filed with the Ministry of the Environment. The houses remain empty.
In 2000, one of the houses is occupied.
The National Board of Antiquities and Historical Monuments releases a statement about the preservation of the houses.
The Ministry of the Environment leaves the plan unratified.
The city appeals the decision to the Supreme Administrative Court.
The occupiers hold on to the house at Kyllikki Street 6 for over a year.

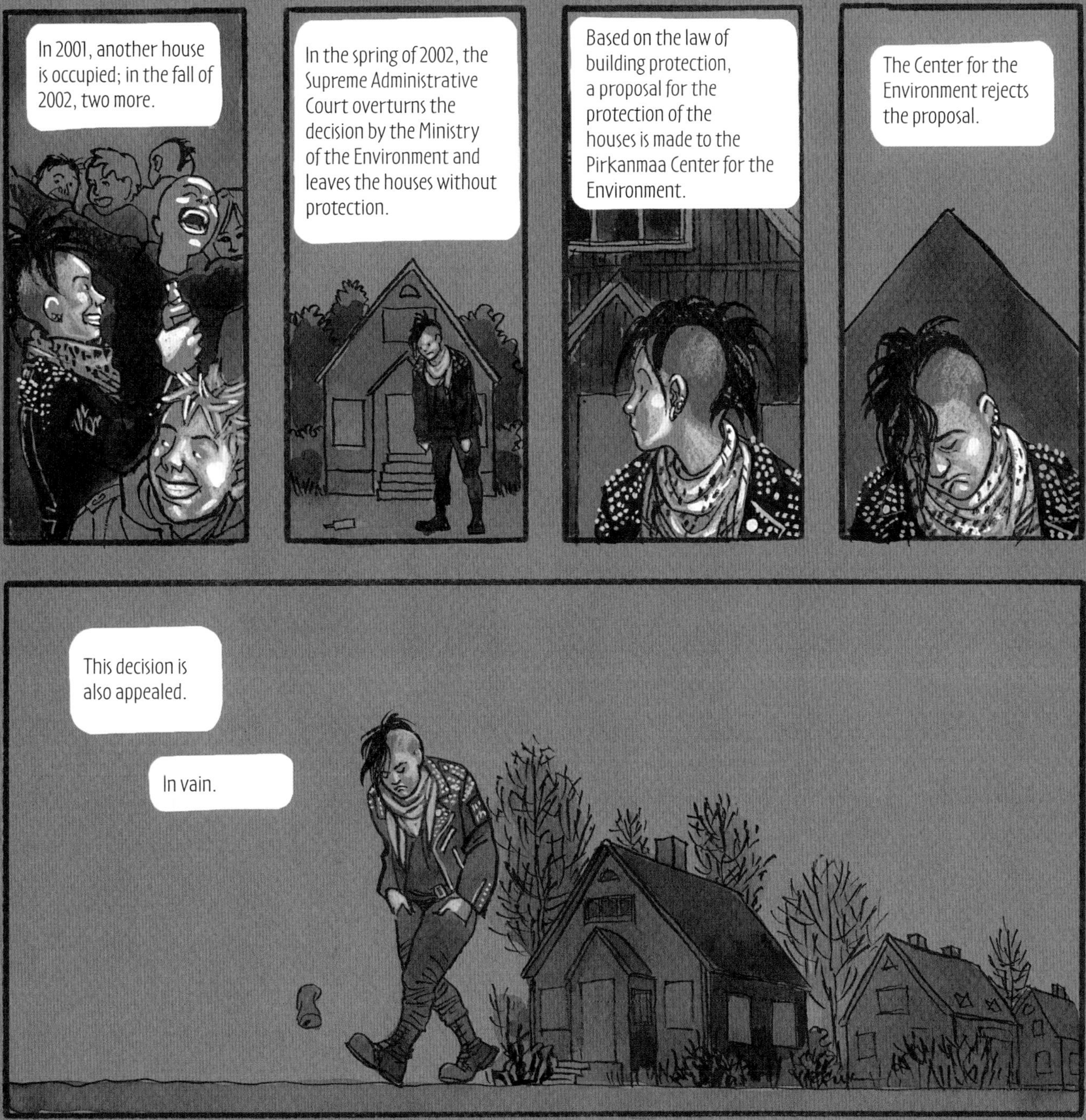
In 2001, another house is occupied; in the fall of 2002, two more.
In the spring of 2002, the Supreme Administrative Court overturns the decision by the Ministry of the Environment and leaves the houses without protection.
Based on the law of building protection, a proposal for the protection of the houses is made to the Pirkanmaa Center for the Environment.
The Center for the Environment rejects the proposal.
This decision is also appealed.
In vain.

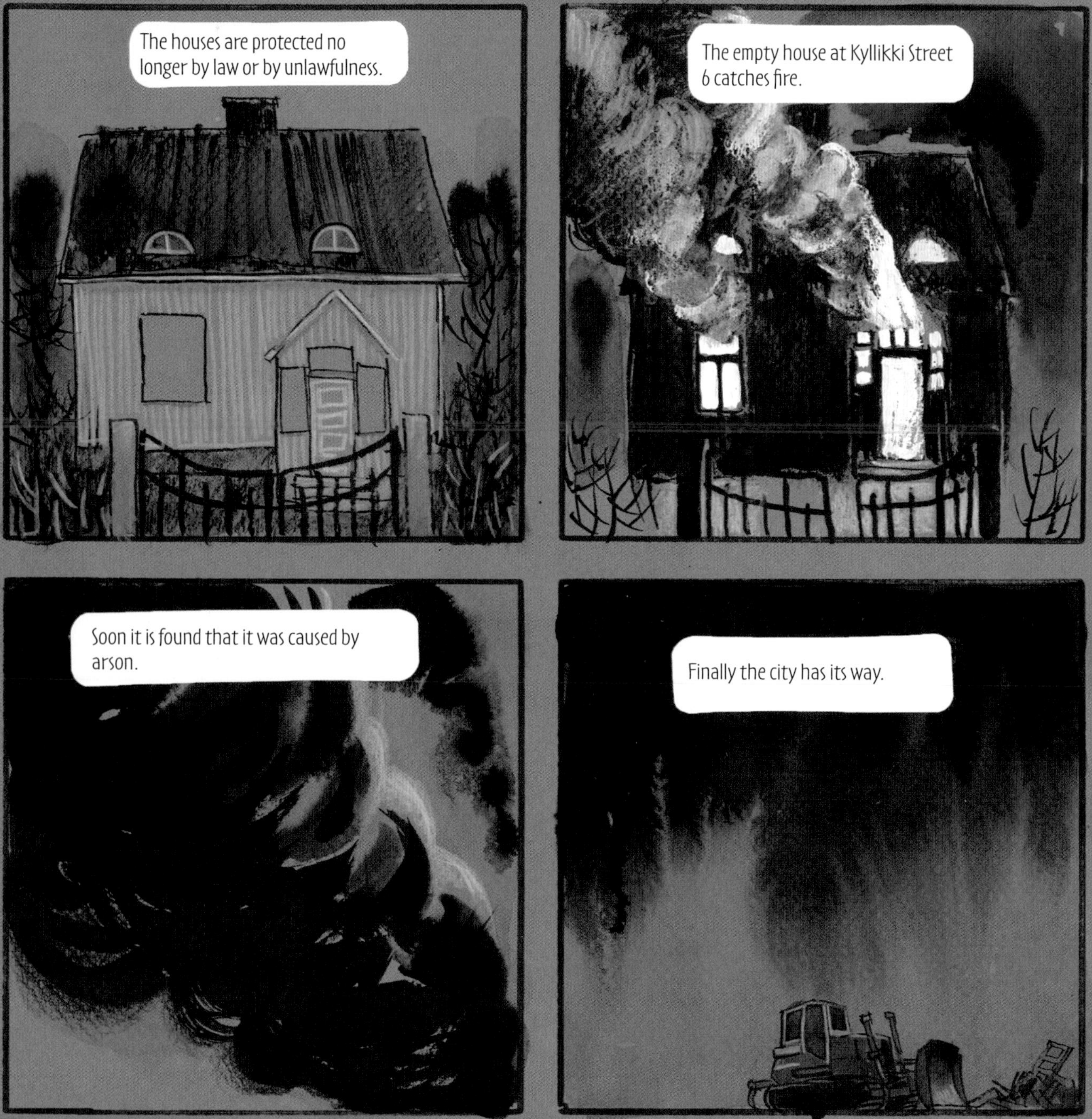
The houses are protected no longer by law or by unlawfulness.
The empty house at Kyllikki Street 6 catches fire.
Soon it is found that it was caused by arson.
Finally the city has its way.

A BITTER NIGHT

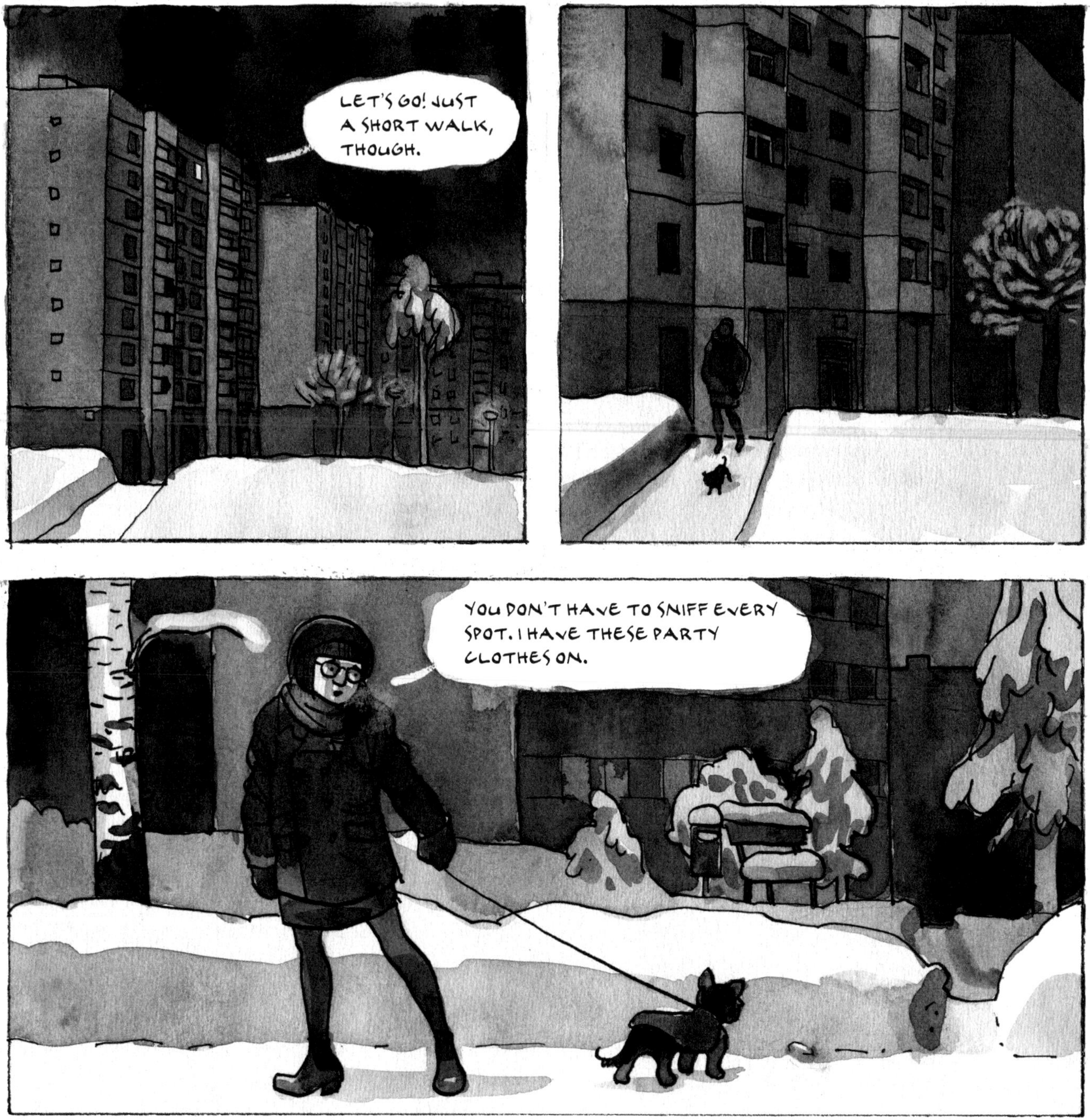
LET'S GO! JUST A SHORT WALK, THOUGH.
YOU DON'T HAVE TO SNIFF EVERY SPOT. I HAVE THESE PARTY CLOTHES ON.

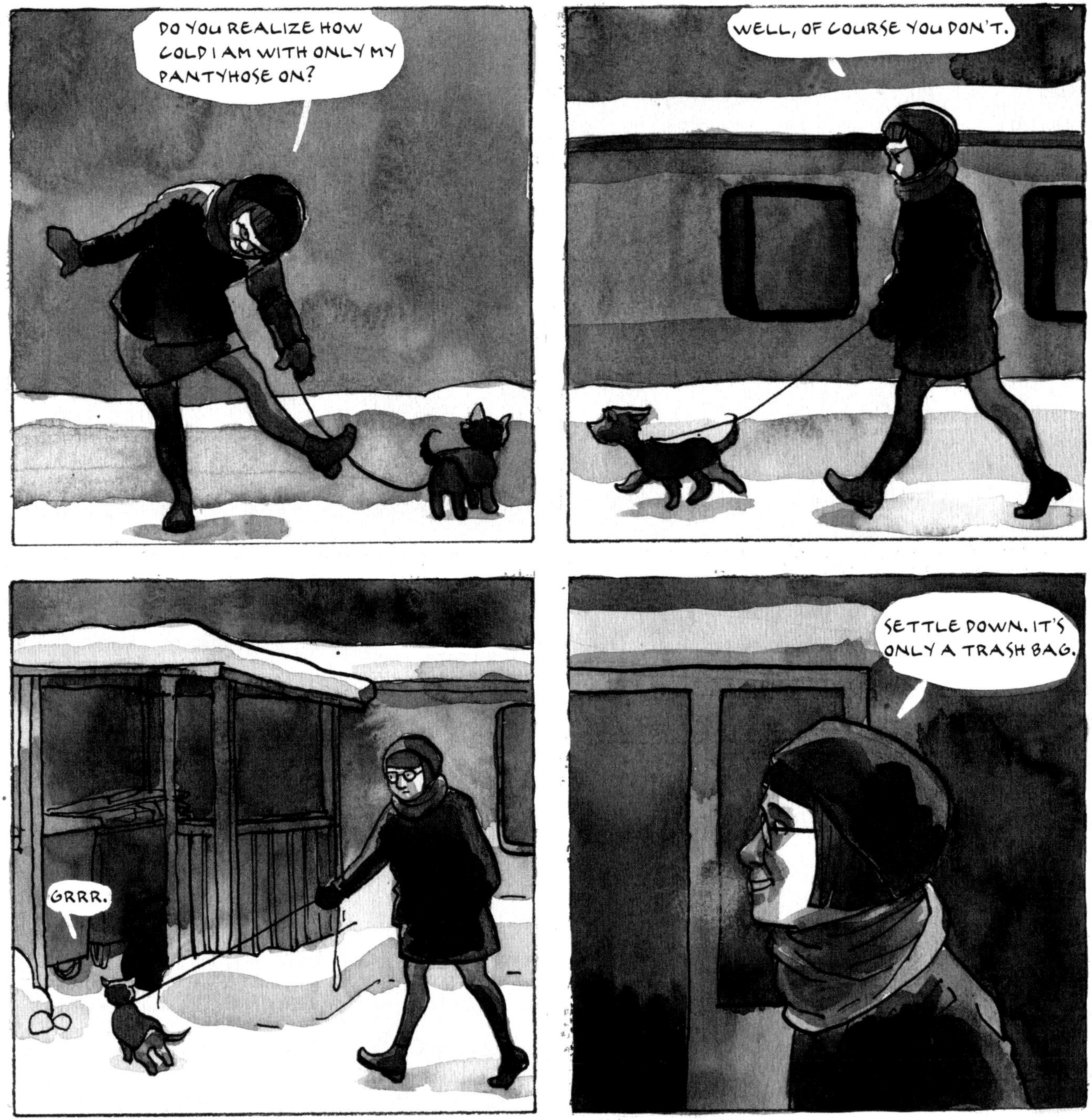
DO YOU REALIZE HOW COLD I AM WITH ONLY MY PANTYHOSE ON?
WELL, OF COURSE YOU DON'T.
GRRR.
SETTLE DOWN. IT'S ONLY A TRASH BAG.

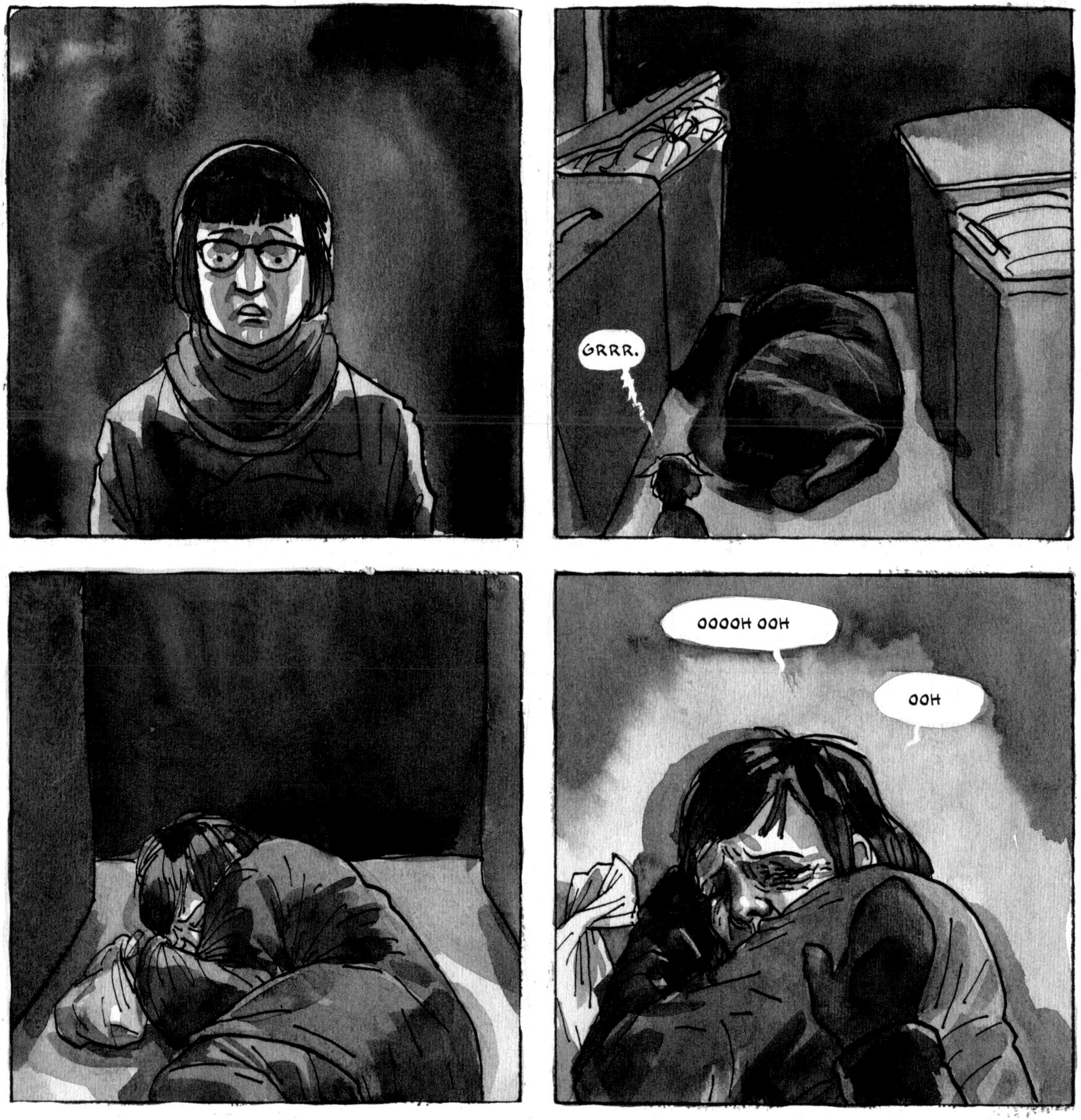
GRRR.
OOOOH OOH
OOH

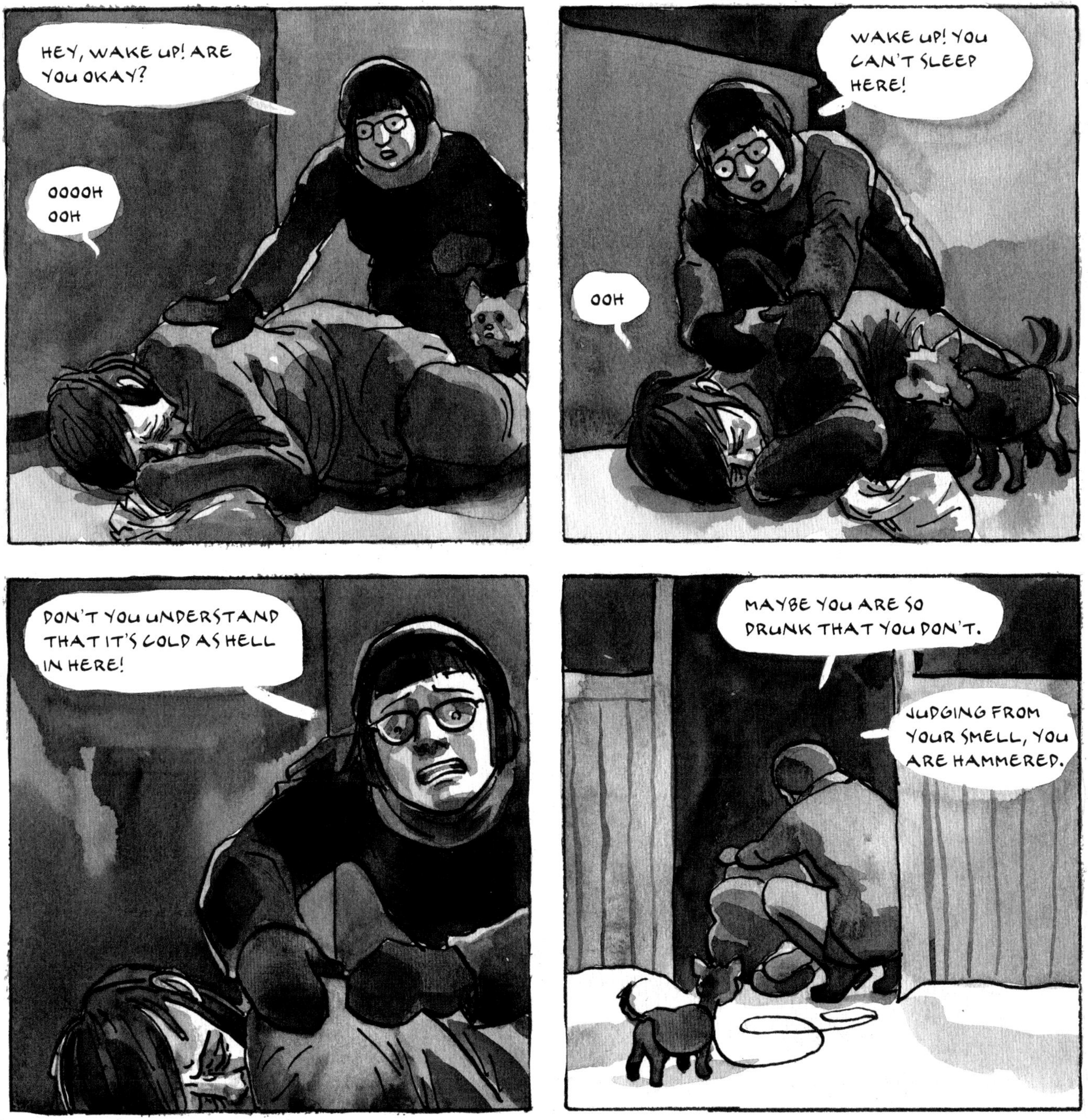
HEY, WAKE UP! ARE YOU OKAY?
OOOOH OOH
WAKE UP! YOU CAN'T SLEEP HERE!
OOH
DON'T YOU UNDERSTAND THAT IT'S COLD AS HELL IN HERE!
MAYBE YOU ARE SO DRUNK THAT YOU DON'T.
JUDGING FROM YOUR SMELL, YOU ARE HAMMERED.

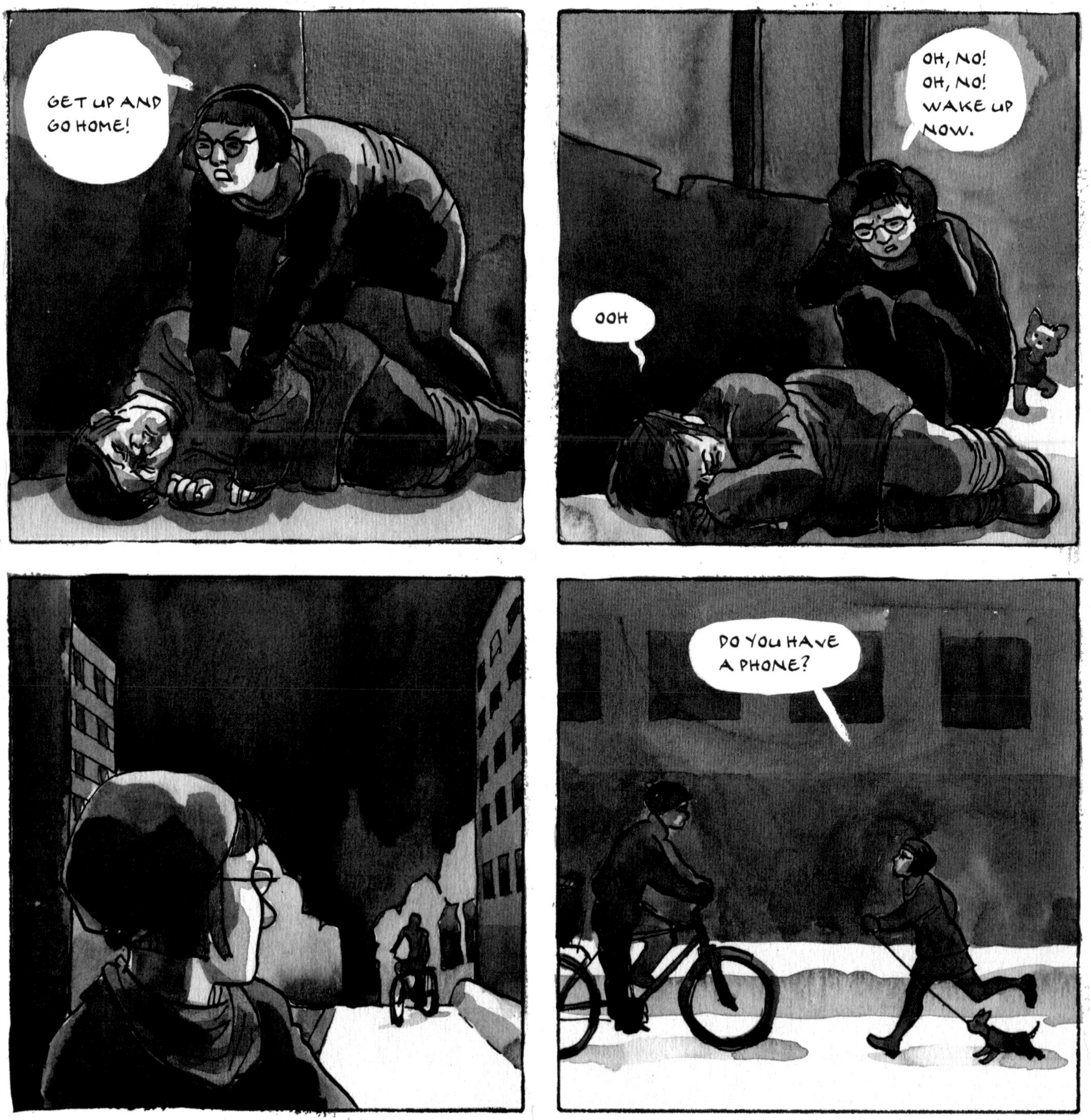
GET UP AND GO HOME!
OH, NO! OH, NO! WAKE UP NOW.
OOH
DO YOU HAVE A PHONE?

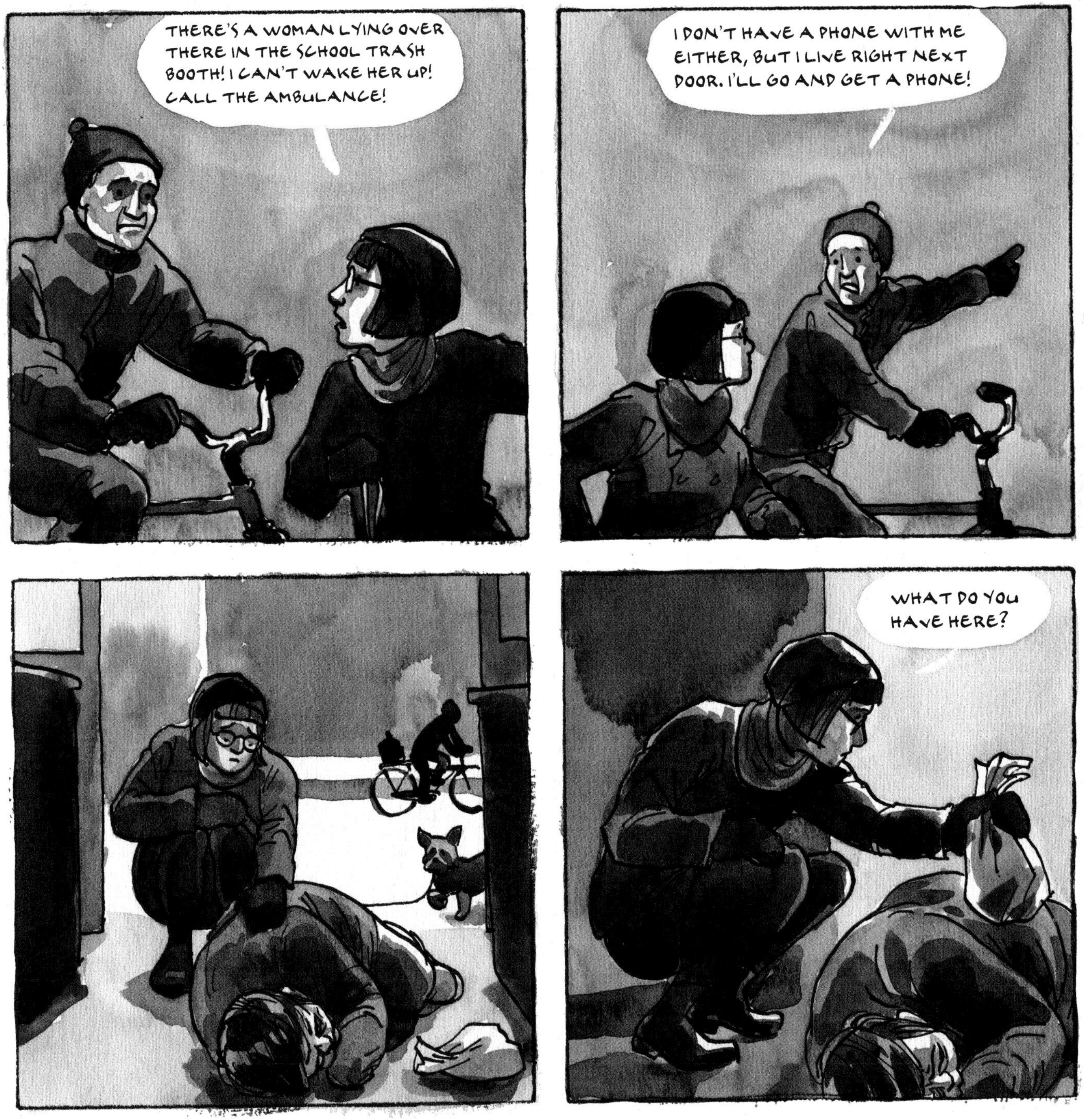
THERE'S A WOMAN LYING OVER THERE IN THE SCHOOL TRASH BOOTH! I CAN'T WAKE HER UP! CALL THE AMBULANCE!
I DON'T HAVE A PHONE WITH ME EITHER, BUT I LIVE RIGHT NEXT DOOR. I'LL GO AND GET A PHONE!
WHAT DO YOU HAVE HERE?

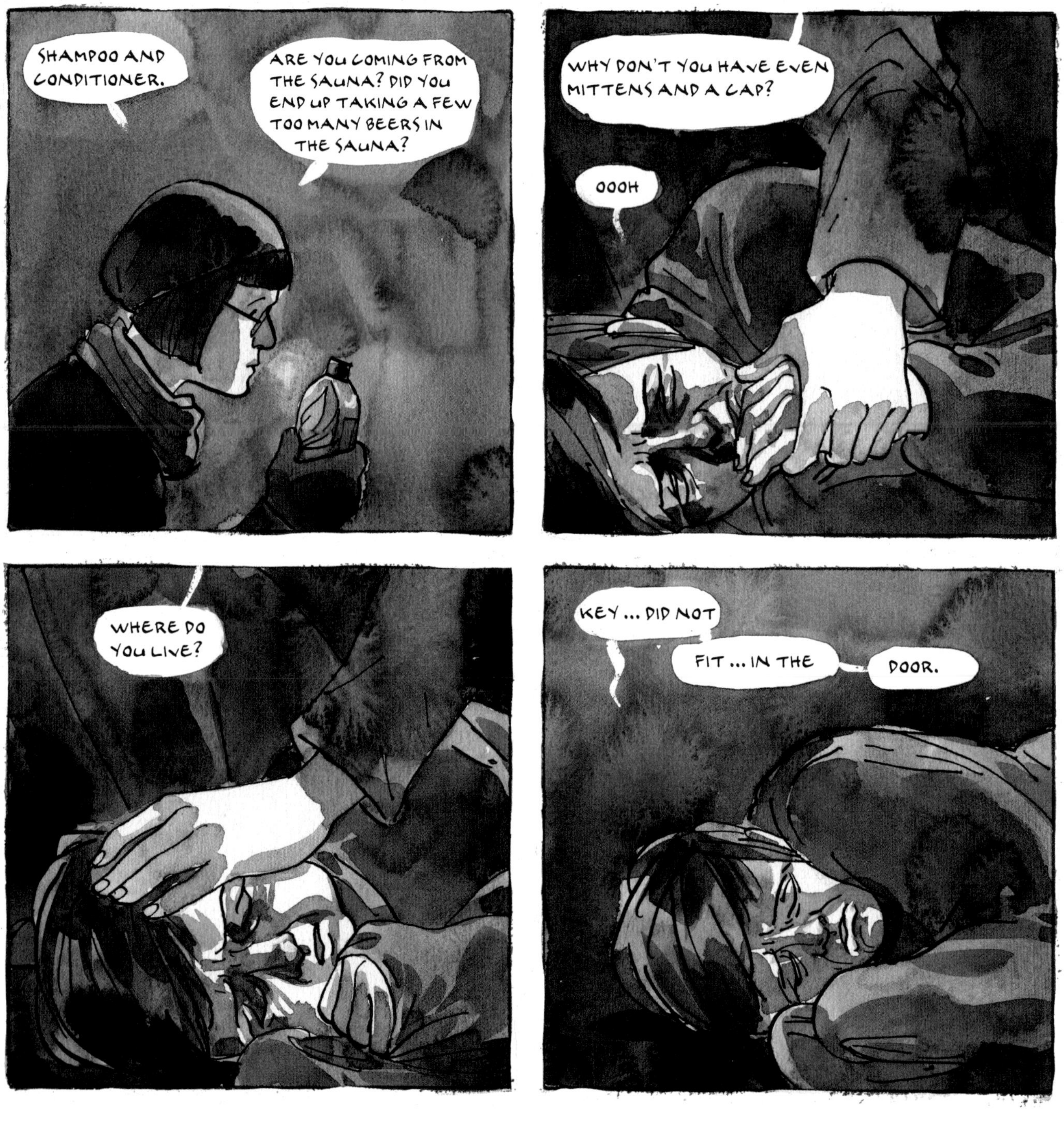
SHAMPOO AND CONDITIONER.
ARE YOU COMING FROM THE SAUNA? DID YOU END UP TAKING A FEW TOO MANY BEERS IN THE SAUNA?
WHY DON'T YOU HAVE EVEN MITTENS AND A CAP?
OOOH
WHERE DO YOU LIVE?
KEY ... DID NOT
FIT ... IN THE
DOOR.

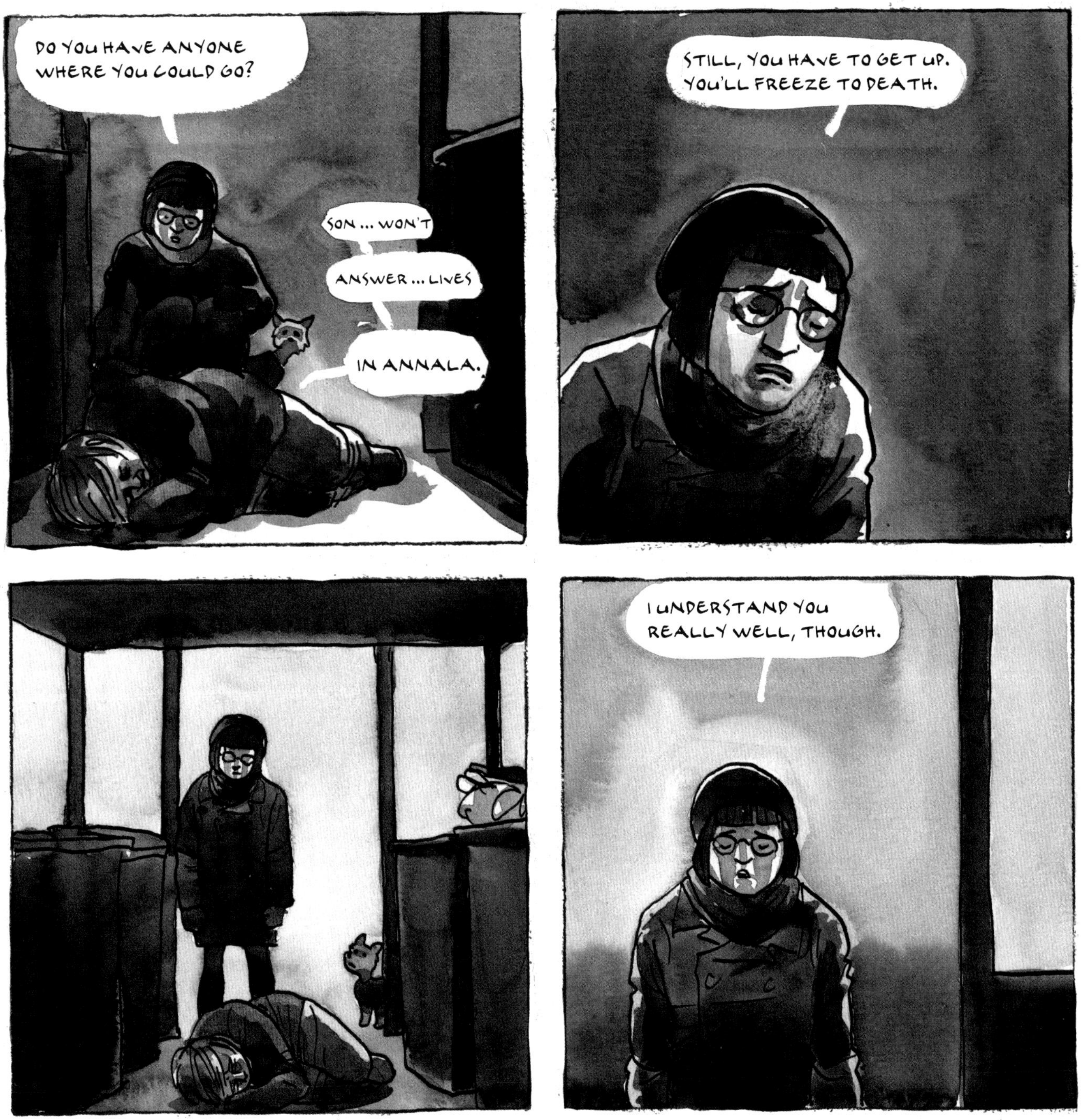
DO YOU HAVE ANYONE WHERE YOU COULD GO?
SON ... WON'T
ANSWER ... LIVES
IN ANNALA.
STILL, YOU HAVE TO GET UP. YOU'LL FREEZE TO DEATH.
I UNDERSTAND YOU REALLY WELL, THOUGH.

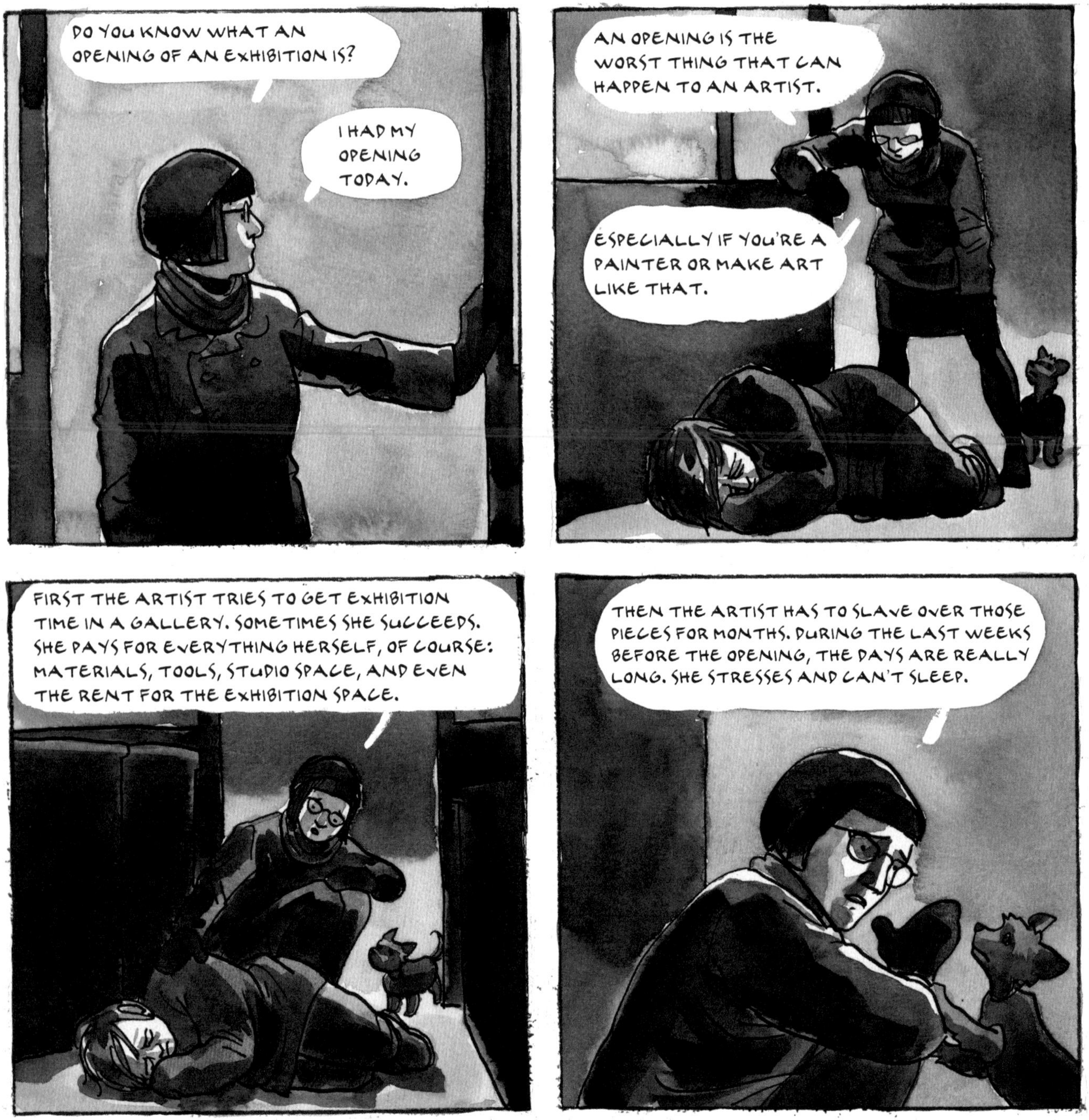
DO YOU KNOW WHAT AN OPENING OF AN EXHIBITION IS?
I HAD MY OPENING TODAY.
AN OPENING IS THE WORST THING THAT CAN HAPPEN TO AN ARTIST.
ESPECIALLY IF YOU'RE A PAINTER OR MAKE ART LIKE THAT.
FIRST THE ARTIST TRIES TO GET EXHIBITION TIME IN A GALLERY. SOMETIMES SHE SUCCEEDS. SHE PAYS FOR EVERYTHING HERSELF, OF COURSE: MATERIALS, TOOLS, STUDIO SPACE, AND EVEN THE RENT FOR THE EXHIBITION SPACE.
THEN THE ARTIST HAS TO SLAVE OVER THOSE PIECES FOR MONTHS. DURING THE LAST WEEKS BEFORE THE OPENING, THE DAYS ARE REALLY LONG. SHE STRESSES AND CAN'T SLEEP.

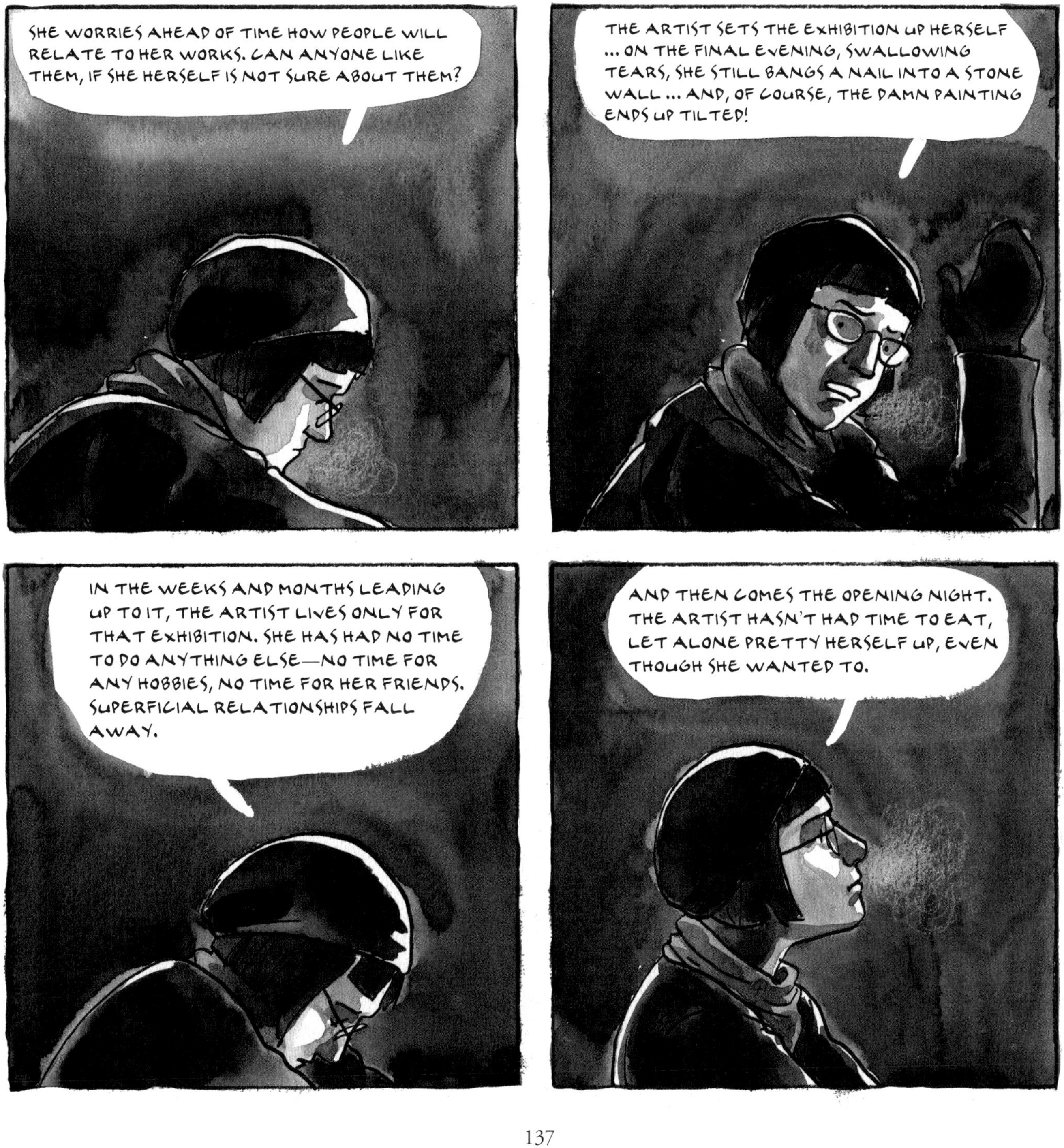
SHE WORRIES AHEAD OF TIME HOW PEOPLE WILL RELATE TO HER WORKS. CAN ANYONE LIKE THEM, IF SHE HERSELF IS NOT SURE ABOUT THEM?
THE ARTIST SETS THE EXHIBITION UP HERSELF ... ON THE FINAL EVENING, SWALLOWING TEARS, SHE STILL BANGS A NAIL INTO A STONE WALL ... AND, OF COURSE, THE DAMN PAINTING ENDS UP TILTED!
IN THE WEEKS AND MONTHS LEADING UP TO IT, THE ARTIST LIVES ONLY FOR THAT EXHIBITION. SHE HAS HAD NO TIME TO DO ANYTHING ELSE—NO TIME FOR ANY HOBBIES, NO TIME FOR HER FRIENDS. SUPERFICIAL RELATIONSHIPS FALL AWAY.
AND THEN COMES THE OPENING NIGHT. THE ARTIST HASN'T HAD TIME TO EAT, LET ALONE PRETTY HERSELF UP, EVEN THOUGH SHE WANTED TO.

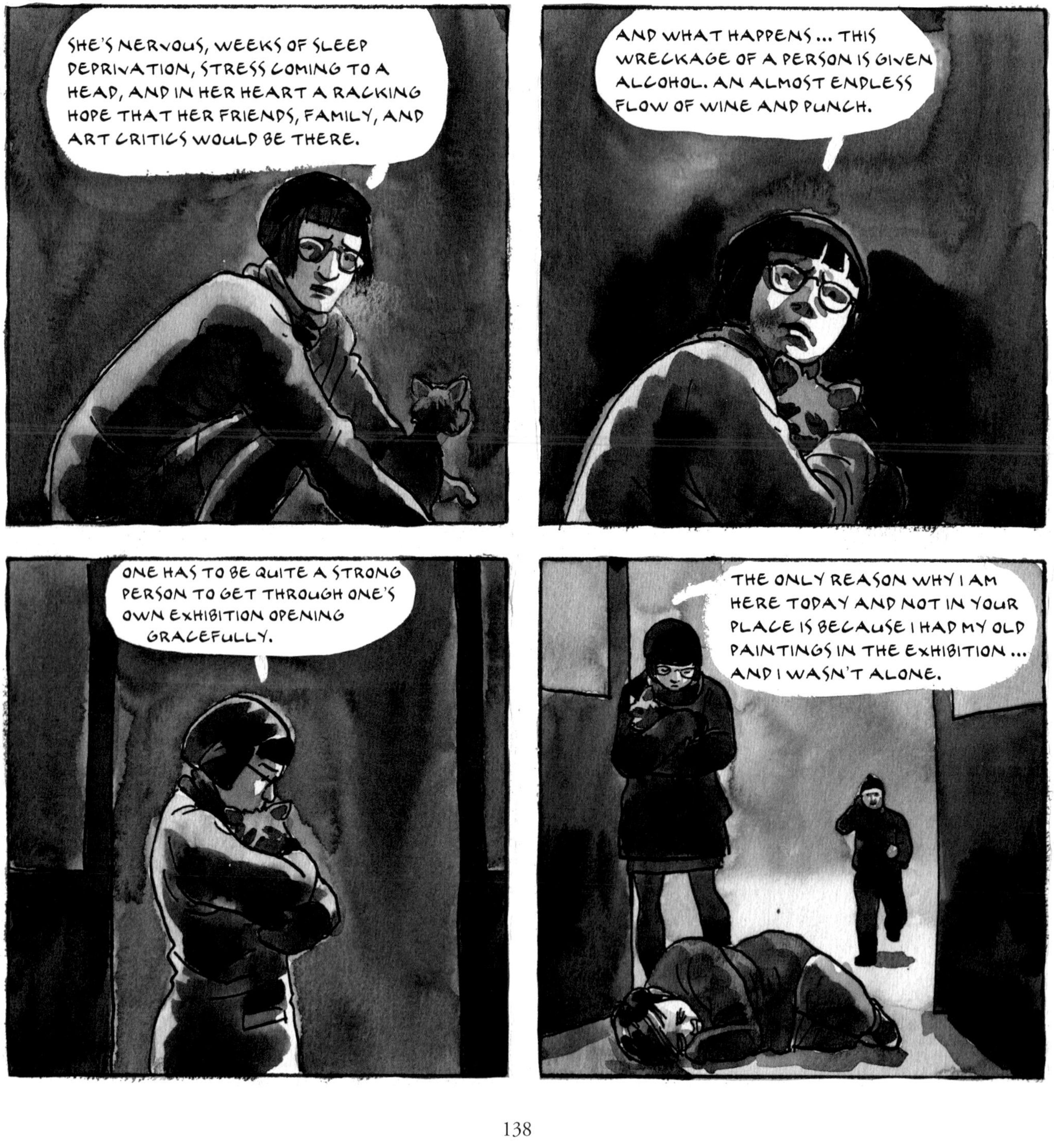
SHE'S NERVOUS, WEEKS OF SLEEP DEPRIVATION, STRESS COMING TO A HEAD, AND IN HER HEART A RACKING HOPE THAT HER FRIENDS, FAMILY, AND ART CRITICS WOULD BE THERE.
AND WHAT HAPPENS... THIS WRECKAGE OF A PERSON IS GIVEN ALCOHOL. AN ALMOST ENDLESS FLOW OF WINE AND PUNCH.
ONE HAS TO BE QUITE A STRONG PERSON TO GET THROUGH ONE'S OWN EXHIBITION OPENING GRACEFULLY.
THE ONLY REASON WHY I AM HERE TODAY AND NOT IN YOUR PLACE IS BECAUSE I HAD MY OLD PAINTINGS IN THE EXHIBITION... AND I WASN'T ALONE.

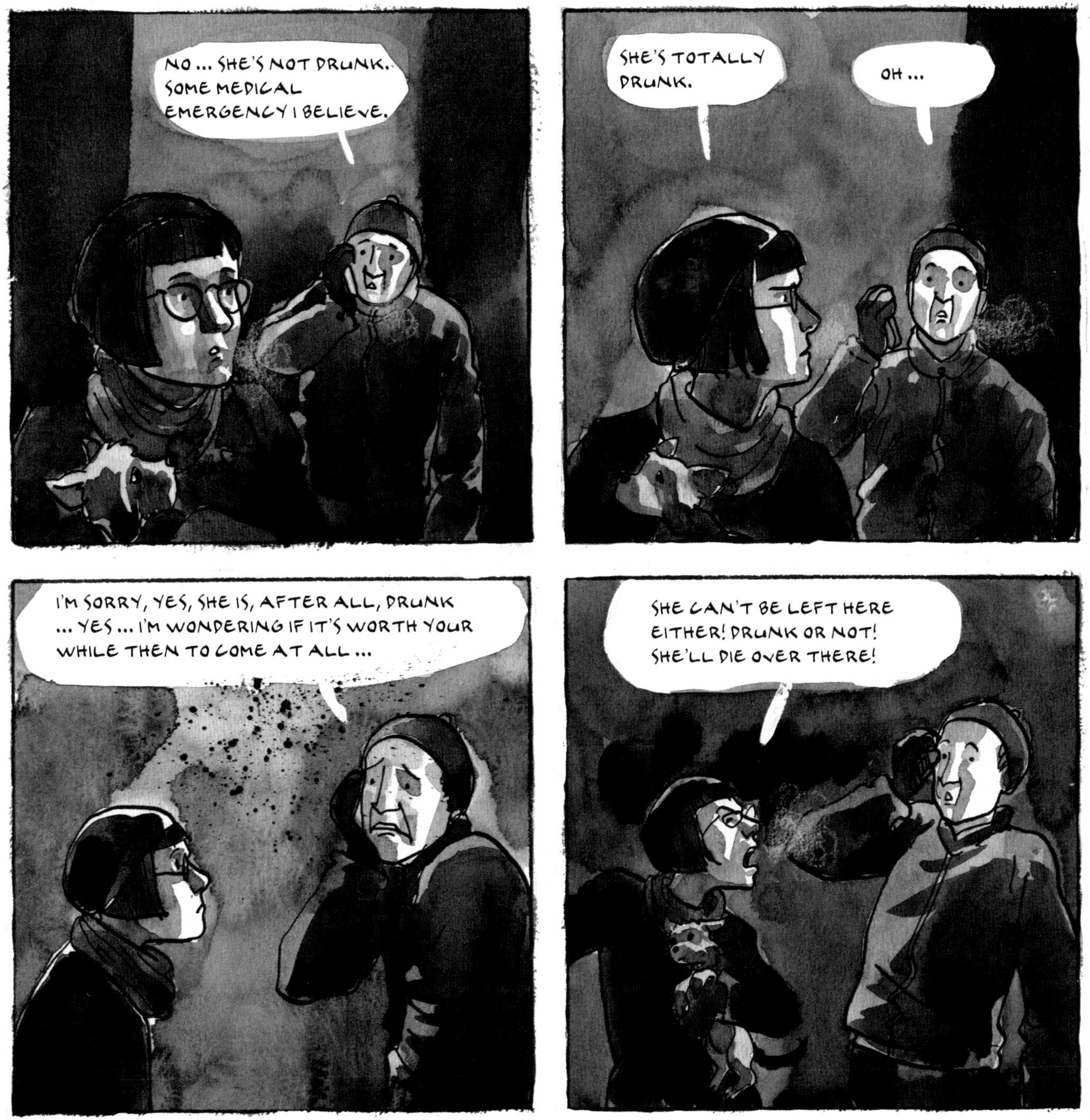
NO ... SHE'S NOT DRUNK. SOME MEDICAL EMERGENCY I BELIEVE.
SHE'S TOTALLY DRUNK.
OH ...
I'M SORRY, YES, SHE IS, AFTER ALL, DRUNK ... YES ... I'M WONDERING IF IT'S WORTH YOUR WHILE THEN TO COME AT ALL ...
SHE CAN'T BE LEFT HERE EITHER! DRUNK OR NOT! SHE'LL DIE OVER THERE!

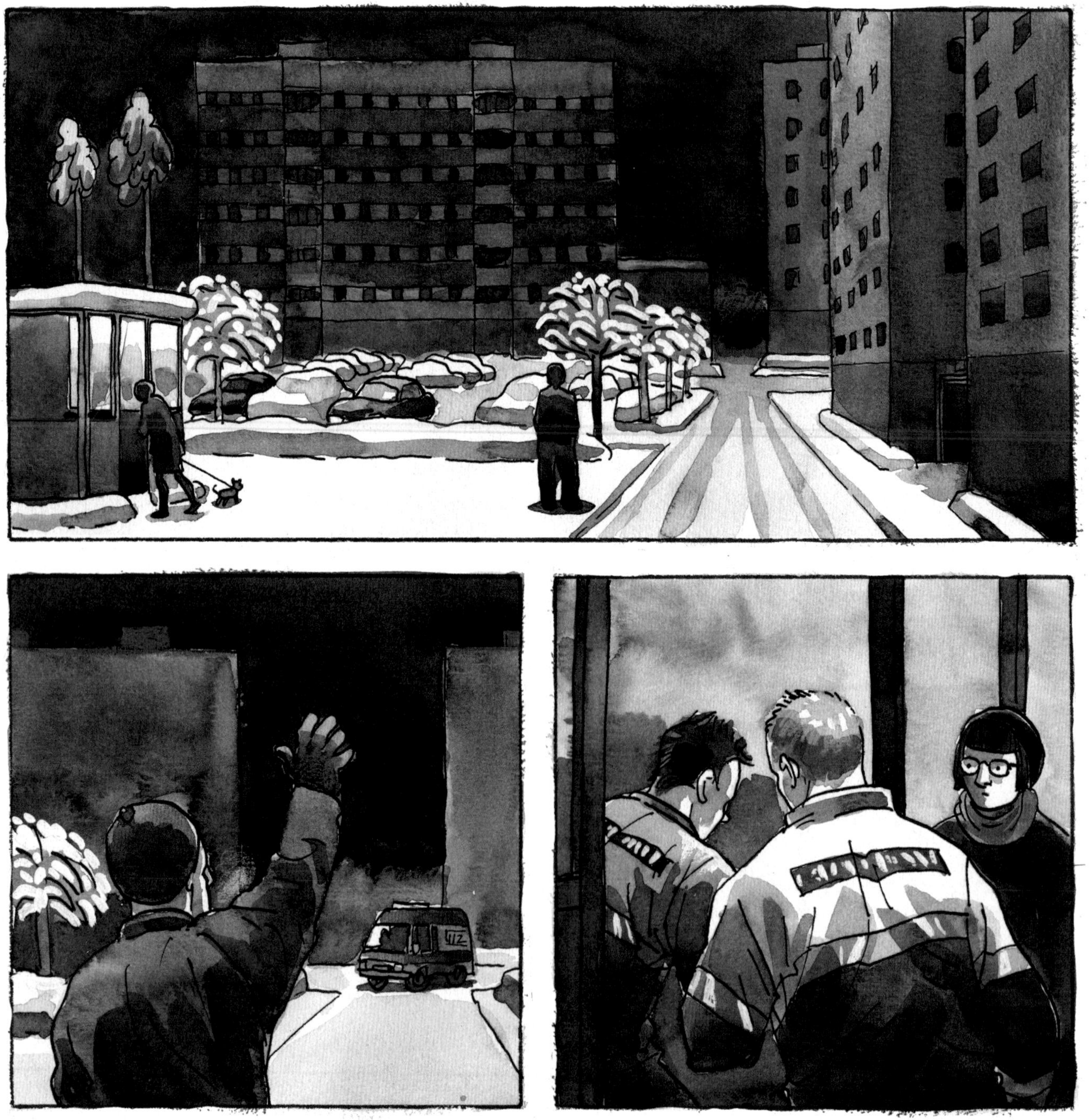

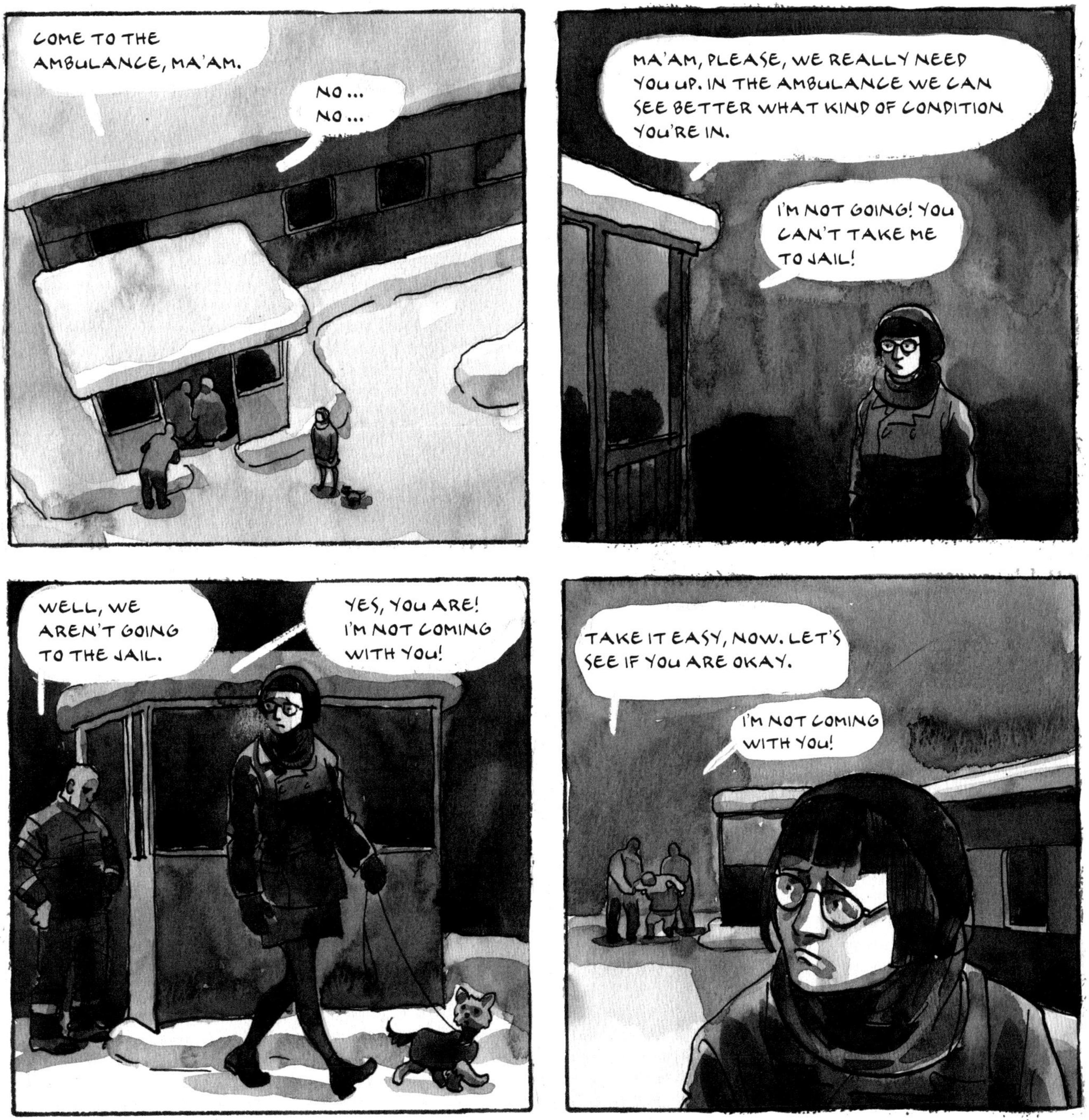
COME TO THE AMBULANCE, MA'AM.
NO ... NO ...
MA'AM, PLEASE, WE REALLY NEED YOU UP. IN THE AMBULANCE WE CAN SEE BETTER WHAT KIND OF CONDITION YOU'RE IN.
I'M NOT GOING! YOU CAN'T TAKE ME TO JAIL!
WELL, WE AREN'T GOING TO THE JAIL.
YES, YOU ARE! I'M NOT COMING WITH YOU!
TAKE IT EASY, NOW. LET'S SEE IF YOU ARE OKAY.
I'M NOT COMING WITH YOU!

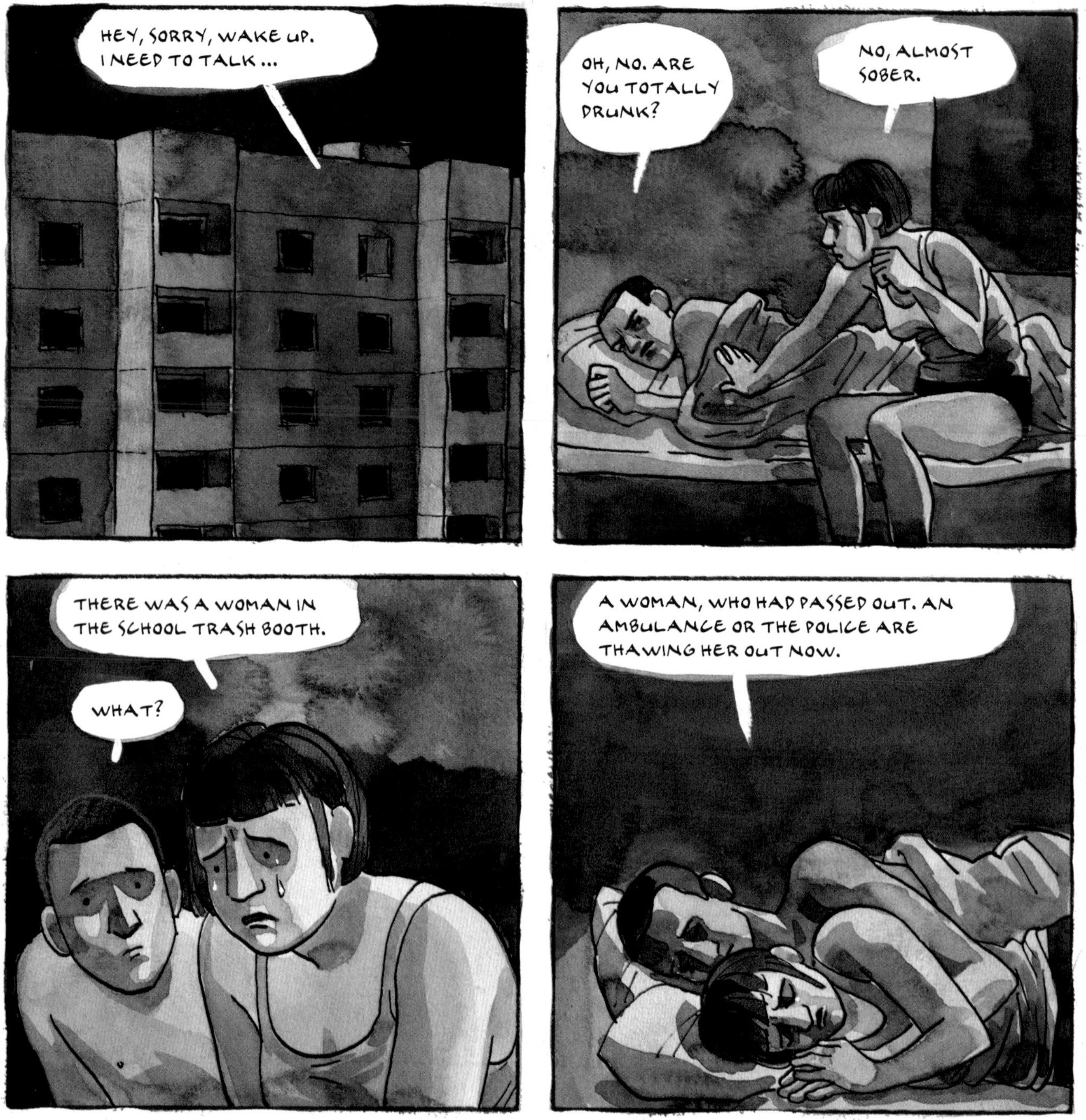
HEY, SORRY, WAKE UP. I NEED TO TALK...
OH, NO. ARE YOU TOTALLY DRUNK?
NO, ALMOST SOBER.
THERE WAS A WOMAN IN THE SCHOOL TRASH BOOTH.
WHAT?
A WOMAN, WHO HAD PASSED OUT. AN AMBULANCE OR THE POLICE ARE THAWING HER OUT NOW.

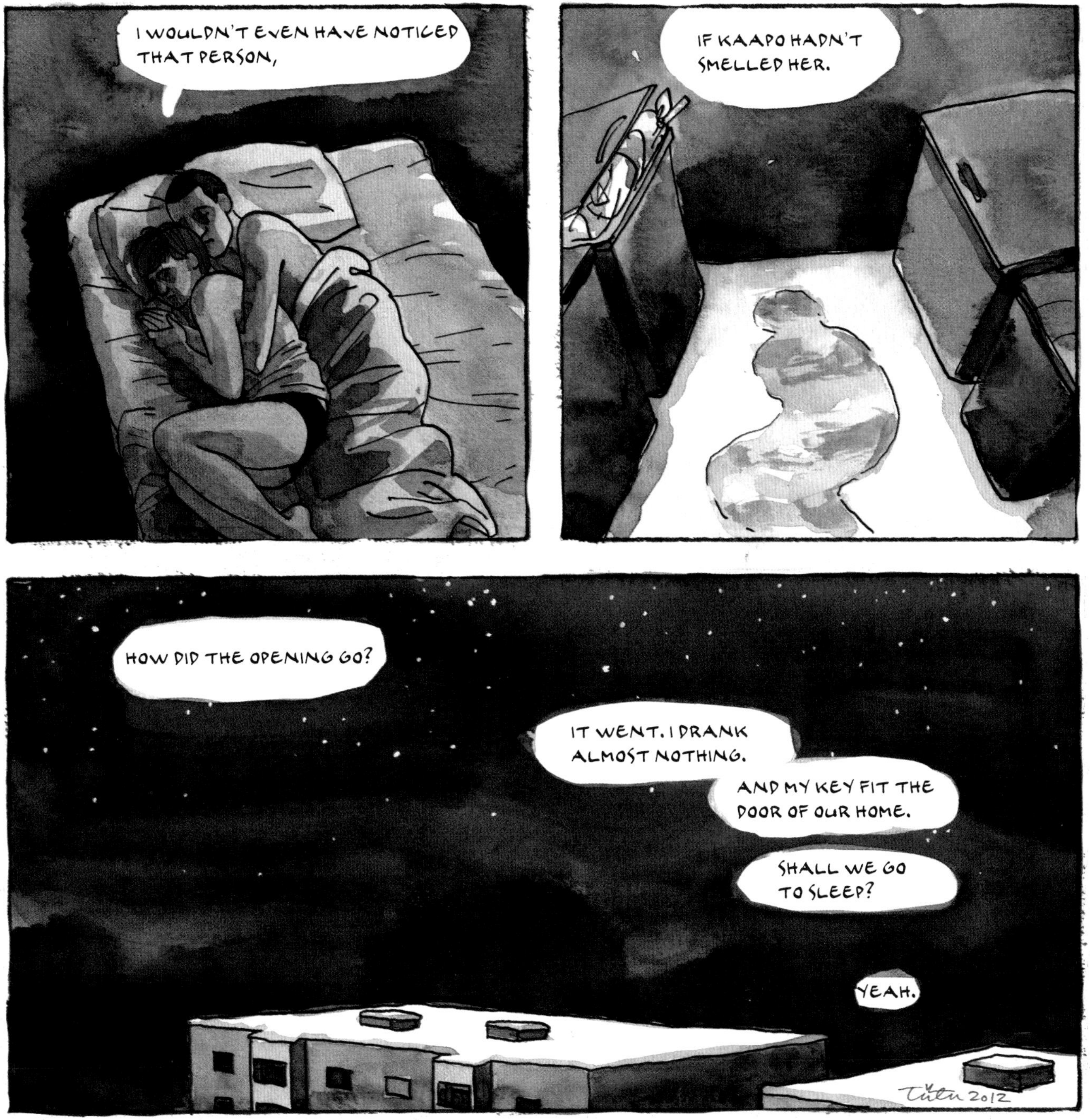
I WOULDN'T EVEN HAVE NOTICED THAT PERSON,
IF KAAPO HADN'T SMELLED HER.
HOW DID THE OPENING GO?
IT WENT. I DRANK ALMOST NOTHING.
AND MY KEY FIT THE DOOR OF OUR HOME.
SHALL WE GO TO SLEEP?
YEAH.
Tiitu 2012

THE BATTLE FOR ANNIKKI

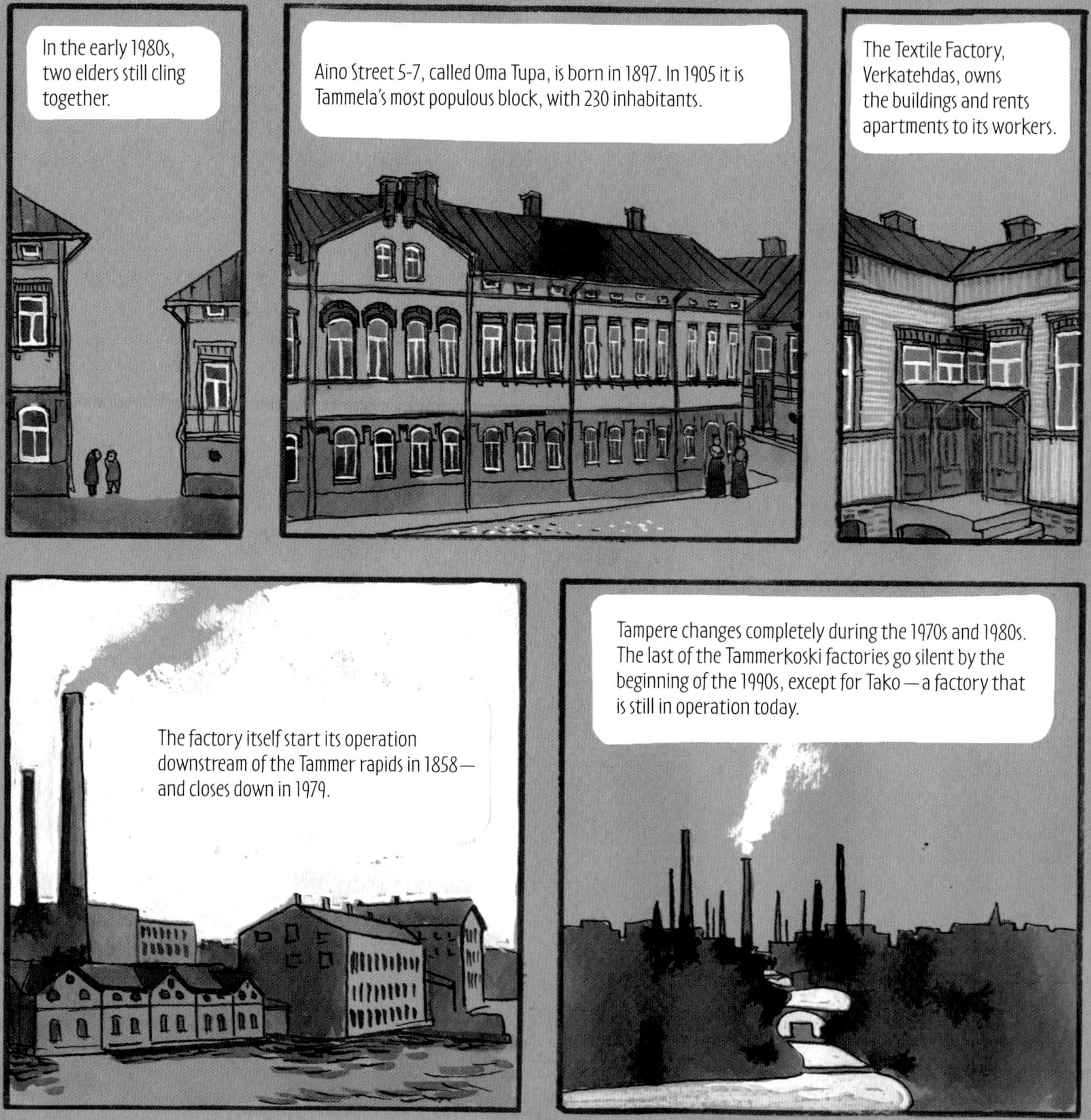
In the early 1980s, two elders still cling together.
Aino Street 5-7, called Oma Tupa, is born in 1897. In 1905 it is Tammela's most populous block, with 230 inhabitants.
The Textile Factory, Verkatehdas, owns the buildings and rents apartments to its workers.
The factory itself start its operation downstream of the Tammer rapids in 1858—and closes down in 1979.
Tampere changes completely during the 1970s and 1980s. The last of the Tammerkoski factories go silent by the beginning of the 1990s, except for Tako—a factory that is still in operation today.

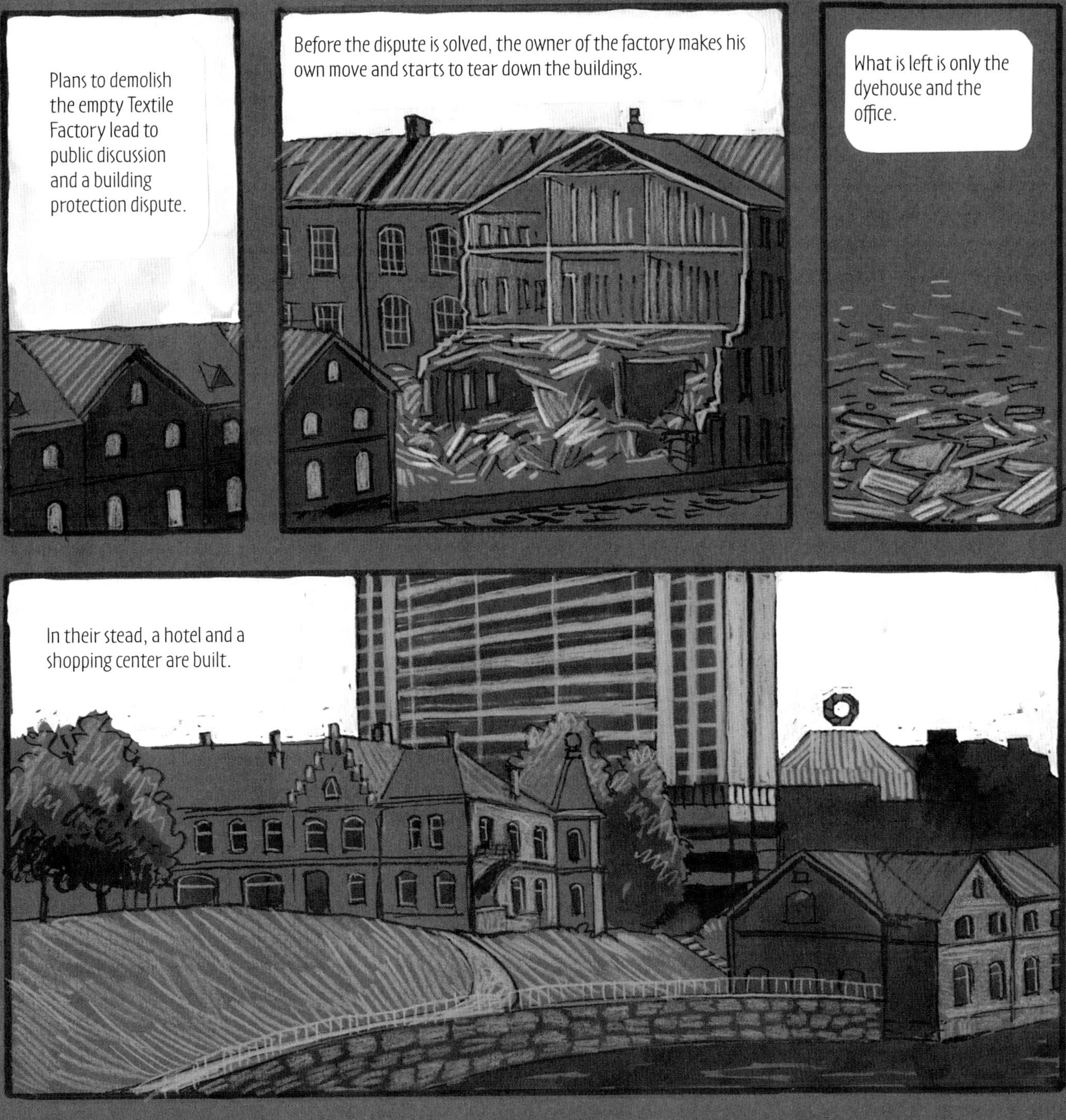
Plans to demolish the empty Textile Factory lead to public discussion and a building protection dispute.
Before the dispute is solved, the owner of the factory makes his own move and starts to tear down the buildings.
What is left is only the dyehouse and the office.
In their stead, a hotel and a shopping center are built.

The demolition of the Textile Factory, however, serves as the trigger for thoughts of building protection in Tampere. It awakens people to the realization that the old buildings are disappearing around them.

Much has already disappeared during the 1960s and 1970s.

In 1972, there's also a demolition threat over the Market Hall's office house. People argue about tearing down this house for a long time, and it also gets occupied.

In 1983, the bank that owned the house promises not to demolish it for ten years. This is enough. After a decade, nobody even talks about tearing it down.

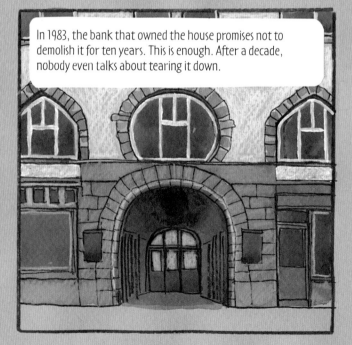

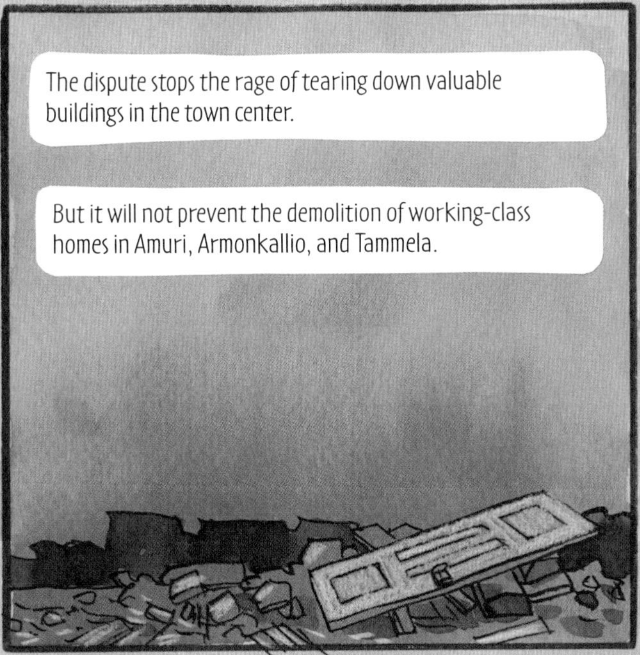
The dispute stops the rage of tearing down valuable buildings in the town center.
But it will not prevent the demolition of working-class homes in Amuri, Armonkallio, and Tammela.

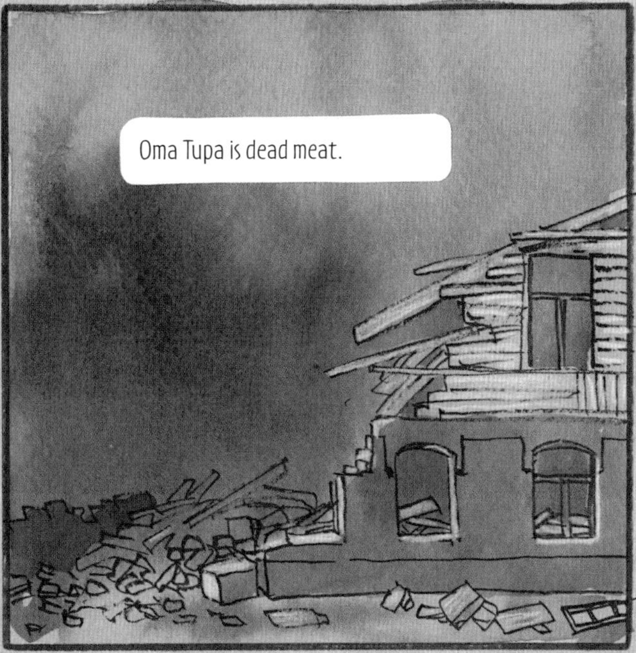
Oma Tupa is dead meat.

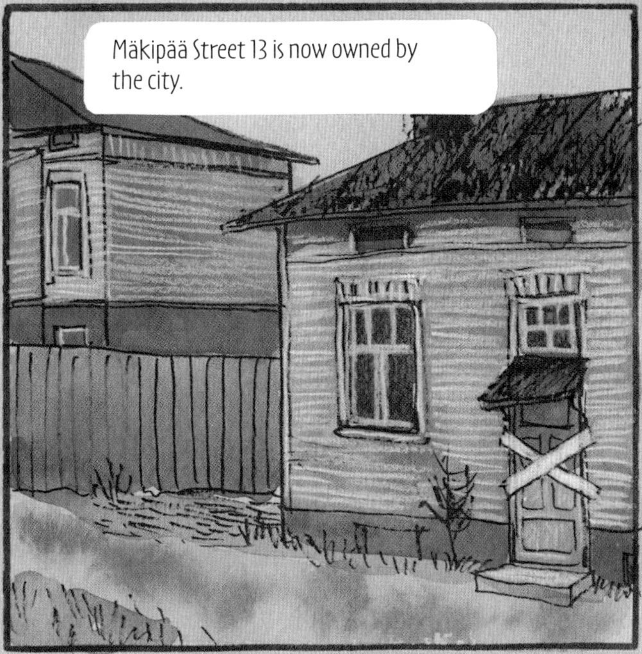
Mäkipää Street 13 is now owned by the city.

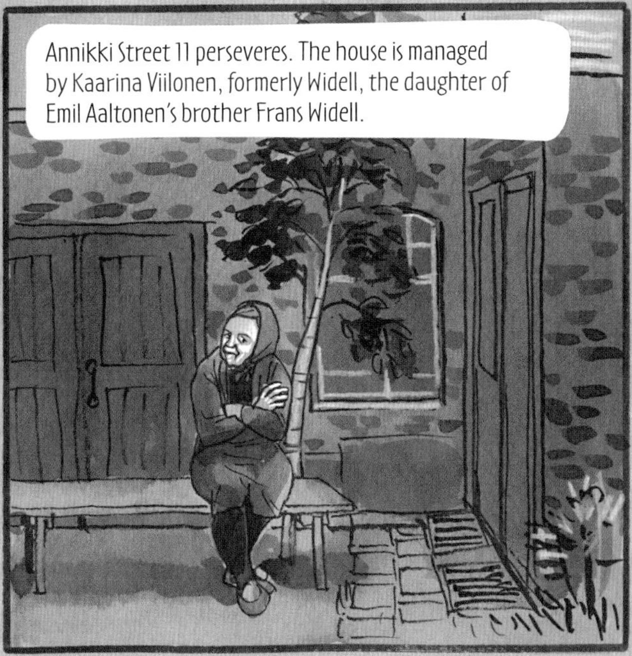
Annikki Street 11 perseveres. The house is managed by Kaarina Viilonen, formerly Widell, the daughter of Emil Aaltonen's brother Frans Widell.

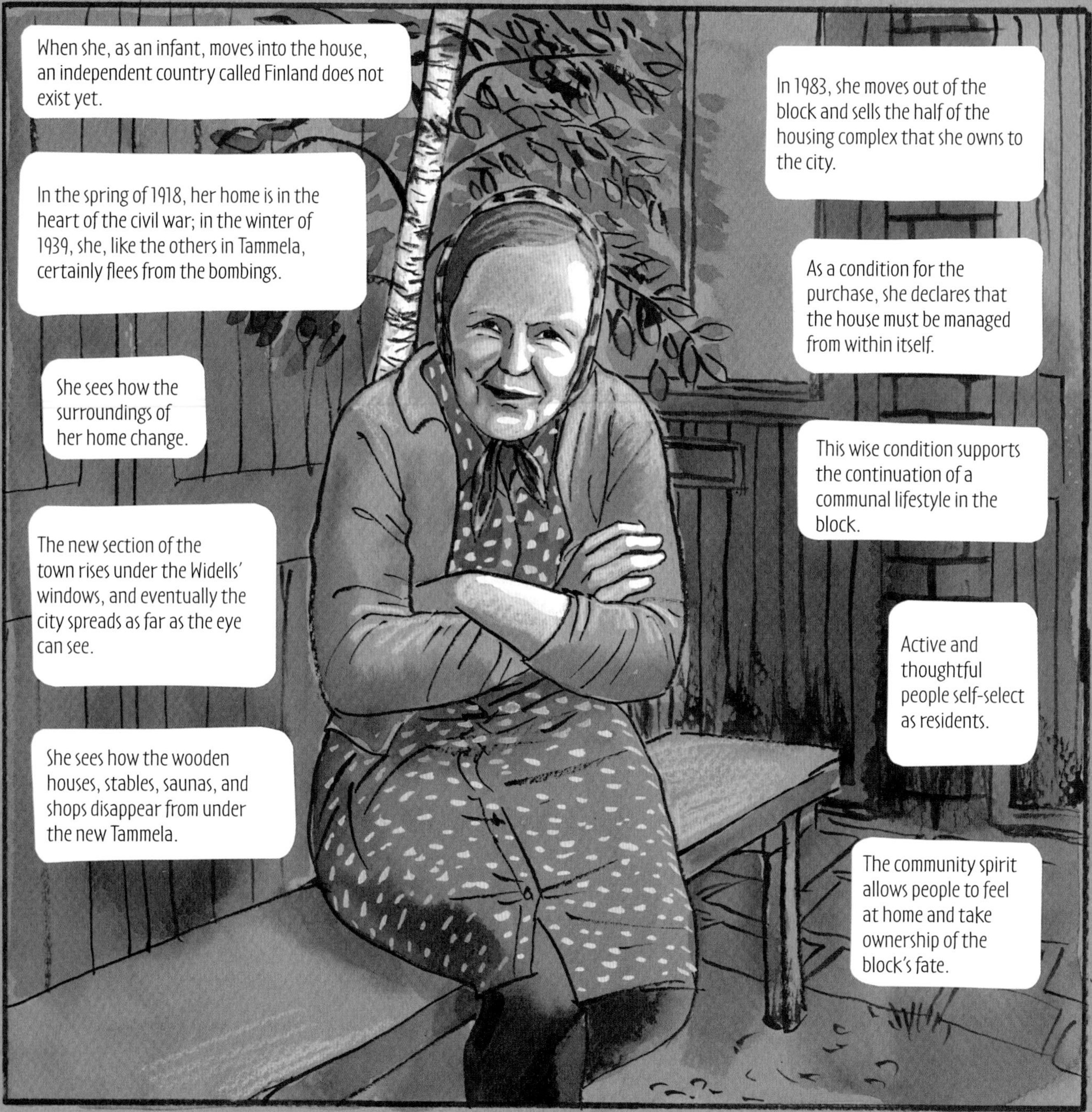
When she, as an infant, moves into the house, an independent country called Finland does not exist yet.
In the spring of 1918, her home is in the heart of the civil war; in the winter of 1939, she, like the others in Tammela, certainly flees from the bombings.
She sees how the surroundings of her home change.
The new section of the town rises under the Widells' windows, and eventually the city spreads as far as the eye can see.
She sees how the wooden houses, stables, saunas, and shops disappear from under the new Tammela.
In 1983, she moves out of the block and sells the half of the housing complex that she owns to the city.
As a condition for the purchase, she declares that the house must be managed from within itself.
This wise condition supports the continuation of a communal lifestyle in the block.
Active and thoughtful people self-select as residents.
The community spirit allows people to feel at home and take ownership of the block's fate.

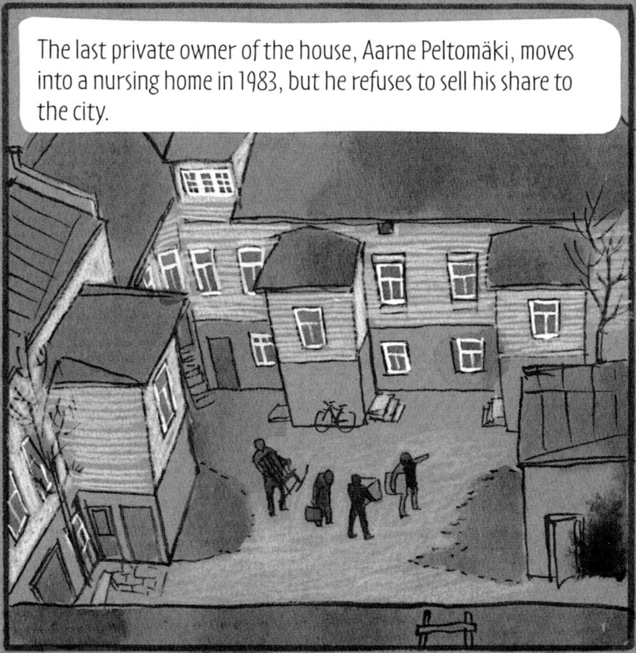
The last private owner of the house, Aarne Peltomäki, moves into a nursing home in 1983, but he refuses to sell his share to the city.

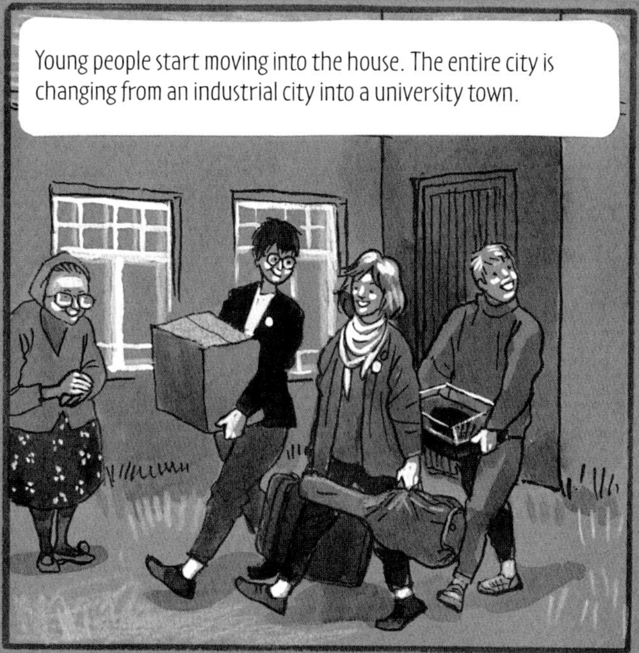
Young people start moving into the house. The entire city is changing from an industrial city into a university town.

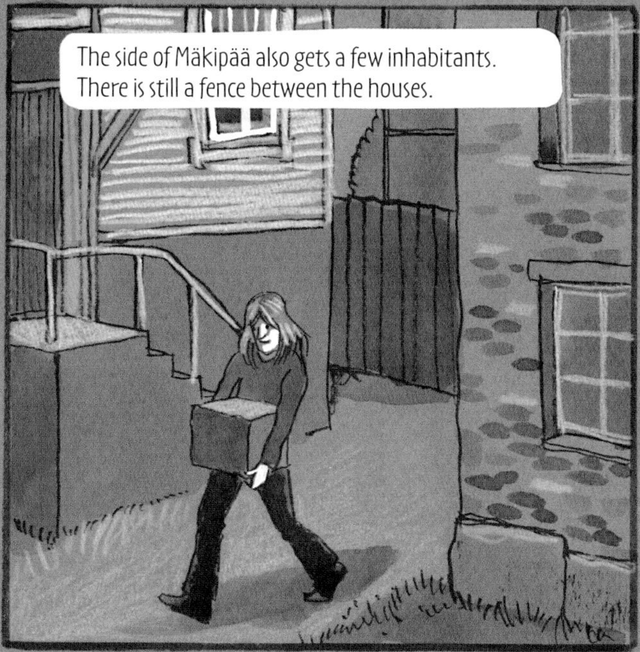
The side of Mäkipää also gets a few inhabitants. There is still a fence between the houses.

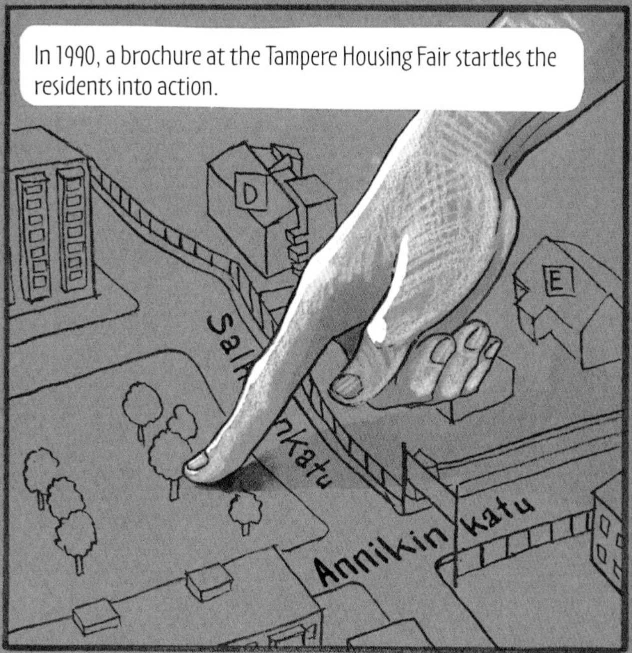
In 1990, a brochure at the Tampere Housing Fair startles the residents into action.
D
E
nkatu
Annikin katu

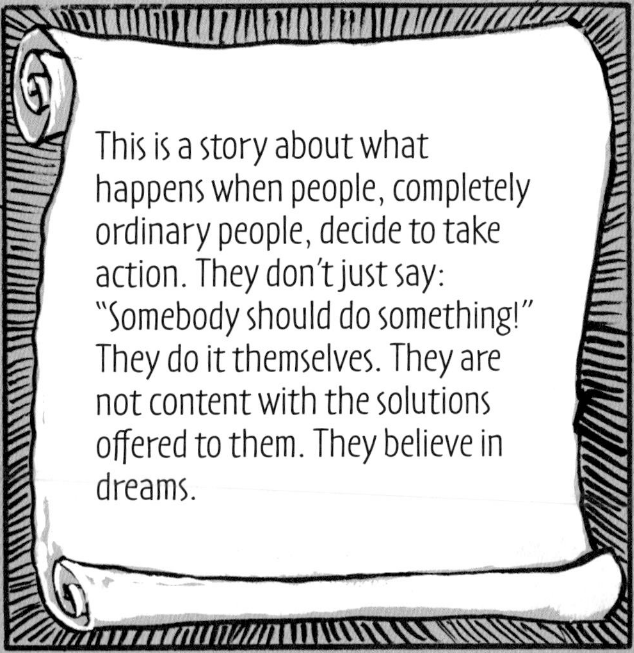
This is a story about what happens when people, completely ordinary people, decide to take action. They don't just say: "Somebody should do something!" They do it themselves. They are not content with the solutions offered to them. They believe in dreams.

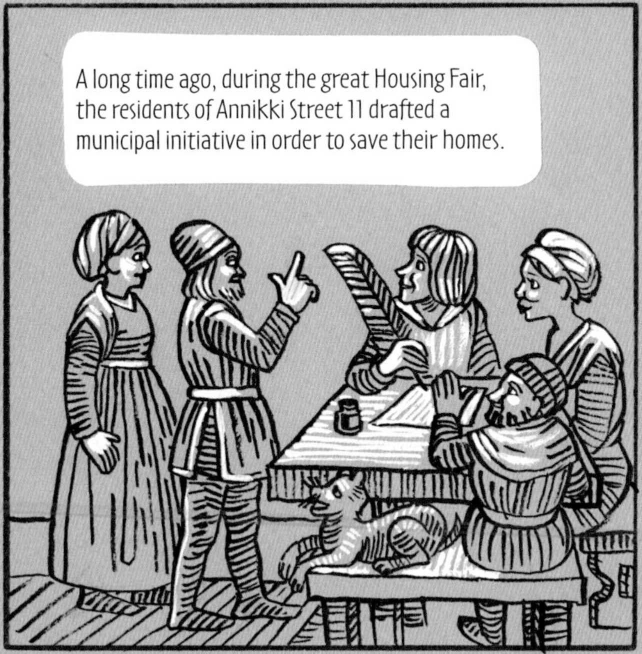
A long time ago, during the great Housing Fair, the residents of Annikki Street 11 drafted a municipal initiative in order to save their homes.

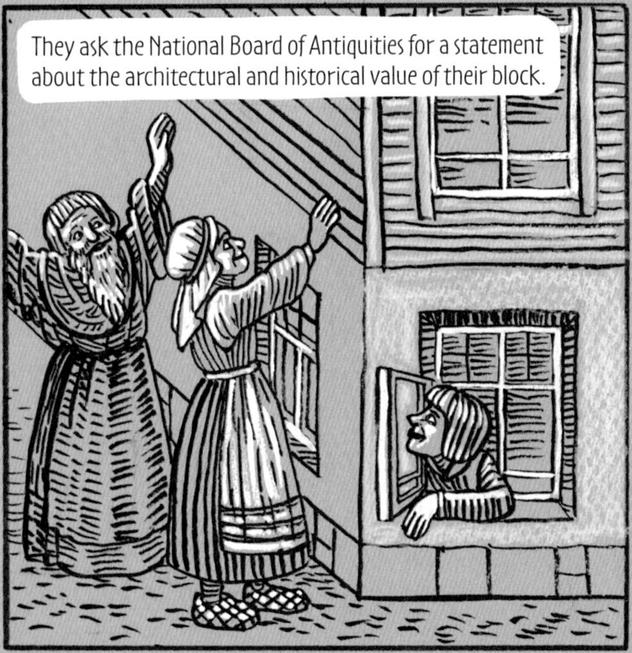
They ask the National Board of Antiquities for a statement about the architectural and historical value of their block.

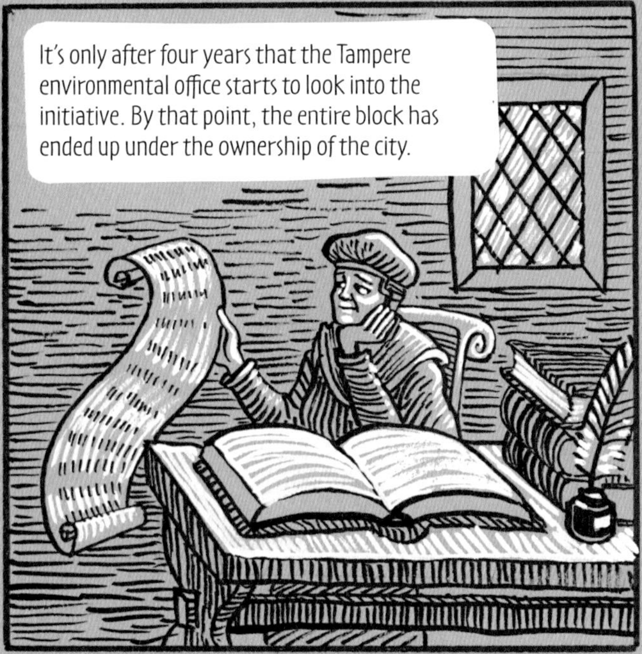
It's only after four years that the Tampere environmental office starts to look into the initiative. By that point, the entire block has ended up under the ownership of the city.

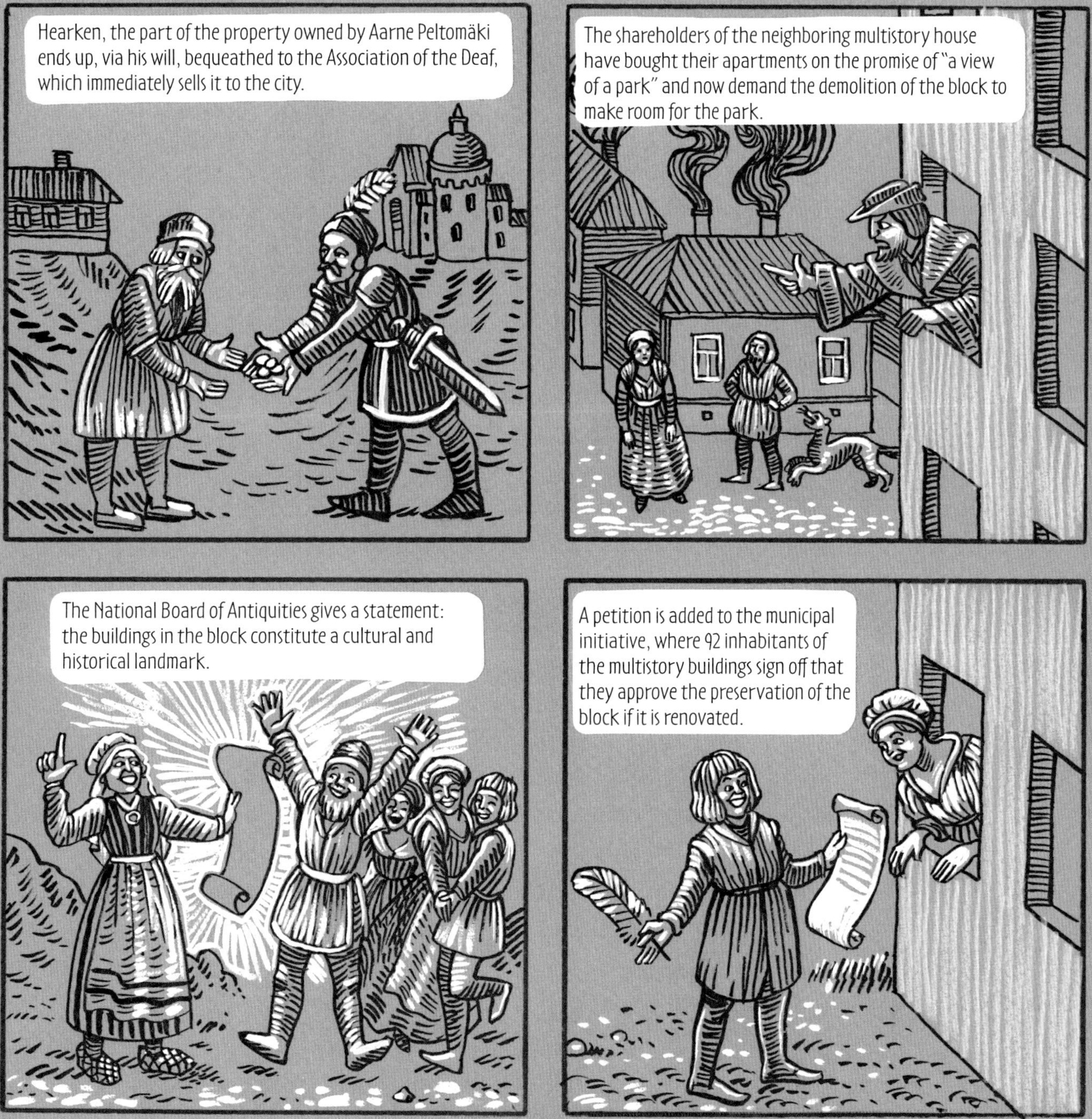
Hearken, the part of the property owned by Aarne Peltomäki ends up, via his will, bequeathed to the Association of the Deaf, which immediately sells it to the city.
The shareholders of the neighboring multistory house have bought their apartments on the promise of "a view of a park" and now demand the demolition of the block to make room for the park.
The National Board of Antiquities gives a statement: the buildings in the block constitute a cultural and historical landmark.
A petition is added to the municipal initiative, where 92 inhabitants of the multistory buildings sign off that they approve the preservation of the block if it is renovated.

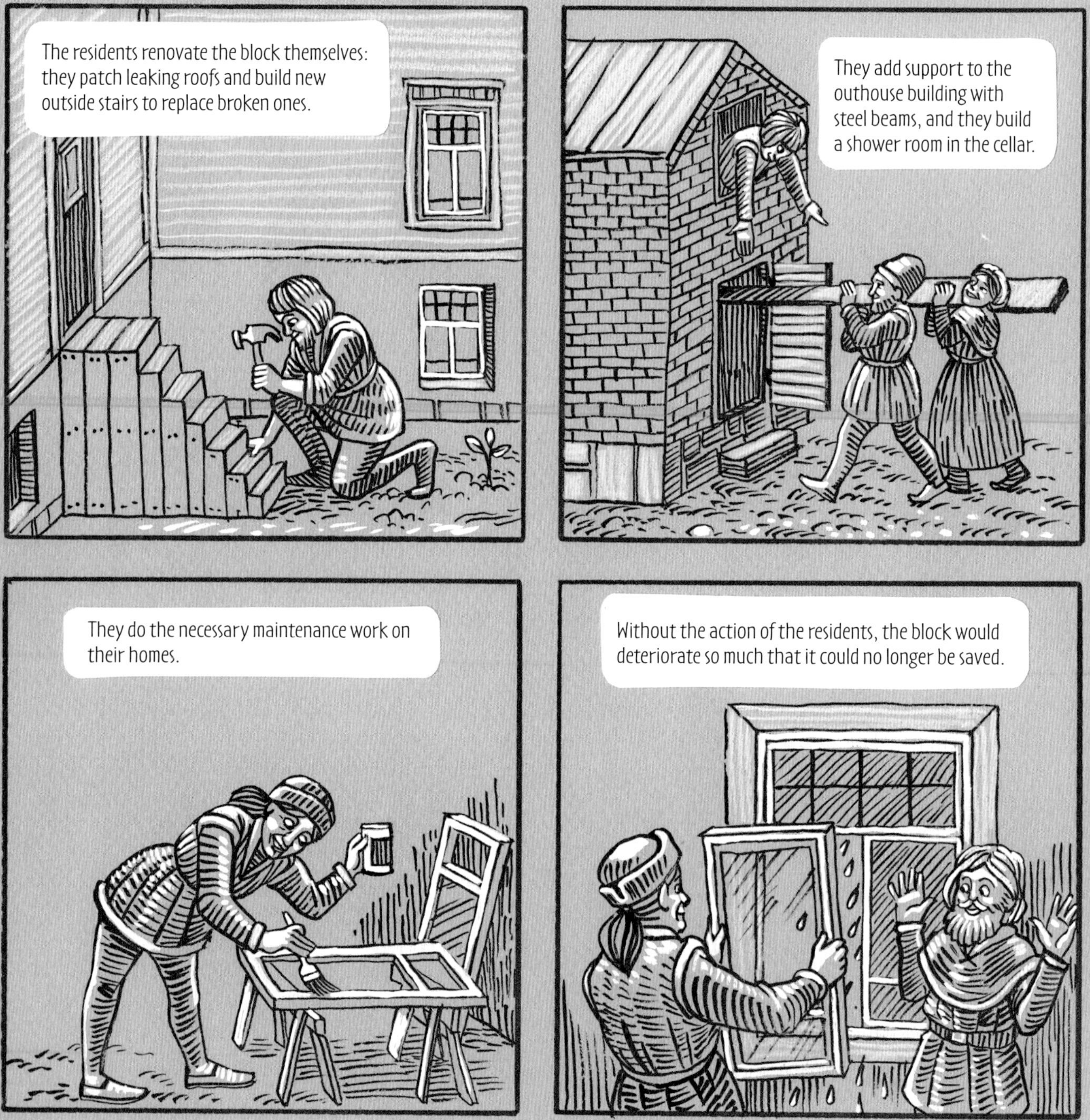
The residents renovate the block themselves: they patch leaking roofs and build new outside stairs to replace broken ones.
They add support to the outhouse building with steel beams, and they build a shower room in the cellar.
They do the necessary maintenance work on their homes.
Without the action of the residents, the block would deteriorate so much that it could no longer be saved.

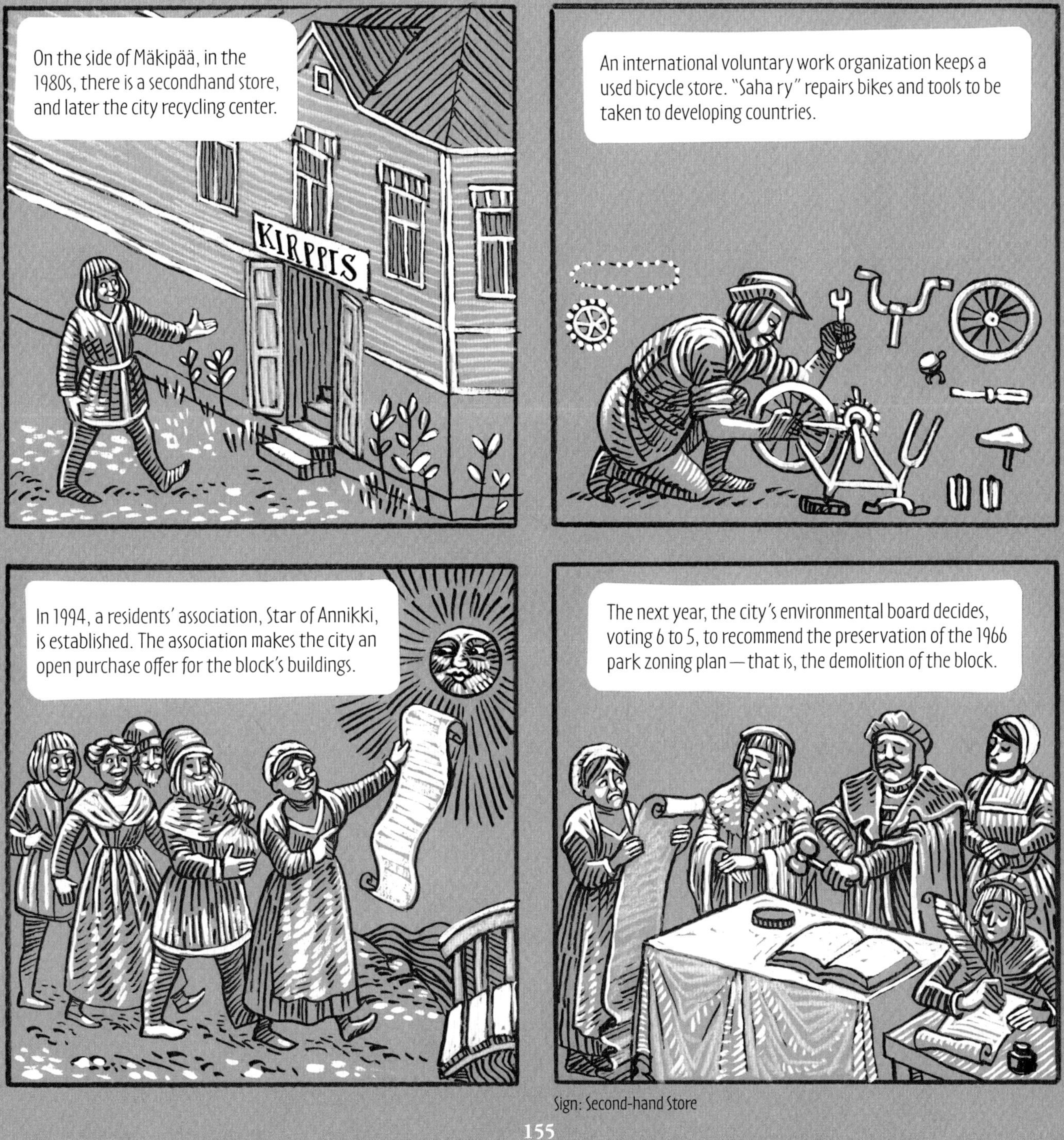
On the side of Mäkipää, in the 1980s, there is a secondhand store, and later the city recycling center.
KIRPPIS
An international voluntary work organization keeps a used bicycle store. "Saha ry" repairs bikes and tools to be taken to developing countries.
In 1994, a residents' association, Star of Annikki, is established. The association makes the city an open purchase offer for the block's buildings.
The next year, the city's environmental board decides, voting 6 to 5, to recommend the preservation of the 1966 park zoning plan — that is, the demolition of the block.

Sign: Second-hand Store

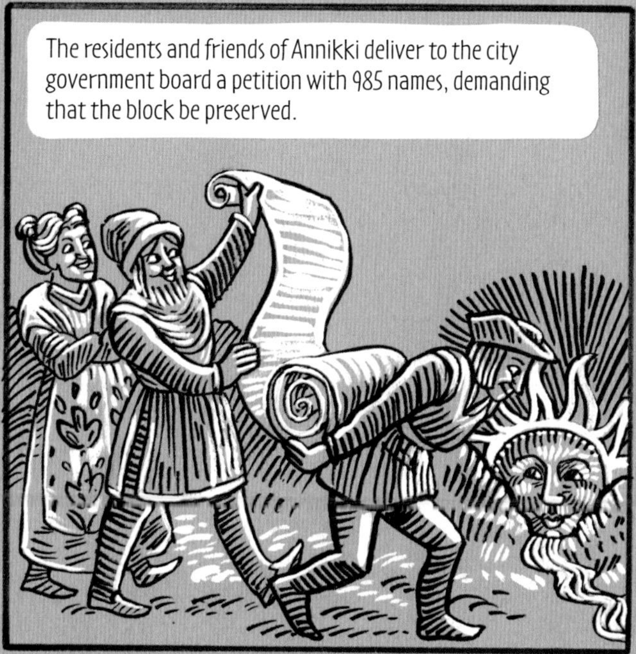
The residents and friends of Annikki deliver to the city government board a petition with 985 names, demanding that the block be preserved.

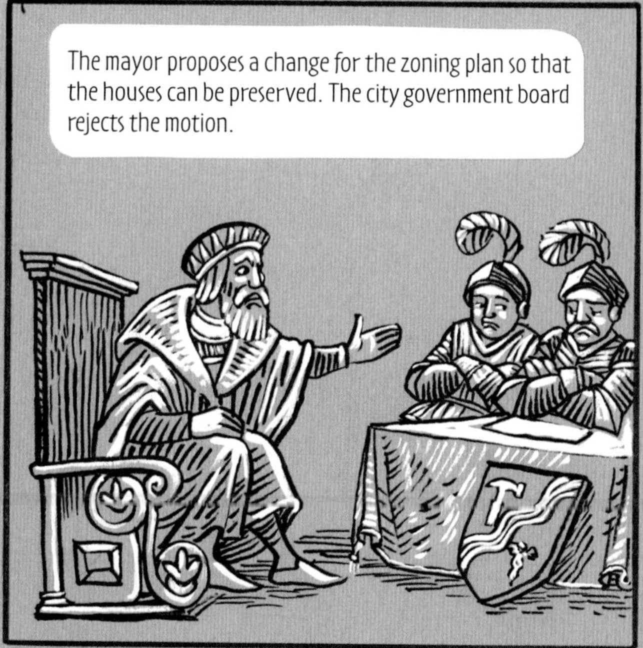
The mayor proposes a change for the zoning plan so that the houses can be preserved. The city government board rejects the motion.

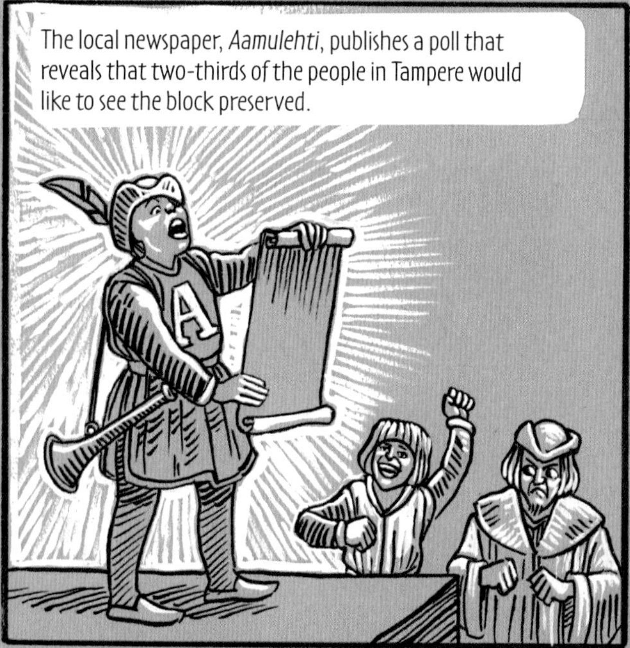
The local newspaper, *Aamulehti*, publishes a poll that reveals that two-thirds of the people in Tampere would like to see the block preserved.

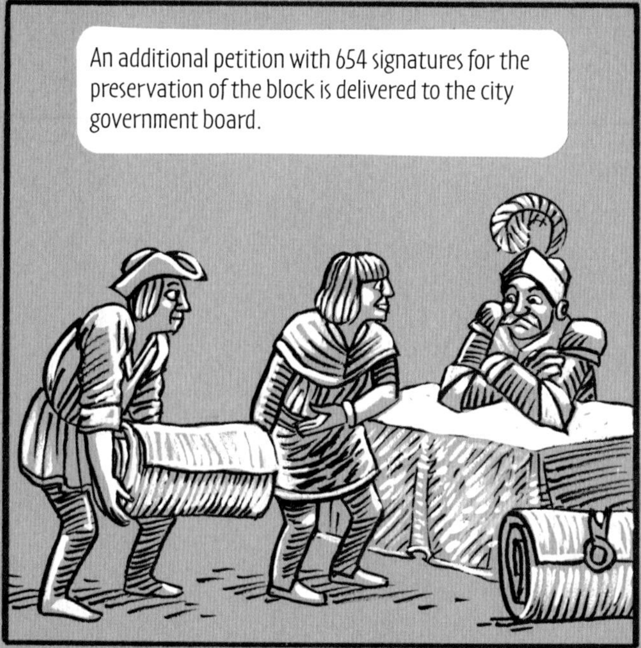
An additional petition with 654 signatures for the preservation of the block is delivered to the city government board.

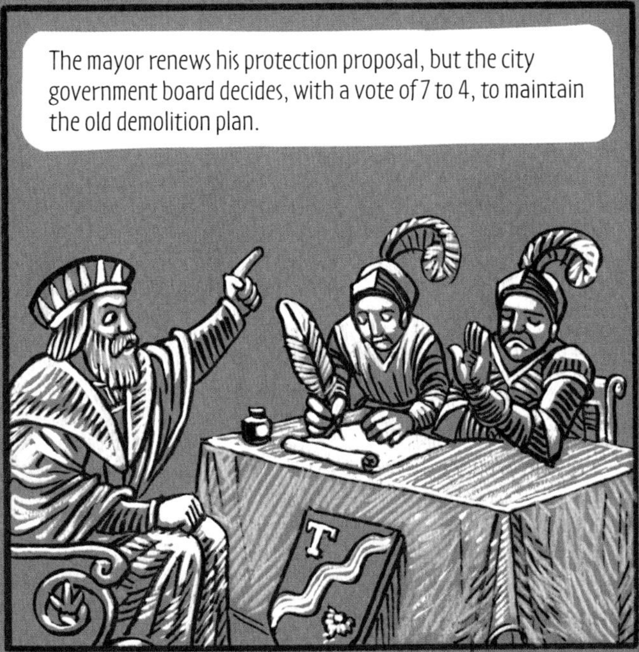
The mayor renews his protection proposal, but the city government board decides, with a vote of 7 to 4, to maintain the old demolition plan.
T

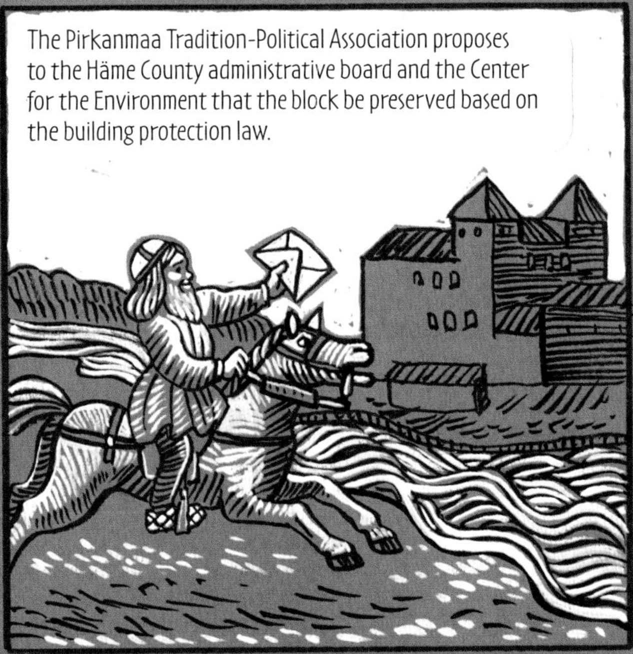
The Pirkanmaa Tradition-Political Association proposes to the Häme County administrative board and the Center for the Environment that the block be preserved based on the building protection law.

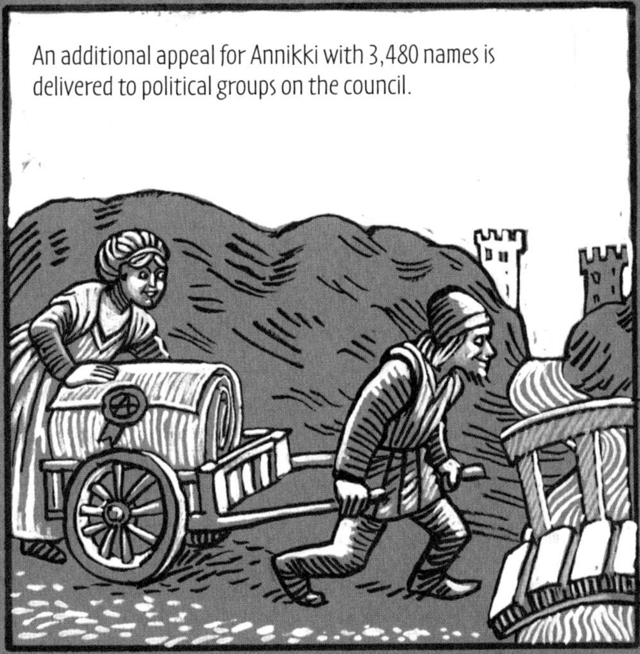
An additional appeal for Annikki with 3,480 names is delivered to political groups on the council.

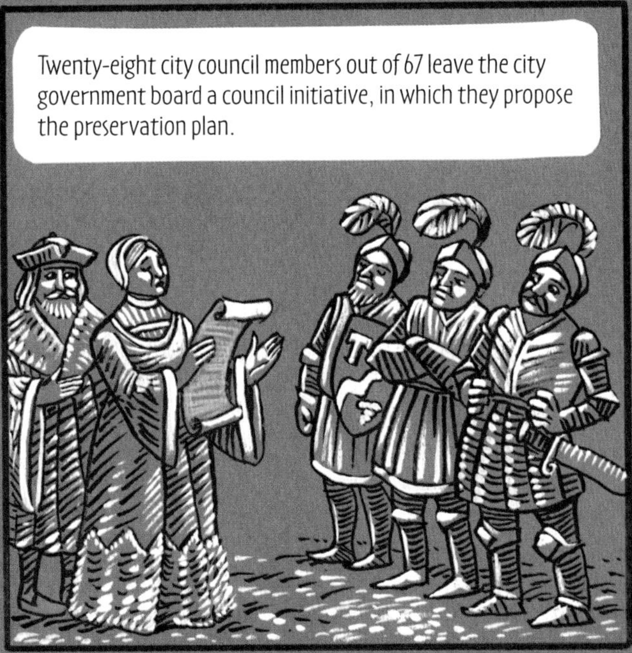
Twenty-eight city council members out of 67 leave the city government board a council initiative, in which they propose the preservation plan.
T

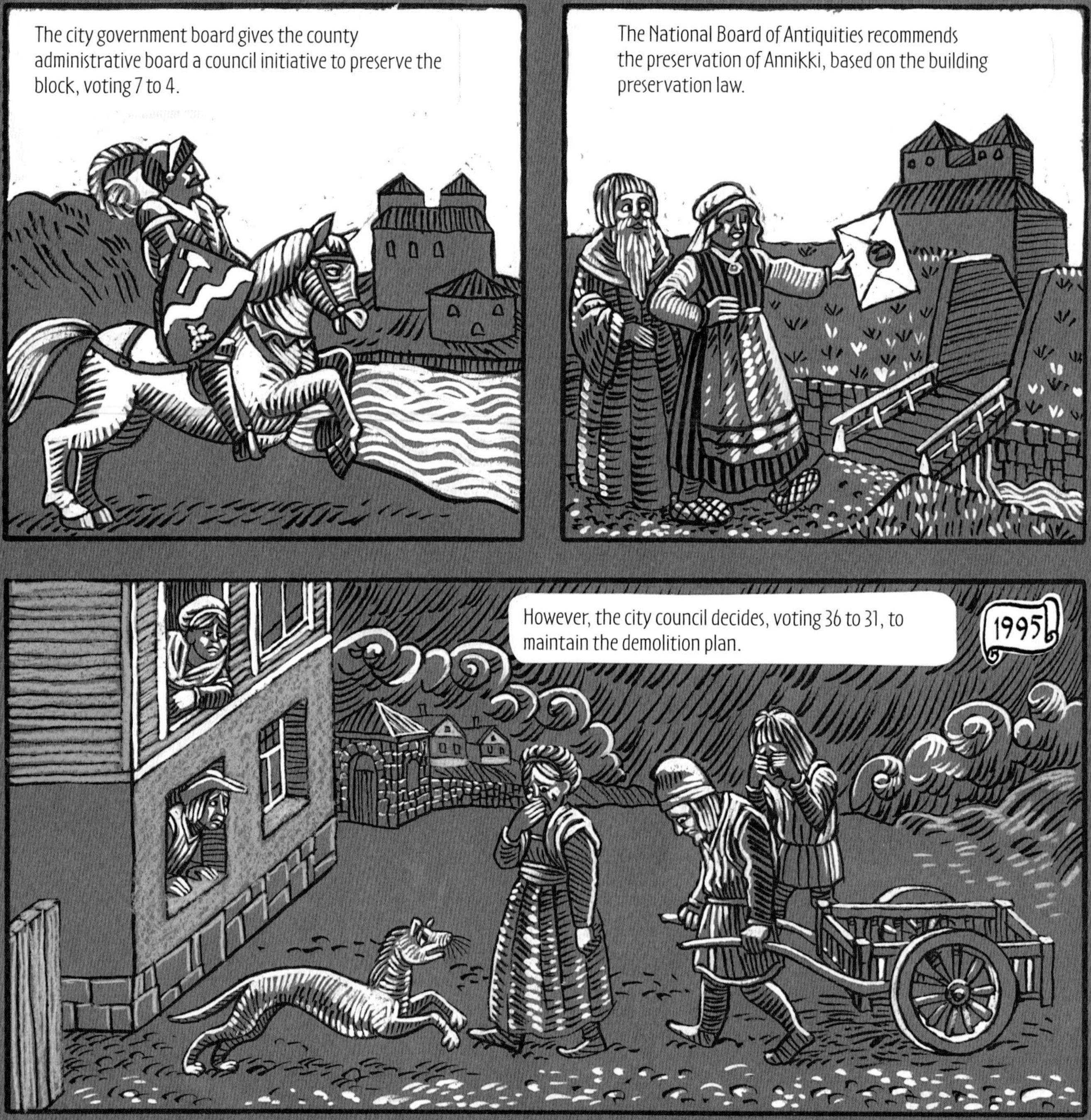
The city government board gives the county administrative board a council initiative to preserve the block, voting 7 to 4.
The National Board of Antiquities recommends the preservation of Annikki, based on the building preservation law.
However, the city council decides, voting 36 to 31, to maintain the demolition plan.
1995

TRASH MOUNTAIN

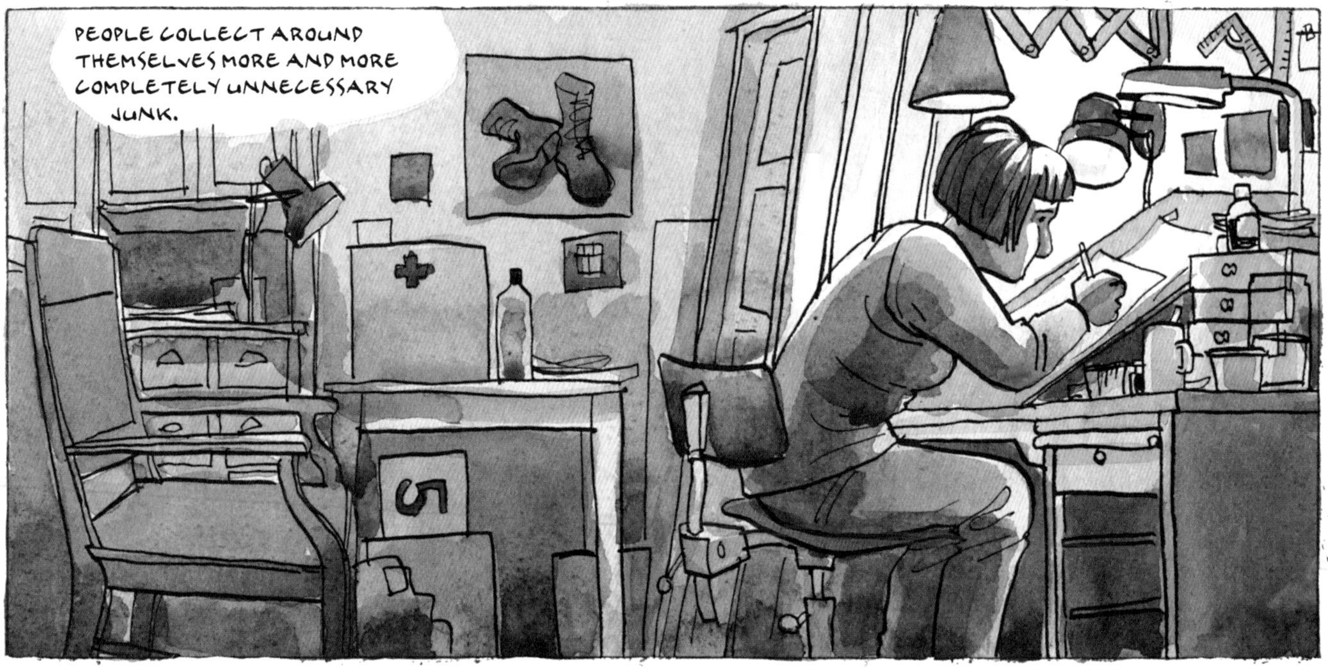
PEOPLE COLLECT AROUND THEMSELVES MORE AND MORE COMPLETELY UNNECESSARY JUNK.

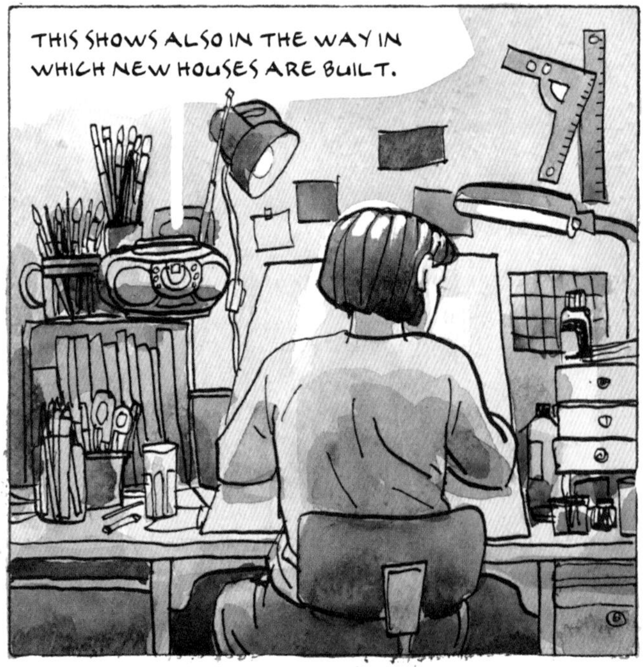
THIS SHOWS ALSO IN THE WAY IN WHICH NEW HOUSES ARE BUILT.

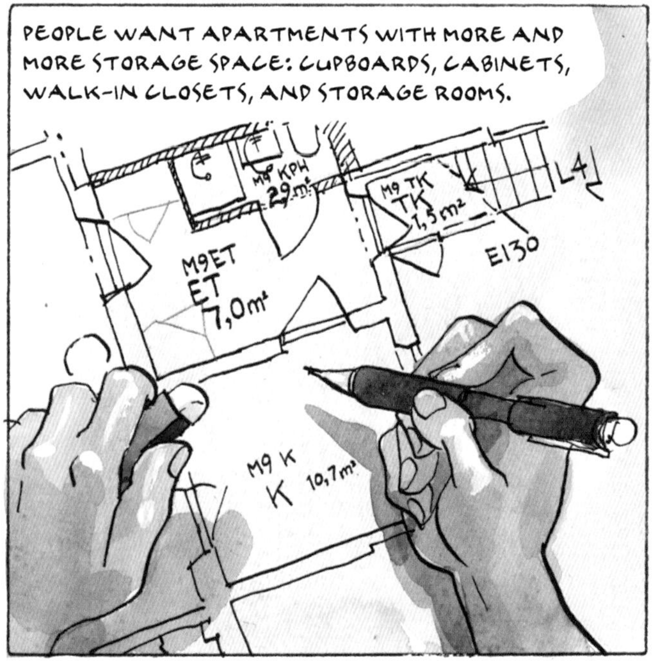
PEOPLE WANT APARTMENTS WITH MORE AND MORE STORAGE SPACE: CUPBOARDS, CABINETS, WALK-IN CLOSETS, AND STORAGE ROOMS.
M9ET
ET
7,0m²
E130
M9 K
K
10,7m²

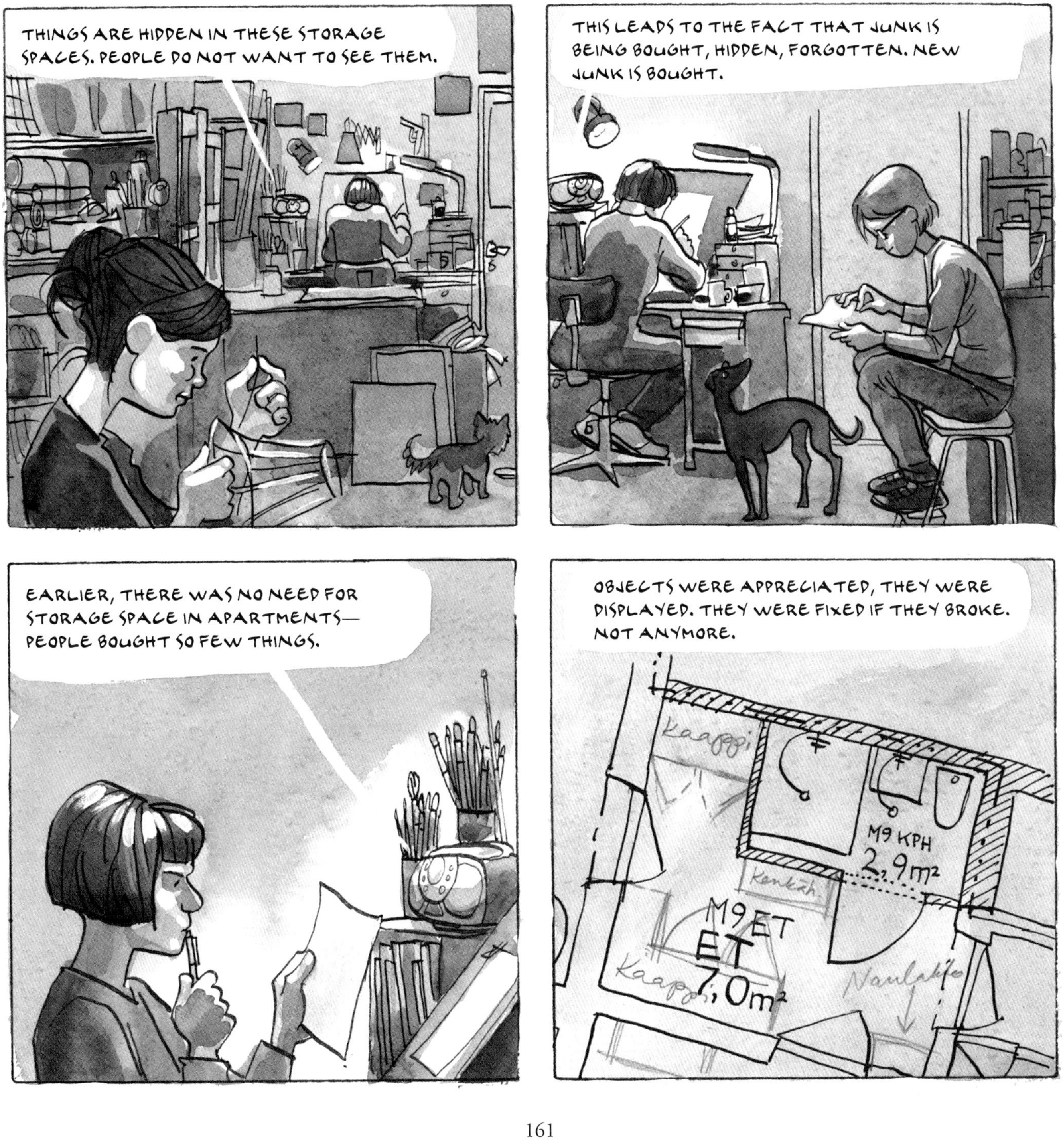
THINGS ARE HIDDEN IN THESE STORAGE SPACES. PEOPLE DO NOT WANT TO SEE THEM.
THIS LEADS TO THE FACT THAT JUNK IS BEING BOUGHT, HIDDEN, FORGOTTEN. NEW JUNK IS BOUGHT.
EARLIER, THERE WAS NO NEED FOR STORAGE SPACE IN APARTMENTS—PEOPLE BOUGHT SO FEW THINGS.
OBJECTS WERE APPRECIATED, THEY WERE DISPLAYED. THEY WERE FIXED IF THEY BROKE. NOT ANYMORE.
Kaappi
M9 KPH
2,9m²
Kenkäh.
M9 ET
ET
Kaappi
7,0m²

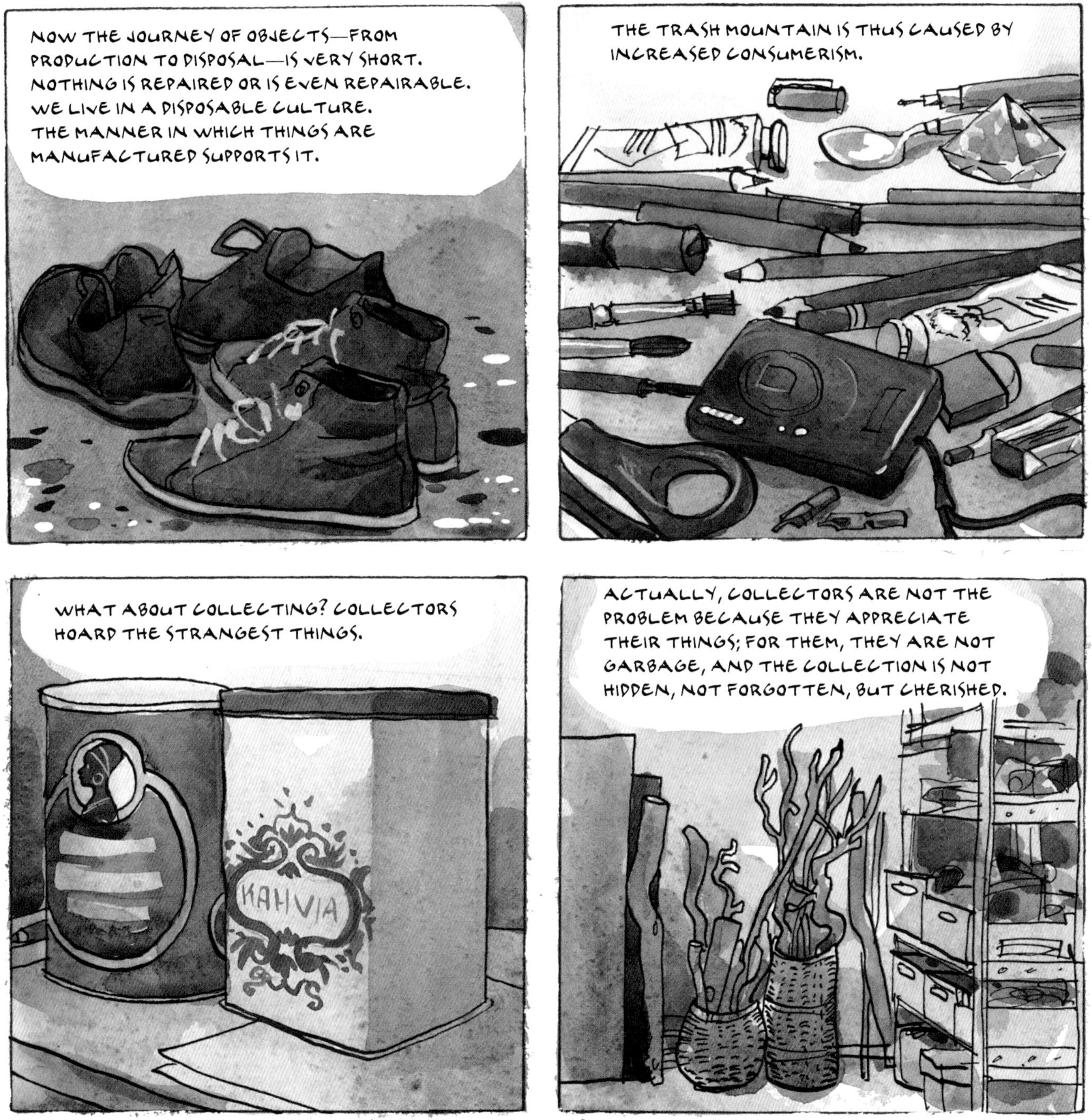
NOW THE JOURNEY OF OBJECTS—FROM PRODUCTION TO DISPOSAL—IS VERY SHORT. NOTHING IS REPAIRED OR IS EVEN REPAIRABLE. WE LIVE IN A DISPOSABLE CULTURE. THE MANNER IN WHICH THINGS ARE MANUFACTURED SUPPORTS IT.
THE TRASH MOUNTAIN IS THUS CAUSED BY INCREASED CONSUMERISM.
WHAT ABOUT COLLECTING? COLLECTORS HOARD THE STRANGEST THINGS.
KAHVIA
ACTUALLY, COLLECTORS ARE NOT THE PROBLEM BECAUSE THEY APPRECIATE THEIR THINGS; FOR THEM, THEY ARE NOT GARBAGE, AND THE COLLECTION IS NOT HIDDEN, NOT FORGOTTEN, BUT CHERISHED.

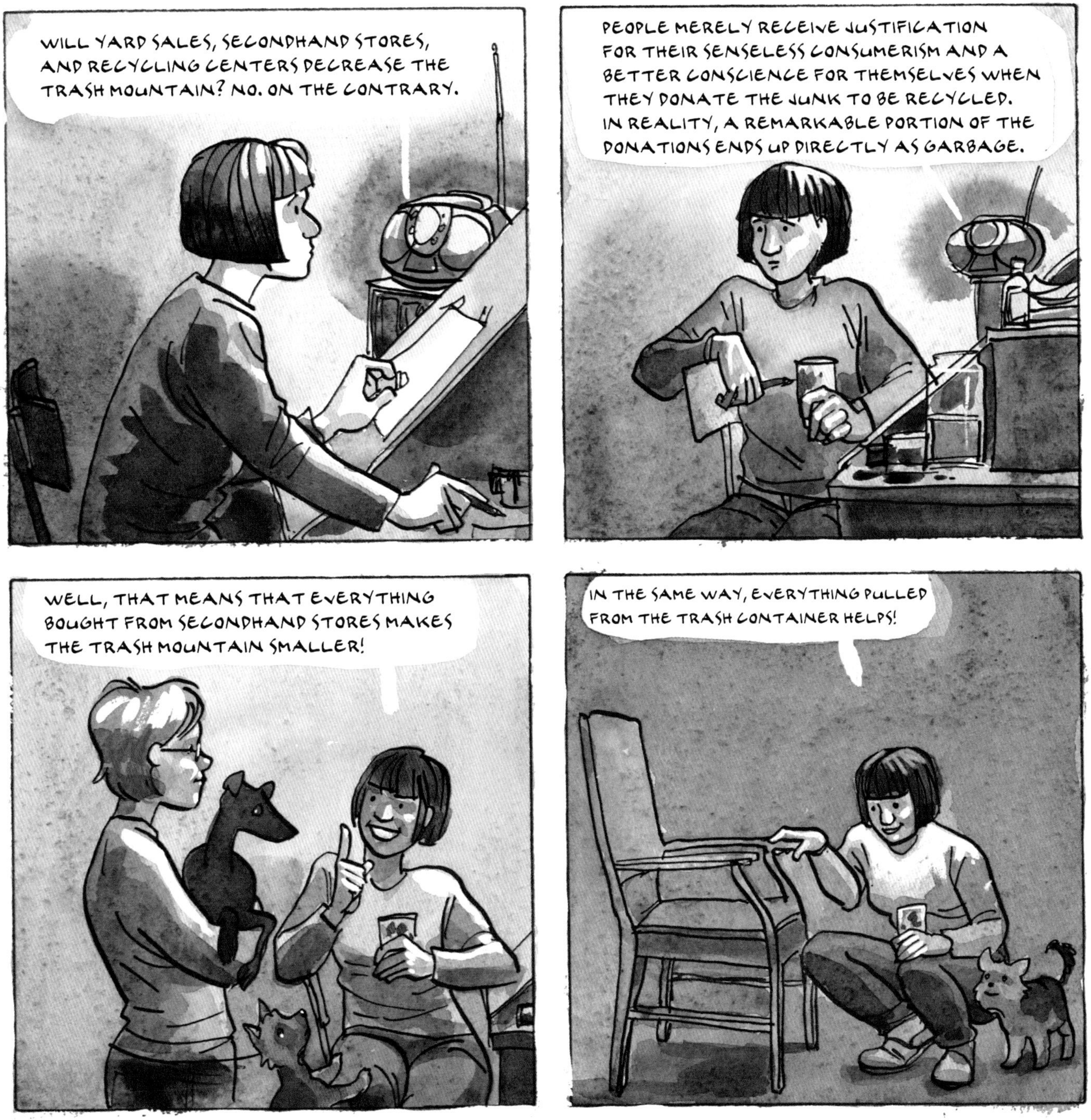
WILL YARD SALES, SECONDHAND STORES, AND RECYCLING CENTERS DECREASE THE TRASH MOUNTAIN? NO. ON THE CONTRARY.
PEOPLE MERELY RECEIVE JUSTIFICATION FOR THEIR SENSELESS CONSUMERISM AND A BETTER CONSCIENCE FOR THEMSELVES WHEN THEY DONATE THE JUNK TO BE RECYCLED. IN REALITY, A REMARKABLE PORTION OF THE DONATIONS ENDS UP DIRECTLY AS GARBAGE.
WELL, THAT MEANS THAT EVERYTHING BOUGHT FROM SECONDHAND STORES MAKES THE TRASH MOUNTAIN SMALLER!
IN THE SAME WAY, EVERYTHING PULLED FROM THE TRASH CONTAINER HELPS!

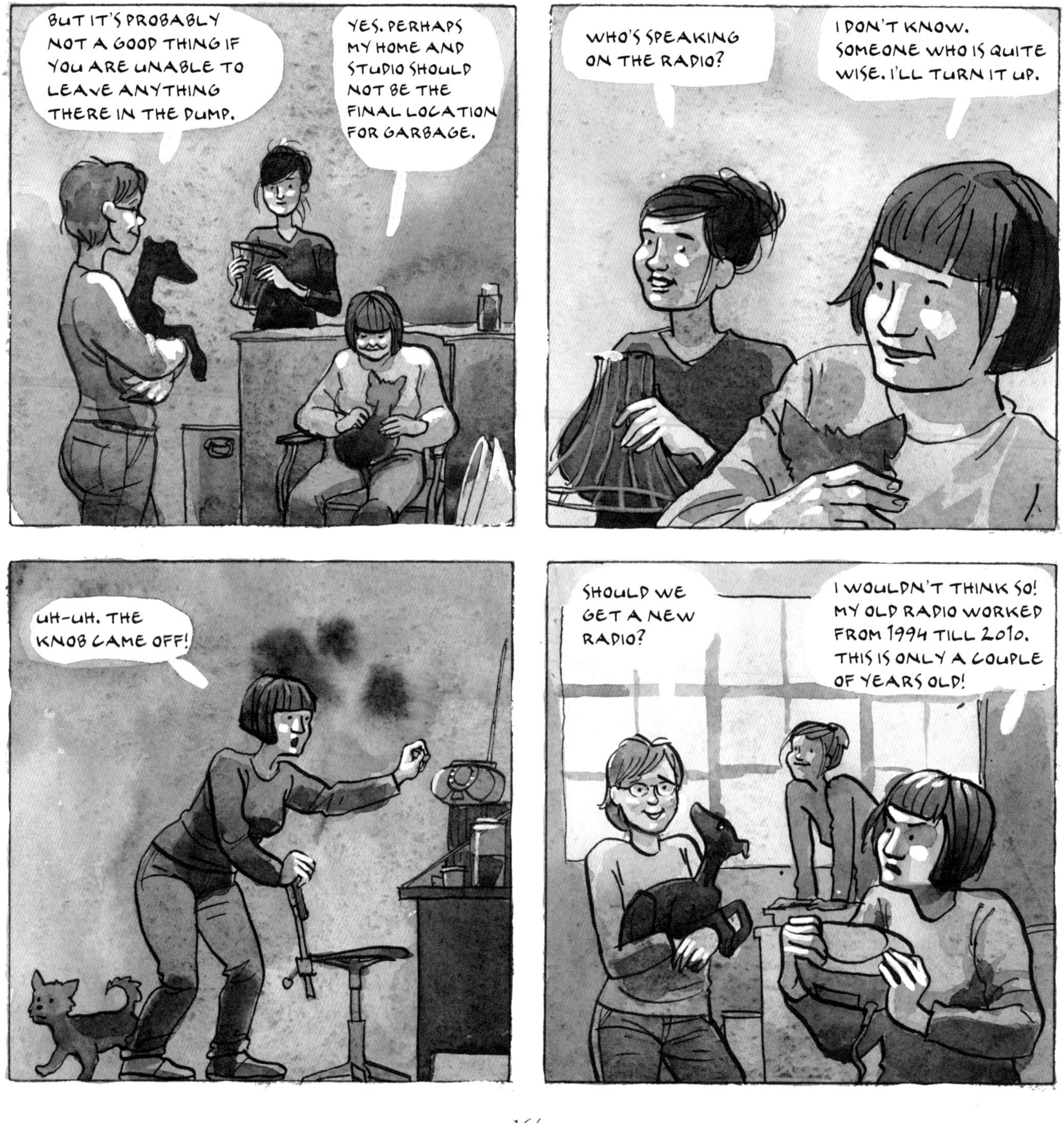
BUT IT'S PROBABLY NOT A GOOD THING IF YOU ARE UNABLE TO LEAVE ANYTHING THERE IN THE DUMP.
YES. PERHAPS MY HOME AND STUDIO SHOULD NOT BE THE FINAL LOCATION FOR GARBAGE.
WHO'S SPEAKING ON THE RADIO?
I DON'T KNOW. SOMEONE WHO IS QUITE WISE. I'LL TURN IT UP.
UH-UH. THE KNOB CAME OFF!
SHOULD WE GET A NEW RADIO?
I WOULDN'T THINK SO! MY OLD RADIO WORKED FROM 1994 TILL 2010. THIS IS ONLY A COUPLE OF YEARS OLD!

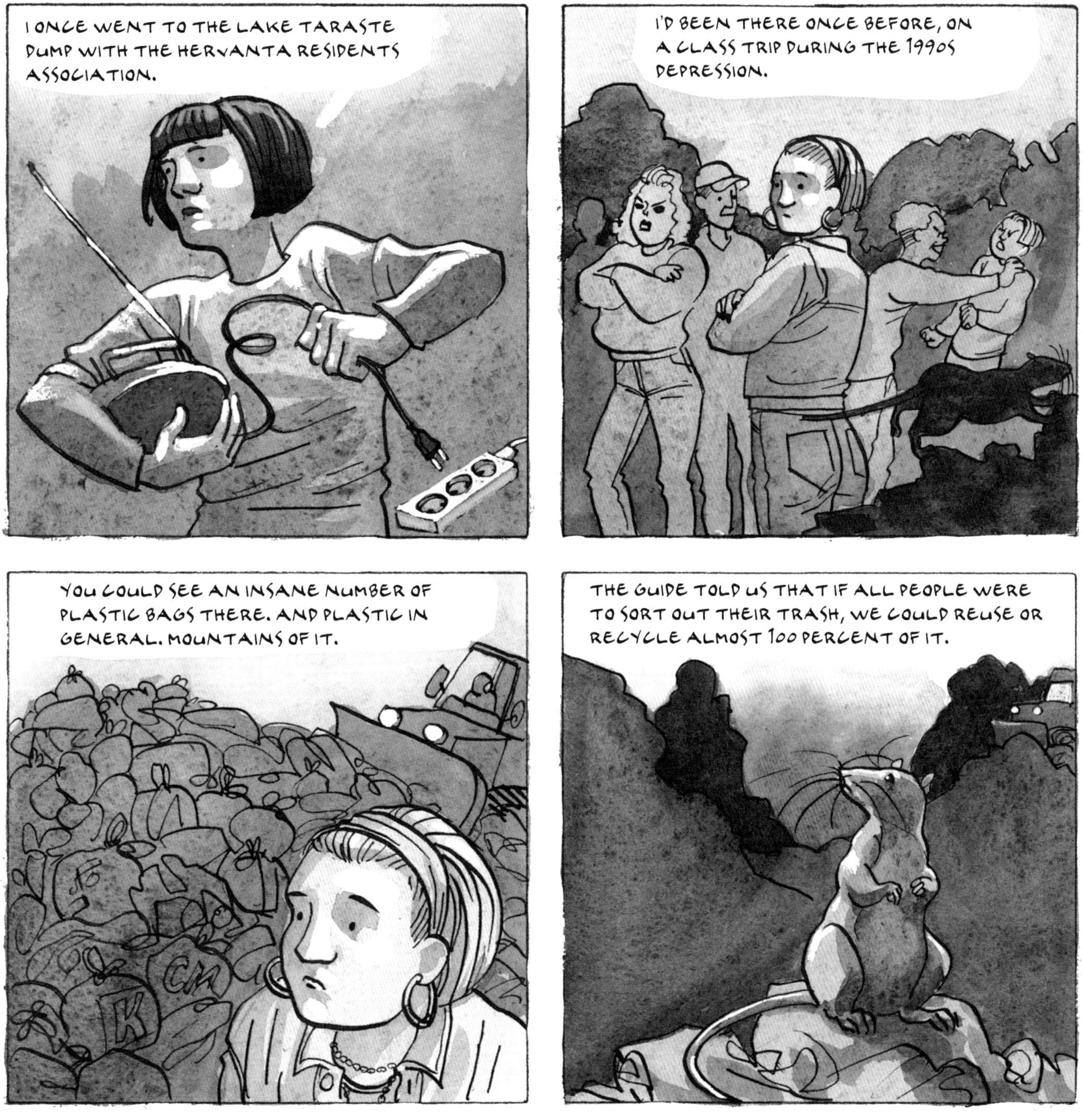
I ONCE WENT TO THE LAKE TARASTE DUMP WITH THE HERVANTA RESIDENTS ASSOCIATION.
I'D BEEN THERE ONCE BEFORE, ON A CLASS TRIP DURING THE 1990S DEPRESSION.
YOU COULD SEE AN INSANE NUMBER OF PLASTIC BAGS THERE. AND PLASTIC IN GENERAL. MOUNTAINS OF IT.
THE GUIDE TOLD US THAT IF ALL PEOPLE WERE TO SORT OUT THEIR TRASH, WE COULD REUSE OR RECYCLE ALMOST 100 PERCENT OF IT.

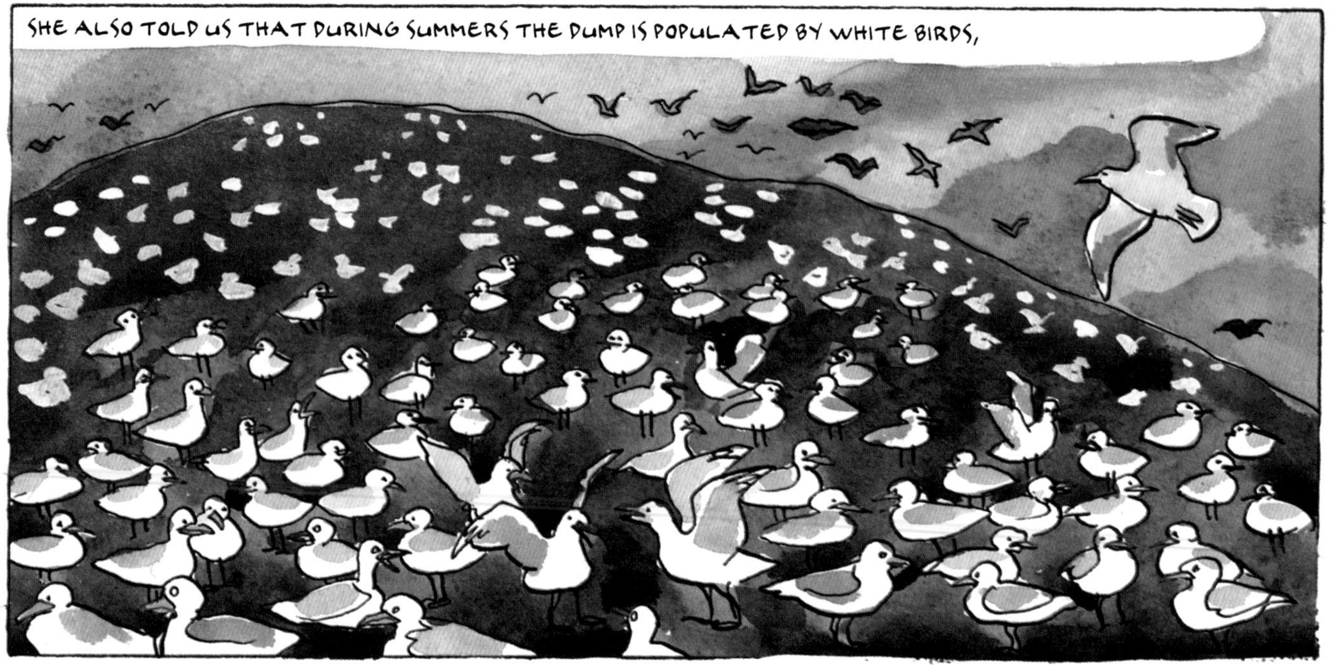
SHE ALSO TOLD US THAT DURING SUMMERS THE DUMP IS POPULATED BY WHITE BIRDS,

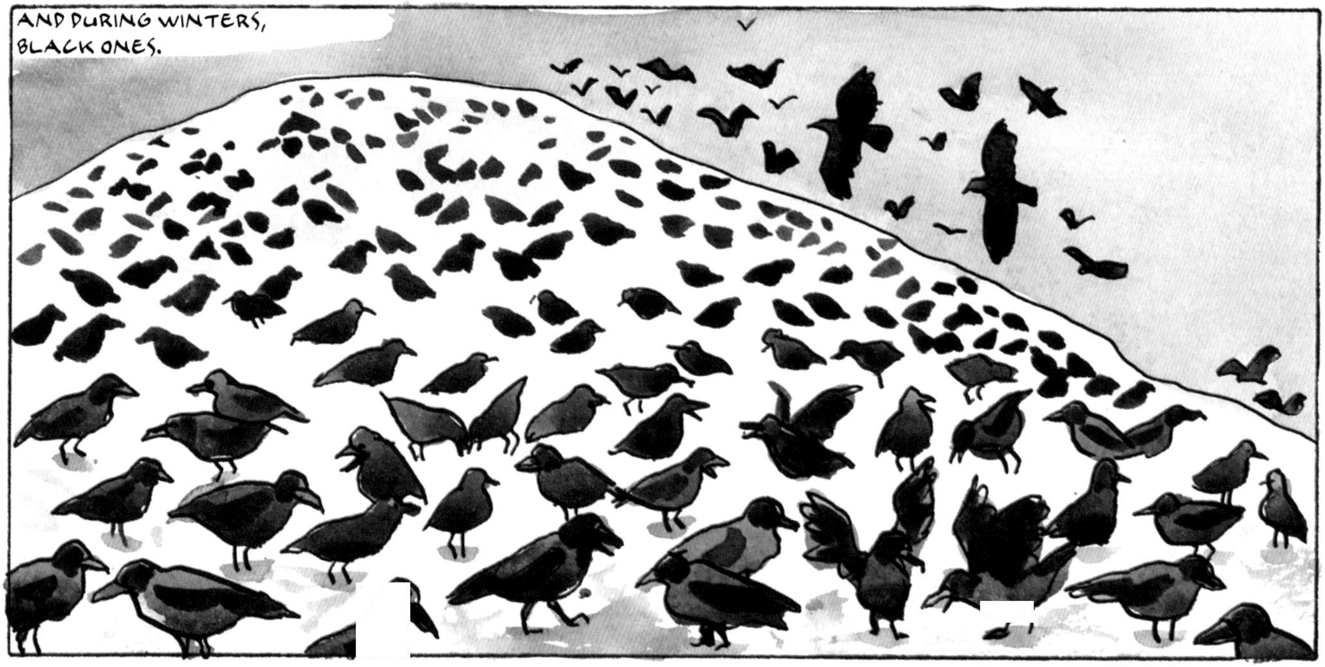
AND DURING WINTERS,
BLACK ONES.

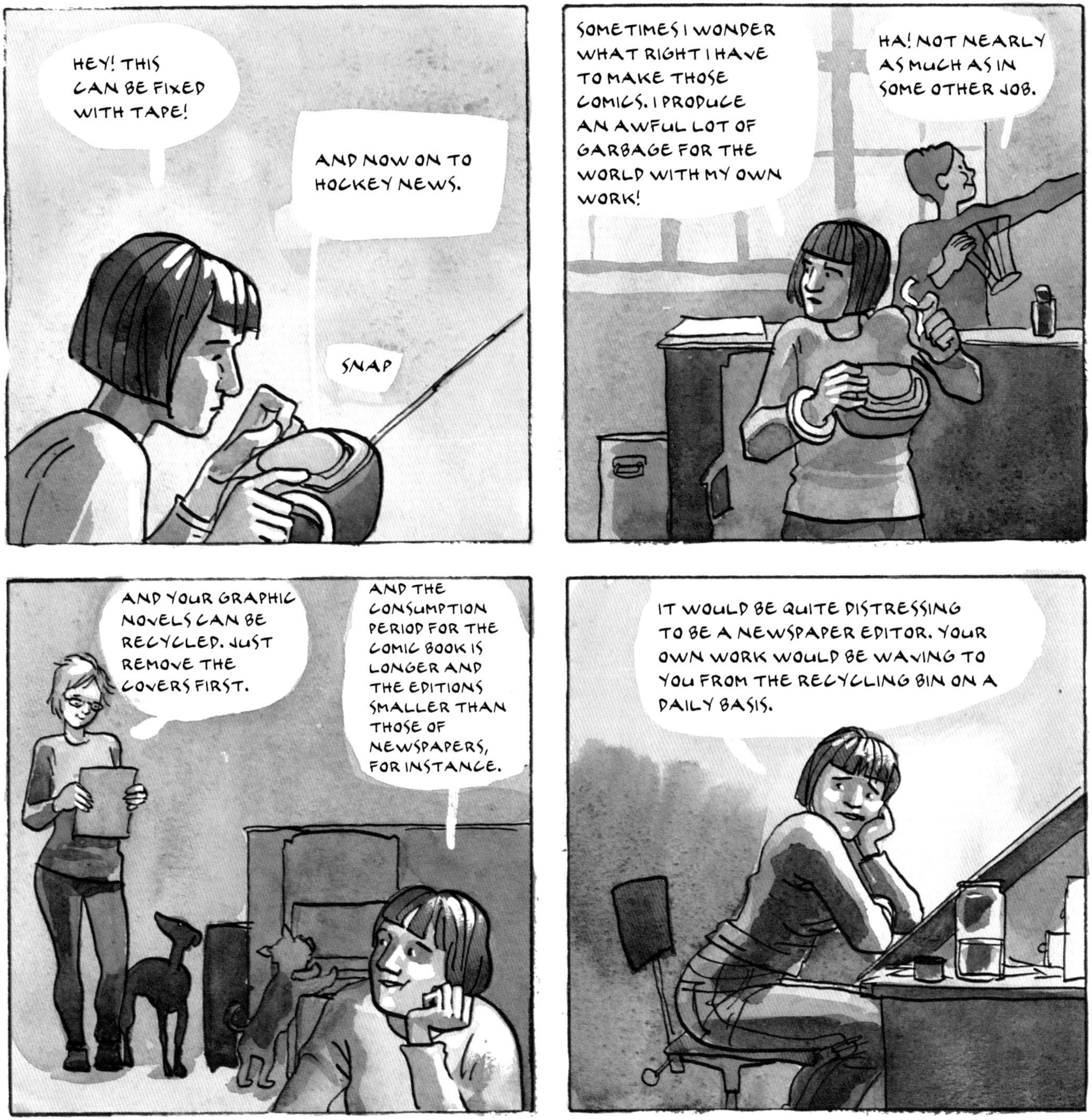
HEY! THIS CAN BE FIXED WITH TAPE!
AND NOW ON TO HOCKEY NEWS.
SNAP
SOMETIMES I WONDER WHAT RIGHT I HAVE TO MAKE THOSE COMICS. I PRODUCE AN AWFUL LOT OF GARBAGE FOR THE WORLD WITH MY OWN WORK!
HA! NOT NEARLY AS MUCH AS IN SOME OTHER JOB.
AND YOUR GRAPHIC NOVELS CAN BE RECYCLED. JUST REMOVE THE COVERS FIRST.
AND THE CONSUMPTION PERIOD FOR THE COMIC BOOK IS LONGER AND THE EDITIONS SMALLER THAN THOSE OF NEWSPAPERS, FOR INSTANCE.
IT WOULD BE QUITE DISTRESSING TO BE A NEWSPAPER EDITOR. YOUR OWN WORK WOULD BE WAVING TO YOU FROM THE RECYCLING BIN ON A DAILY BASIS.

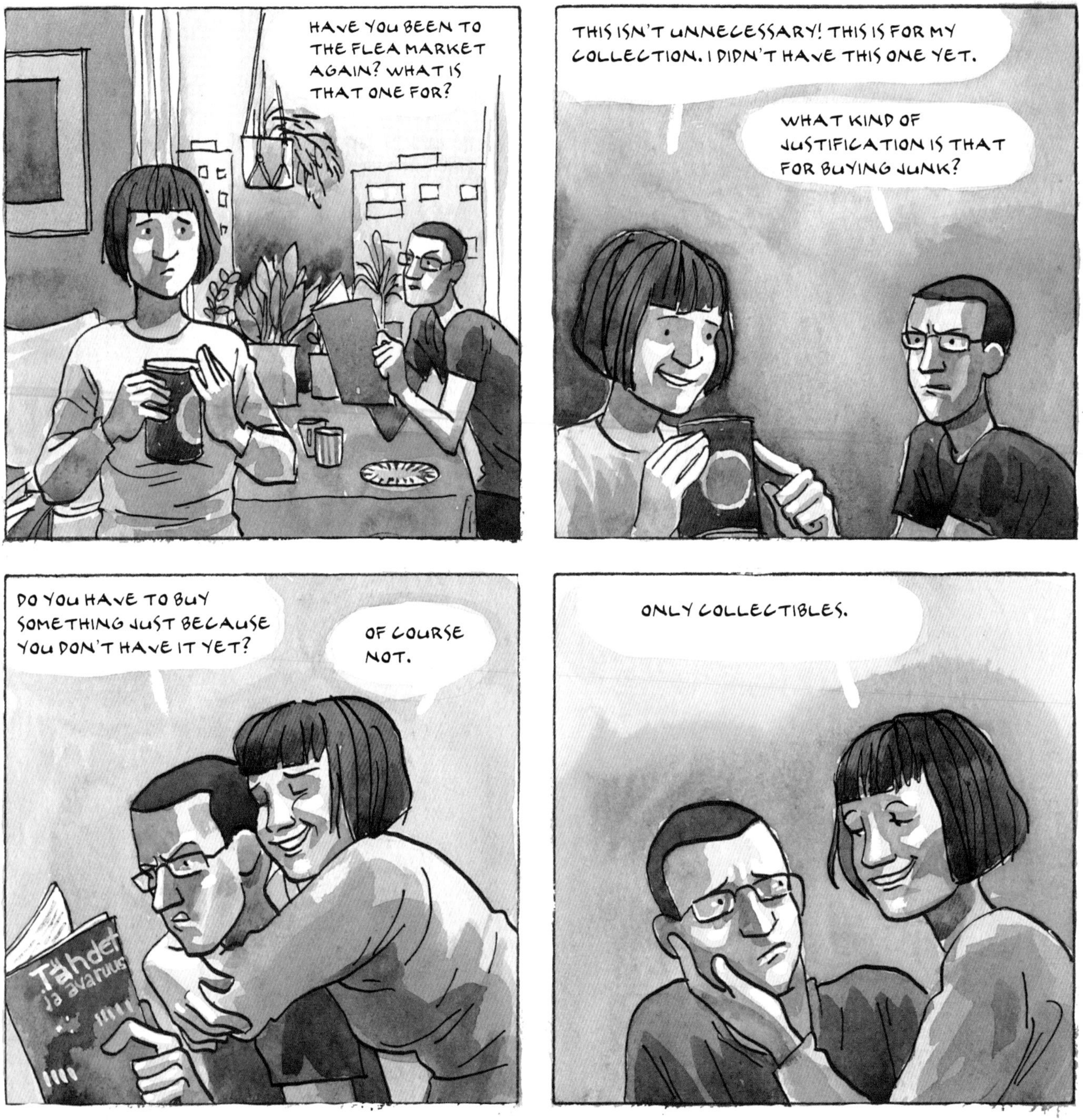
HAVE YOU BEEN TO THE FLEA MARKET AGAIN? WHAT IS THAT ONE FOR?
THIS ISN'T UNNECESSARY! THIS IS FOR MY COLLECTION. I DIDN'T HAVE THIS ONE YET.
WHAT KIND OF JUSTIFICATION IS THAT FOR BUYING JUNK?
DO YOU HAVE TO BUY SOMETHING JUST BECAUSE YOU DON'T HAVE IT YET?
OF COURSE NOT.
Tähdet ja avaruus
ONLY COLLECTIBLES.

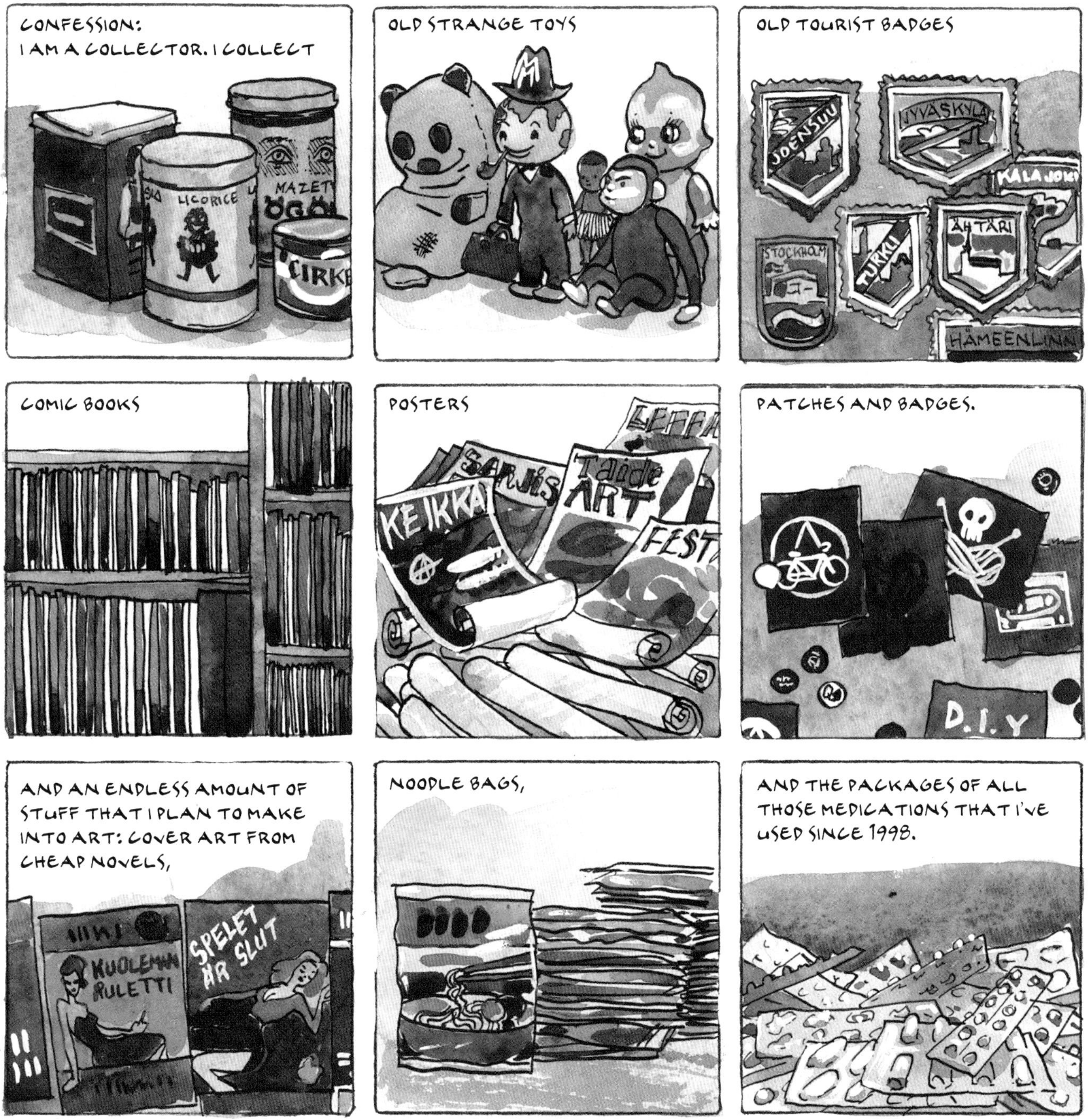
CONFESSION:
I AM A COLLECTOR. I COLLECT
LICORICE
OLD STRANGE TOYS
OLD TOURIST BADGES
JOENSUU
JYVÄSKYLÄ
STOCKHOLM
TURKU
ÄHTÄRI
COMIC BOOKS
POSTERS
KEIKKA
SARJIS
Taide
ART
PATCHES AND BADGES.
D.I.Y
AND AN ENDLESS AMOUNT OF STUFF THAT I PLAN TO MAKE INTO ART: COVER ART FROM CHEAP NOVELS,
KUOLEMAN RULETTI
SPELET ÄR SLUT
NOODLE BAGS,
AND THE PACKAGES OF ALL THOSE MEDICATIONS THAT I'VE USED SINCE 1998.

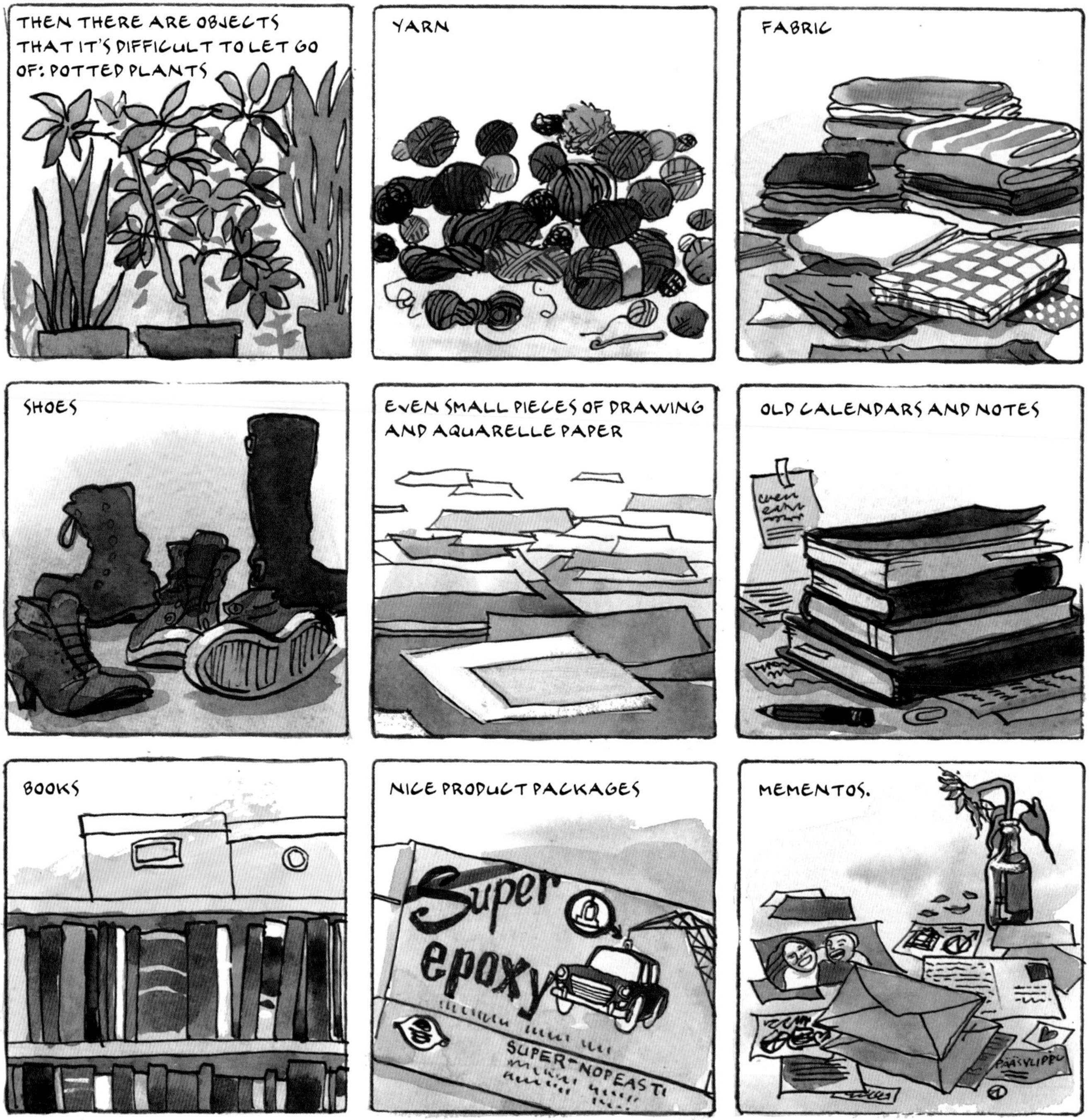
THEN THERE ARE OBJECTS THAT IT'S DIFFICULT TO LET GO OF: POTTED PLANTS
YARN
FABRIC
SHOES
EVEN SMALL PIECES OF DRAWING AND AQUARELLE PAPER
OLD CALENDARS AND NOTES
BOOKS
NICE PRODUCT PACKAGES
Super epoxy
MEMENTOS.

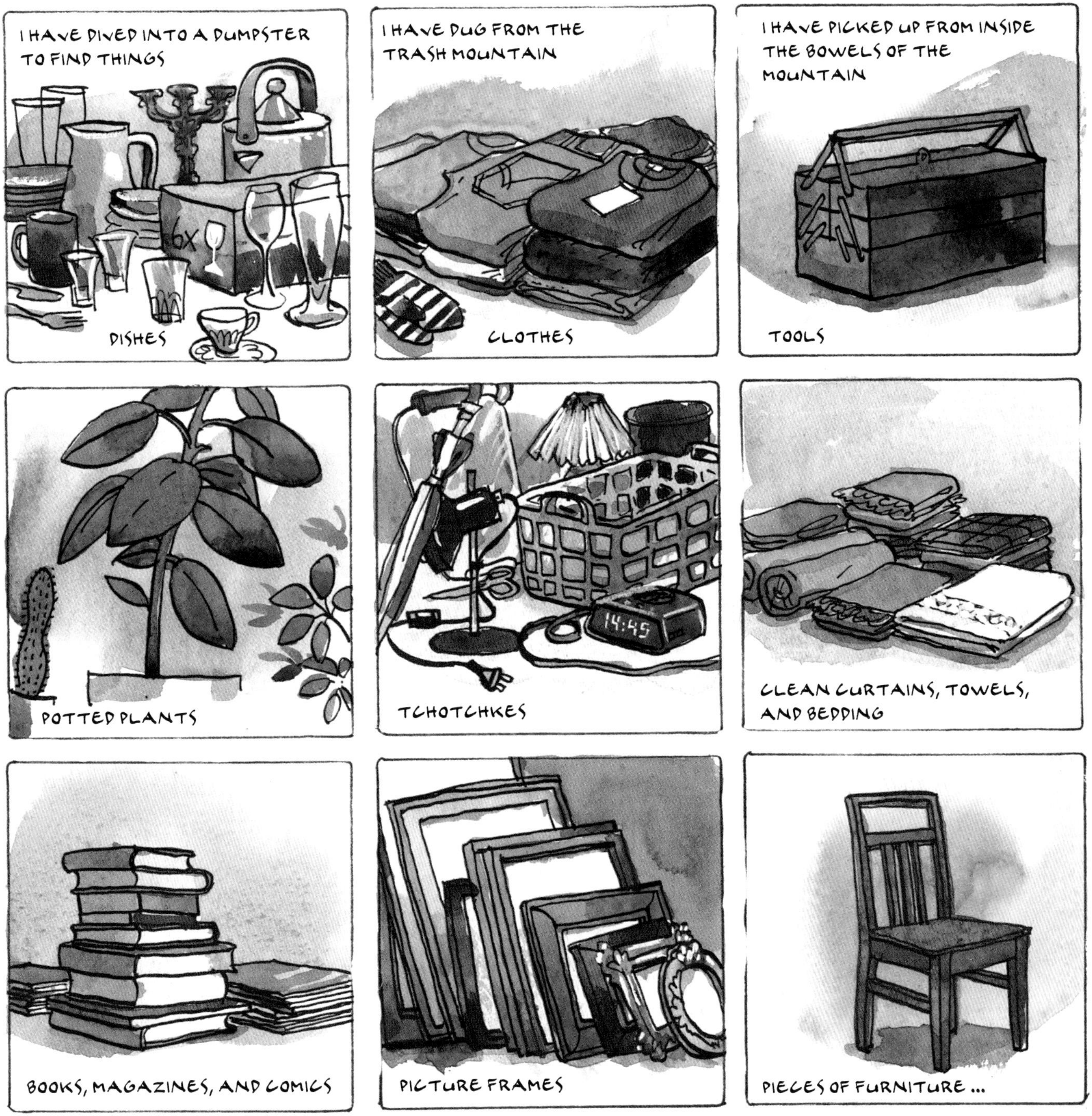
I HAVE DIVED INTO A DUMPSTER TO FIND THINGS
6X
DISHES
I HAVE DUG FROM THE TRASH MOUNTAIN
CLOTHES
I HAVE PICKED UP FROM INSIDE THE BOWELS OF THE MOUNTAIN
TOOLS
POTTED PLANTS
14:45
TCHOTCHKES
CLEAN CURTAINS, TOWELS, AND BEDDING
BOOKS, MAGAZINES, AND COMICS
PICTURE FRAMES
PIECES OF FURNITURE ...

ESPECIALLY FURNITURE.

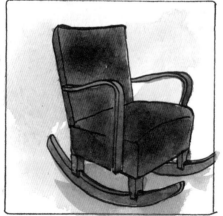

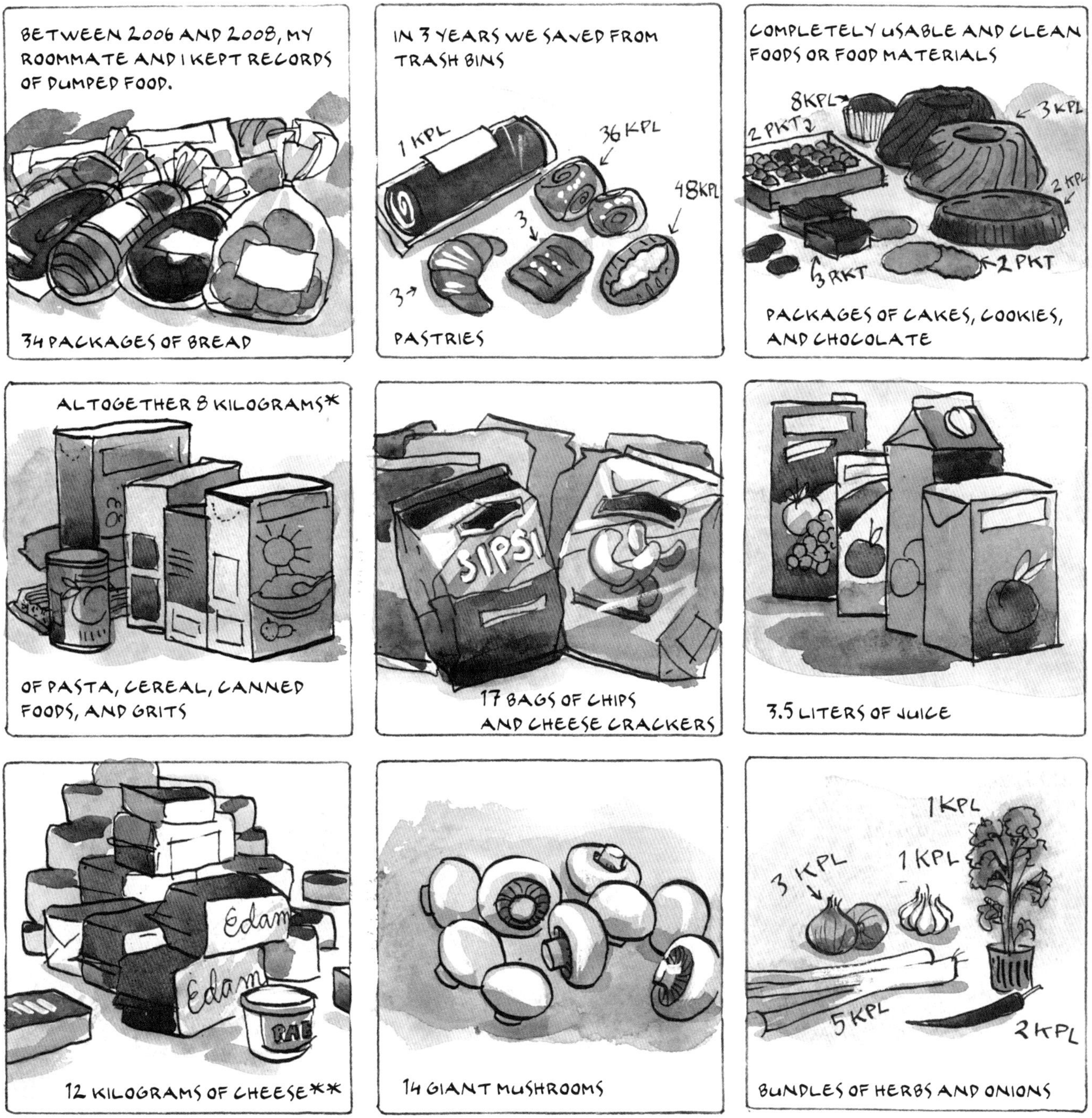
BETWEEN 2006 AND 2008, MY ROOMMATE AND I KEPT RECORDS OF DUMPED FOOD.
34 PACKAGES OF BREAD
IN 3 YEARS WE SAVED FROM TRASH BINS
1 KPL
36 KPL
48 KPL
3
3
PASTRIES
COMPLETELY USABLE AND CLEAN FOODS OR FOOD MATERIALS
8 KPL
2 PKT 2
3 KPL
2 KPL
3 PKT
2 PKT
PACKAGES OF CAKES, COOKIES, AND CHOCOLATE
ALTOGETHER 8 KILOGRAMS*
OF PASTA, CEREAL, CANNED FOODS, AND GRITS
SIPSI
17 BAGS OF CHIPS AND CHEESE CRACKERS
3.5 LITERS OF JUICE
Edam
Edam
12 KILOGRAMS OF CHEESE**
14 GIANT MUSHROOMS
1 KPL
3 KPL
1 KPL
5 KPL
2 KPL
BUNDLES OF HERBS AND ONIONS

*18 pounds

**26 pounds of cheese

WE WEREN'T EVEN VERY DILIGENT.

6 KPL

5 KPL

PINEAPPLES AND MELONS

AND WE TOOK ONLY WHAT WE NEEDED

10 KPL

LETTUCE

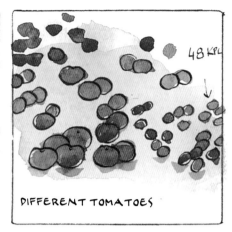

48 KPL

DIFFERENT TOMATOES

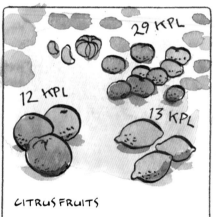

29 KPL

12 KPL

13 KPL

CITRUS FRUITS

98 APPLES

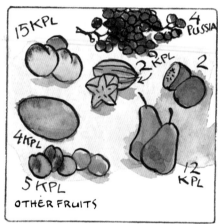

15 KPL

4 RUSSIA

29 KPL

2

4 KPL

5 KPL

12 KPL

OTHER FRUITS

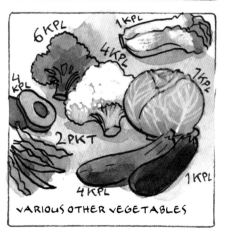

6 KPL

1 KPL

4 KPL

4 KPL

1 KPL

2 PKT

4 KPL

1 KPL

VARIOUS OTHER VEGETABLES

4 KPL

23 KPL

6 KPL

2 KPL

ROOT VEGETABLES

AND 18 CUCUMBERS

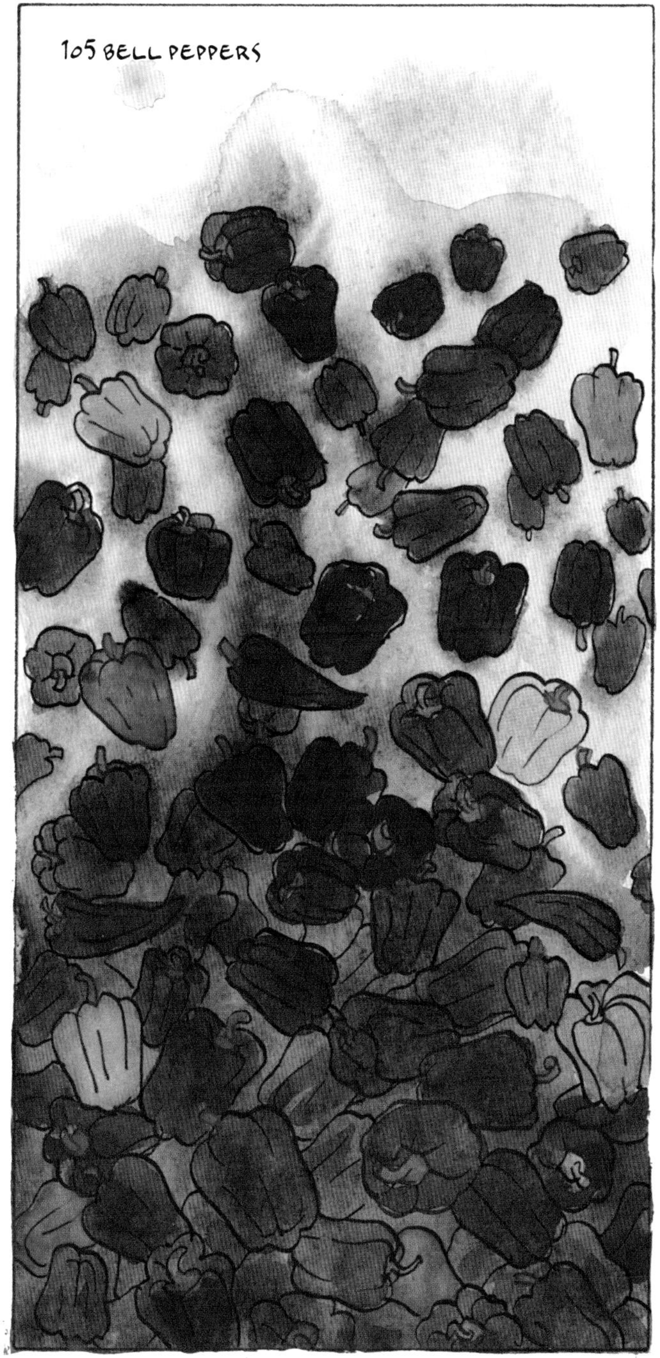
105 BELL PEPPERS

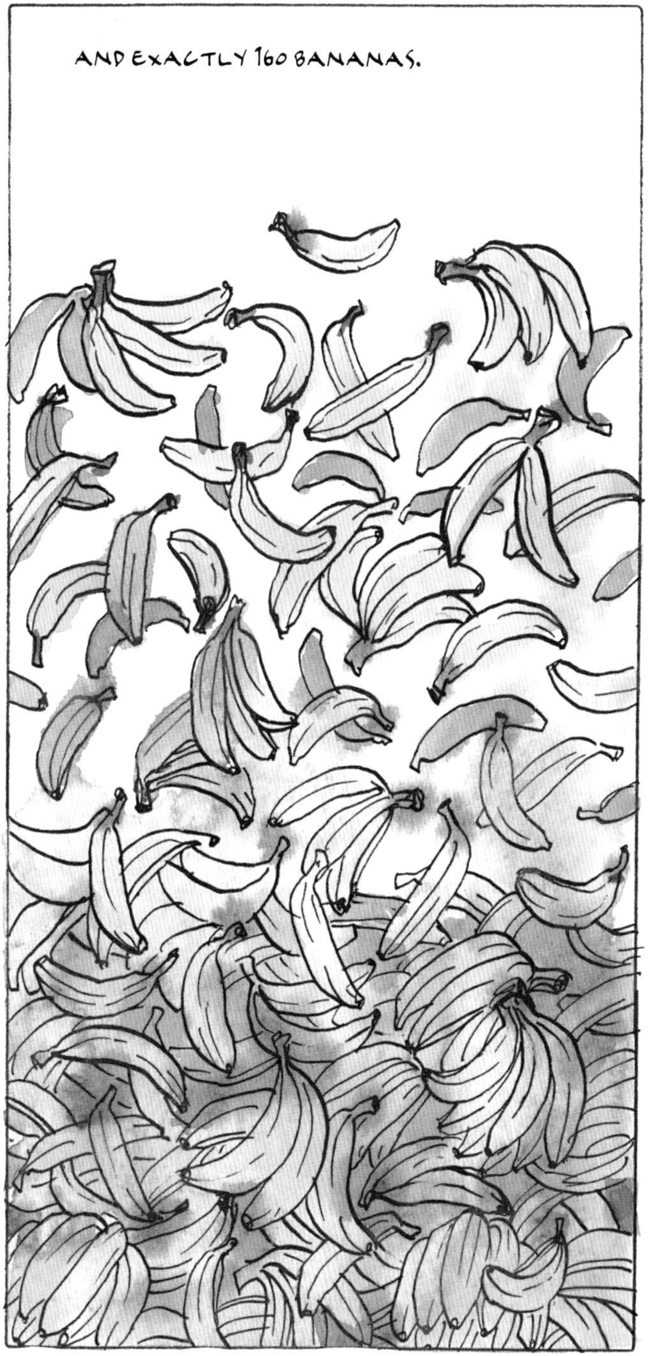
AND EXACTLY 160 BANANAS.

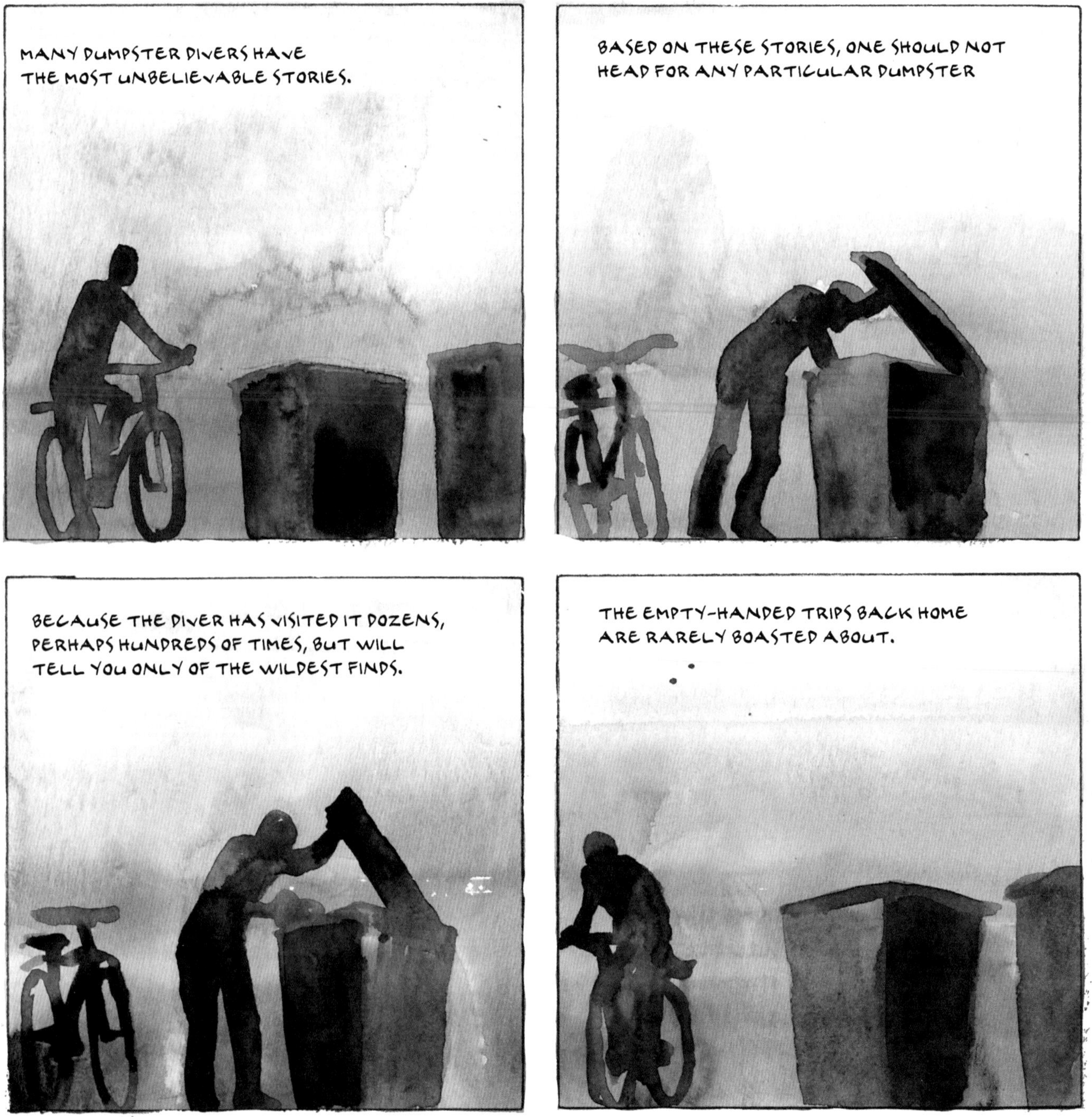
MANY DUMPSTER DIVERS HAVE THE MOST UNBELIEVABLE STORIES.
BASED ON THESE STORIES, ONE SHOULD NOT HEAD FOR ANY PARTICULAR DUMPSTER
BECAUSE THE DIVER HAS VISITED IT DOZENS, PERHAPS HUNDREDS OF TIMES, BUT WILL TELL YOU ONLY OF THE WILDEST FINDS.
THE EMPTY-HANDED TRIPS BACK HOME ARE RARELY BOASTED ABOUT.

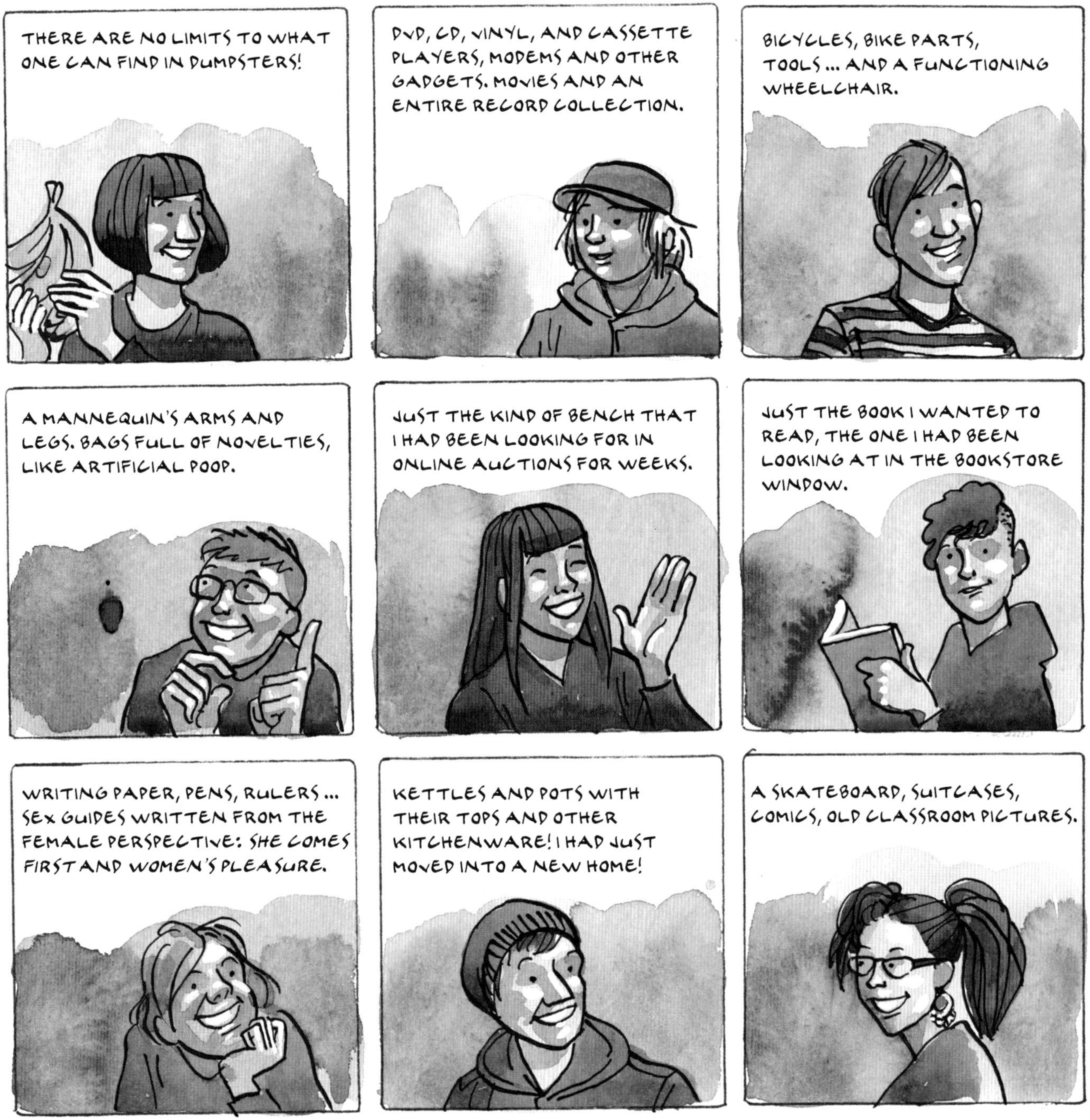
THERE ARE NO LIMITS TO WHAT ONE CAN FIND IN DUMPSTERS!
DVD, CD, VINYL, AND CASSETTE PLAYERS, MODEMS AND OTHER GADGETS. MOVIES AND AN ENTIRE RECORD COLLECTION.
BICYCLES, BIKE PARTS, TOOLS ... AND A FUNCTIONING WHEELCHAIR.
A MANNEQUIN'S ARMS AND LEGS. BAGS FULL OF NOVELTIES, LIKE ARTIFICIAL POOP.
JUST THE KIND OF BENCH THAT I HAD BEEN LOOKING FOR IN ONLINE AUCTIONS FOR WEEKS.
JUST THE BOOK I WANTED TO READ, THE ONE I HAD BEEN LOOKING AT IN THE BOOKSTORE WINDOW.
WRITING PAPER, PENS, RULERS ... SEX GUIDES WRITTEN FROM THE FEMALE PERSPECTIVE: SHE COMES FIRST AND WOMEN'S PLEASURE.
KETTLES AND POTS WITH THEIR TOPS AND OTHER KITCHENWARE! I HAD JUST MOVED INTO A NEW HOME!
A SKATEBOARD, SUITCASES, COMICS, OLD CLASSROOM PICTURES.

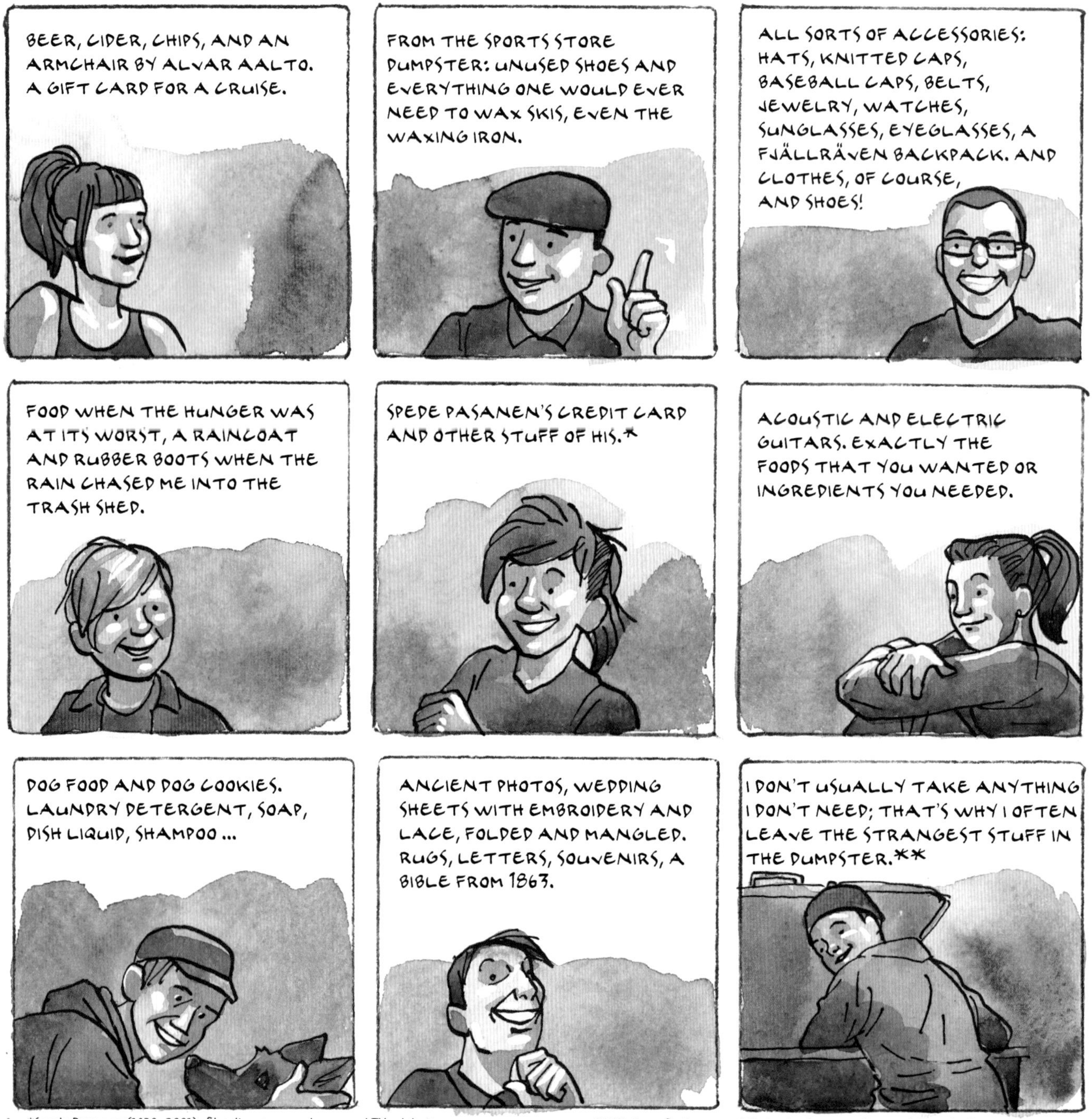
BEER, CIDER, CHIPS, AND AN ARMCHAIR BY ALVAR AALTO. A GIFT CARD FOR A CRUISE.
FROM THE SPORTS STORE DUMPSTER: UNUSED SHOES AND EVERYTHING ONE WOULD EVER NEED TO WAX SKIS, EVEN THE WAXING IRON.
ALL SORTS OF ACCESSORIES: HATS, KNITTED CAPS, BASEBALL CAPS, BELTS, JEWELRY, WATCHES, SUNGLASSES, EYEGLASSES, A FJÄLLRÄVEN BACKPACK. AND CLOTHES, OF COURSE, AND SHOES!
FOOD WHEN THE HUNGER WAS AT ITS WORST, A RAINCOAT AND RUBBER BOOTS WHEN THE RAIN CHASED ME INTO THE TRASH SHED.
SPEDE PASANEN'S CREDIT CARD AND OTHER STUFF OF HIS.*
ACOUSTIC AND ELECTRIC GUITARS. EXACTLY THE FOODS THAT YOU WANTED OR INGREDIENTS YOU NEEDED.
DOG FOOD AND DOG COOKIES. LAUNDRY DETERGENT, SOAP, DISH LIQUID, SHAMPOO ...
ANCIENT PHOTOS, WEDDING SHEETS WITH EMBROIDERY AND LACE, FOLDED AND MANGLED. RUGS, LETTERS, SOUVENIRS, A BIBLE FROM 1863.
I DON'T USUALLY TAKE ANYTHING I DON'T NEED; THAT'S WHY I OFTEN LEAVE THE STRANGEST STUFF IN THE DUMPSTER.**

*Spede Pasanen (1930–2001), film director, producer, and TV celebrity

**All these finds are real! Only the faces are fictional. Thanks for the help, divers!

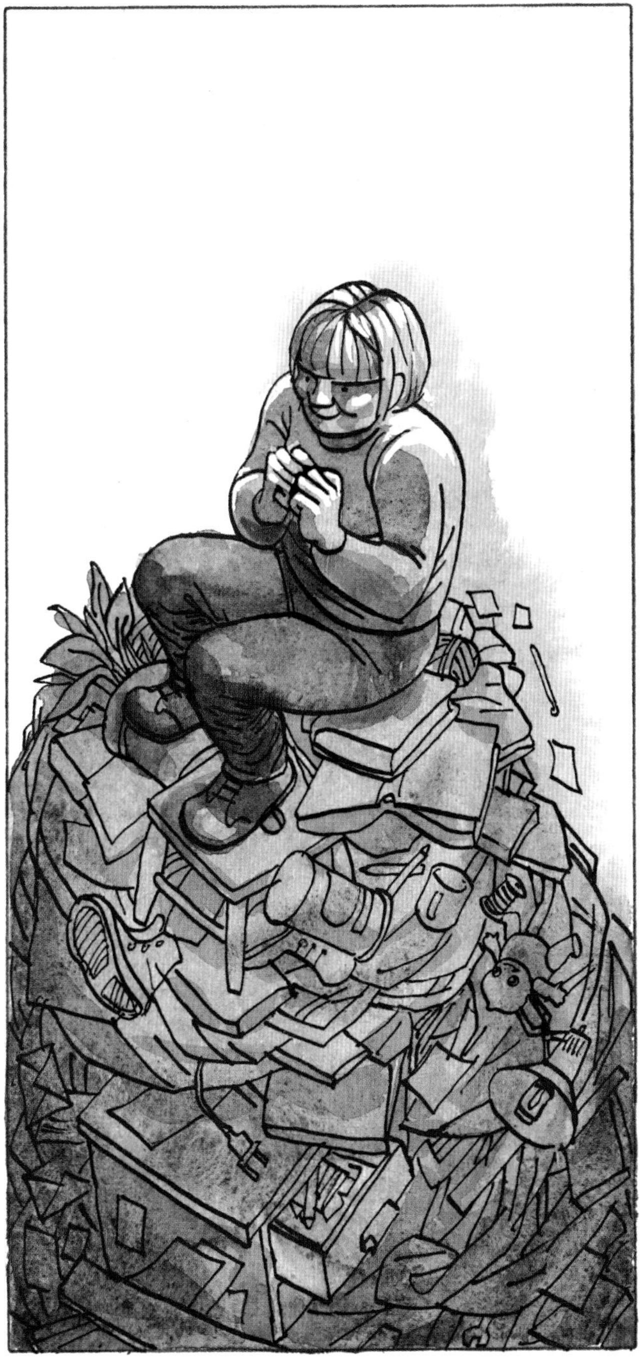

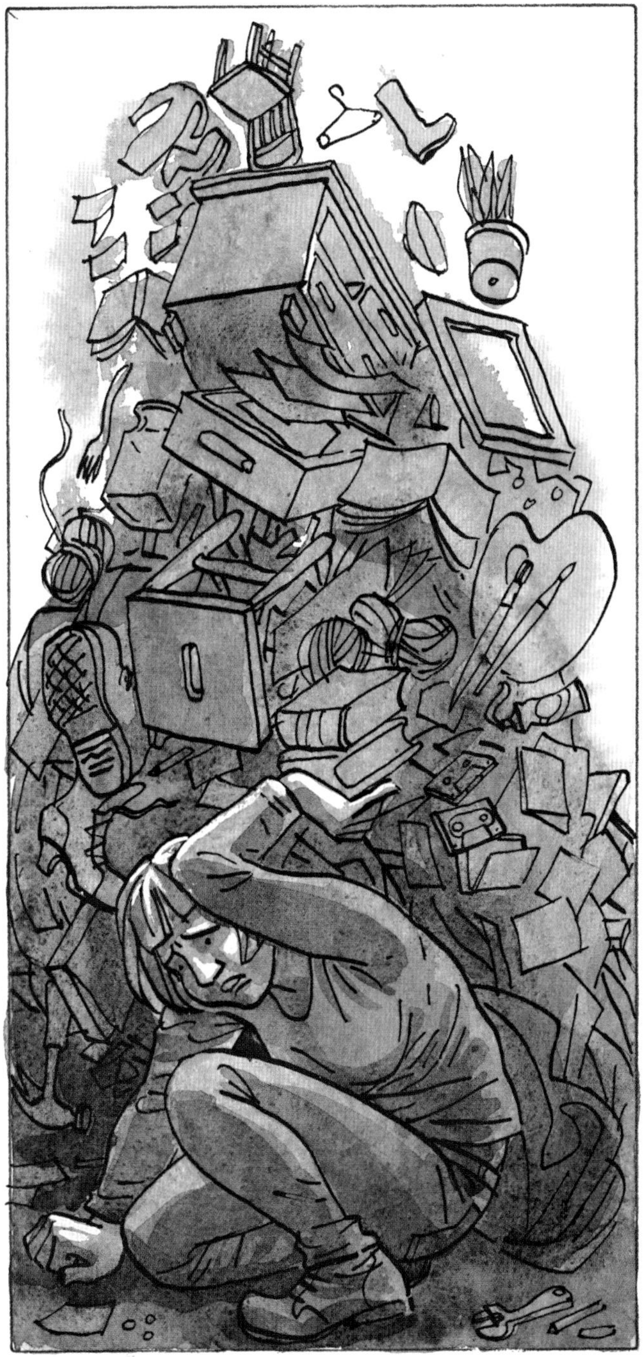

IN 1995, A TEENAGER FROM GOTHENBURG IS IN COPENHAGEN WITH THEIR MOTHER AND THE MOTHER'S BOYFRIEND. IT'S THERE WHERE THEY FALL IN LOVE WITH SHOES OF THE TANK GIRL BRAND.

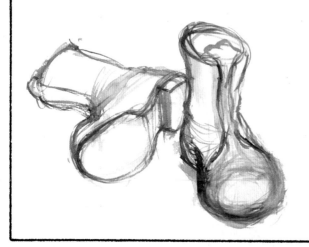

THE SHOES WERE BROWN, WITH MASSIVE IRON TIPS, AND ON THE BOTTOM A PICTURE OF A COMIC BOOK CHARACTER ON A TURQUOISE RUBBER SOLE. THEY MUST HAVE THE SHOES—WHICH ARE EVEN ON SALE.

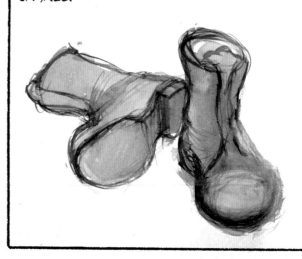

DURING THE TRIP HOME, THEY WALK IN THEIR NEW SHOES ALONG THE SEASHORE AT THE KULLABERG NATURE RESERVE. THE NEW SHOES AND THE ROUGH TERRAIN MAKE THE YOUNG ADVENTURER DISAPPEAR FOR A MOMENT ON THEIR OWN PONDEROUS PATHS.

THE NEXT YEAR THEY LEAVE HOME TO MOVE TO FINLAND, TO INARI. THE SHOES ARE NOT WARM ENOUGH FOR THE LAPLAND WINTER. OFTEN THEY STILL HITCHHIKE IN THE SHOES FOR THEIR FRIDAY TRIPS TO IVALO AND BACK.

THE YEARS TAKE THE YOUNG PERSON AND THEIR SHOES FROM ONE PLACE TO ANOTHER: TO KUOPIO, TO LAHTI, TO TAMPERE. THE SHOES HAVEN'T BEEN WORN MUCH, AND THEY CHANGE OWNERS.

THE NEXT OWNER WEARS THEM OCCASIONALLY, BUT DECIDES TO GIVE THEM UP. I END UP HAVING THE SHOES IN 2005. THEY ARE ACTUALLY SOMEWHAT WORN NOW, AND THE IRON TIP OF ONE HAS BEEN BENT. BUT THE GIRL ON THE SOLE STILL GRINS.

I WEAR THE SHOES FOR BAND GIGS, FOR INTERNATIONAL WOMEN'S DAY IN 2006 IN JYVÄSKYLÄ, FOR YEARS I SELL ZINES AT PUNTALA-ROCK WEARING THE SHOES, AND THEY WALK WITH ME ON THE STAIRS OF THE COLOGNE CATHEDRAL BELL TOWER.

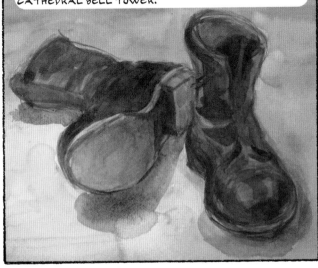

WITH ME, THE SHOES WITNESS HOW THE YEAR CHANGES TO ANOTHER ON THE STREETS OF LONDON. TOGETHER WE CHANGE TRAINS IN BELGIUM, AND EVEN THOUGH WE RUN, WE NARROWLY MISS IT. THEY ARE MY MAIN WINTER BOOTS UNTIL 2012.

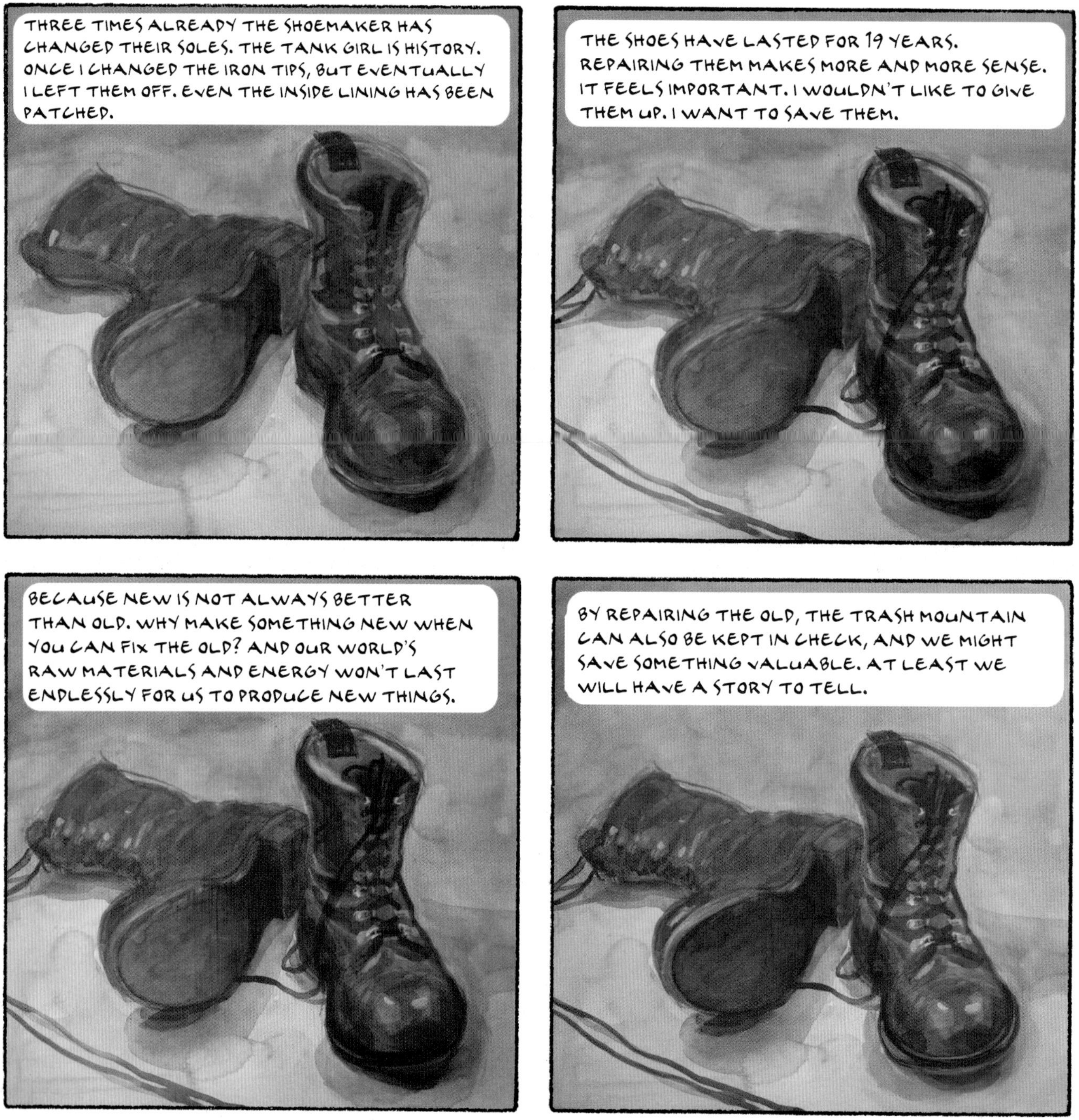
THREE TIMES ALREADY THE SHOEMAKER HAS CHANGED THEIR SOLES. THE TANK GIRL IS HISTORY. ONCE I CHANGED THE IRON TIPS, BUT EVENTUALLY I LEFT THEM OFF. EVEN THE INSIDE LINING HAS BEEN PATCHED.
THE SHOES HAVE LASTED FOR 19 YEARS. REPAIRING THEM MAKES MORE AND MORE SENSE. IT FEELS IMPORTANT. I WOULDN'T LIKE TO GIVE THEM UP. I WANT TO SAVE THEM.
BECAUSE NEW IS NOT ALWAYS BETTER THAN OLD. WHY MAKE SOMETHING NEW WHEN YOU CAN FIX THE OLD? AND OUR WORLD'S RAW MATERIALS AND ENERGY WON'T LAST ENDLESSLY FOR US TO PRODUCE NEW THINGS.
BY REPAIRING THE OLD, THE TRASH MOUNTAIN CAN ALSO BE KEPT IN CHECK, AND WE MIGHT SAVE SOMETHING VALUABLE. AT LEAST WE WILL HAVE A STORY TO TELL.

THE BATTLE FOR ANNIKKI: PART II

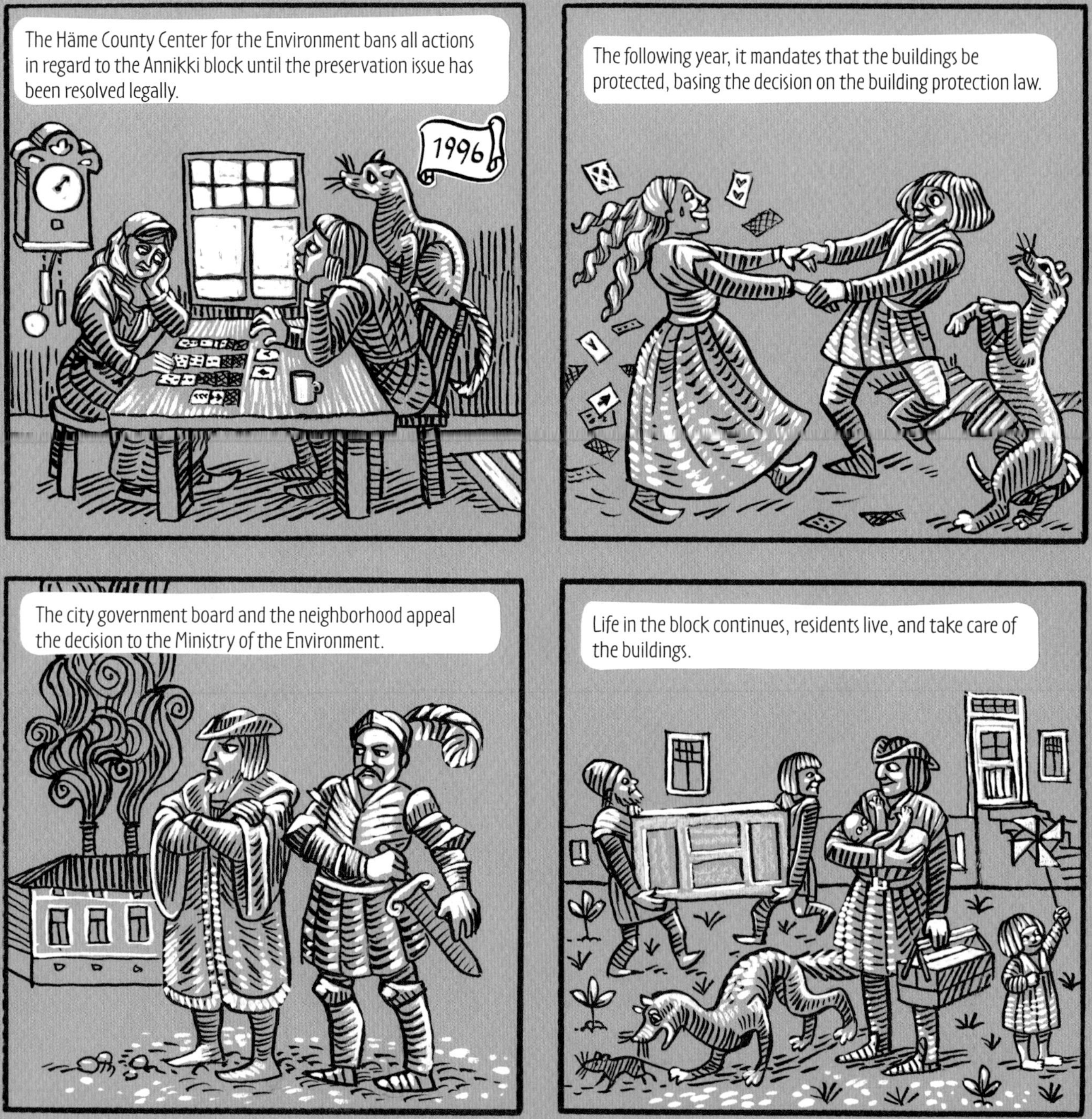
The Häme County Center for the Environment bans all actions in regard to the Annikki block until the preservation issue has been resolved legally.
1996
The following year, it mandates that the buildings be protected, basing the decision on the building protection law.
The city government board and the neighborhood appeal the decision to the Ministry of the Environment.
Life in the block continues, residents live, and take care of the buildings.

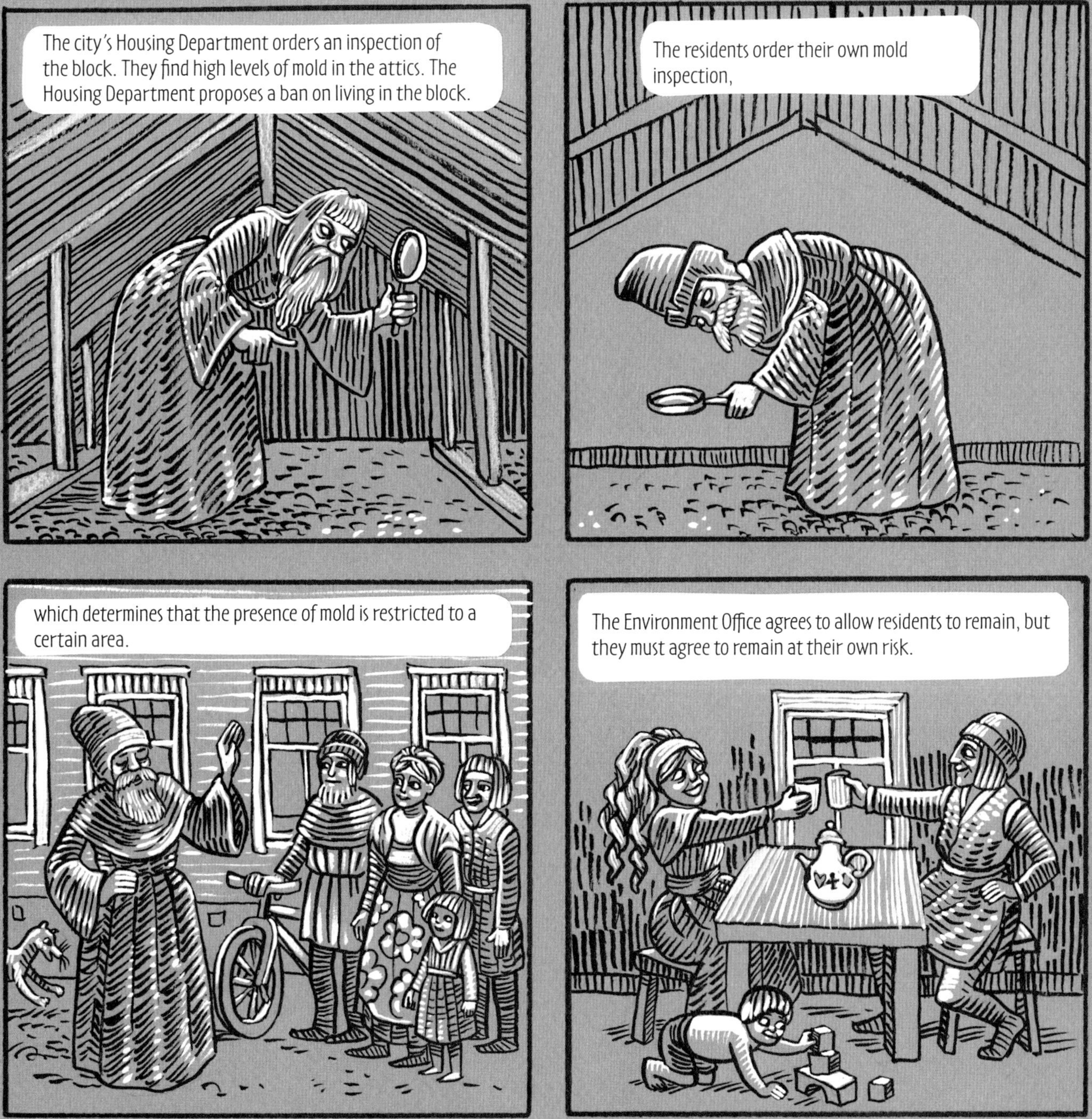
The city's Housing Department orders an inspection of the block. They find high levels of mold in the attics. The Housing Department proposes a ban on living in the block.
The residents order their own mold inspection,
which determines that the presence of mold is restricted to a certain area.
The Environment Office agrees to allow residents to remain, but they must agree to remain at their own risk.

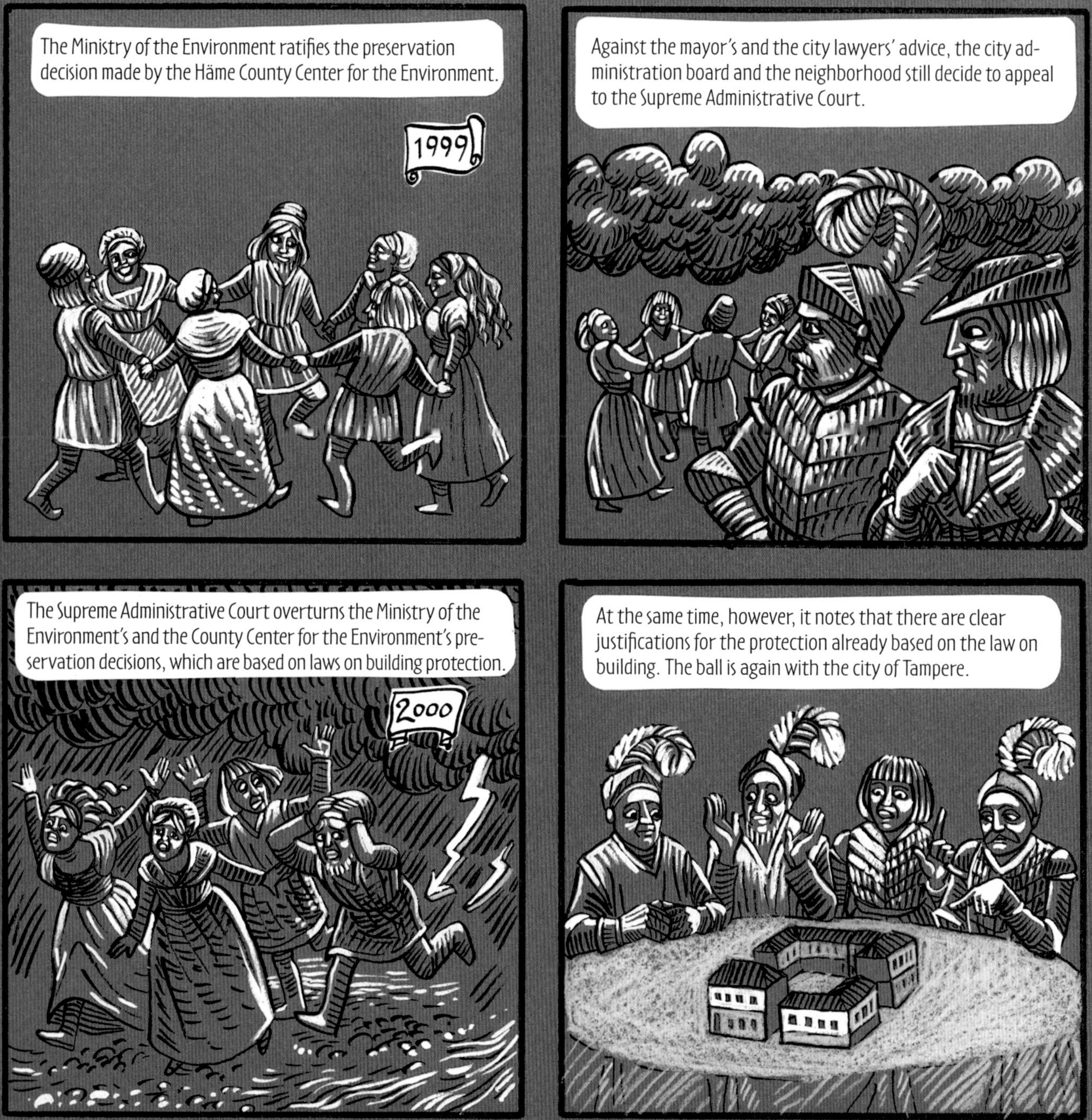
The Ministry of the Environment ratifies the preservation decision made by the Häme County Center for the Environment.
1999
Against the mayor's and the city lawyers' advice, the city administration board and the neighborhood still decide to appeal to the Supreme Administrative Court.
The Supreme Administrative Court overturns the Ministry of the Environment's and the County Center for the Environment's preservation decisions, which are based on laws on building protection.
2000
At the same time, however, it notes that there are clear justifications for the protection already based on the law on building. The ball is again with the city of Tampere.

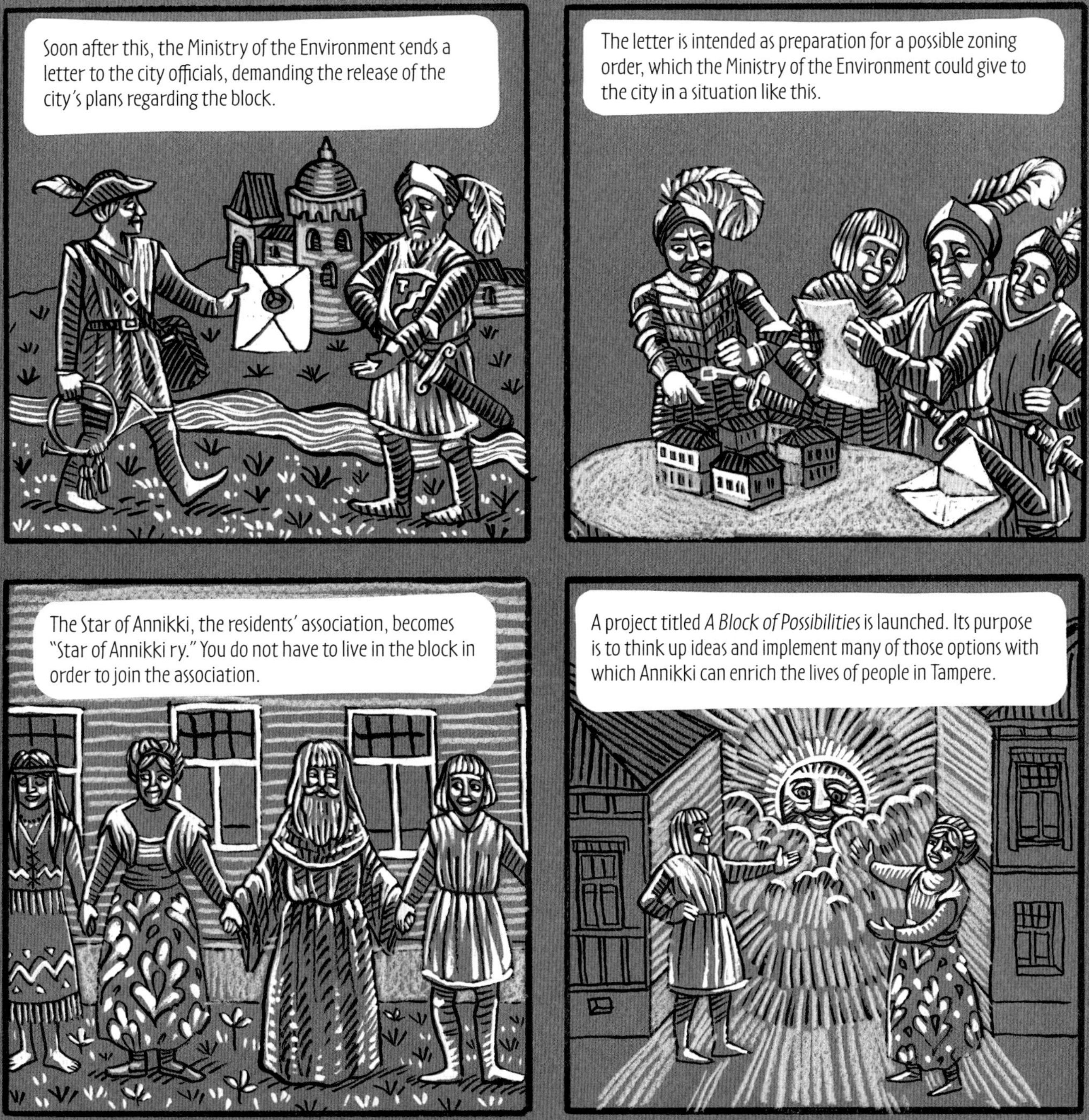
Soon after this, the Ministry of the Environment sends a letter to the city officials, demanding the release of the city's plans regarding the block.
The letter is intended as preparation for a possible zoning order, which the Ministry of the Environment could give to the city in a situation like this.
The Star of Annikki, the residents' association, becomes "Star of Annikki ry." You do not have to live in the block in order to join the association.
A project titled *A Block of Possibilities* is launched. Its purpose is to think up ideas and implement many of those options with which Annikki can enrich the lives of people in Tampere.

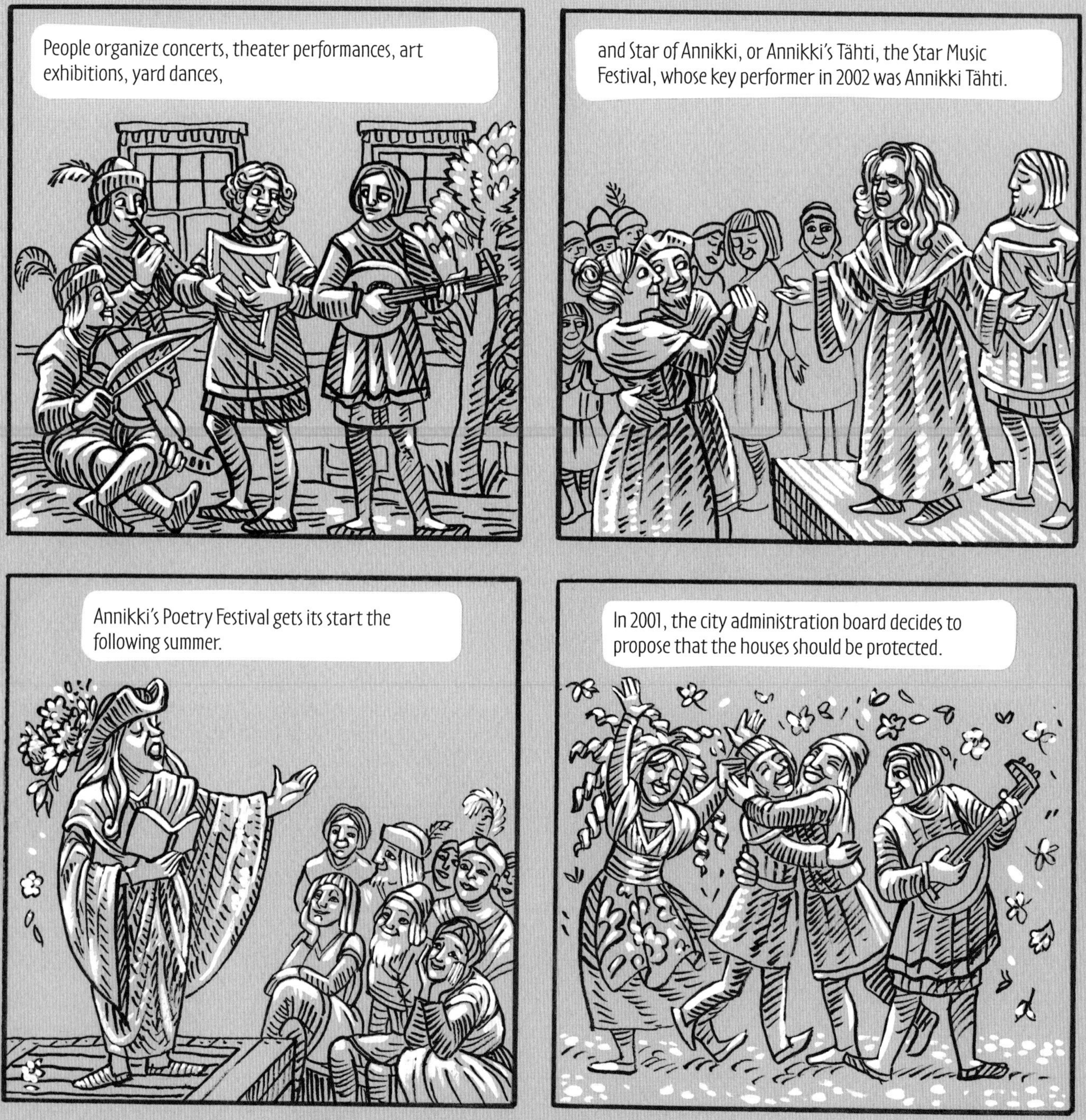
People organize concerts, theater performances, art exhibitions, yard dances,
and Star of Annikki, or Annikki's Tähti, the Star Music Festival, whose key performer in 2002 was Annikki Tähti.
Annikki's Poetry Festival gets its start the following summer.
In 2001, the city administration board decides to propose that the houses should be protected.

The preparations for protection zoning start. The multistory buildings on both sides are going to complain about the plan if there are to be parking lots under their windows.

Star of Annikki suggests that the block have a limited number of cars or even be an experimental block without cars.

The residents begin to prepare for the purchase project of the Annikki block.

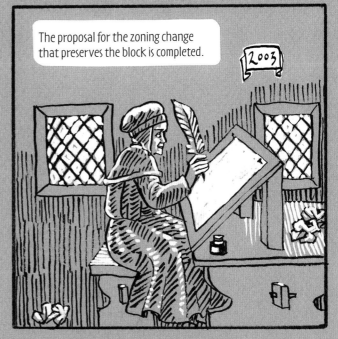

The proposal for the zoning change that preserves the block is completed.

2003

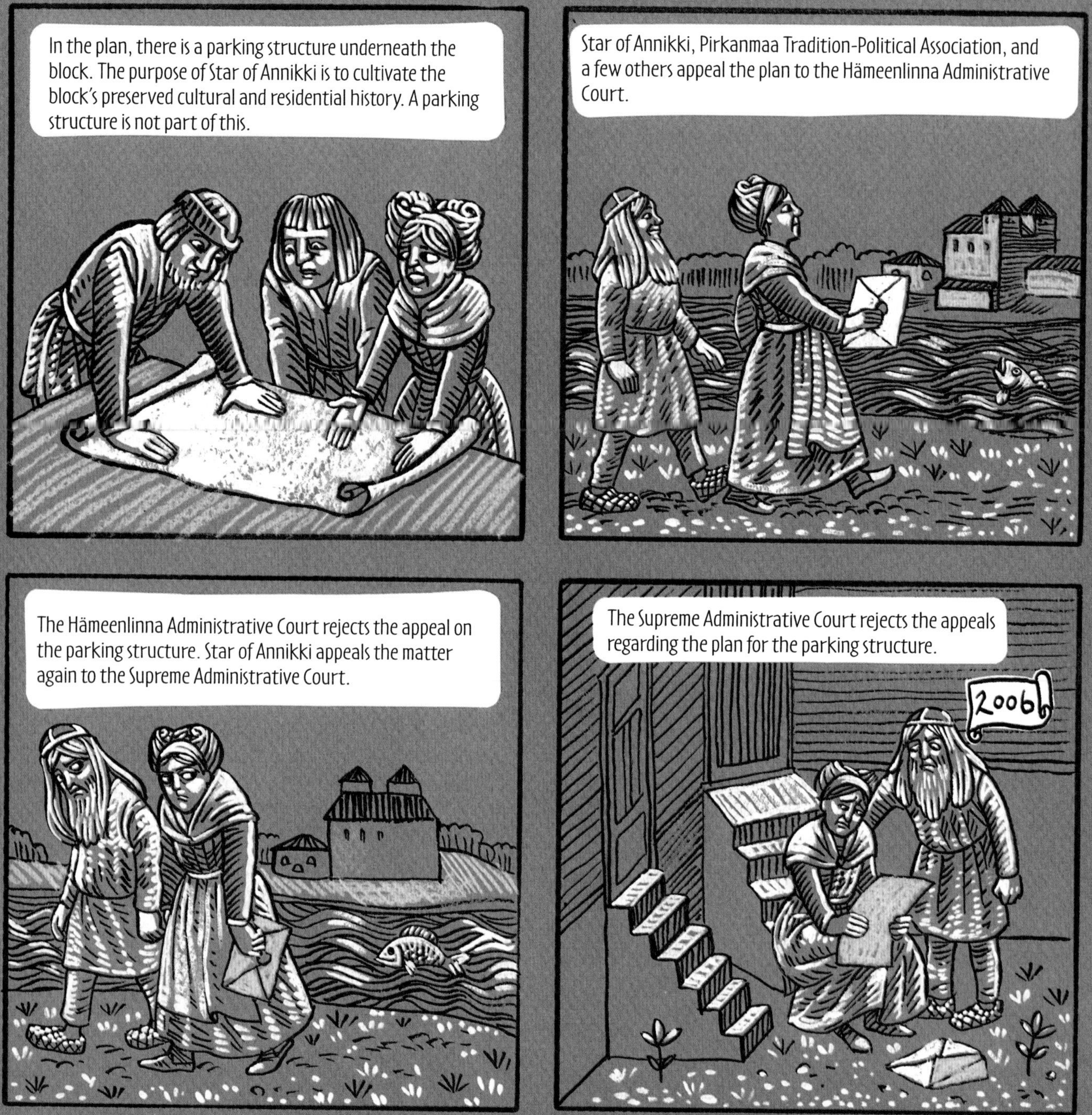
In the plan, there is a parking structure underneath the block. The purpose of Star of Annikki is to cultivate the block's preserved cultural and residential history. A parking structure is not part of this.
Star of Annikki, Pirkanmaa Tradition-Political Association, and a few others appeal the plan to the Hämeenlinna Administrative Court.
The Hämeenlinna Administrative Court rejects the appeal on the parking structure. Star of Annikki appeals the matter again to the Supreme Administrative Court.
The Supreme Administrative Court rejects the appeals regarding the plan for the parking structure.
2006

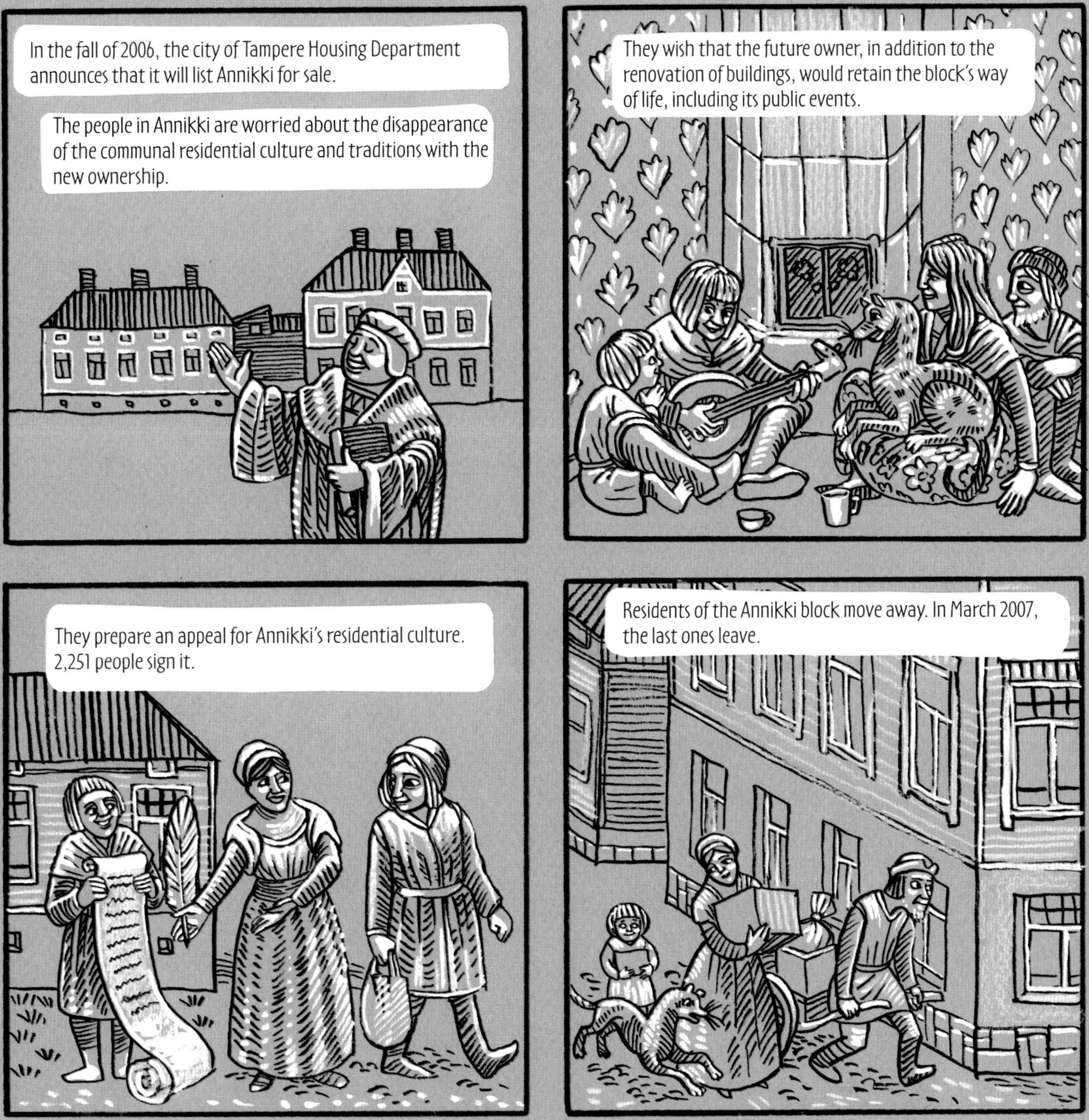
In the fall of 2006, the city of Tampere Housing Department announces that it will list Annikki for sale.
The people in Annikki are worried about the disappearance of the communal residential culture and traditions with the new ownership.
They wish that the future owner, in addition to the renovation of buildings, would retain the block's way of life, including its public events.
They prepare an appeal for Annikki's residential culture. 2,251 people sign it.
Residents of the Annikki block move away. In March 2007, the last ones leave.

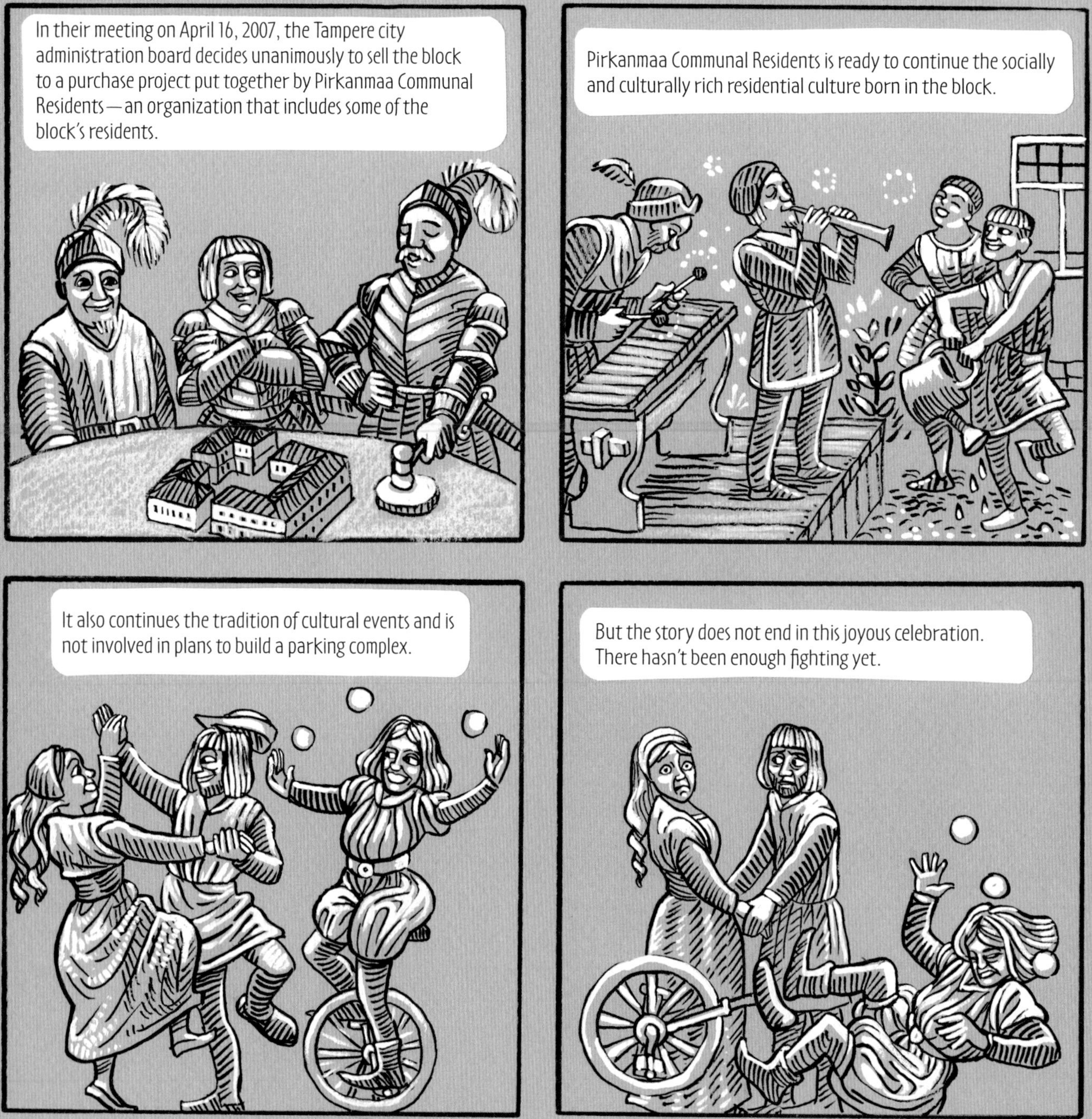
In their meeting on April 16, 2007, the Tampere city administration board decides unanimously to sell the block to a purchase project put together by Pirkanmaa Communal Residents—an organization that includes some of the block's residents.
Pirkanmaa Communal Residents is ready to continue the socially and culturally rich residential culture born in the block.
It also continues the tradition of cultural events and is not involved in plans to build a parking complex.
But the story does not end in this joyous celebration. There hasn't been enough fighting yet.

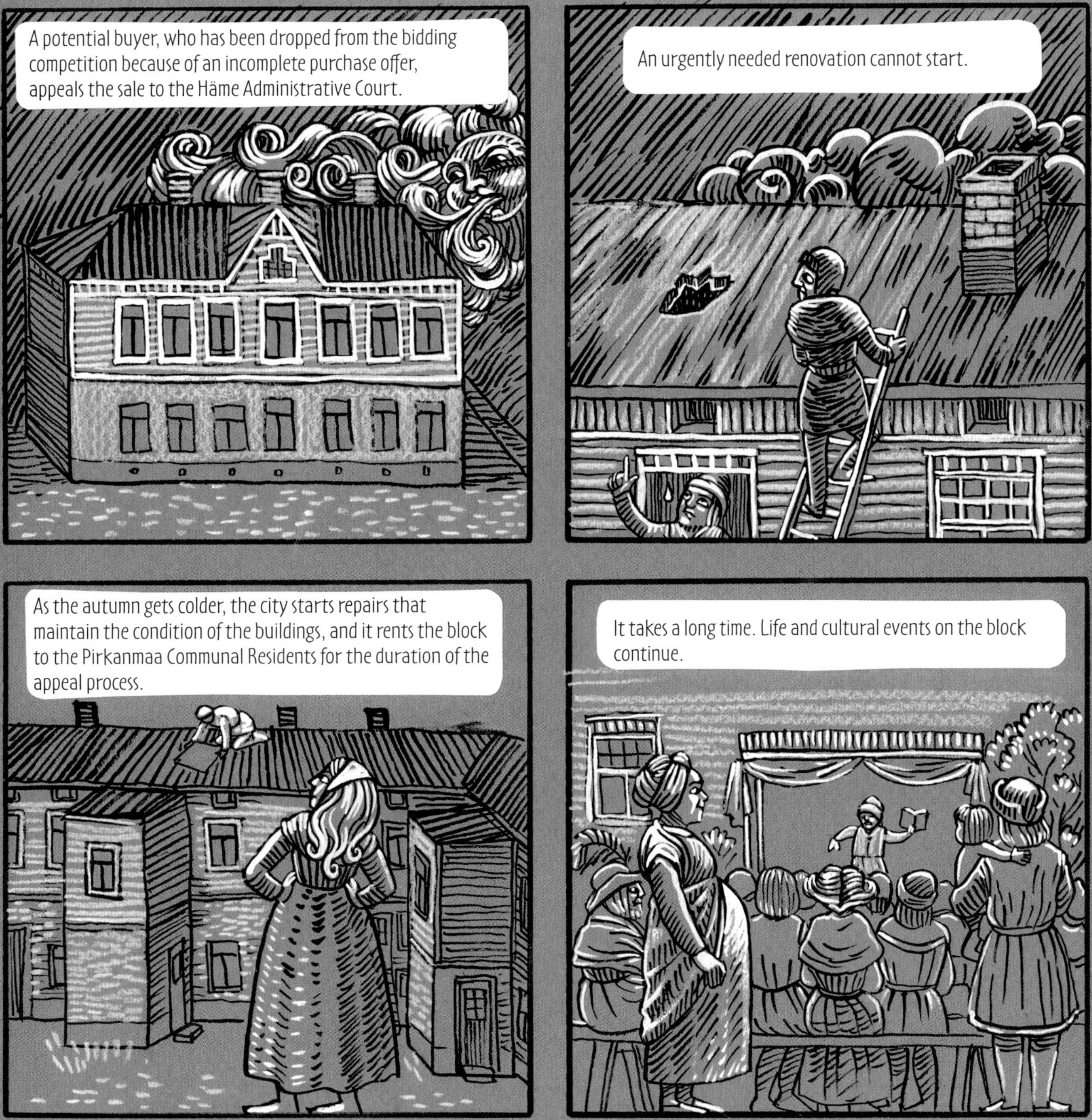
A potential buyer, who has been dropped from the bidding competition because of an incomplete purchase offer, appeals the sale to the Häme Administrative Court.
An urgently needed renovation cannot start.
As the autumn gets colder, the city starts repairs that maintain the condition of the buildings, and it rents the block to the Pirkanmaa Communal Residents for the duration of the appeal process.
It takes a long time. Life and cultural events on the block continue.

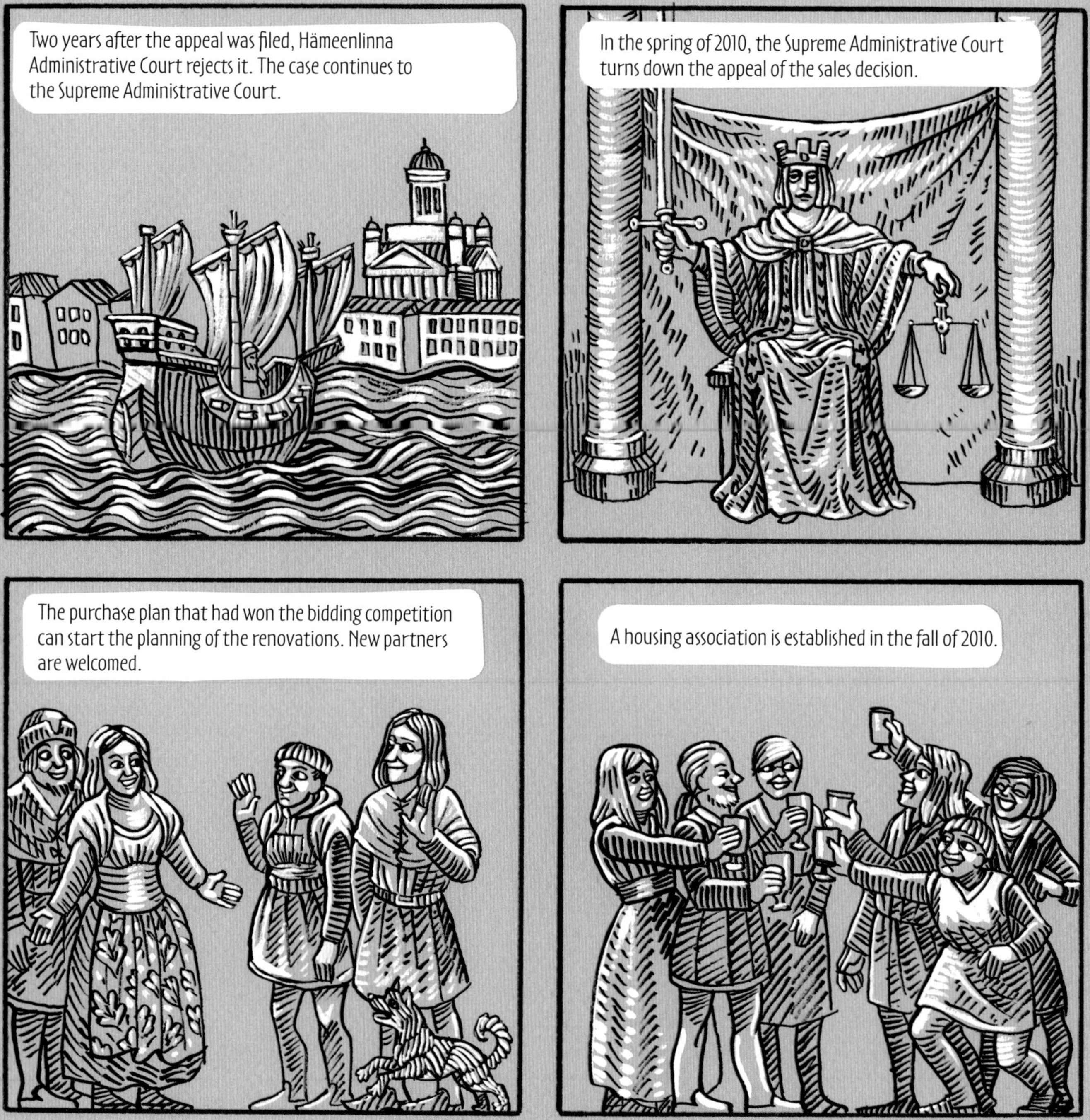
Two years after the appeal was filed, Hämeenlinna Administrative Court rejects it. The case continues to the Supreme Administrative Court.
In the spring of 2010, the Supreme Administrative Court turns down the appeal of the sales decision.
The purchase plan that had won the bidding competition can start the planning of the renovations. New partners are welcomed.
A housing association is established in the fall of 2010.

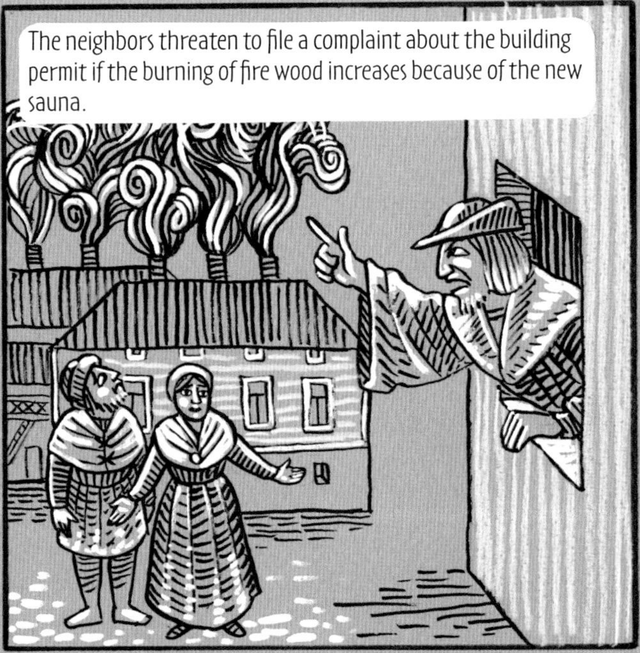
The neighbors threaten to file a complaint about the building permit if the burning of fire wood increases because of the new sauna.

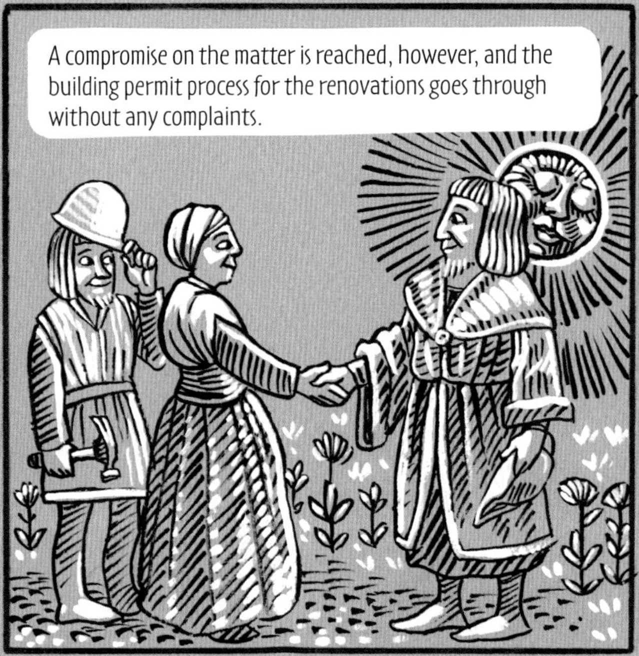
A compromise on the matter is reached, however, and the building permit process for the renovations goes through without any complaints.

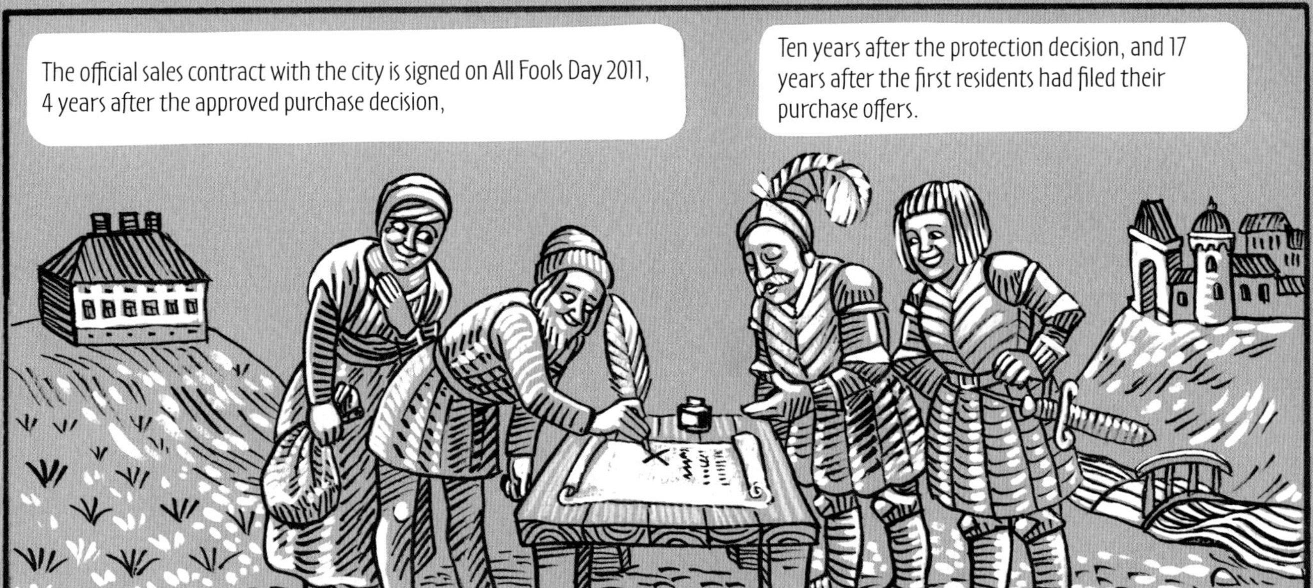
The official sales contract with the city is signed on All Fools Day 2011, 4 years after the approved purchase decision,
Ten years after the protection decision, and 17 years after the first residents had filed their purchase offers.

CONSTRUCTION SITE

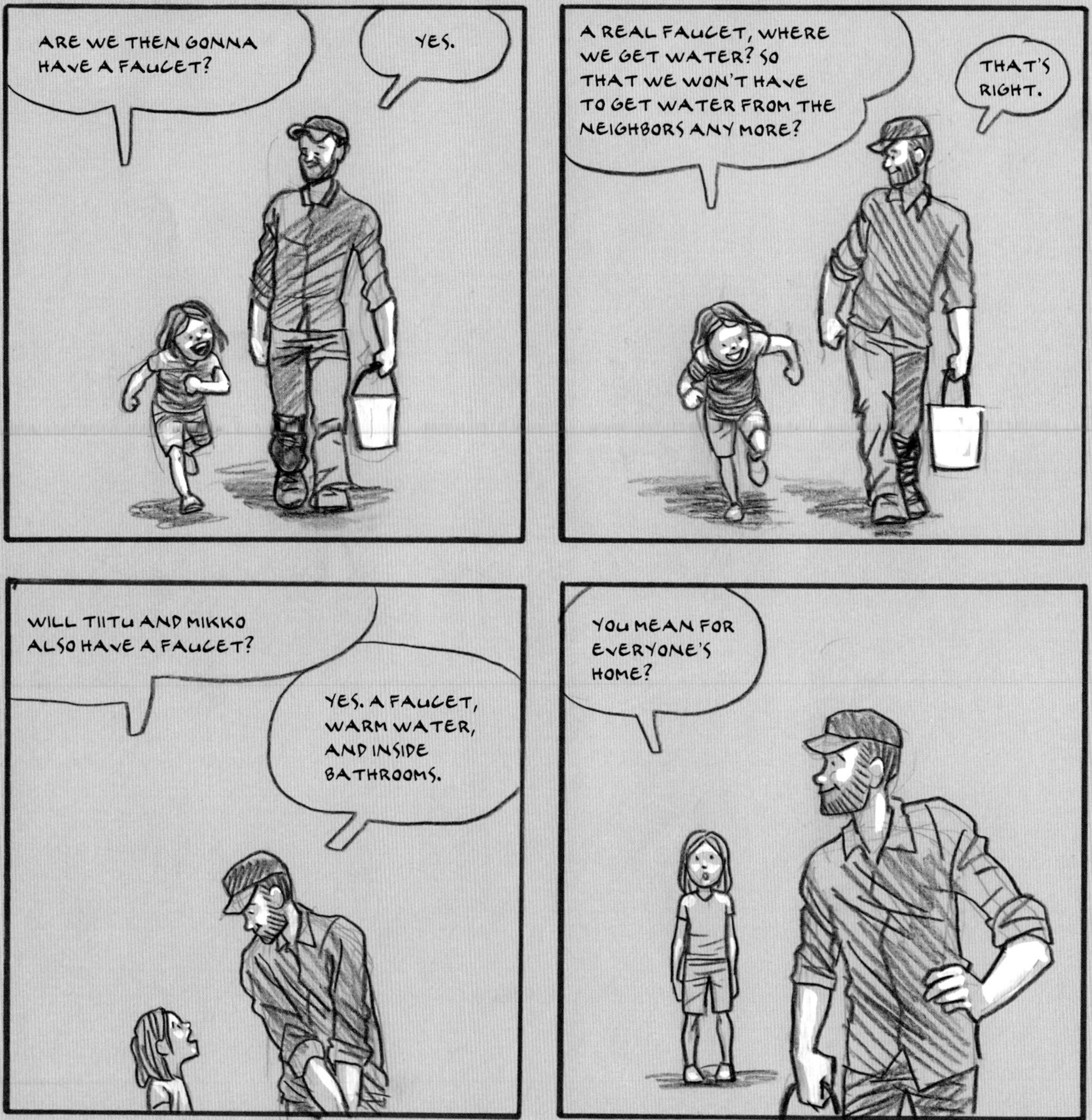
ARE WE THEN GONNA HAVE A FAUCET?
YES.
A REAL FAUCET, WHERE WE GET WATER? SO THAT WE WON'T HAVE TO GET WATER FROM THE NEIGHBORS ANY MORE?
THAT'S RIGHT.
WILL TIITU AND MIKKO ALSO HAVE A FAUCET?
YES. A FAUCET, WARM WATER, AND INSIDE BATHROOMS.
YOU MEAN FOR EVERYONE'S HOME?

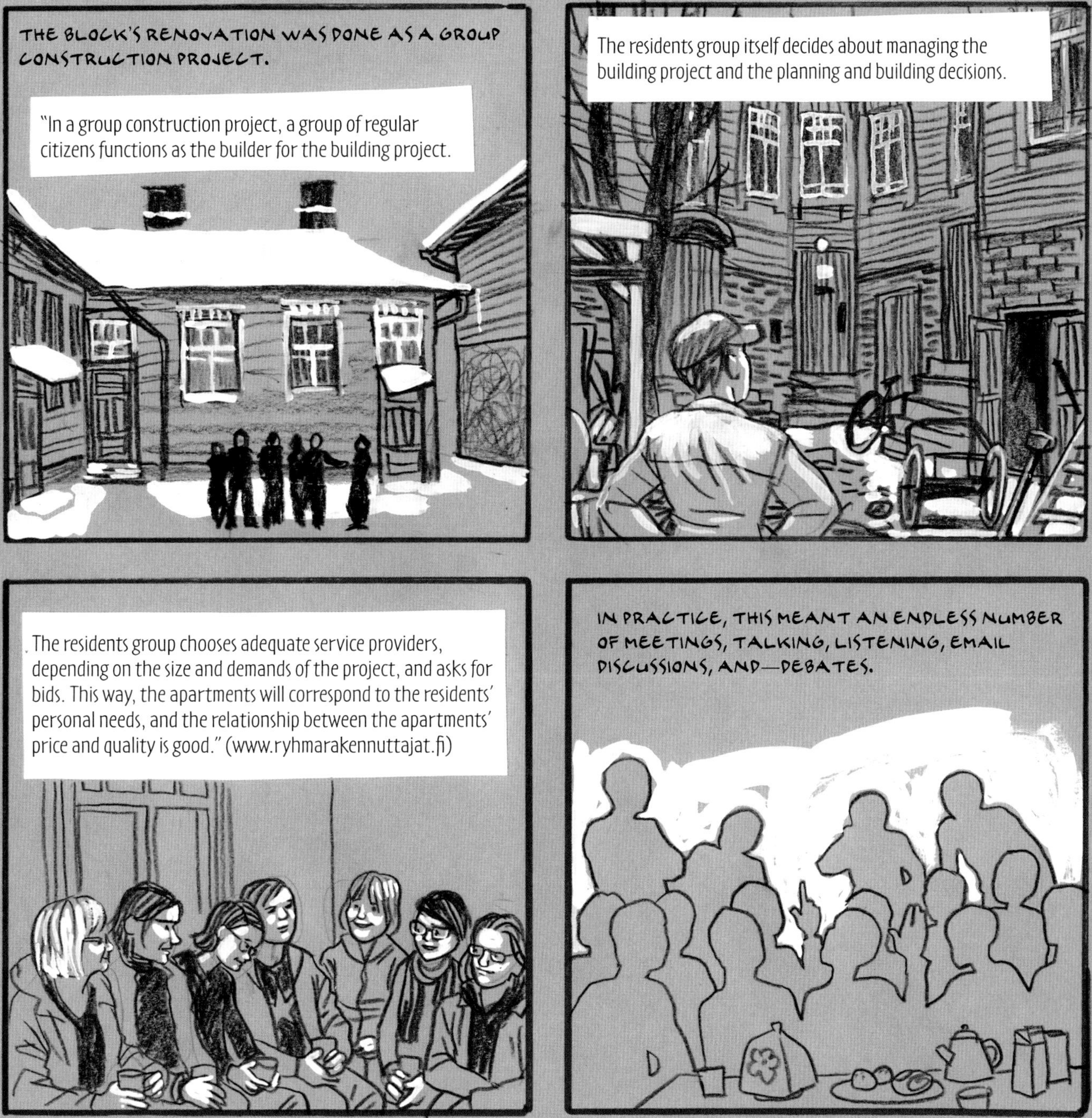
THE BLOCK'S RENOVATION WAS DONE AS A GROUP CONSTRUCTION PROJECT.
"In a group construction project, a group of regular citizens functions as the builder for the building project.
The residents group itself decides about managing the building project and the planning and building decisions.
The residents group chooses adequate service providers, depending on the size and demands of the project, and asks for bids. This way, the apartments will correspond to the residents' personal needs, and the relationship between the apartments' price and quality is good." (www.ryhmarakennuttajat.fi)
IN PRACTICE, THIS MEANT AN ENDLESS NUMBER OF MEETINGS, TALKING, LISTENING, EMAIL DISCUSSIONS, AND—DEBATES.

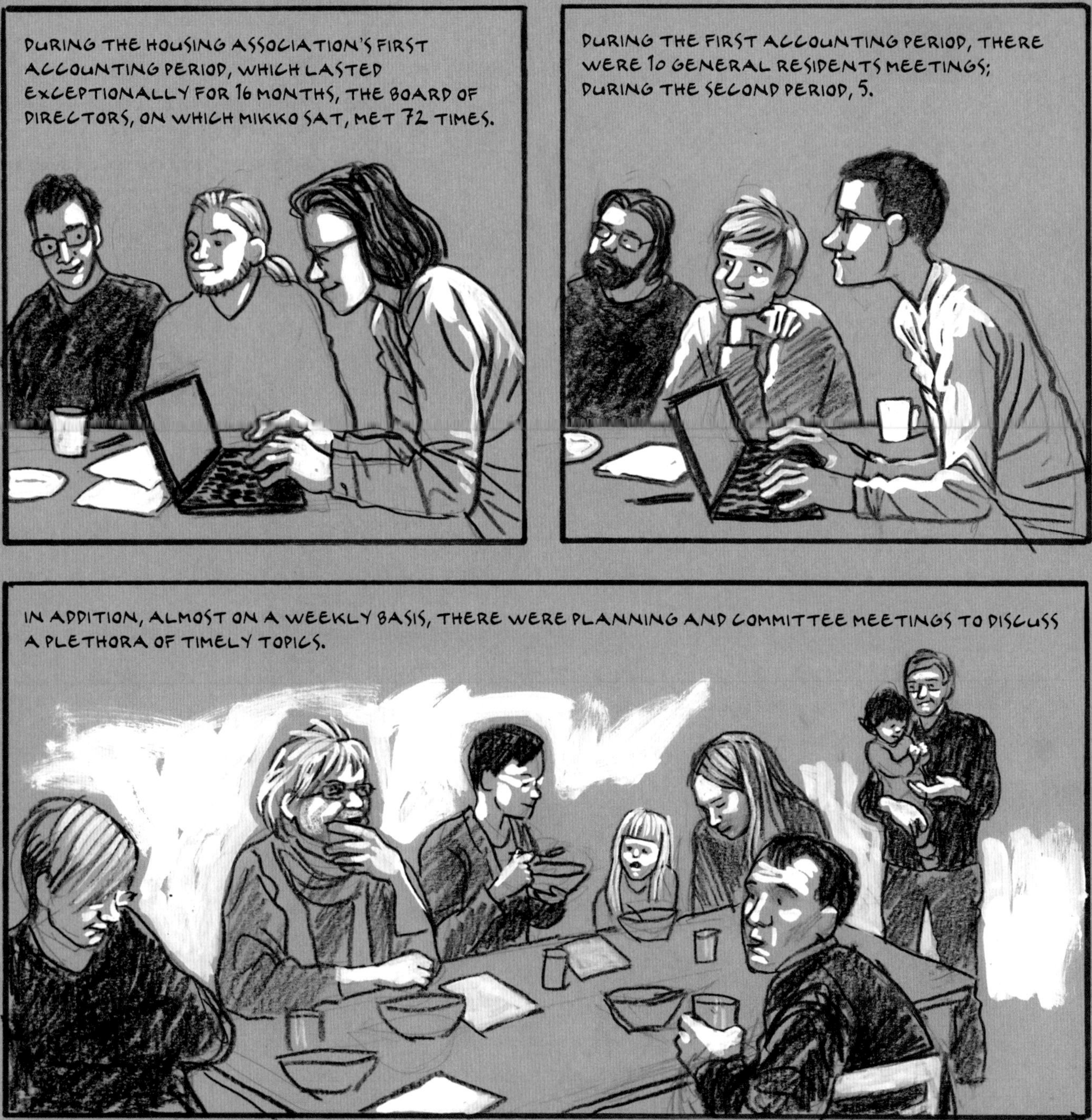
DURING THE HOUSING ASSOCIATION'S FIRST ACCOUNTING PERIOD, WHICH LASTED EXCEPTIONALLY FOR 16 MONTHS, THE BOARD OF DIRECTORS, ON WHICH MIKKO SAT, MET 72 TIMES.
DURING THE FIRST ACCOUNTING PERIOD, THERE WERE 10 GENERAL RESIDENTS MEETINGS; DURING THE SECOND PERIOD, 5.
IN ADDITION, ALMOST ON A WEEKLY BASIS, THERE WERE PLANNING AND COMMITTEE MEETINGS TO DISCUSS A PLETHORA OF TIMELY TOPICS.

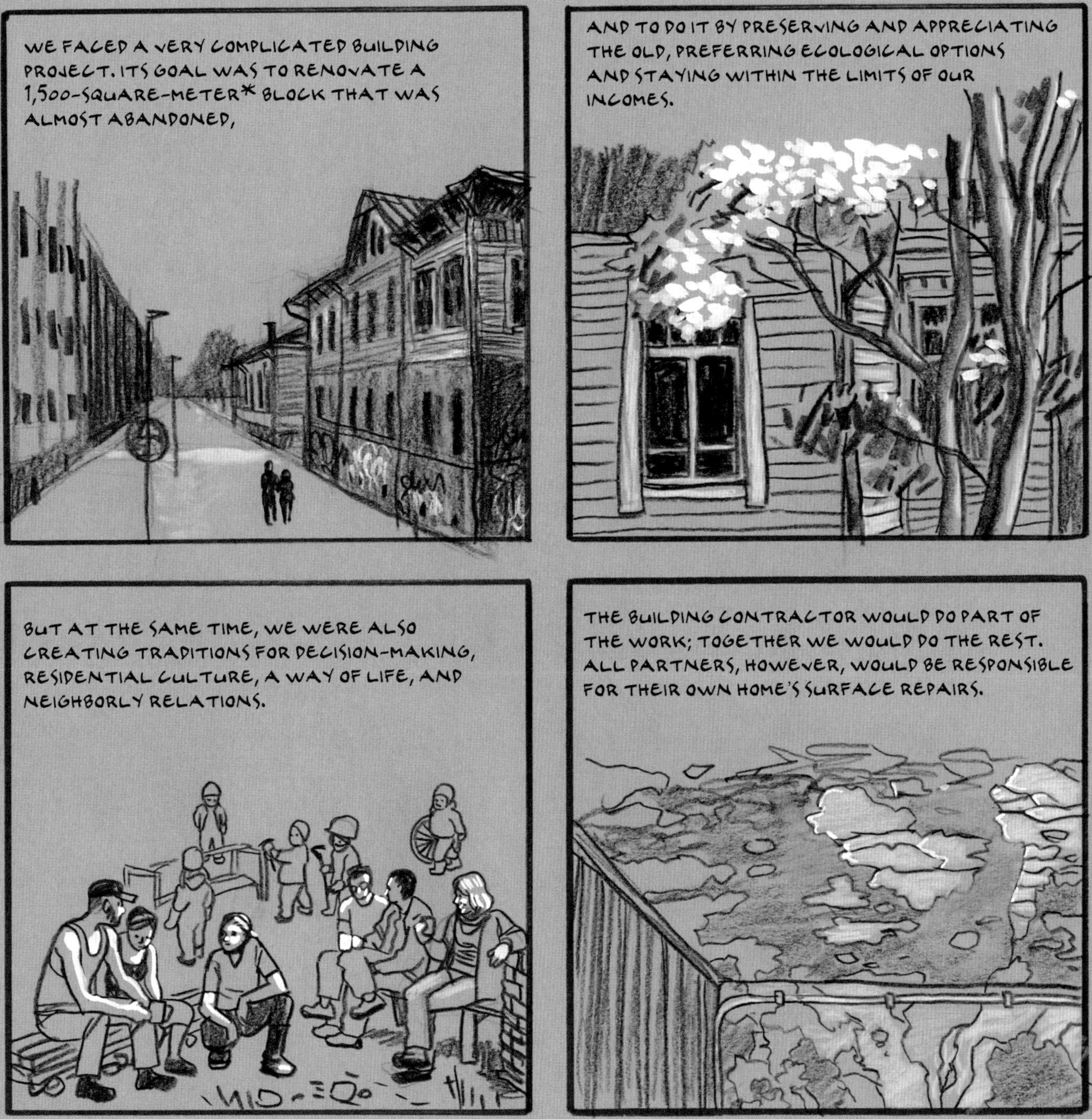
WE FACED A VERY COMPLICATED BUILDING PROJECT. ITS GOAL WAS TO RENOVATE A 1,500-SQUARE-METER* BLOCK THAT WAS ALMOST ABANDONED,
AND TO DO IT BY PRESERVING AND APPRECIATING THE OLD, PREFERRING ECOLOGICAL OPTIONS AND STAYING WITHIN THE LIMITS OF OUR INCOMES.
BUT AT THE SAME TIME, WE WERE ALSO CREATING TRADITIONS FOR DECISION-MAKING, RESIDENTIAL CULTURE, A WAY OF LIFE, AND NEIGHBORLY RELATIONS.
THE BUILDING CONTRACTOR WOULD DO PART OF THE WORK; TOGETHER WE WOULD DO THE REST. ALL PARTNERS, HOWEVER, WOULD BE RESPONSIBLE FOR THEIR OWN HOME'S SURFACE REPAIRS.

*16,000 square feet

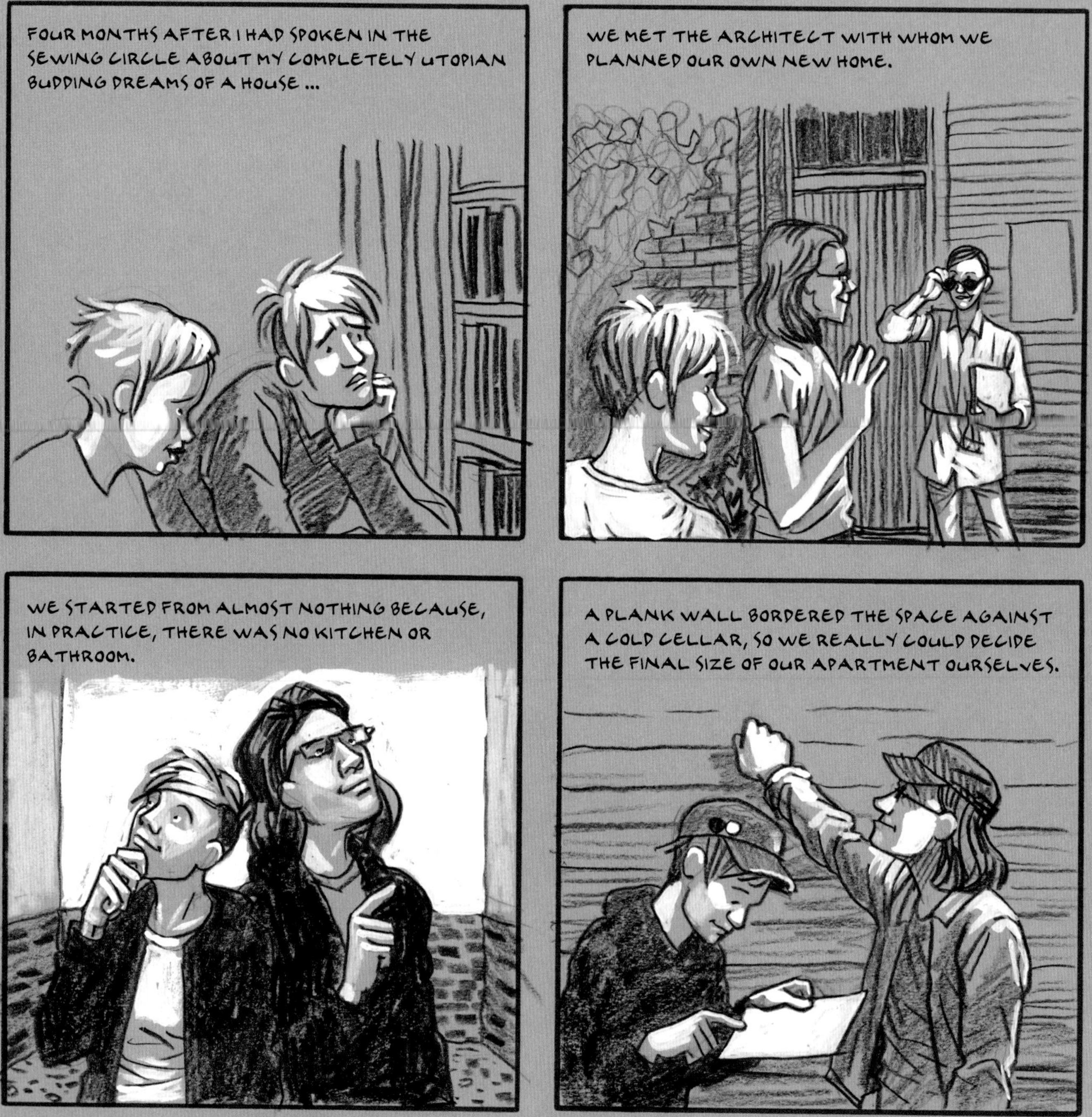
FOUR MONTHS AFTER I HAD SPOKEN IN THE SEWING CIRCLE ABOUT MY COMPLETELY UTOPIAN BUDDING DREAMS OF A HOUSE ...
WE MET THE ARCHITECT WITH WHOM WE PLANNED OUR OWN NEW HOME.
WE STARTED FROM ALMOST NOTHING BECAUSE, IN PRACTICE, THERE WAS NO KITCHEN OR BATHROOM.
A PLANK WALL BORDERED THE SPACE AGAINST A COLD CELLAR, SO WE REALLY COULD DECIDE THE FINAL SIZE OF OUR APARTMENT OURSELVES.

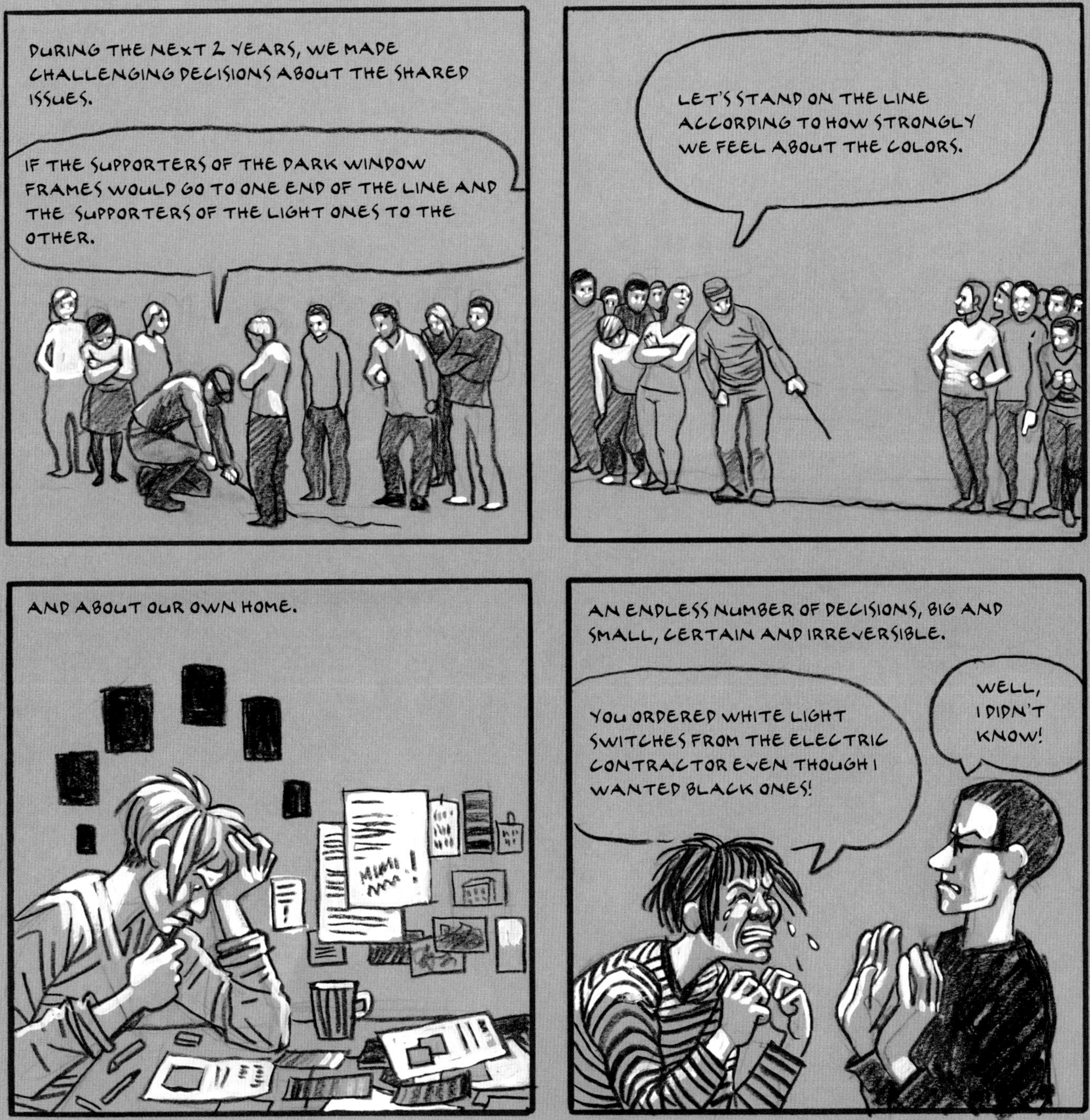
DURING THE NEXT 2 YEARS, WE MADE CHALLENGING DECISIONS ABOUT THE SHARED ISSUES.
IF THE SUPPORTERS OF THE DARK WINDOW FRAMES WOULD GO TO ONE END OF THE LINE AND THE SUPPORTERS OF THE LIGHT ONES TO THE OTHER.
LET'S STAND ON THE LINE ACCORDING TO HOW STRONGLY WE FEEL ABOUT THE COLORS.
AND ABOUT OUR OWN HOME.
AN ENDLESS NUMBER OF DECISIONS, BIG AND SMALL, CERTAIN AND IRREVERSIBLE.
YOU ORDERED WHITE LIGHT SWITCHES FROM THE ELECTRIC CONTRACTOR EVEN THOUGH I WANTED BLACK ONES!
WELL, I DIDN'T KNOW!

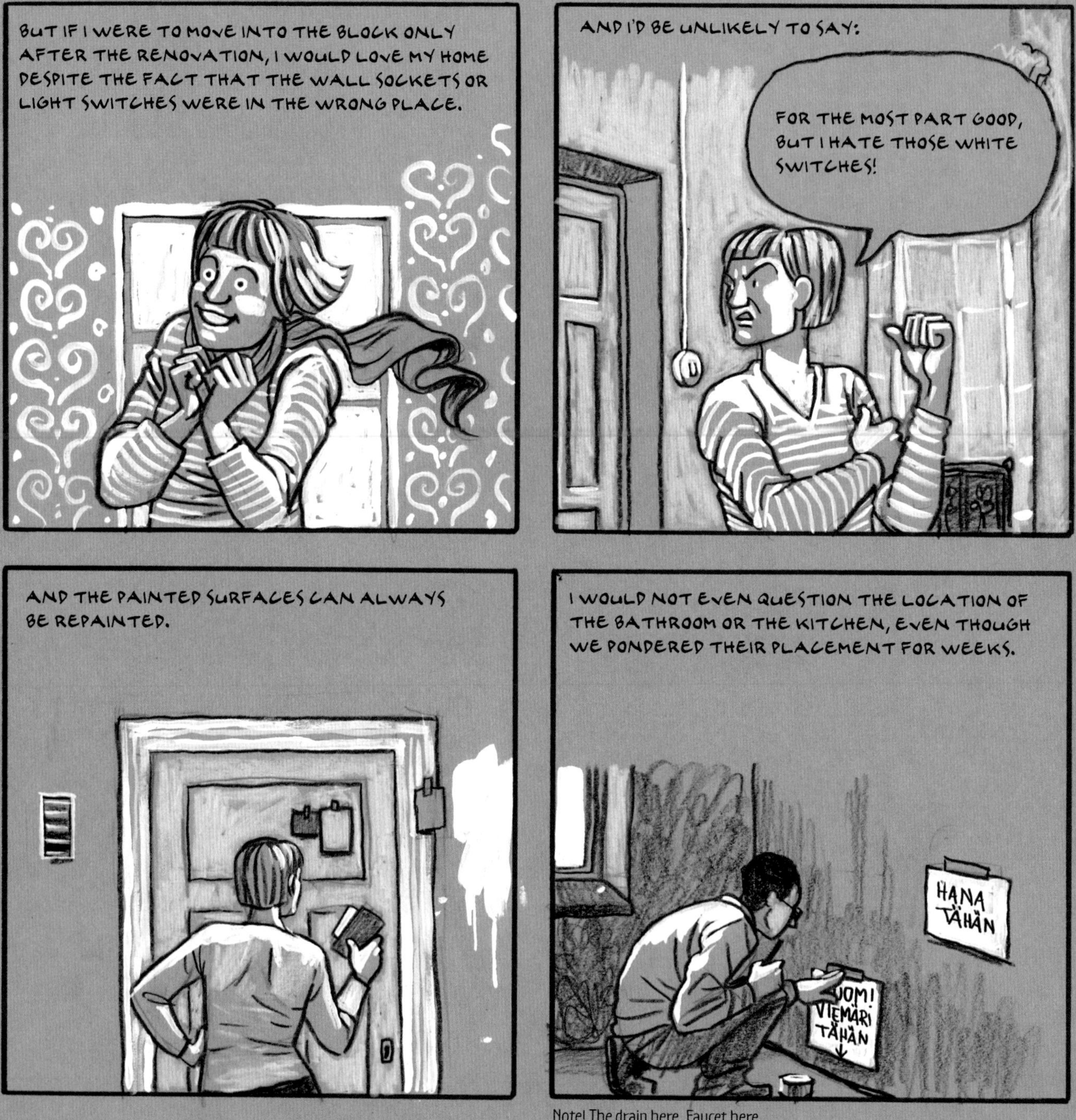
BUT IF I WERE TO MOVE INTO THE BLOCK ONLY AFTER THE RENOVATION, I WOULD LOVE MY HOME DESPITE THE FACT THAT THE WALL SOCKETS OR LIGHT SWITCHES WERE IN THE WRONG PLACE.
AND I'D BE UNLIKELY TO SAY:
FOR THE MOST PART GOOD, BUT I HATE THOSE WHITE SWITCHES!
AND THE PAINTED SURFACES CAN ALWAYS BE REPAINTED.
I WOULD NOT EVEN QUESTION THE LOCATION OF THE BATHROOM OR THE KITCHEN, EVEN THOUGH WE PONDERED THEIR PLACEMENT FOR WEEKS.
HANA TÄHÄN
UOM! VIEMÄRI TÄHÄN

Note! The drain here. Faucet here

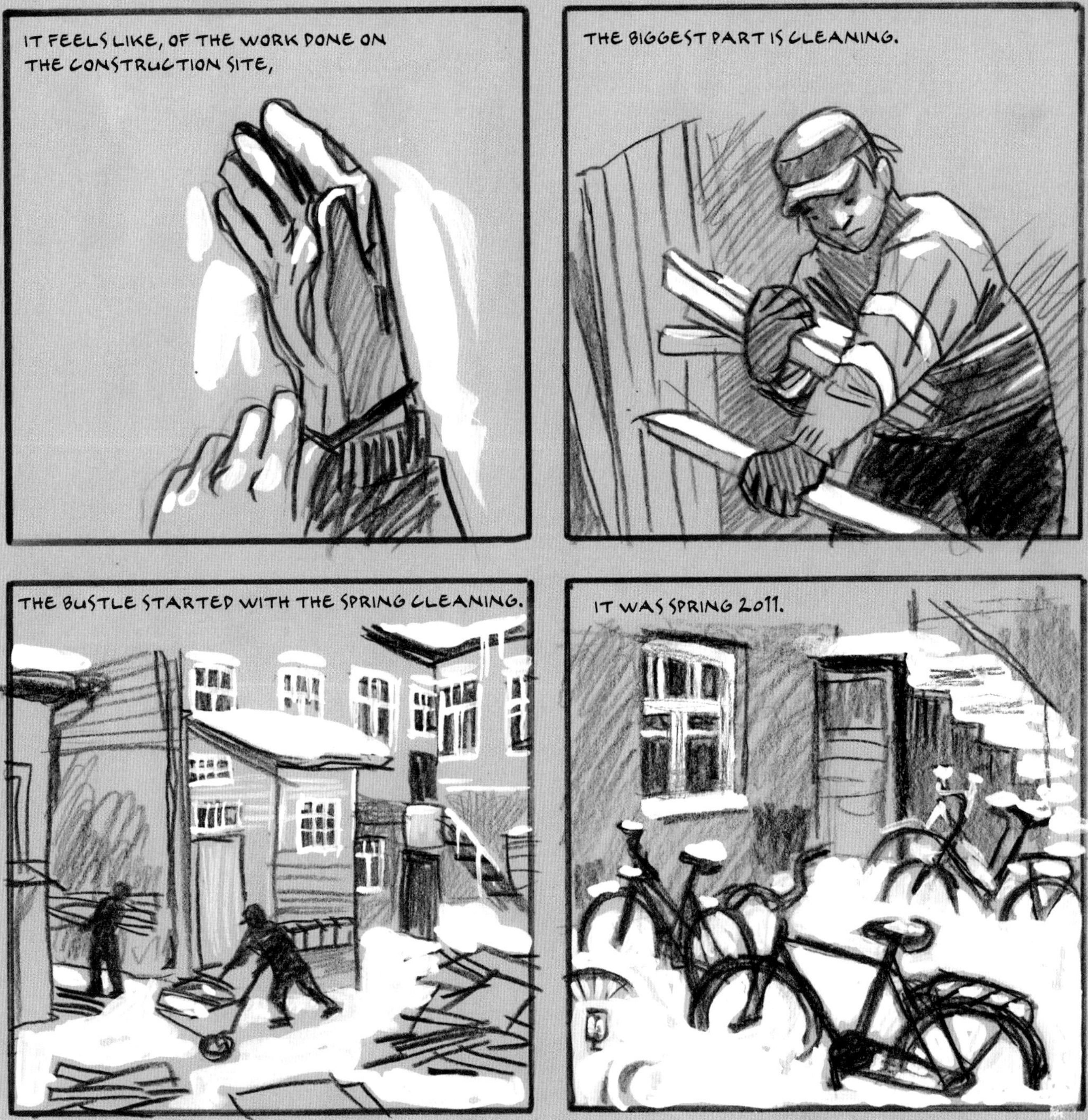
IT FEELS LIKE, OF THE WORK DONE ON THE CONSTRUCTION SITE,
THE BIGGEST PART IS CLEANING.
THE BUSTLE STARTED WITH THE SPRING CLEANING.
IT WAS SPRING 2011.

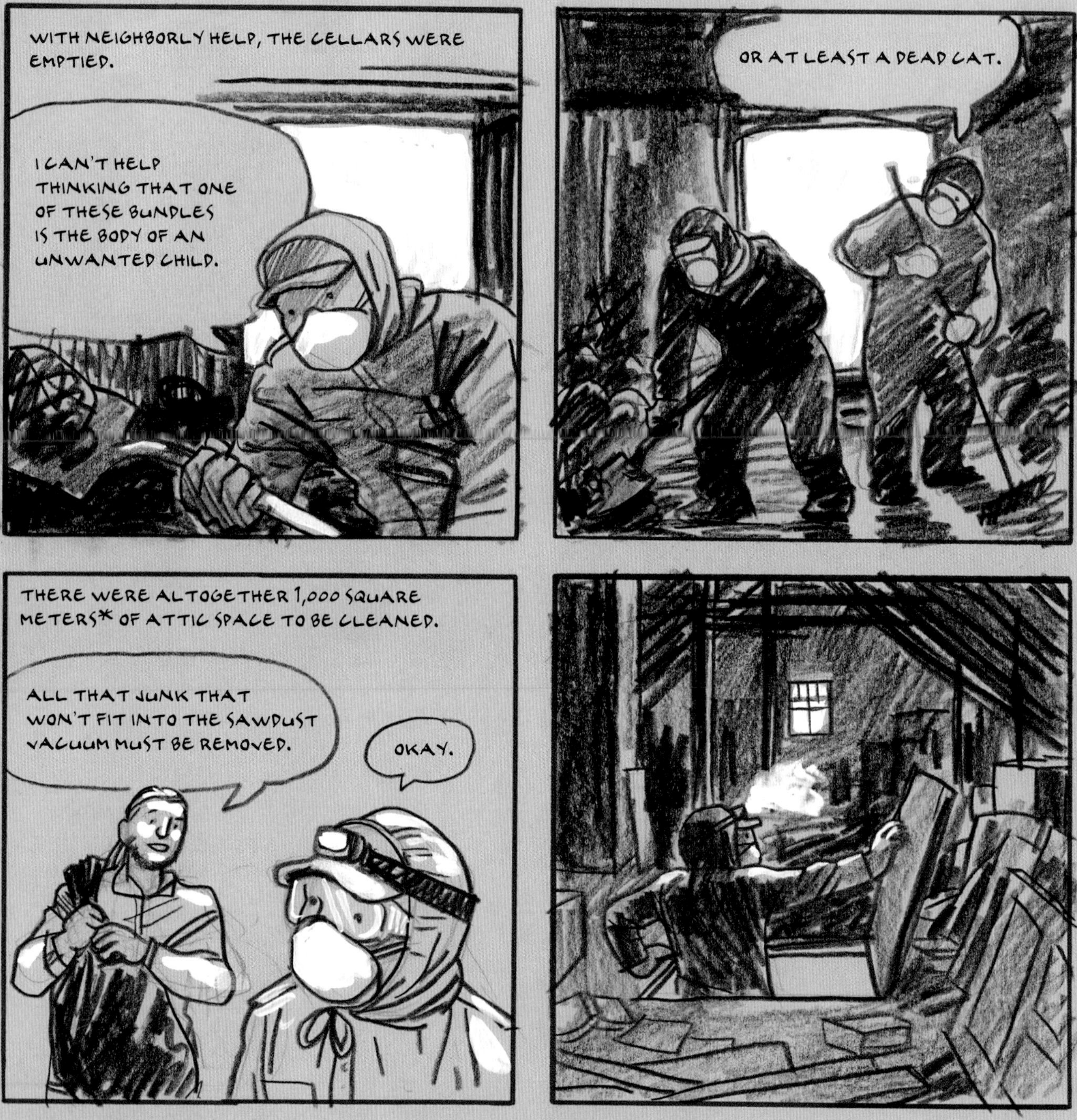
WITH NEIGHBORLY HELP, THE CELLARS WERE EMPTIED.
I CAN'T HELP THINKING THAT ONE OF THESE BUNDLES IS THE BODY OF AN UNWANTED CHILD.
OR AT LEAST A DEAD CAT.
THERE WERE ALTOGETHER 1,000 SQUARE METERS* OF ATTIC SPACE TO BE CLEANED.
ALL THAT JUNK THAT WON'T FIT INTO THE SAWDUST VACUUM MUST BE REMOVED.
OKAY.

*over 10,000 square feet

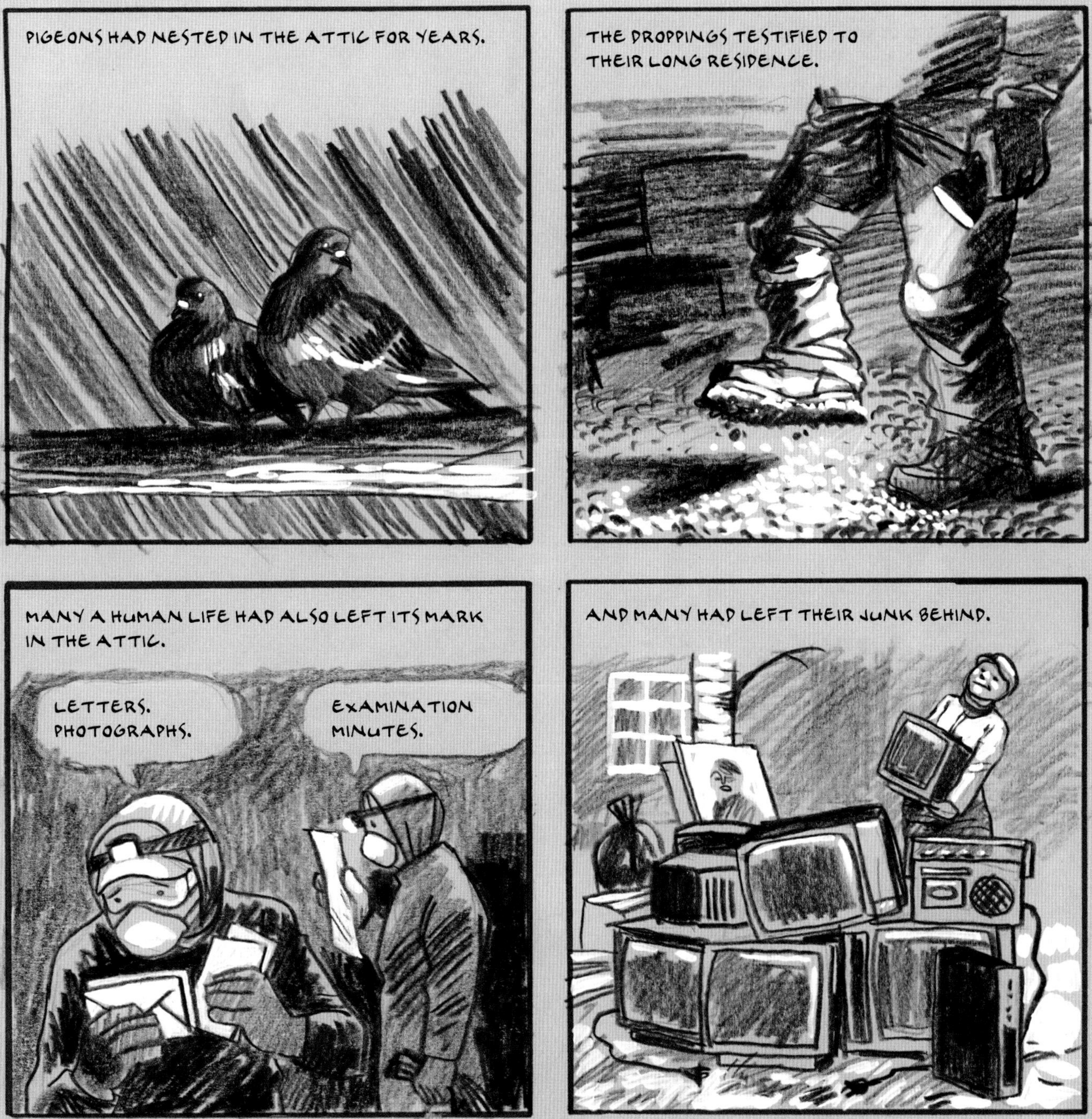
PIGEONS HAD NESTED IN THE ATTIC FOR YEARS.
THE DROPPINGS TESTIFIED TO THEIR LONG RESIDENCE.
MANY A HUMAN LIFE HAD ALSO LEFT ITS MARK IN THE ATTIC.
LETTERS. PHOTOGRAPHS.
EXAMINATION MINUTES.
AND MANY HAD LEFT THEIR JUNK BEHIND.

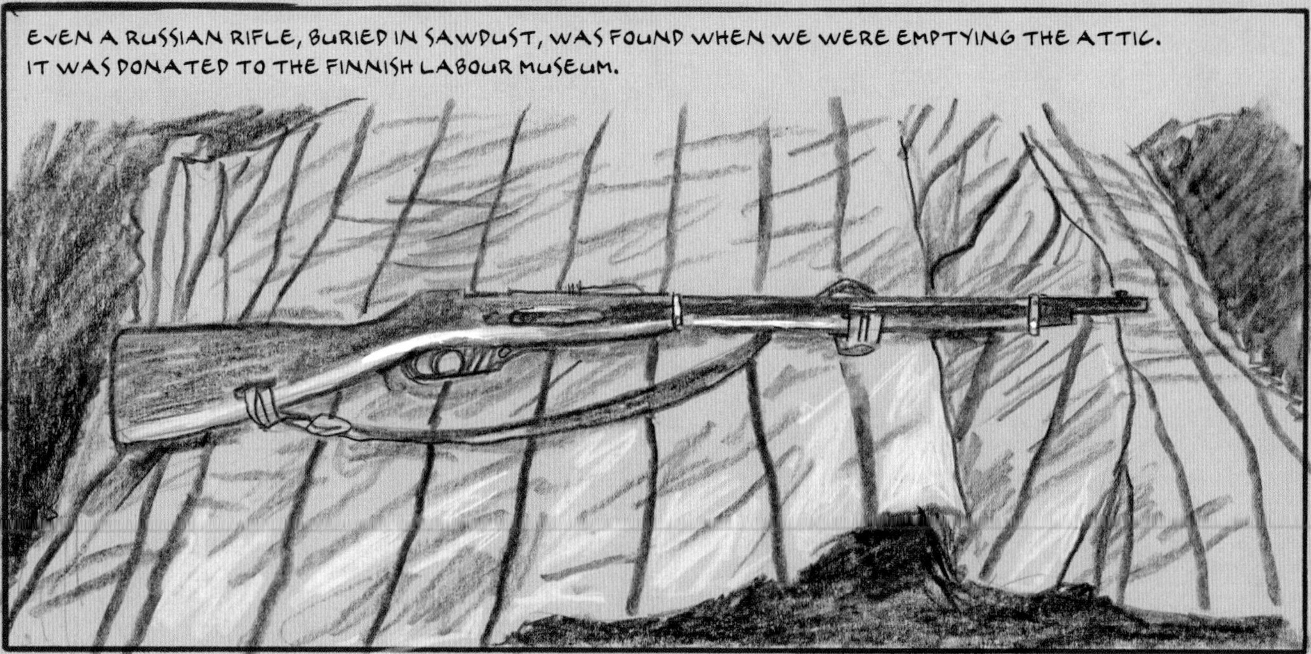
EVEN A RUSSIAN RIFLE, BURIED IN SAWDUST, WAS FOUND WHEN WE WERE EMPTYING THE ATTIC. IT WAS DONATED TO THE FINNISH LABOUR MUSEUM.

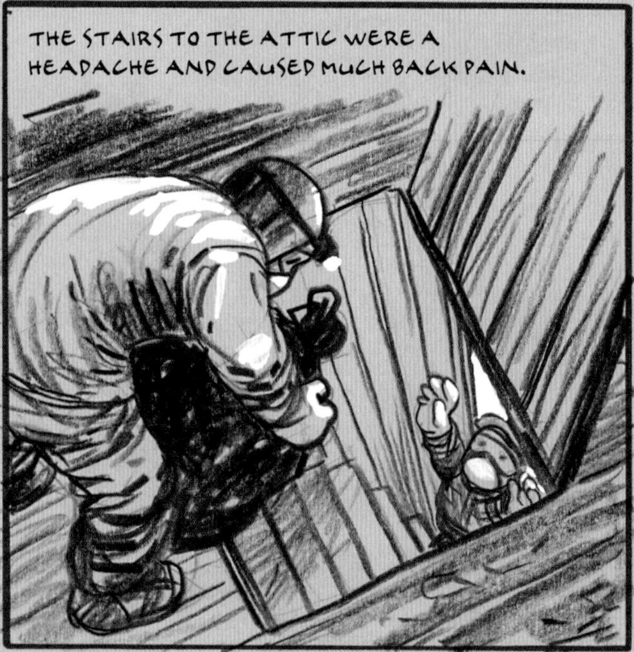
THE STAIRS TO THE ATTIC WERE A HEADACHE AND CAUSED MUCH BACK PAIN.

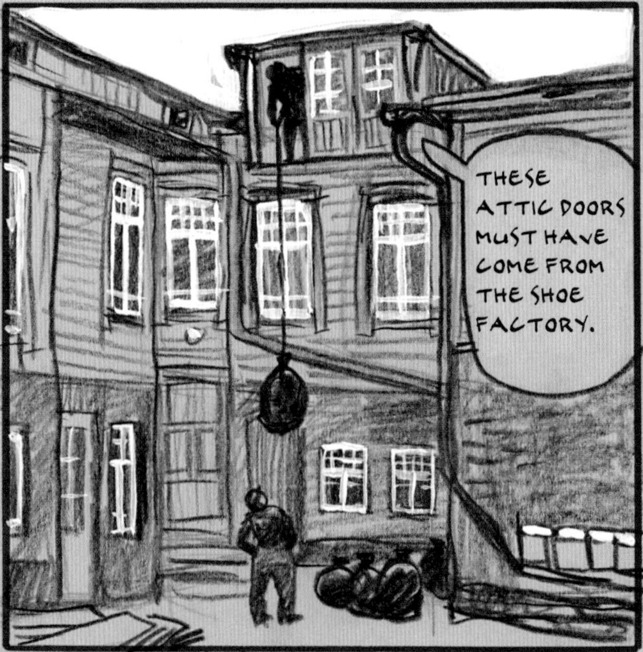
THESE ATTIC DOORS MUST HAVE COME FROM THE SHOE FACTORY.

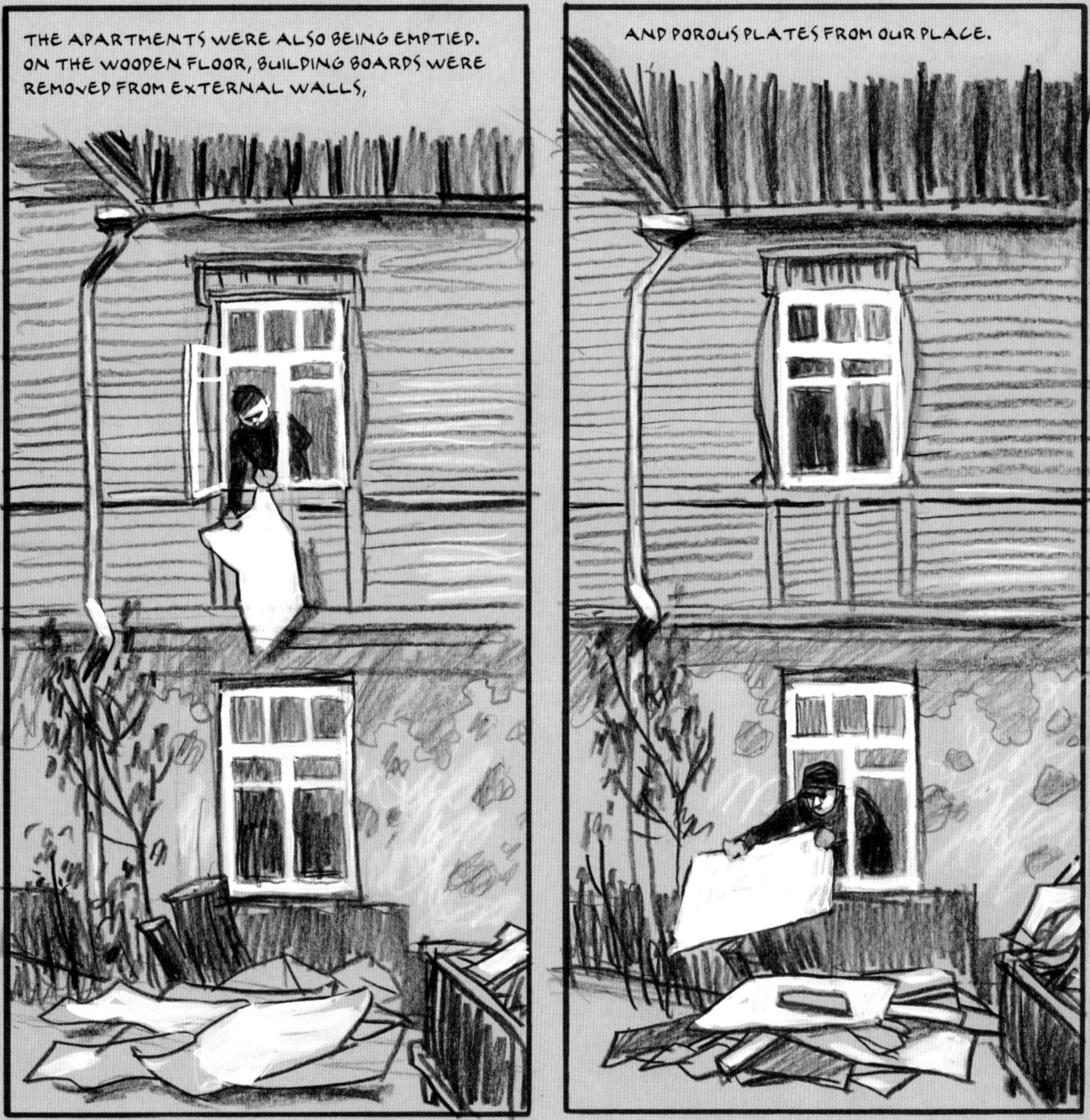
THE APARTMENTS WERE ALSO BEING EMPTIED. ON THE WOODEN FLOOR, BUILDING BOARDS WERE REMOVED FROM EXTERNAL WALLS,
AND POROUS PLATES FROM OUR PLACE.

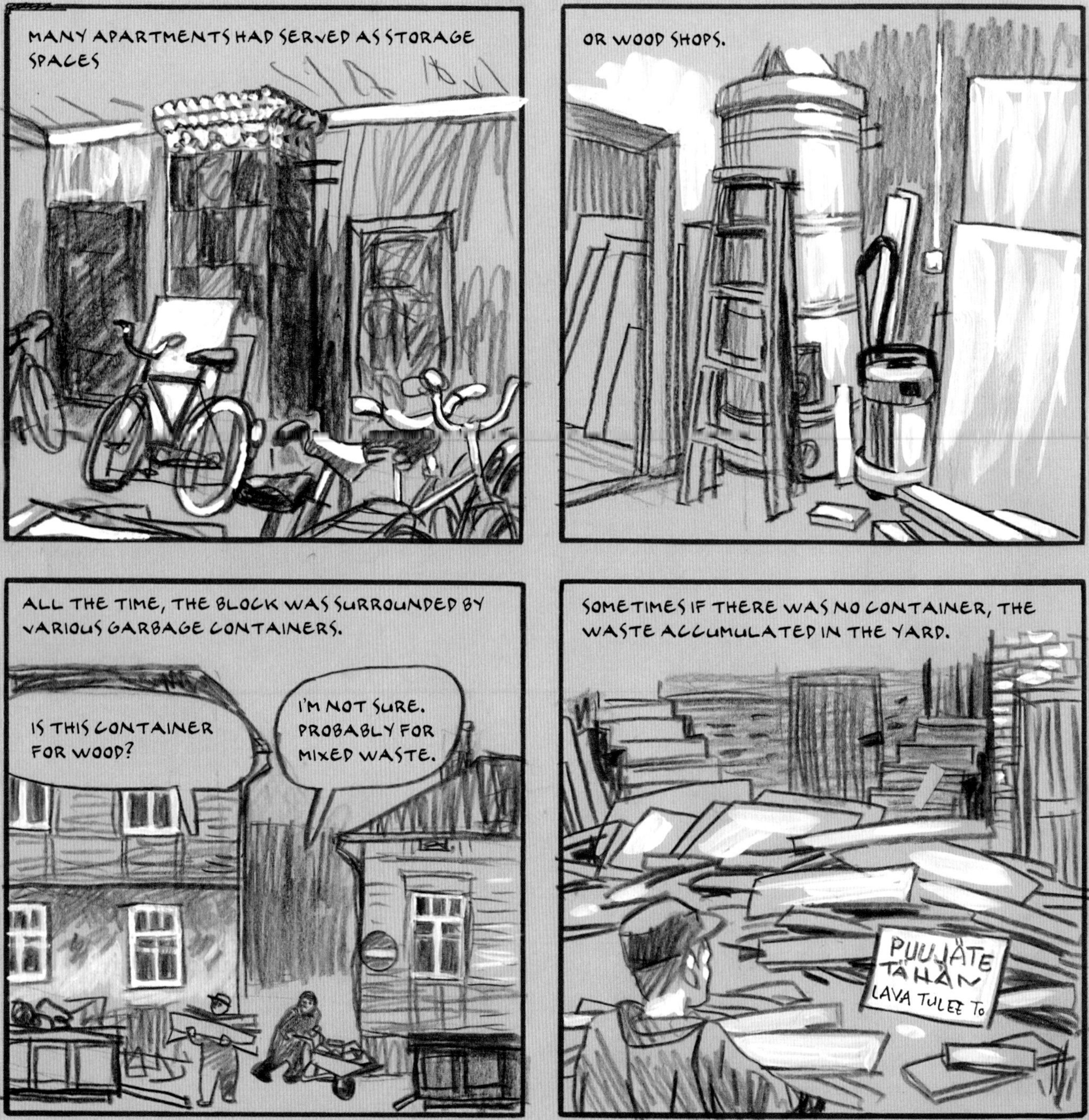
MANY APARTMENTS HAD SERVED AS STORAGE SPACES
OR WOOD SHOPS.
ALL THE TIME, THE BLOCK WAS SURROUNDED BY VARIOUS GARBAGE CONTAINERS.
IS THIS CONTAINER FOR WOOD?
I'M NOT SURE. PROBABLY FOR MIXED WASTE.
SOMETIMES IF THERE WAS NO CONTAINER, THE WASTE ACCUMULATED IN THE YARD.
PUUJÄTE TÄHÄN
LAVA TULEE To

Sign reads: Wood waste here. Platform arrives on Thursday.

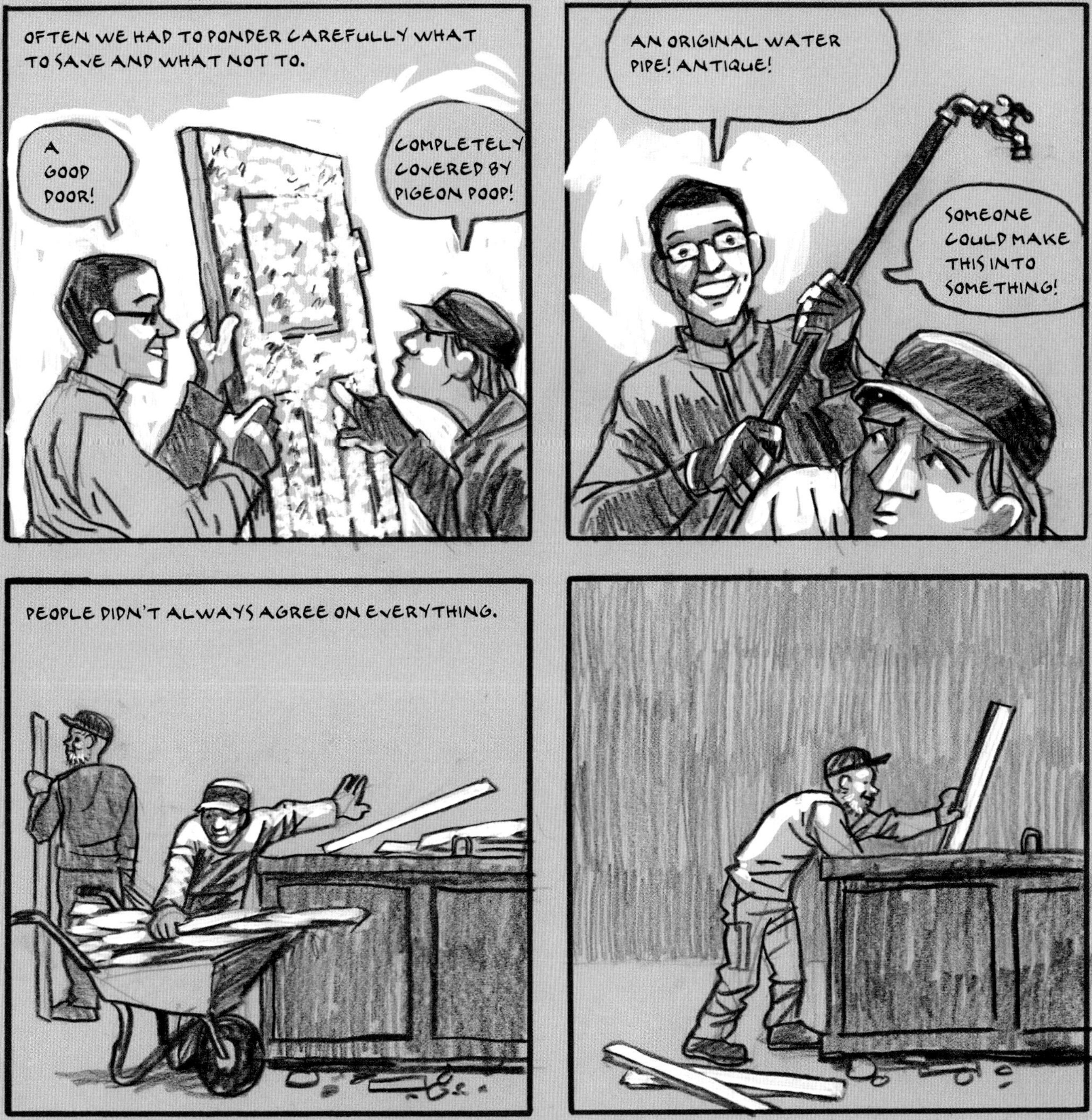
OFTEN WE HAD TO PONDER CAREFULLY WHAT TO SAVE AND WHAT NOT TO.
A GOOD DOOR!
COMPLETELY COVERED BY PIGEON POOP!
AN ORIGINAL WATER PIPE! ANTIQUE!
SOMEONE COULD MAKE THIS INTO SOMETHING!
PEOPLE DIDN'T ALWAYS AGREE ON EVERYTHING.

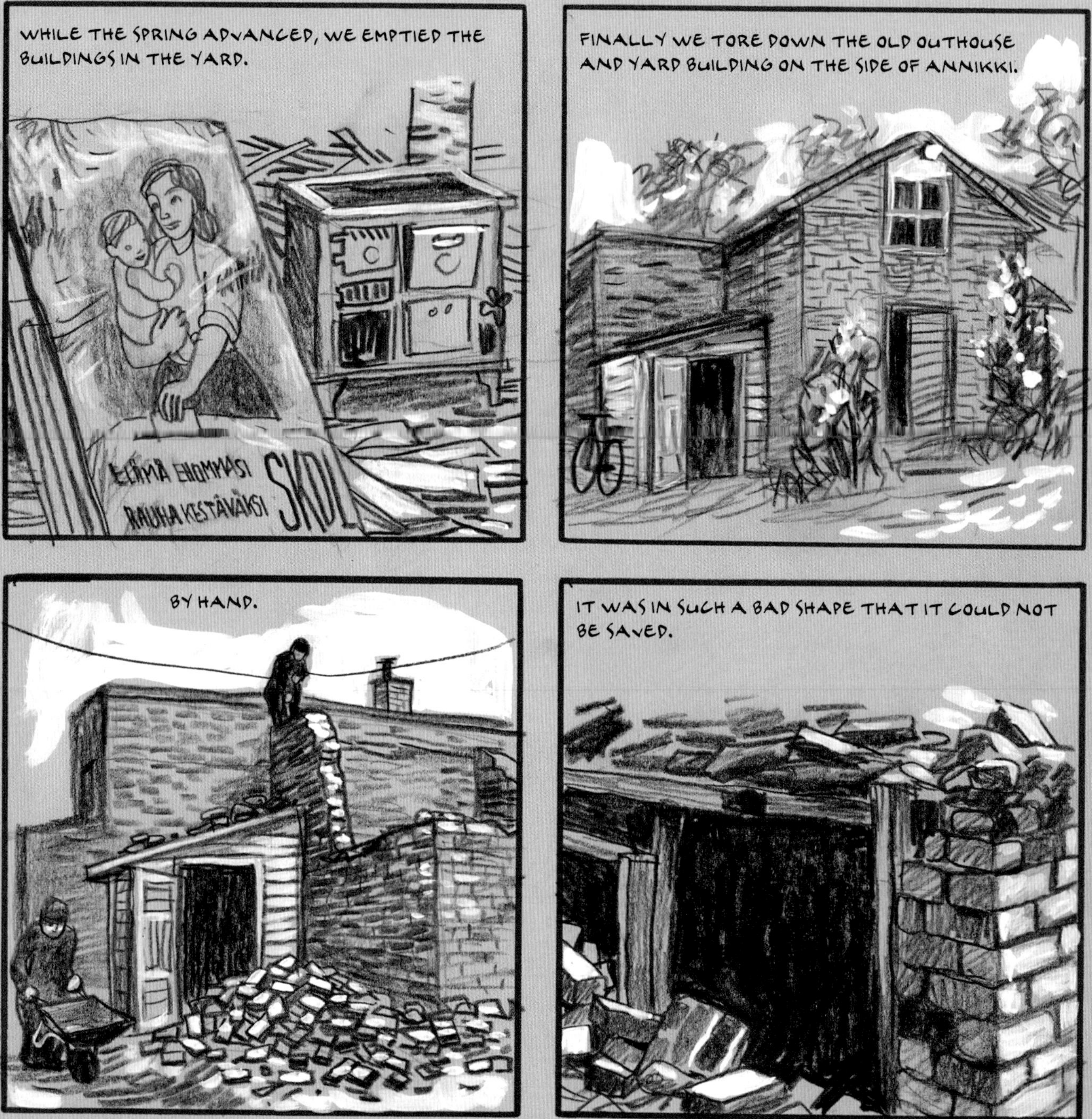
WHILE THE SPRING ADVANCED, WE EMPTIED THE BUILDINGS IN THE YARD.
ELÄMÄ EHOMMASI
RAUHA KESTÄVÄKSI
SKDL
FINALLY WE TORE DOWN THE OLD OUTHOUSE AND YARD BUILDING ON THE SIDE OF ANNIKKI.
BY HAND.
IT WAS IN SUCH A BAD SHAPE THAT IT COULD NOT BE SAVED.

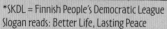

*SKDL = Finnish People's Democratic League
Slogan reads: Better Life, Lasting Peace

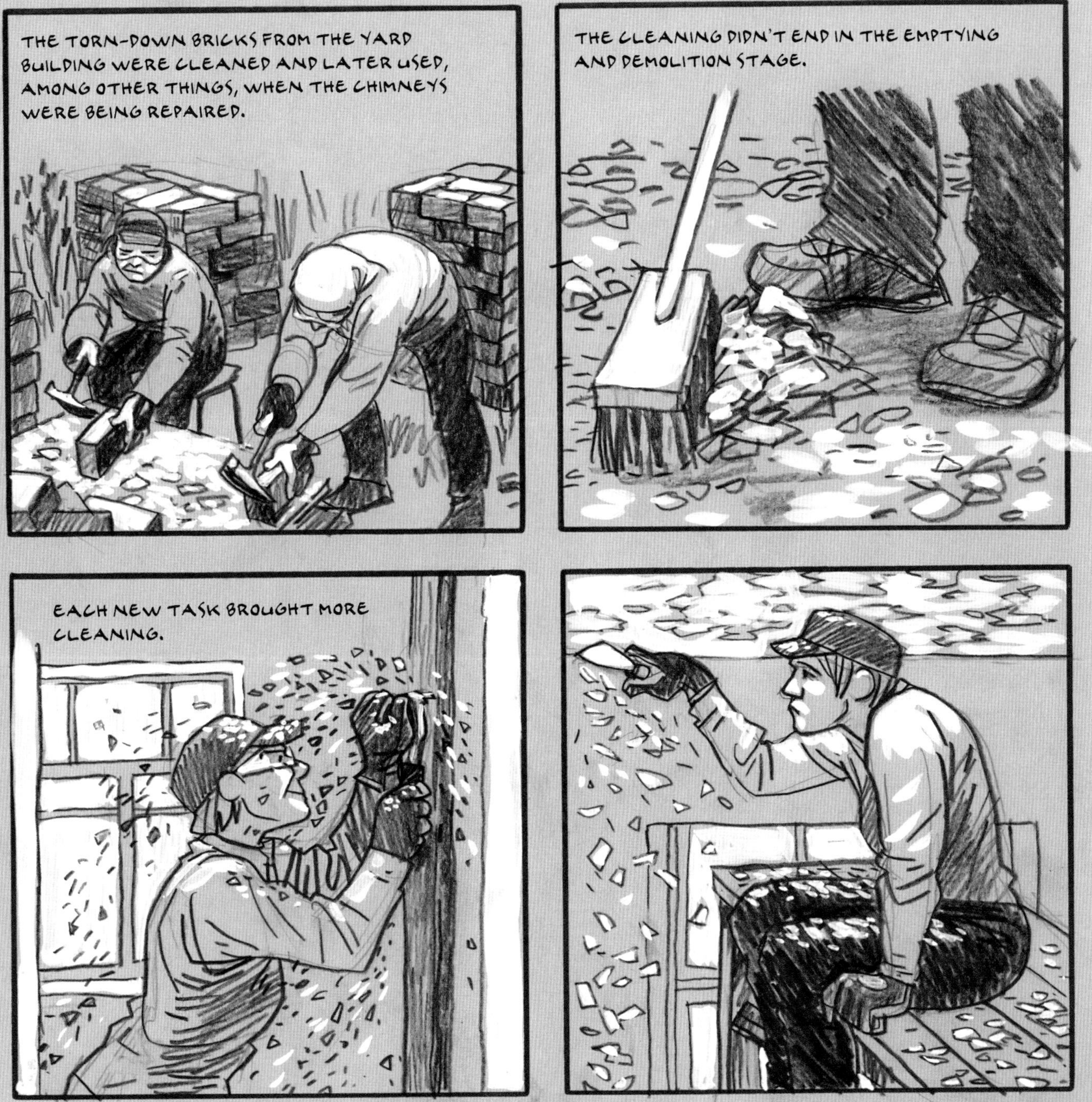
THE TORN-DOWN BRICKS FROM THE YARD BUILDING WERE CLEANED AND LATER USED, AMONG OTHER THINGS, WHEN THE CHIMNEYS WERE BEING REPAIRED.
THE CLEANING DIDN'T END IN THE EMPTYING AND DEMOLITION STAGE.
EACH NEW TASK BROUGHT MORE CLEANING.

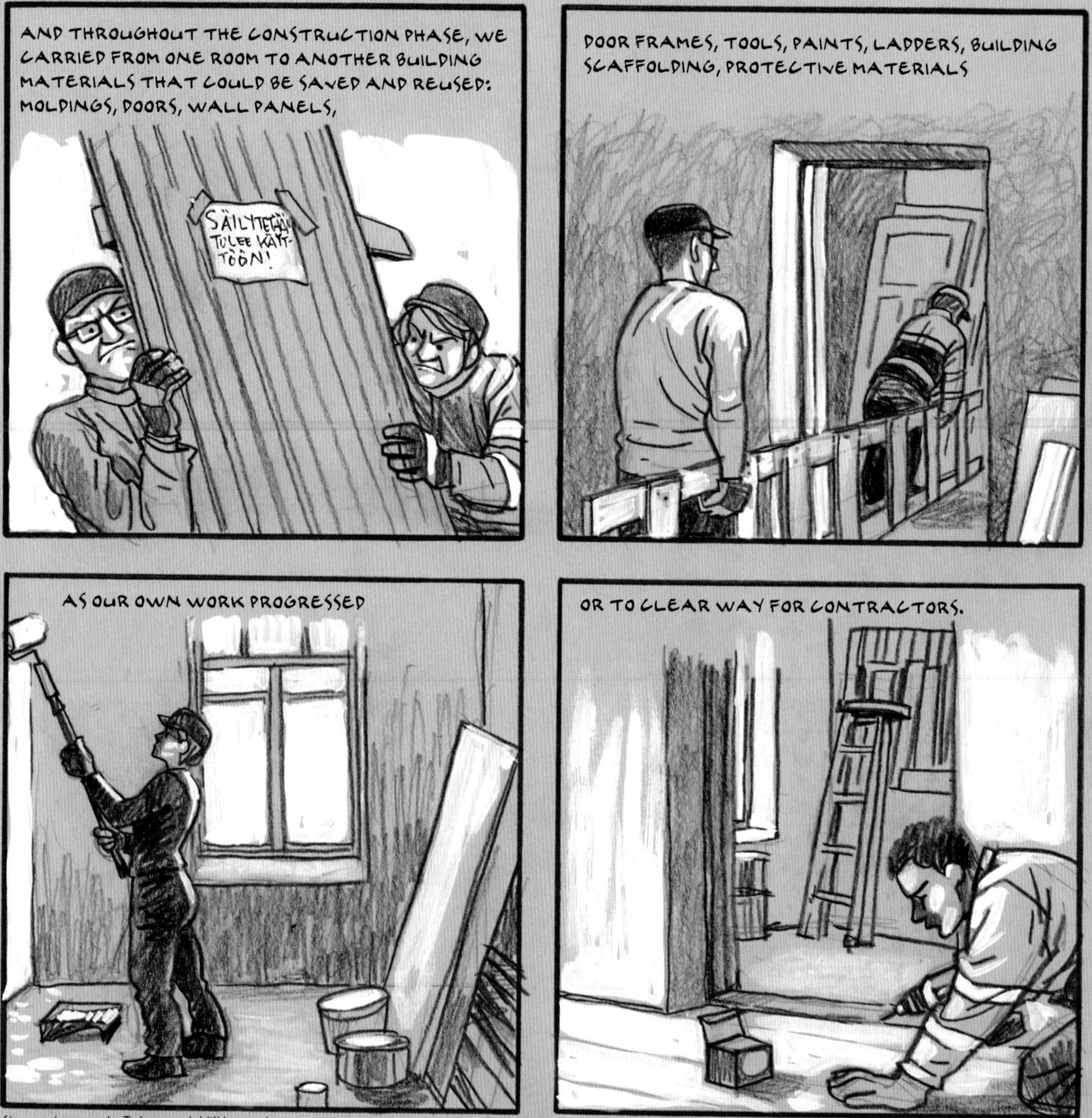
AND THROUGHOUT THE CONSTRUCTION PHASE, WE CARRIED FROM ONE ROOM TO ANOTHER BUILDING MATERIALS THAT COULD BE SAVED AND REUSED: MOLDINGS, DOORS, WALL PANELS,
SÄILYTETÄÄN TULEE KÄYT-TÖÖN!
DOOR FRAMES, TOOLS, PAINTS, LADDERS, BUILDING SCAFFOLDING, PROTECTIVE MATERIALS
AS OUR OWN WORK PROGRESSED
OR TO CLEAR WAY FOR CONTRACTORS.
Sign on door reads: To be saved. Will be used.

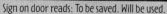

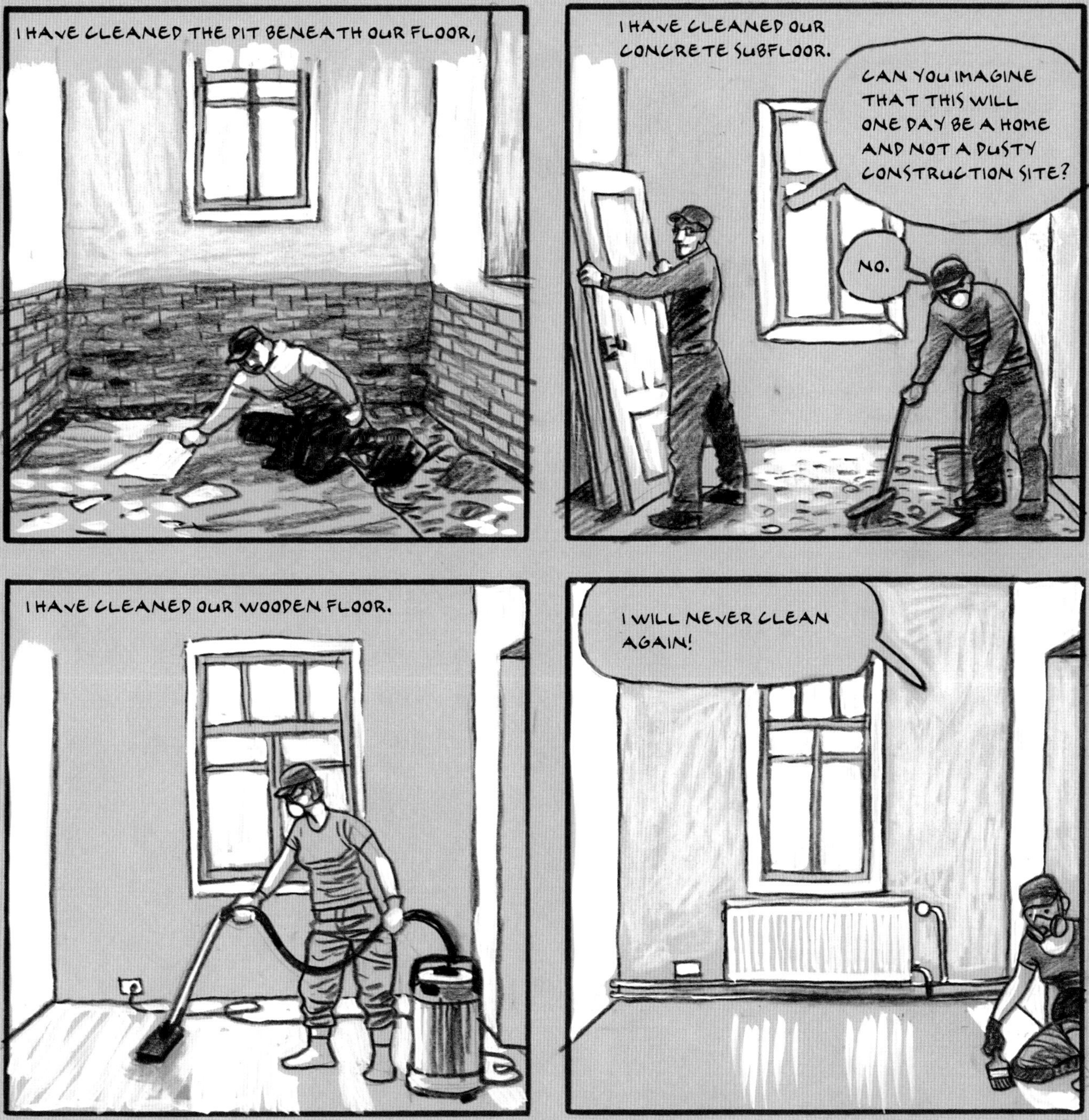
I HAVE CLEANED THE PIT BENEATH OUR FLOOR,
I HAVE CLEANED OUR CONCRETE SUBFLOOR.
CAN YOU IMAGINE THAT THIS WILL ONE DAY BE A HOME AND NOT A DUSTY CONSTRUCTION SITE?
NO.
I HAVE CLEANED OUR WOODEN FLOOR.
I WILL NEVER CLEAN AGAIN!

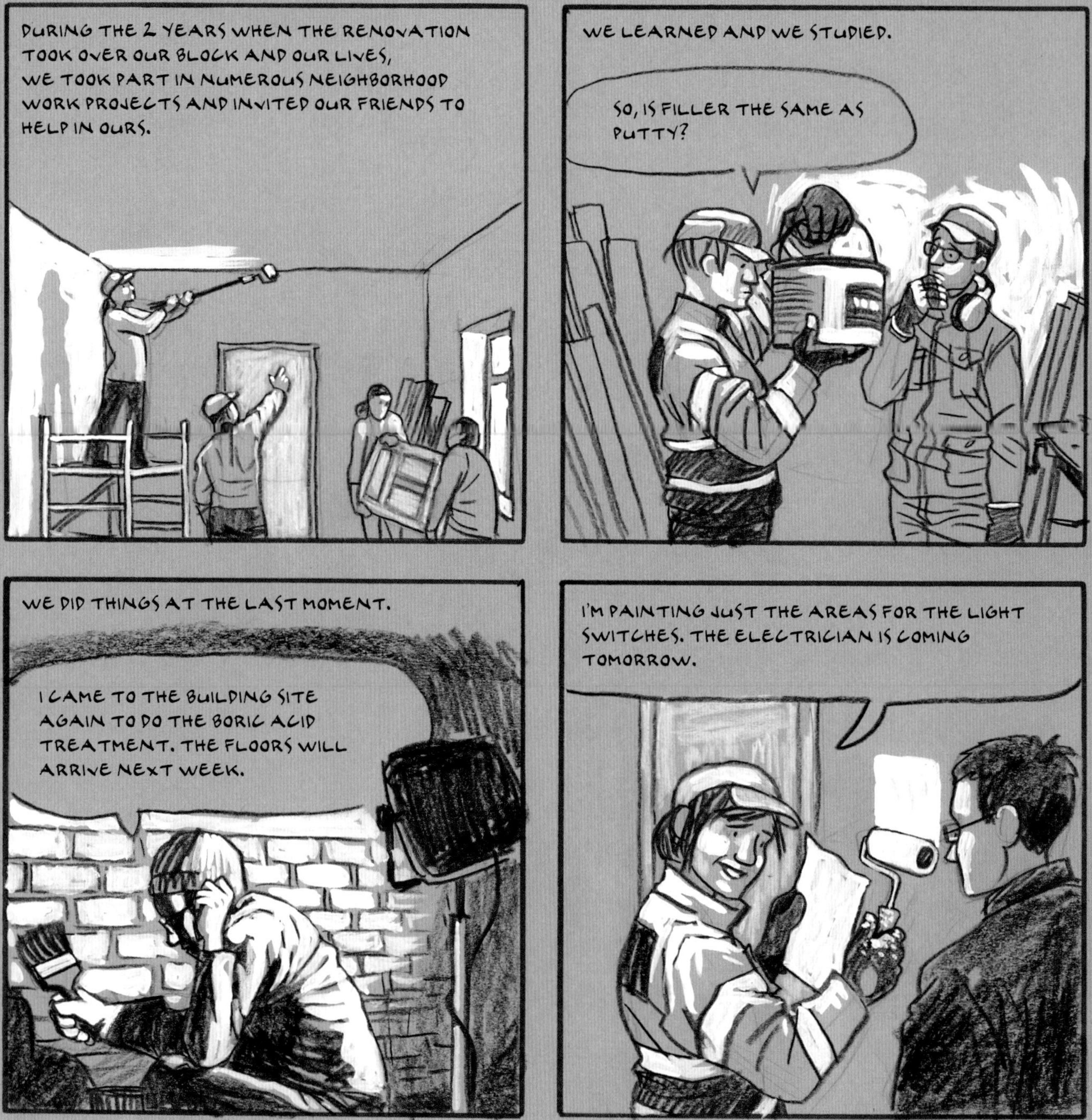
DURING THE 2 YEARS WHEN THE RENOVATION TOOK OVER OUR BLOCK AND OUR LIVES, WE TOOK PART IN NUMEROUS NEIGHBORHOOD WORK PROJECTS AND INVITED OUR FRIENDS TO HELP IN OURS.
WE LEARNED AND WE STUDIED.
SO, IS FILLER THE SAME AS PUTTY?
WE DID THINGS AT THE LAST MOMENT.
I CAME TO THE BUILDING SITE AGAIN TO DO THE BORIC ACID TREATMENT. THE FLOORS WILL ARRIVE NEXT WEEK.
I'M PAINTING JUST THE AREAS FOR THE LIGHT SWITCHES. THE ELECTRICIAN IS COMING TOMORROW.

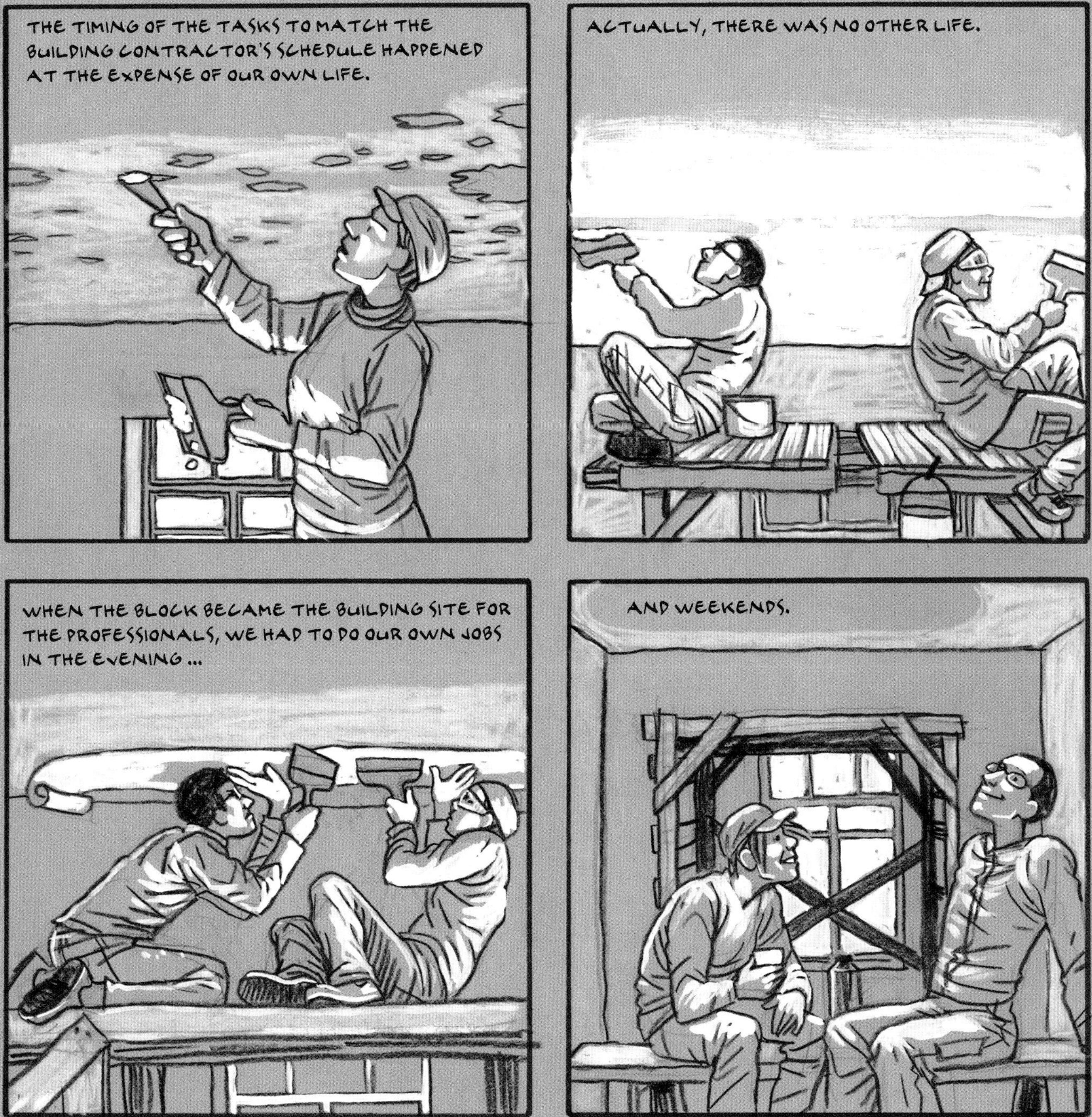
THE TIMING OF THE TASKS TO MATCH THE BUILDING CONTRACTOR'S SCHEDULE HAPPENED AT THE EXPENSE OF OUR OWN LIFE.
ACTUALLY, THERE WAS NO OTHER LIFE.
WHEN THE BLOCK BECAME THE BUILDING SITE FOR THE PROFESSIONALS, WE HAD TO DO OUR OWN JOBS IN THE EVENING ...
AND WEEKENDS.

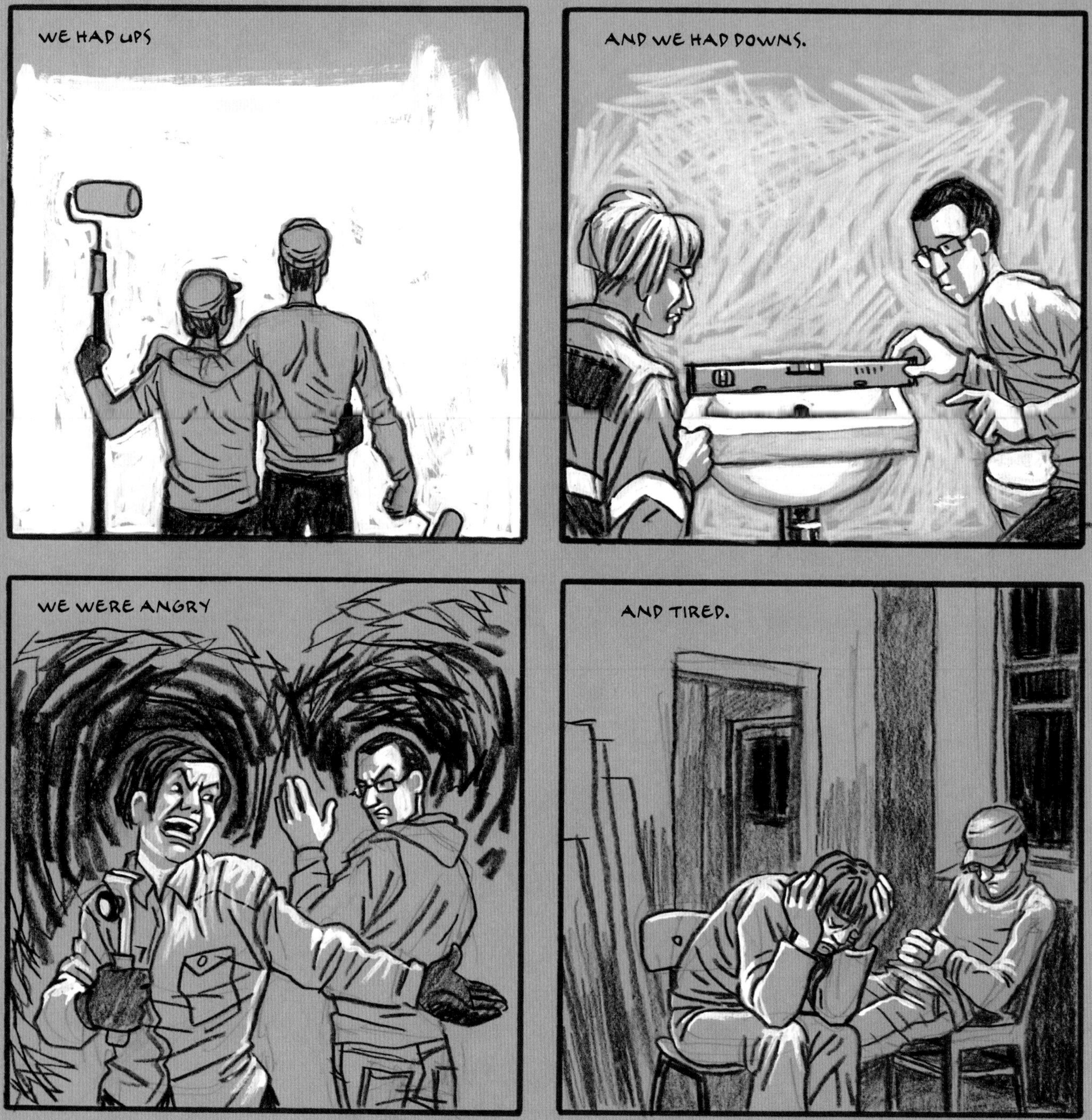
WE HAD UPS
AND WE HAD DOWNS.
WE WERE ANGRY
AND TIRED.

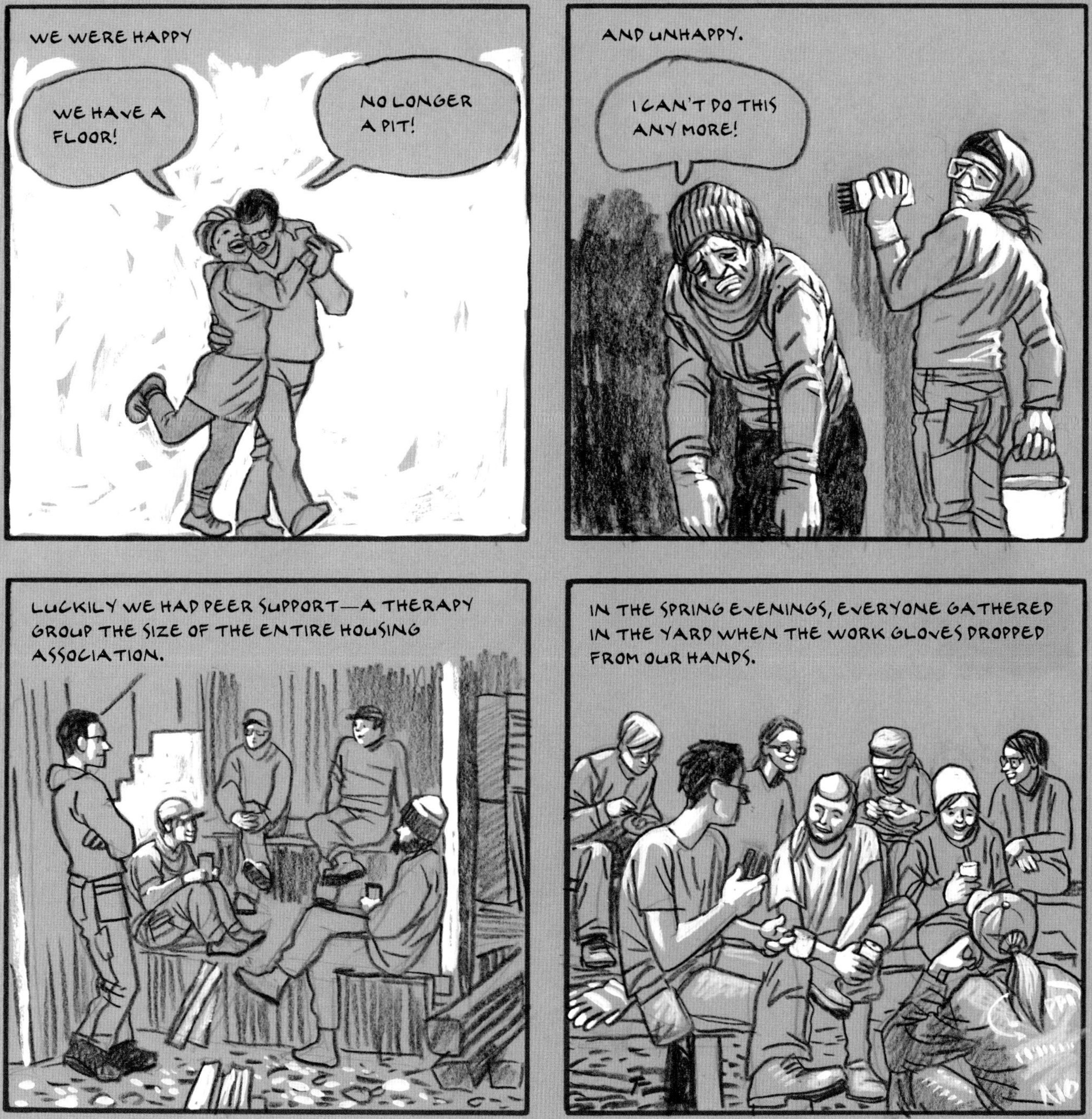
WE WERE HAPPY
WE HAVE A FLOOR!
NO LONGER A PIT!
AND UNHAPPY.
I CAN'T DO THIS ANY MORE!
LUCKILY WE HAD PEER SUPPORT—A THERAPY GROUP THE SIZE OF THE ENTIRE HOUSING ASSOCIATION.
IN THE SPRING EVENINGS, EVERYONE GATHERED IN THE YARD WHEN THE WORK GLOVES DROPPED FROM OUR HANDS.

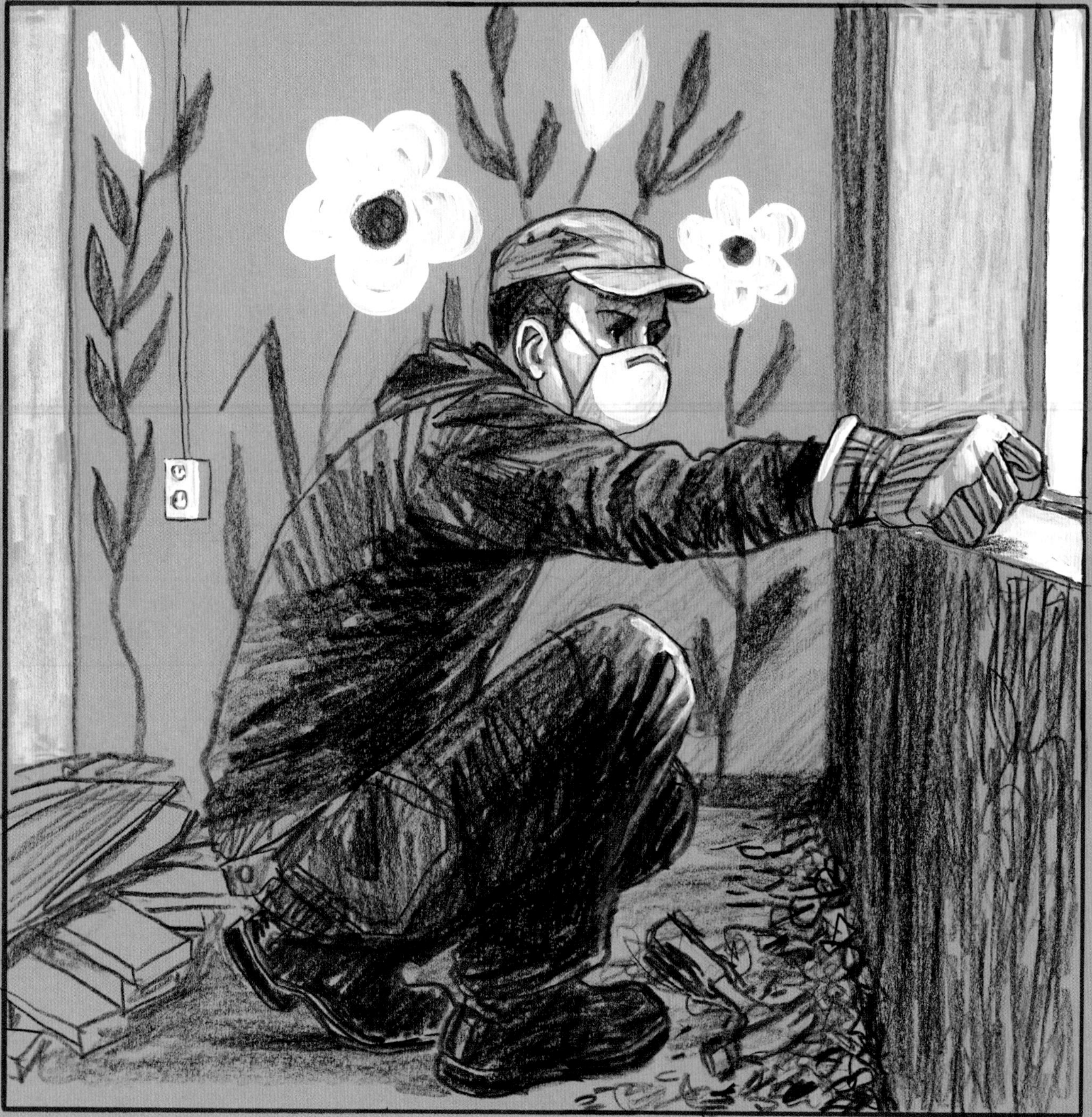
The bicycle shop wall paintings in the future living room.

HOME

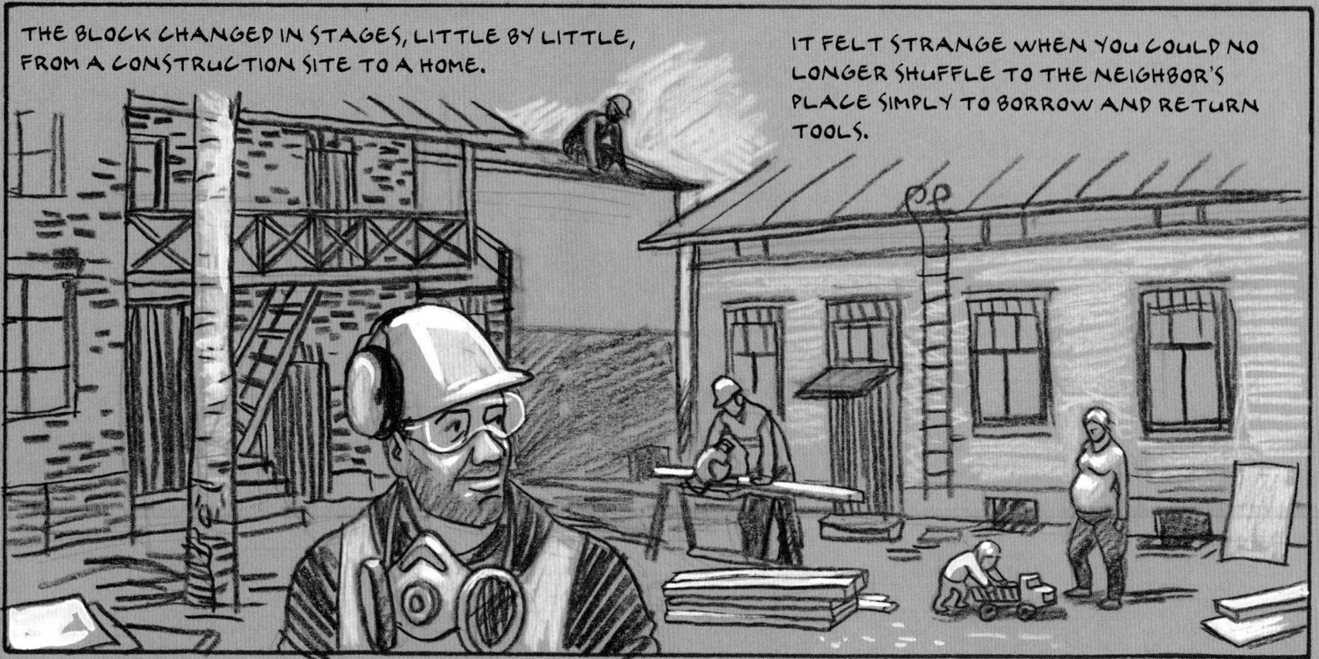
THE BLOCK CHANGED IN STAGES, LITTLE BY LITTLE, FROM A CONSTRUCTION SITE TO A HOME.
IT FELT STRANGE WHEN YOU COULD NO LONGER SHUFFLE TO THE NEIGHBOR'S PLACE SIMPLY TO BORROW AND RETURN TOOLS.

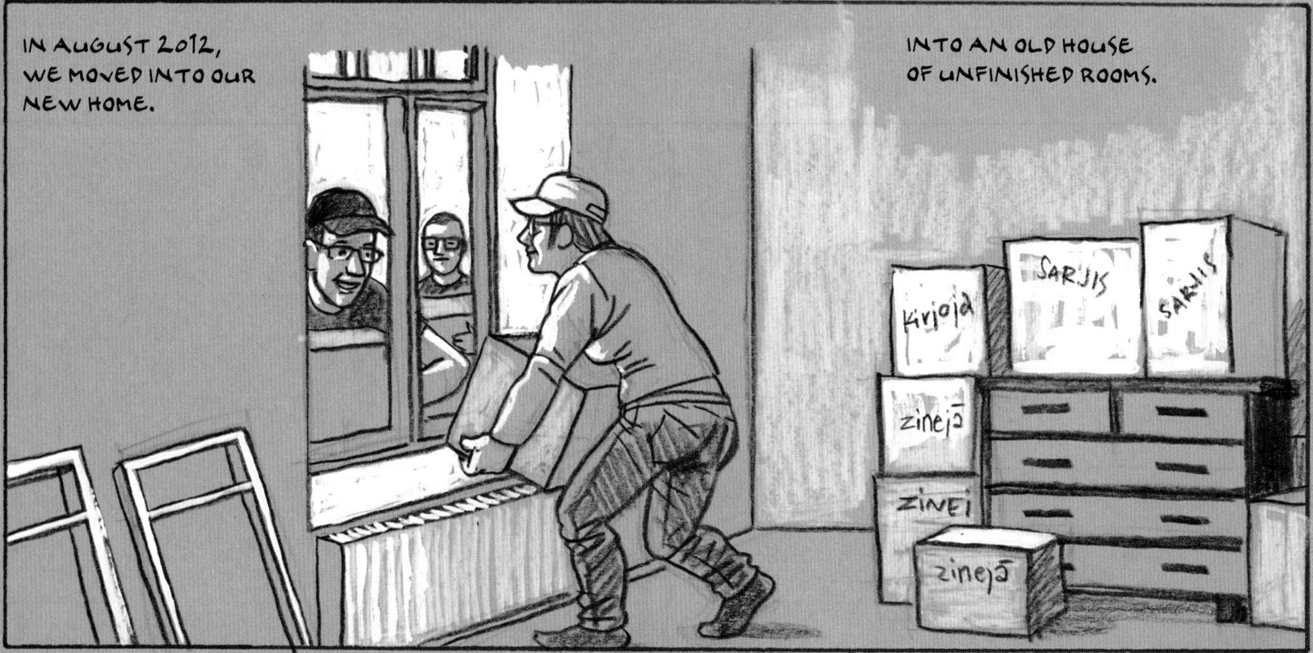
IN AUGUST 2012, WE MOVED INTO OUR NEW HOME.
INTO AN OLD HOUSE OF UNFINISHED ROOMS.
kirjoja
SARJIS
SARJIS
zinejā
ZINEI
zinejā

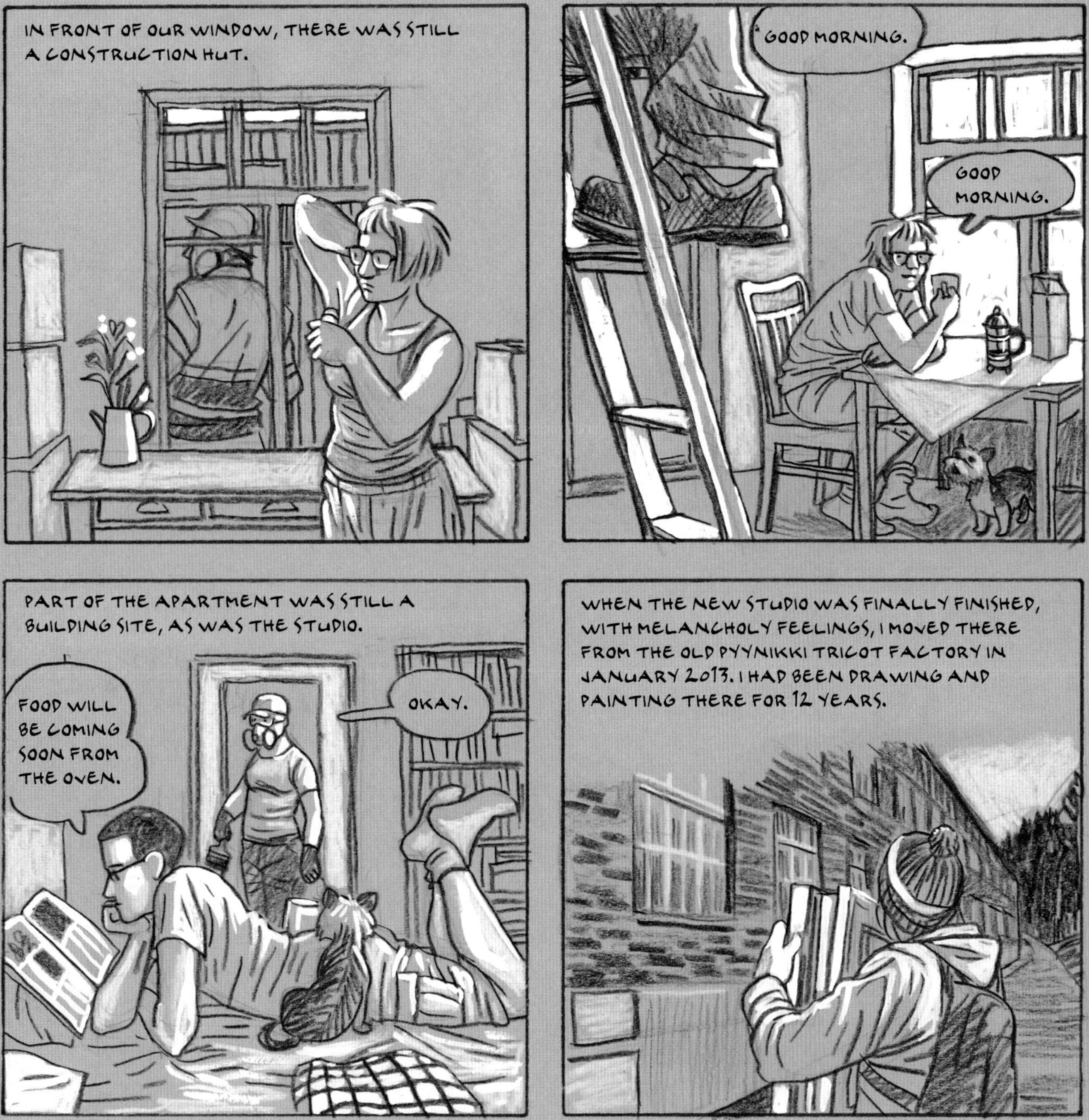
IN FRONT OF OUR WINDOW, THERE WAS STILL A CONSTRUCTION HUT.
GOOD MORNING.
GOOD MORNING.
PART OF THE APARTMENT WAS STILL A BUILDING SITE, AS WAS THE STUDIO.
FOOD WILL BE COMING SOON FROM THE OVEN.
OKAY.
WHEN THE NEW STUDIO WAS FINALLY FINISHED, WITH MELANCHOLY FEELINGS, I MOVED THERE FROM THE OLD PYYNIKKI TRICOT FACTORY IN JANUARY 2013. I HAD BEEN DRAWING AND PAINTING THERE FOR 12 YEARS.

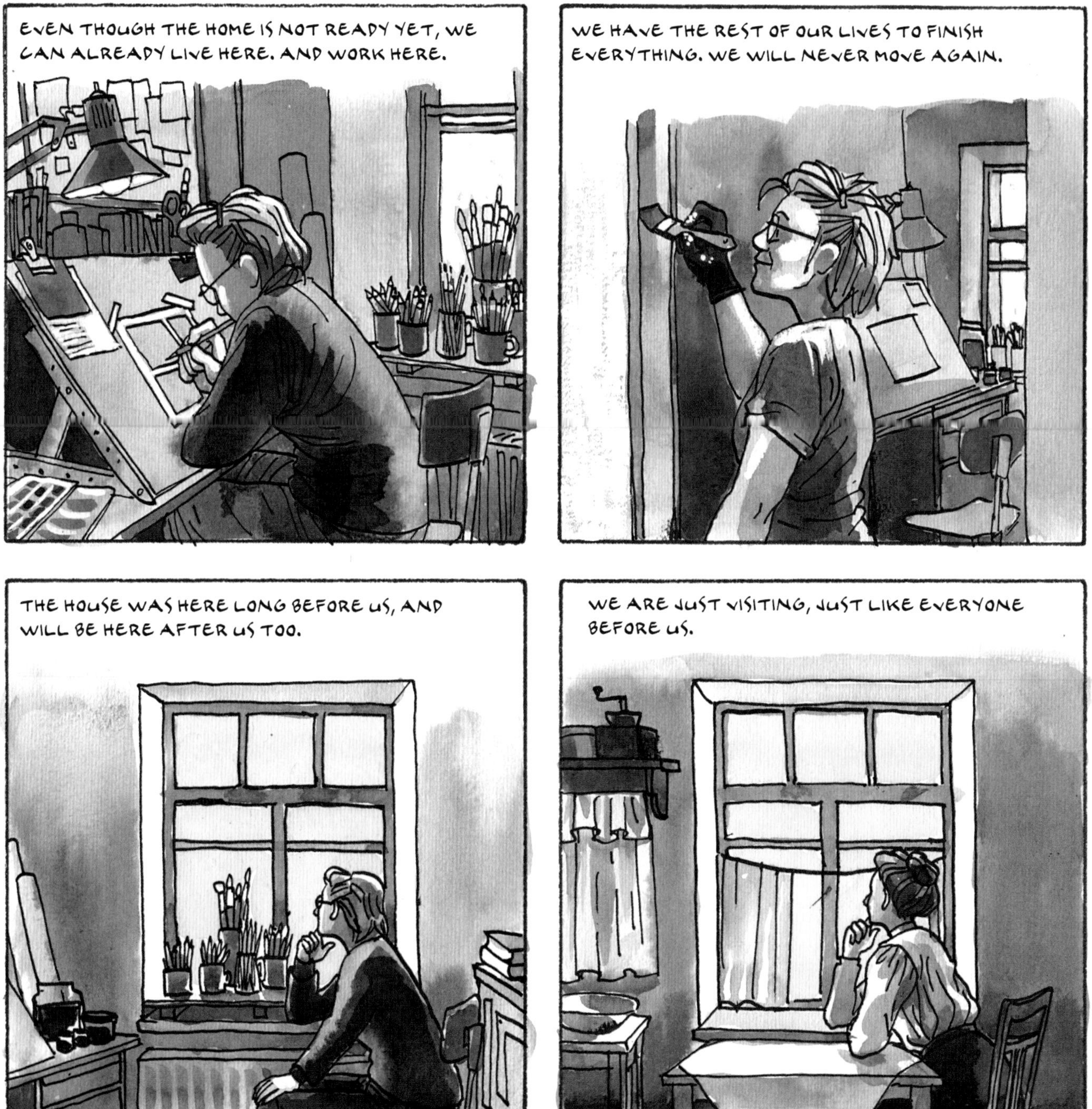
EVEN THOUGH THE HOME IS NOT READY YET, WE CAN ALREADY LIVE HERE. AND WORK HERE.
WE HAVE THE REST OF OUR LIVES TO FINISH EVERYTHING. WE WILL NEVER MOVE AGAIN.
THE HOUSE WAS HERE LONG BEFORE US, AND WILL BE HERE AFTER US TOO.
WE ARE JUST VISITING, JUST LIKE EVERYONE BEFORE US.

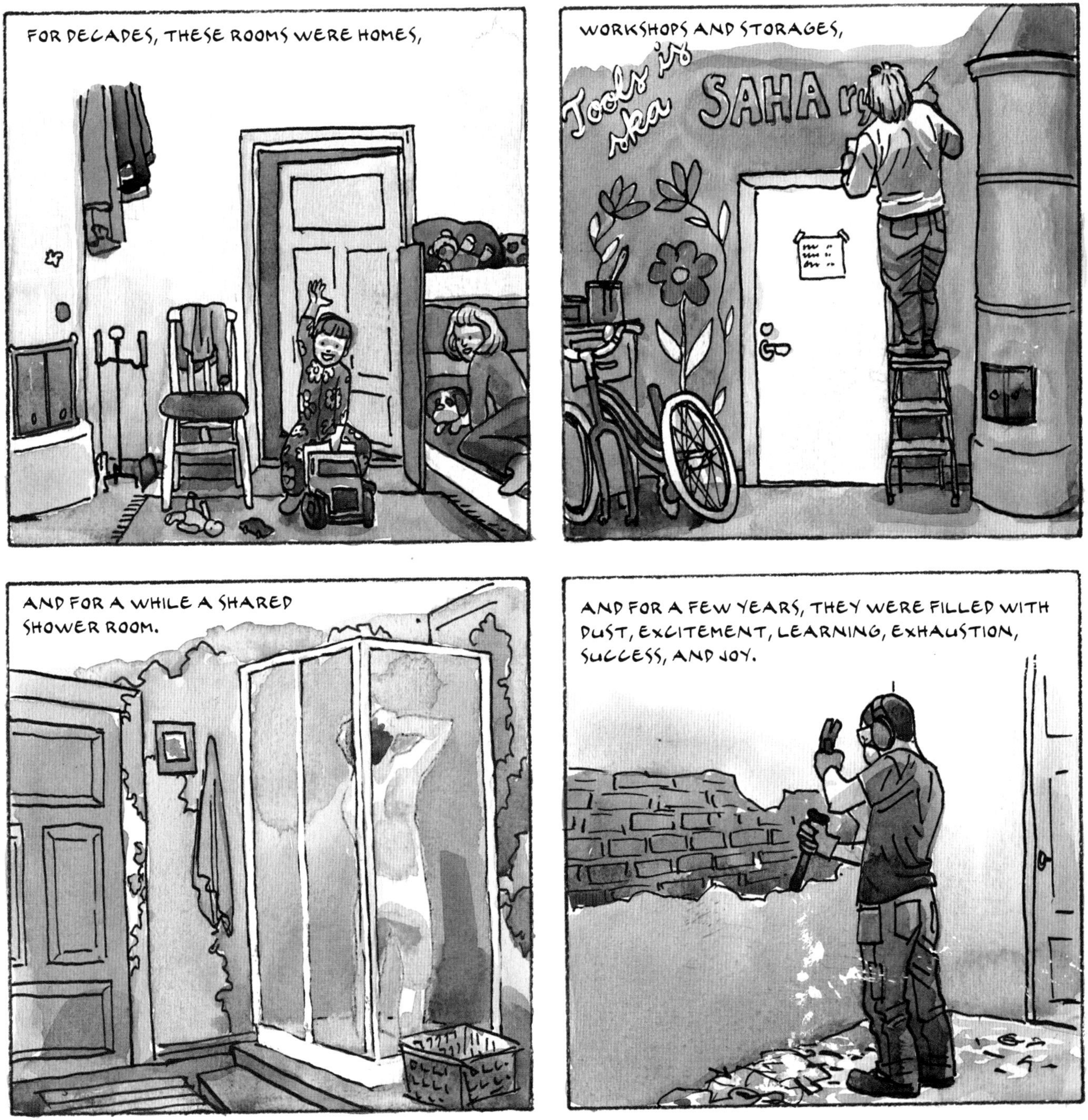
FOR DECADES, THESE ROOMS WERE HOMES,
WORKSHOPS AND STORAGES,
SAHA ry
AND FOR A WHILE A SHARED SHOWER ROOM.
AND FOR A FEW YEARS, THEY WERE FILLED WITH DUST, EXCITEMENT, LEARNING, EXHAUSTION, SUCCESS, AND JOY.

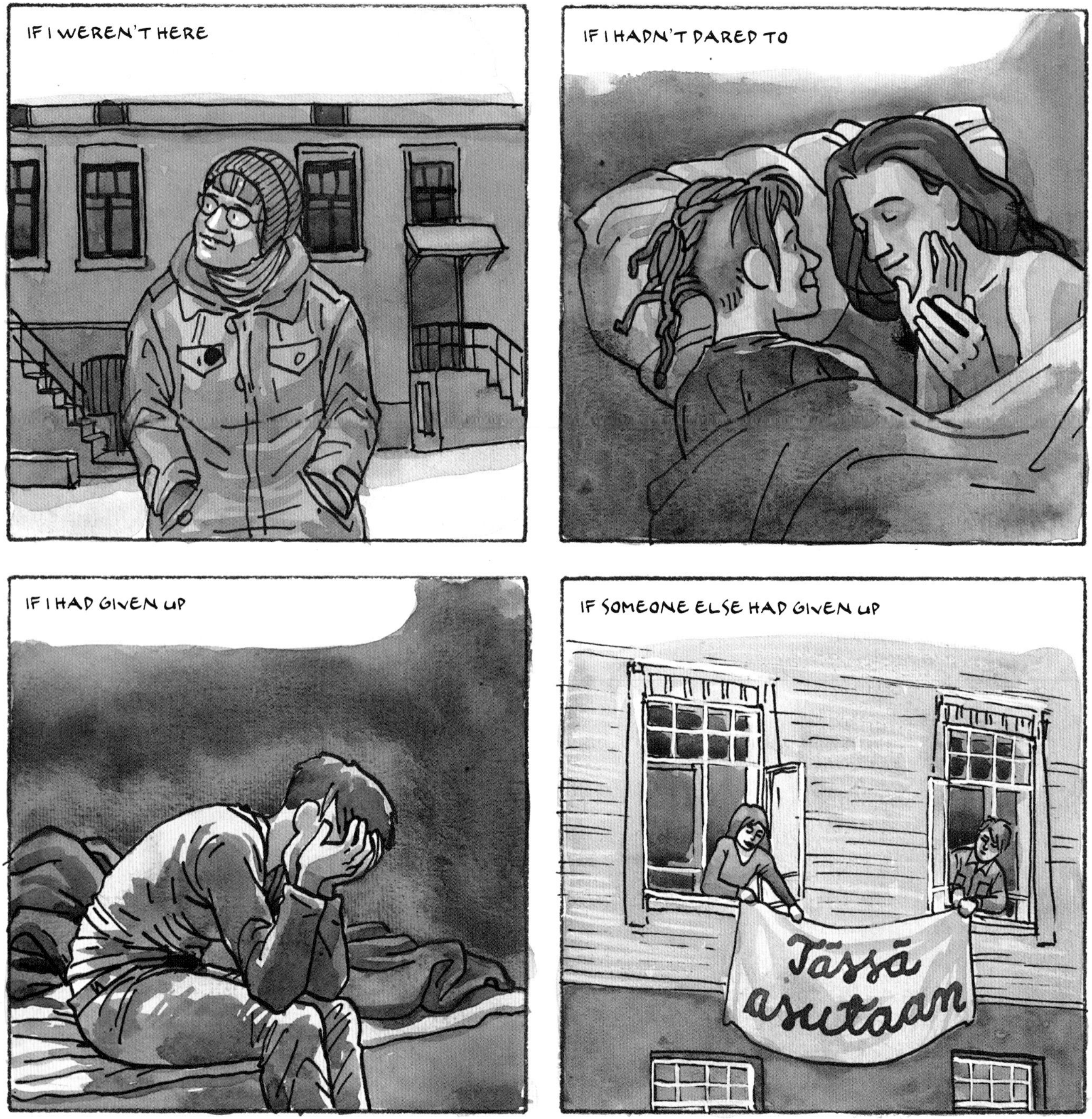
IF I WEREN'T HERE
IF I HADN'T DARED TO
IF I HAD GIVEN UP
IF SOMEONE ELSE HAD GIVEN UP
Tässä asutaan

Sign: People live here

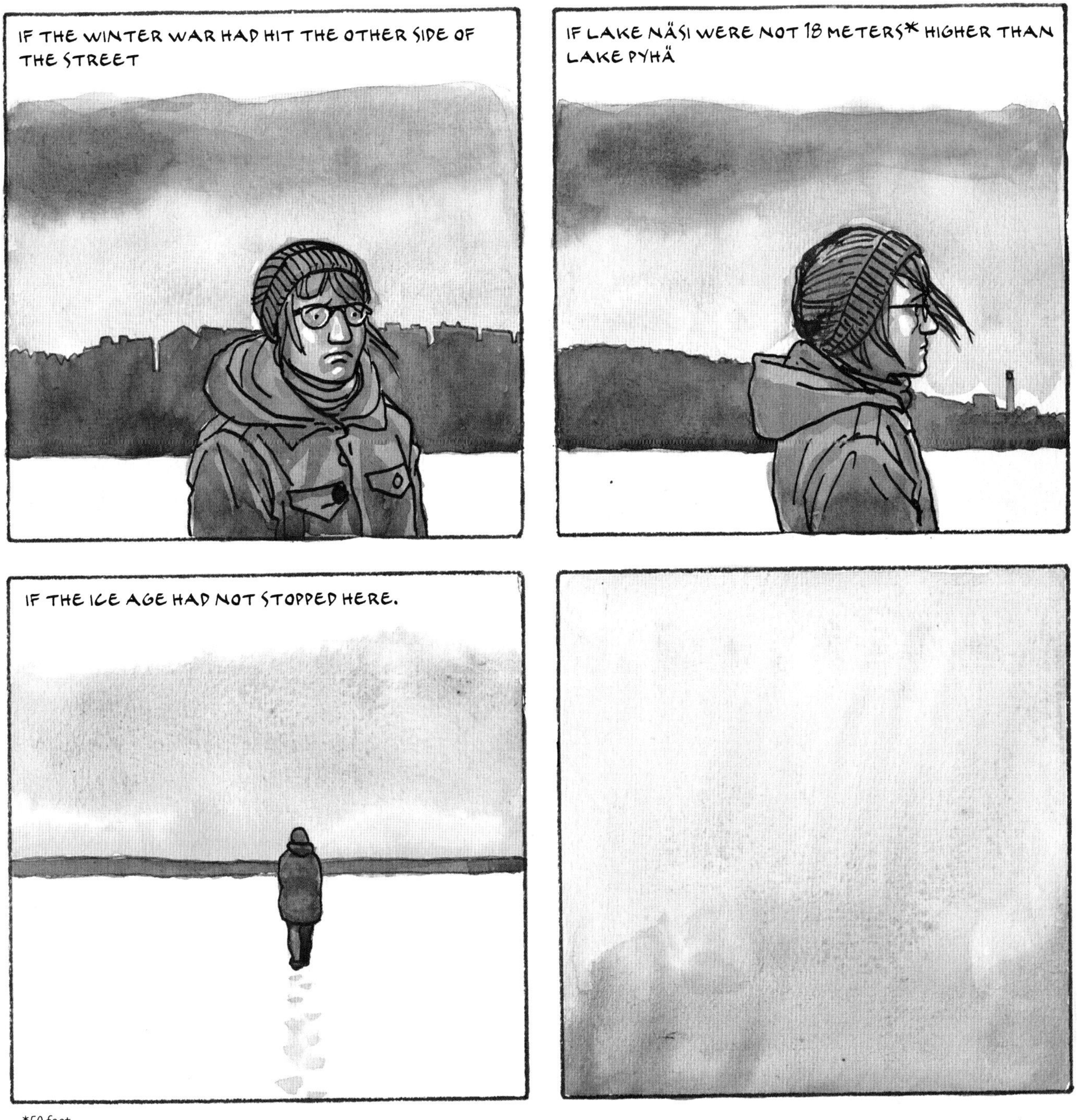
IF THE WINTER WAR HAD HIT THE OTHER SIDE OF THE STREET
IF LAKE NÄSI WERE NOT 18 METERS* HIGHER THAN LAKE PYHÄ
IF THE ICE AGE HAD NOT STOPPED HERE.

*59 feet

ANNIKKI TANGO

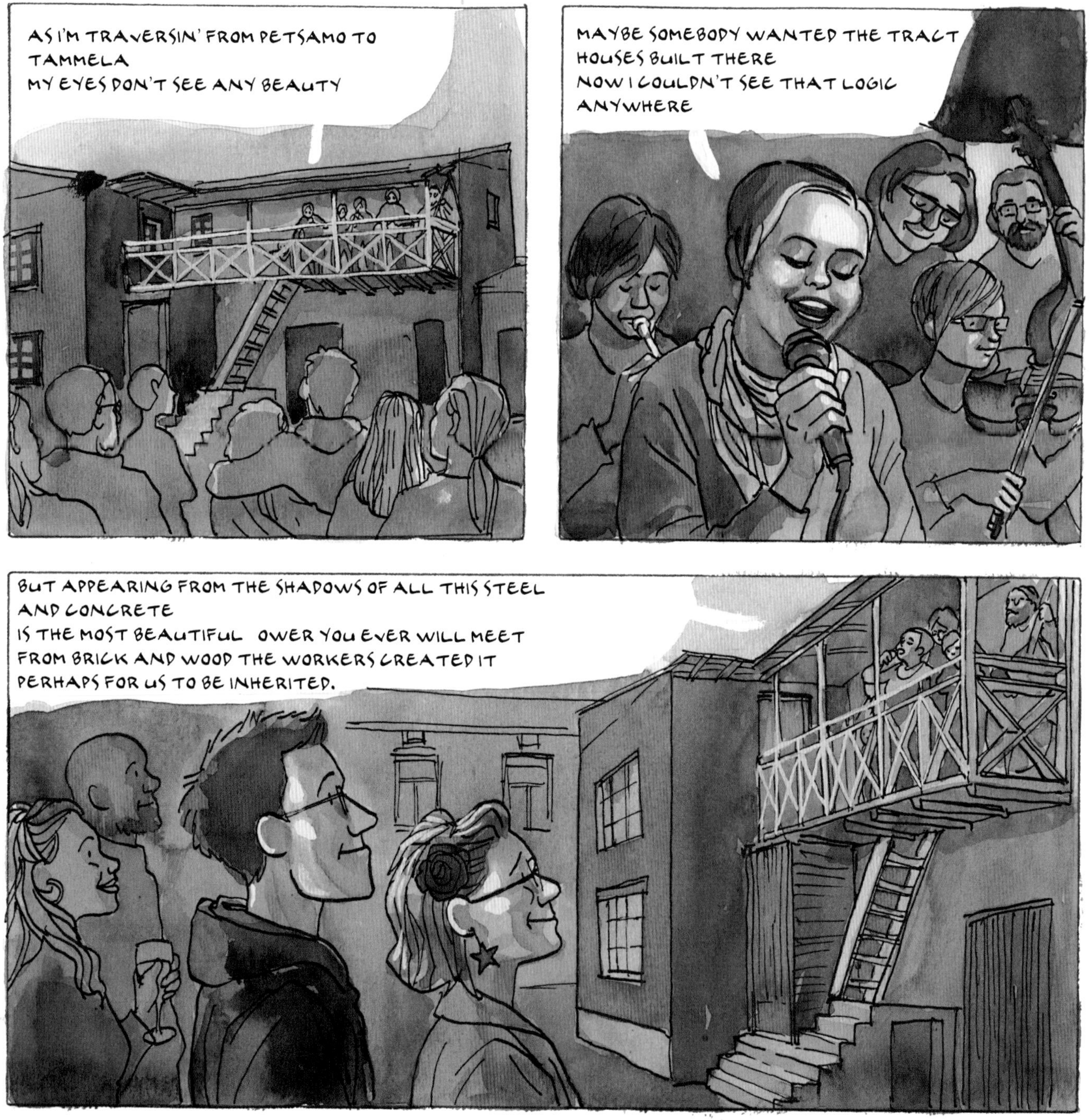
AS I'M TRAVERSIN' FROM PETSAMO TO TAMMELA
MY EYES DON'T SEE ANY BEAUTY
MAYBE SOMEBODY WANTED THE TRACT HOUSES BUILT THERE
NOW I COULDN'T SEE THAT LOGIC ANYWHERE
BUT APPEARING FROM THE SHADOWS OF ALL THIS STEEL AND CONCRETE
IS THE MOST BEAUTIFUL OWER YOU EVER WILL MEET
FROM BRICK AND WOOD THE WORKERS CREATED IT
PERHAPS FOR US TO BE INHERITED.

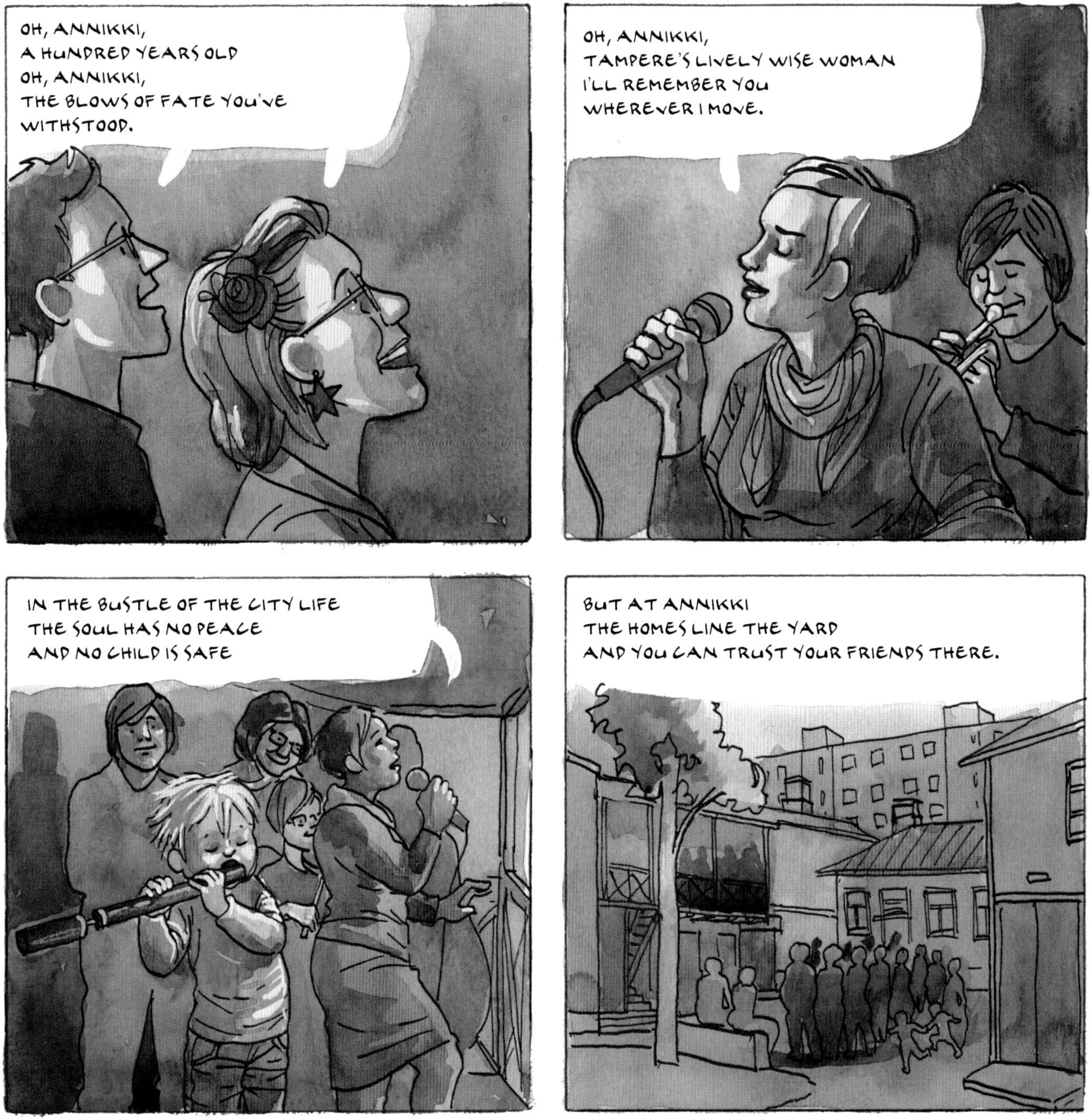
OH, ANNIKKI,
A HUNDRED YEARS OLD
OH, ANNIKKI,
THE BLOWS OF FATE YOU'VE
WITHSTOOD.
OH, ANNIKKI,
TAMPERE'S LIVELY WISE WOMAN
I'LL REMEMBER YOU
WHEREVER I MOVE.
IN THE BUSTLE OF THE CITY LIFE
THE SOUL HAS NO PEACE
AND NO CHILD IS SAFE
BUT AT ANNIKKI
THE HOMES LINE THE YARD
AND YOU CAN TRUST YOUR FRIENDS THERE.

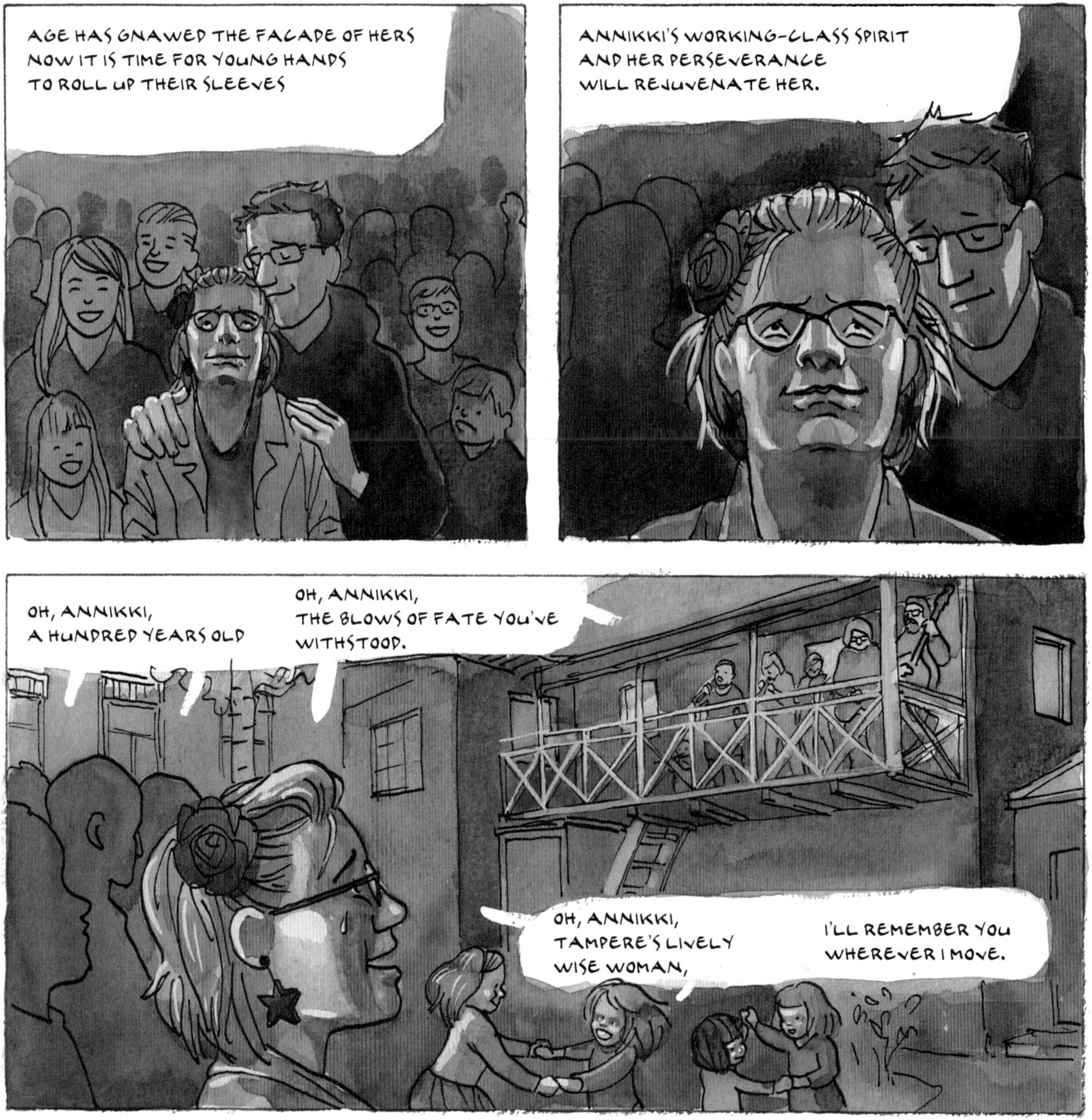
AGE HAS GNAWED THE FACADE OF HERS
NOW IT IS TIME FOR YOUNG HANDS
TO ROLL UP THEIR SLEEVES
ANNIKKI'S WORKING-CLASS SPIRIT
AND HER PERSEVERANCE
WILL REJUVENATE HER.
OH, ANNIKKI,
A HUNDRED YEARS OLD
OH, ANNIKKI,
THE BLOWS OF FATE YOU'VE
WITHSTOOD.
OH, ANNIKKI,
TAMPERE'S LIVELY
WISE WOMAN,
I'LL REMEMBER YOU
WHEREVER I MOVE.

"Annikki-tango," lyrics by Matti Huhta, translated by Samuli Björkling.

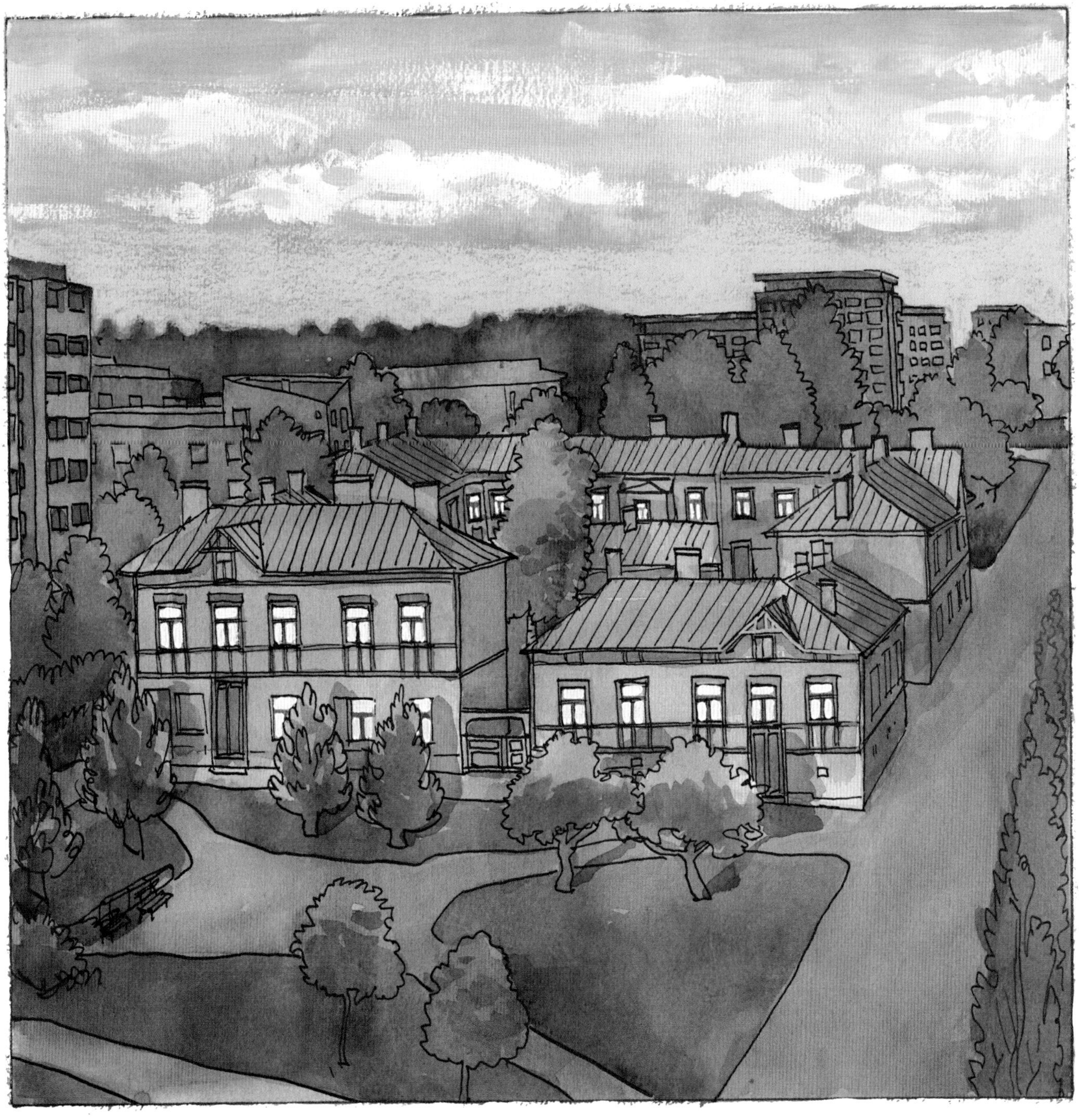

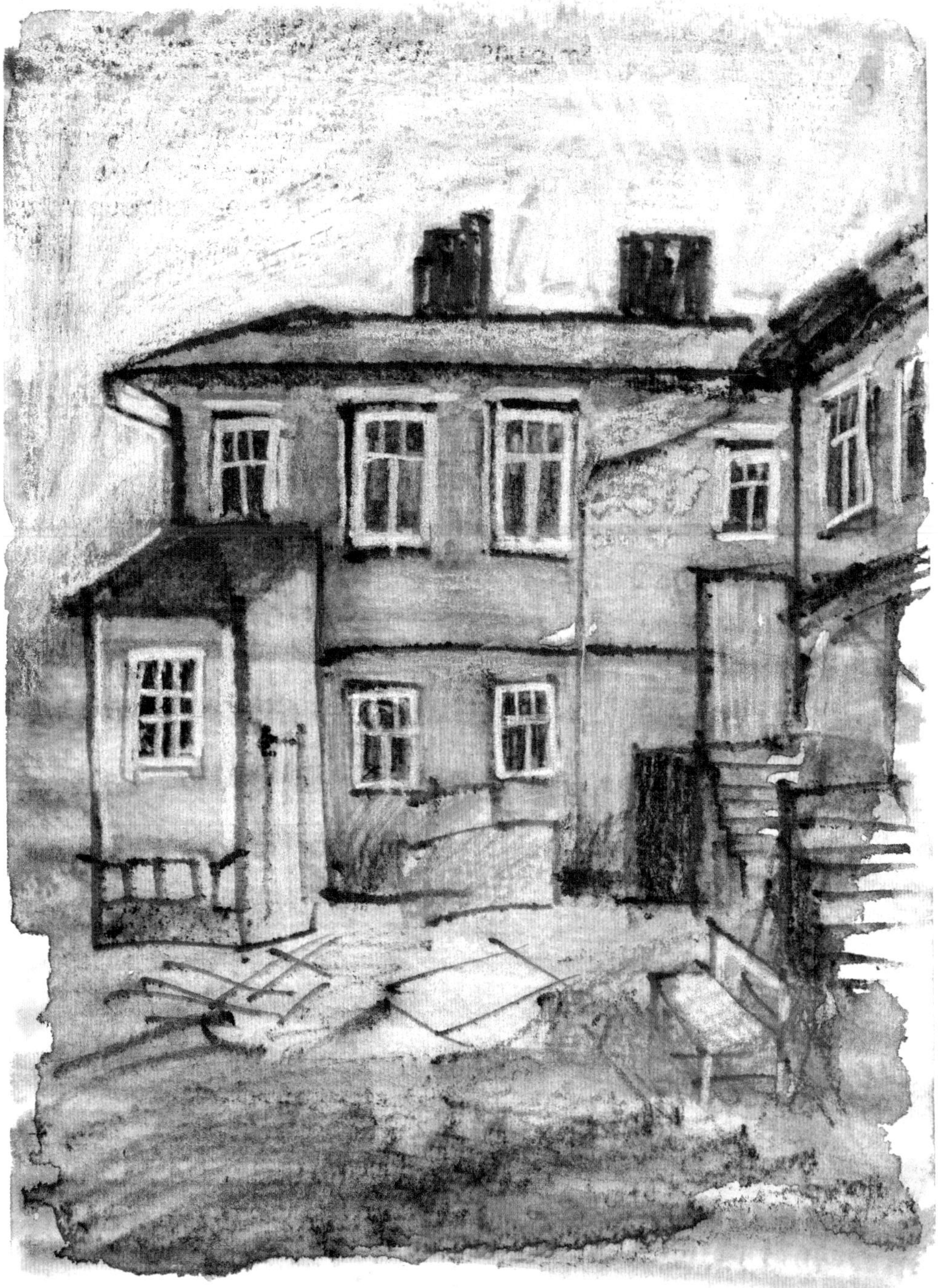

Springtime dusk in the year 2011. The renovation has begun and the yard starts to fill up with junk.

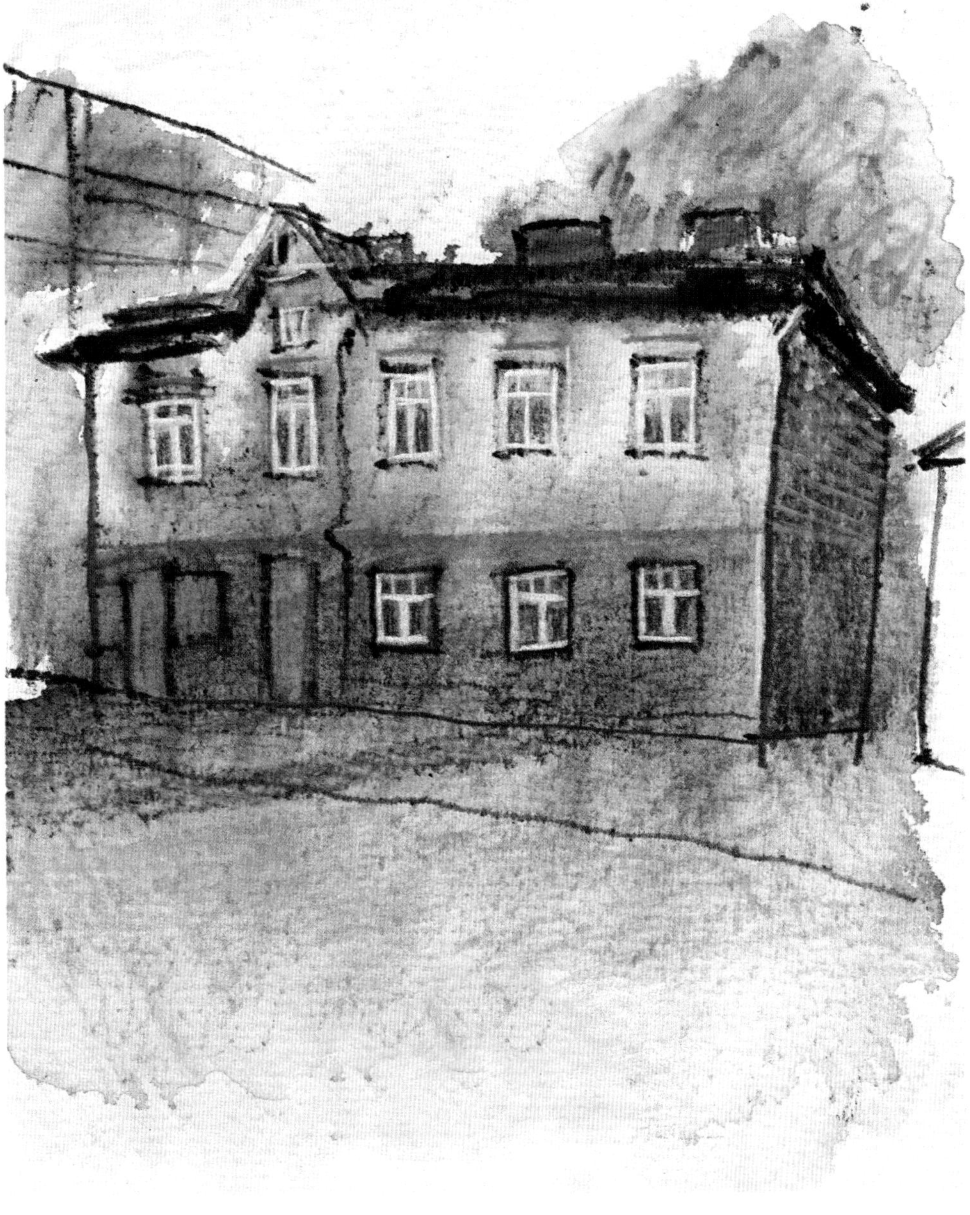

In the spring of 2011 the evening sun hits the old house's exterior, which has witnessed life.

The festival Apple Blossom Time—Wooden Tammela Magic in June 1999. I happened to immortalize a piece of the now disappeared garden in Väinölä Street in my sketchbook.

Right: Mikko and Kaapo in Hervanta in the summer of 2008. Illustration for the Swedish *Allt för konsten* 7 graphic anthology cover.

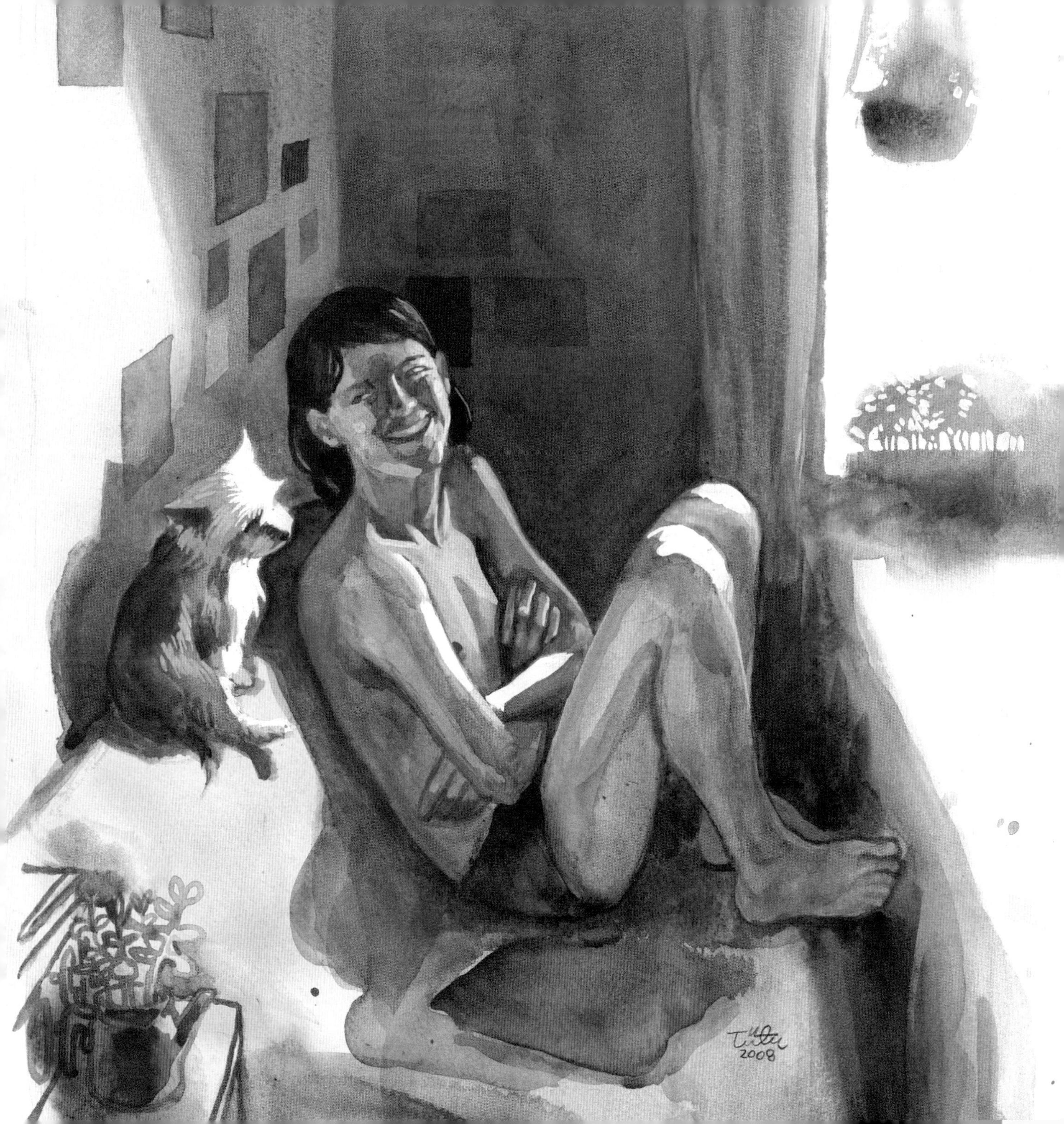
2008

The maple tree grew too close to the house, and it had to be cut down. On the ground next to the tree are boxes full of bricks from the torn-down yard building.

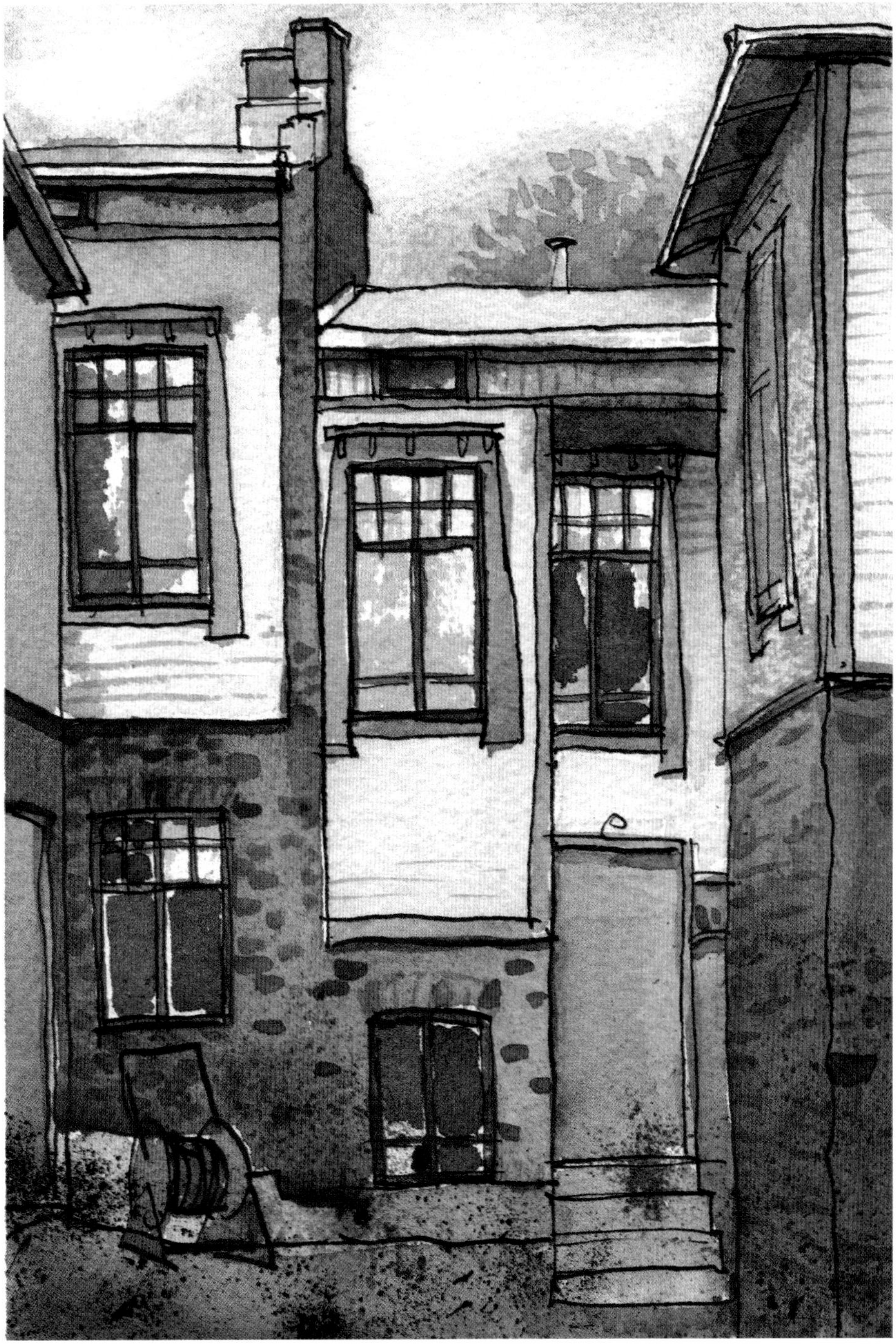

In the summer of 2012, when the renovation starts to be over. The door is being repaired, and a piece of plywood covers the doorway. The unpainted new tin roofs shine.

ANNIKIN
RUNOFESTIVAALI
6.6.2009

RADIKAALIT!

AULIKKI OKSANEN	VILLE HYTÖNEN	TAMPEREELLA
HANNU SALAMA	PEKKA KEJONEN	ANNIKINKADUN
PENTTI SAARITSA	HELI SLUNGA	PUUKORTTELIN
SAILA SUSILUOTO	JARKKO TONTTI	SISÄPIHALLA
CLAES ANDERSSON	ASA & JÄTKÄT	ANNIKINKATU 11
SATU HASSI	IHOTEOLLISUUS	KELLO 11.00-22.00
		PÄÄSYLIPUT 2€
		PUFFETTI, KIRJABASAARI
		LASTEN RUNOTYÖPAJA

JUONTAA:
ROSA MERILÄINEN

MUKANA MYÖS:
KIROILEVA SIILI
JA KATARIINA
LILLQVIST

JÄRJESTÄJÄT: ANNIKIN TÄHTI RY JA PIRKANMAAN YHTEISÖASUJAT RY
KIITOKSET: TAITEEN KESKUSTOIMIKUNTA, TAMPEREEN KULTTUURITOIMI, VASTEDES RY
WWW.ANNIKINKATU.NET/RUNOFESTIVAALI09

Annikki's Poetry Festival
June 6, 2009
Radicals!

(These are the performers, many of whom are big celebrities in Finland)

Aulikki Oksanen Ville Hytönen In Tampere

Hannu Salama Pekka Kejonen
Annikki Street wooden block

Pentti Saaritsa Heli Slunga Inside yard

Saila Susiluoto Jarkko Tontti Annikki Street 11

Claes Andersson Asa & Jätkät 11 a.m.–10 p.m.

Satu Hassi Ihoteollisuus

Tickets €2

Café, book bazaar
Children's poetry workshop

MC: Rosa Meriläinen

Also participating:
Kiroileva siili (The Swearing Hedgehog)
and Katariina Lillqvist

Organizers:
Star of Annikki and Pirkanmaa Communal Residents

Thanks to Taiteen Keskustoimikunta (Central Art Commission), Tampereen Kulttuuritoimi (Tampere Cultural Activities), Vastedes ry

www.annikinkatu.net/runofestivaali09

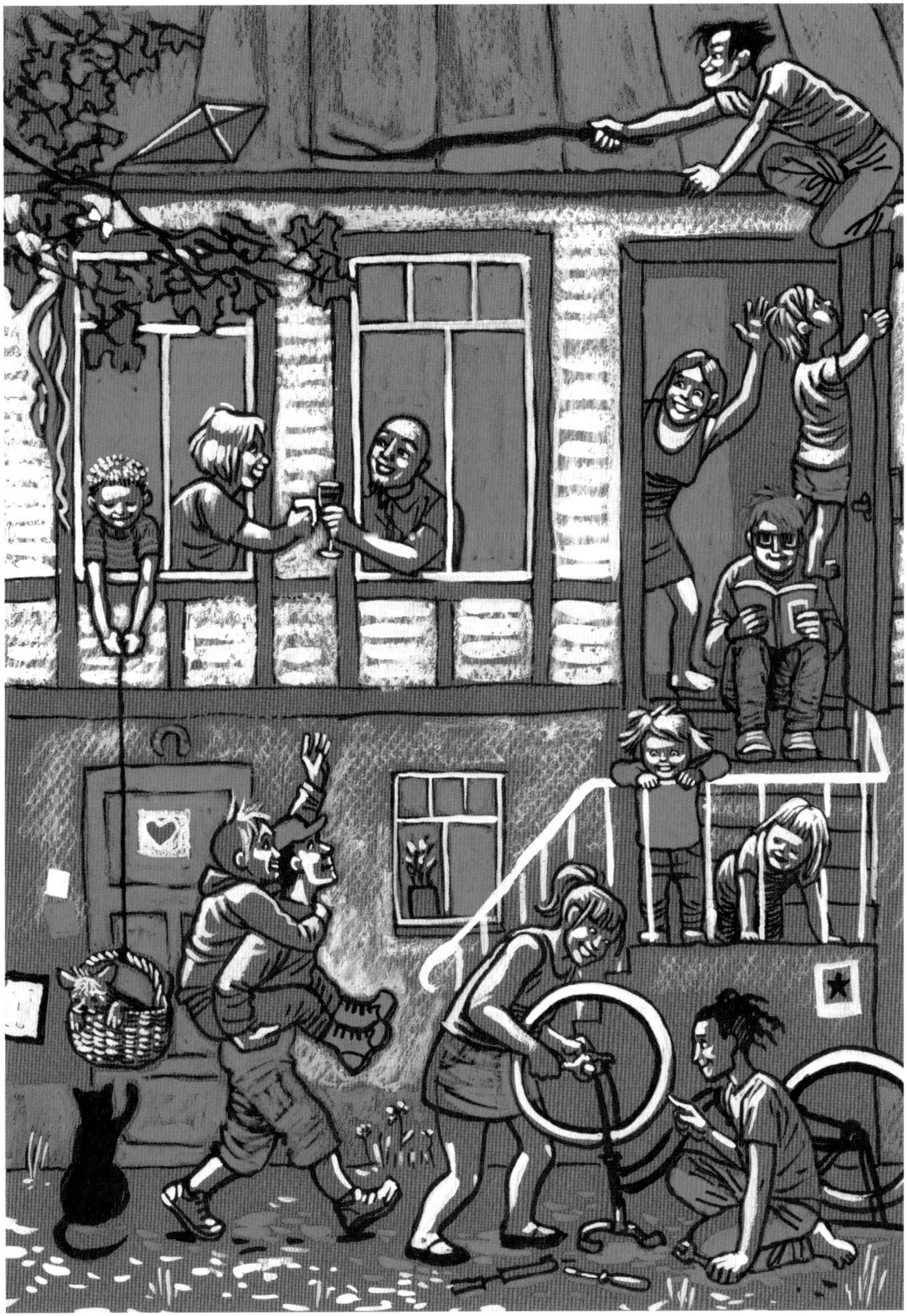

Illustration for the "Kissing behind the barricades" calendar, 2011. Inspiration: Annikki, of course.

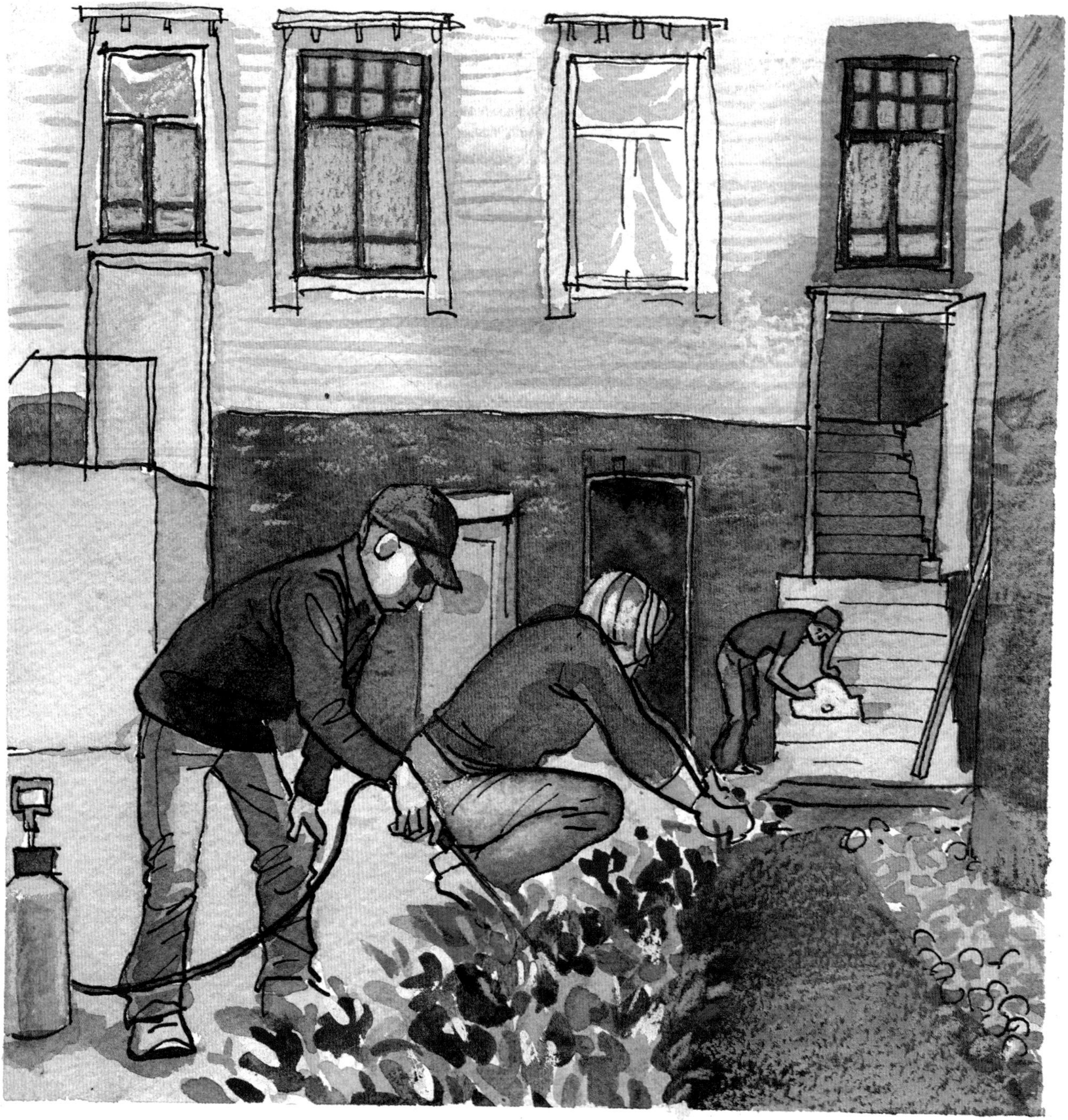

In the summer of 2012, the moment the yard didn't look like a construction site anymore, we planted summer flowers. The windows are still covered by plastic, doors with plywood. In the background, an old washbasin is being washed so that it can be reinstalled for use.

AFTERWORD
An Important Work in Comic Art

Media commentators and art critics, for more than twenty years, have described comic art as coming of age. Such claims can be heard regularly at Comic-Con and similar festivals across the world attended by hundreds of thousands of mostly young people. This book, the unique creation of a new generation, and of a talented Finnish artist influenced by both feminism and anarchism, gives us some definite clues to what comics can do at their most creative.

Readers will know that "the comics," a genre preceding radio, television, and the web, have long since lost their honored place as a central icon of the popular reader and especially the half-literate reader. Printed newspapers are dying, and the popular comic book field that could sell half a million or more per title, month after month, barely survives. What remains for comic art? One of the genre's giants, Art Spiegelman, predicted that it might be reborn as "art." Comic images have indeed sometimes been repurposed for art galleries and museums that few comics readers themselves will ever visit. But comic art, in the hands of a younger generation, has other purposes.

Tiitu Takalo is herself the inheritor of the comic art tradition but also of another just as vital to her work: the constant worldwide struggle for community against often seemingly overwhelming odds. To this point Finland has been rather exceptional in retaining many of the successes of social democracy lost elsewhere: it ranks high in public education and health, while even its sister Scandinavian states have begun to move toward privatization of health services and lower taxes on the wealthy. Everywhere, it seems, the scarcity and rising cost of housing, a key source of misery and of widespread protests since the 1990s, highlight social issues. Add to these gloomy developments the growing ecological crisis and we find a generation discovering that it must fight in order to live.

The struggle has many terrains, none so unimportant that they can be ignored. Struggles themselves have an educational value beyond their immediate purposes. Sometimes the lesson is: you will be crushed. But often, a sense of solidarity can emerge, does emerge, where people intimately involved come to feel differently about themselves and their society. The sense of apathy, of being lost in history and society, falls away, at least for a time, and "strength" is redefined as a common quality that must be shared to be real. "Intellectual" or "leader" and "worker" or "citizen" (or refugee without citizenship), likewise racial and gender assignment, lose their debilitating force for the less fortunate, or at least there is movement in that direction. Life has new purpose, even if this is a feeling that cannot be sustained, through difficulties, over months and years.

Finnish history naturally adds its own special quality to the saga. Other modern societies have seen myriad kinds of cooperative economics and cooperative life. Finns, famed for at least a century for their comprehensive socialistic cooperatives reaching even the distant north woods of the US Midwest, and for a community theater engaging nearly every member of the community, have a vital legacy to build from. Also unique was the accomplishment of women's right to vote in Finland generations before other nations. This success speaks to something else deep in the culture, doubtless to the strength of women individually and as a group within Finnish society.

Too much can easily be made of such legacies, now in the twenty-first century, with global citizens on their smart phones, ordering consumer products produced thousands of miles away. But perhaps we should not be hasty in writing off the past.

The particulars of this comic have to do with the threatened destruction of a community, a physical town, wholesale. Villages across the world face similar destruction, sometimes by damming rivers and flooding regions for assorted purposes, or wiping them out for mineral extraction or even for the creation of shiny new anonymous cities where previous traces of actual community have been wiped out. This village, Takalo's own village, or rather the Tammela section of Tampere, faces a similar calamity, and some of the villagers find their own way to struggle against behemoth. It is a beautiful thing to observe, and the artist has rendered it beautifully.

But there is also a deeper meaning—several deeper meanings—that American audiences may find difficult to grasp fully. Finnish architecture, as the author-artist says, contains precious little of the past, and this very village, with its historic styles and wooden 1910s structures, has every right to be preserved for that reason alone. Across town in Tampere stands the Red Village, known as such because it was settled after 1918 by the widows of a bloody civil war, recalling martyrs in a class conflict that the world has largely forgotten. And then there is the environmental dimension that is not referenced specifically in many places in the book, but is ever present in the background. Around and beyond the settled zones of Finland lies the taiga, the vast forest, with its many lakes. Takalo very much sees herself as part of that setting, shaped by forces older than human experience.

The artist has tapped these meanings in her own way, blending them into and around a love story and a community-wide saga. That she has relied on her conversations with fellow residents raises yet one more crucial point. Oral history as a scholarly field has traveled a long way since its origins in the 1950s efforts to preserve memories of "great men" who had failed to gain biographers. The field changed dramatically, at least across large parts of Europe and especially the United States, during the 1960s. The field worker became an activist, or at least the scholarly-minded comrade of the activists, sometimes gathering minutes of meetings and such. The lives of the activists and the communities they served only emerged in and through the interviews, usually life stories captured with primitive tape recorders. This was a new way of looking at history, breaking down the formal barriers between personal revelations and "historical facts." Here, the orality itself, the memory of persons and events, not the absolute factual accuracy, became the most important consideration. If Chicago's Studs Terkel was the one glittering personality of the field, thousands of interviewers, many of them with part-time academic jobs or no academic jobs, sought to emulate his efforts.

The artist makes her own limitations very clear. If anything, she is overly modest. This is no objective history of the community, and she makes no such claim. What she does say, clearly, and demonstrates with great patience, is that real meaning comes out of plurality. She could say "love," the love of the community in struggle, but that might seem maudlin. It is enough to explain that the effort is collaborative and collective, and that it has been her struggle as well as that of others. She is not absent from this scene even as she makes a significant contribution to it as an artist.

Now we can turn to a crucial particularity of the narrative in the graphic novel. Let us say first, that in the field of graphic novels, the personal story of an adolescent or young woman now has a resonance that could not have been imagined twenty or thirty years ago. *Fun Home* by Alison Bechdel and *Persepolis* by Marjane Satrapi have ascended the heights of international fame and reputation, in ways that only Spiegelman's *Maus* could be said to exceed. Spiegelman barely inserts himself into *Maus*, and only in troubled conversations with his father, the Holocaust survivor. *Fun Home* and *Persepolis* are deeply personal stories, and in that fact lies a great deal of their power and drama. We close this thought with Joe Sacco's several well-known comic art travelogues of war and ethnic violence, among the comics most likely to be seen on the shelves of specialty stores across Europe and the United States. Sacco is personal and appears as himself in all his work. Like Takalo, he is on the scene.

Perhaps it is best to close this note by coming back to the history of Finnish comics. They prospered, in their own way, from the 1910s to World War II, an era ended, as most elsewhere in Europe, because afterward the international comics syndicates took over the "funny pages" of daily newspapers, with few or no local representatives. Formation of the Finnish Comic Society in 1971 and in the following decades at first slow growth, then rapid growth in the new century, changed the scene dramatically. The limits of the language size—there are five million Finnish speakers—mean that few or no full-time artists are paid enough to live on their comic work. On the other hand, the hardscrabble life of the Finnish comic artists can be said to have brought out their rebellious character. An explosion of creativity has taken place, along with the highly popular Helsinki Comics Festival (since 1979) and the annual publication of the best of current work. In other words, Takalo has made colleagues engaged in the highest levels of creativity. Let us hope that the publication of this work will encourage more translations of her work and the work of other Finnish artists.

Paul Buhle, a retired Senior Lecturer at Brown University, has edited a dozen nonfiction graphic novels including *Red Rosa: A Graphic Biography of Rosa Luxemburg* and *Eugene V. Debs: a Graphic Biography*

June 2019

SOURCES

Books and other print sources

Haapala, P. 1986. *Tehtaan valossa: Teollistuminen ja työväestön muodostuminen Tampereella 1820–1920* [In the light of the factory: Industrialization and the formation of a working class in Tampere 1820–1920]. Tampere: Osuuskunta Vastapaino. Suomen historiallinen seura.

Holmberg, R., Virtanen, H., Ylikangas, H. 1996. Tie Tampereelle [The road to Tampere]. [s.l.]: INK Company.

Hoppu, T., Haapala, P., Antila, K., Honkasalo, M., Lind, M., Liuttunen, A., Saloniemi, M. (eds.). 2008. *Tampere 1918*. Tampere: Tampereen museot.

Huhta, L., Meriläinen, R. 2009. *Feministin käsikirja* [A feminist's handbook]. Jyväskylä: Ajatus Kirjat.

Järvelä, A., Malmi T. 2008. *Tampere tulessa 1918* [Tampere in fire 1918]. Jyväskylä: Atena.

Jokinen, A., Juhila, K. 1987. *Asumisen ankeus ja autuus: Tutkimus puu-Tammelasta ja sen asukkaista* [The gloom and bliss of living: A study on Wooden Tammela and its inhabitants]. Tampere: University of Tampere.

Kallio, P., Takalo, T., Antila, K., Koivisto, I., Lind, M., Nissinaho, A. 2011. *Ottopoikia ja työläistyttöjä: Yhdeksän tarinaa Tampereelta* [Foster sons and cotton girls: Nine stories from Tampere]. Tampere: Tampereen museot.

Lilius, M. 1997. *Villan aika: Kuvia Tampereen verkatehtaasta* [The time of wool: Pictures from the Tampere cloth factory]. Tampere: Tampereen museot.

Lind, M., Antila, K., Liuttunen A. (eds.). 2011. *Tammerkoski ja kosken kaupunki* [Tammerkoski and the city on the rapids]. Tampere: Tampereen museot.

Louhivaara, M. 1999. *Tampereen kadunnimet* [Tampere street names]. Tampere: Tampereen museot.

Määttänen, M., Toivonen, P., Järvinen, S., Laine, P. 1994. Muistikuvia vanhasta Tammelasta: Nykyisyydestä entiseen ja takaisin [Memories of old Tammela: From the present to the past and back]. *Tammerkoski-lehti* 8/1994. Tampere-Seura.

Mattila, A. 2002. Annikinkorttelin korjaussuunnitelma [The repair plan for the Annikki block]. Thesis. Tampere University of Technology, School of Architecture.

Pasanen, J. 2012. Keittiö, huone ja ulkohuussi Tammelassa [A kitchen, a room, and an outhouse in Tammela]. Proseminar study. Tampere: University of Tampere.

Voionmaa, Väinö. 1907–1910. *Tampereen kaupungin historia: Tampereen historia viime vuosikymmeninä (1856-1905)* [The History of the City of Tampere], part III. Tampere: Tampereen kaupunki.

Wacklin, M. 2008. *Tammela: Tarinoita torin kulmilta* [Tammela: Stories from market corners]. Tampere: Tampereen tammelalaiset ry.

Wacklin, M. 2010. *Tammela: Suutarien pääkaupunki* [Tammela: The shoemakers' capital]. Tampere: Tampereen tammelalaiset ry, Tampereen kaupunki.

Ylikangas, H. 1993. *Tie Tampereelle* [The road to Tampere]. Porvoo: WSOY.

Online sources

Annikin Tähti ry.—*annikinkatu.net*

Armonkallio—*fi.wikipedia.org/wiki/Armonkallio*

Ihmisoikeudet.net, oppia ihmisyydestä—*ihmisoikeudet.net*

Koskesta voimaa—*historia.tampere.fi*

Ryhmärakennuttajat ry.—*ryhmarakennuttajat.fi*

Tampereen tarina: Teollisuuden synnyttämä kaupunki harjujen ja järvien solmukohdassa—*tampere.fi/liitteet/t/bV6J59ALc/Tampereen_tarina.pdf*

Tasa-arvotiedon keskus Minna—*minna.fi*

Teollisuustyön jäljillä—*pori.fi/kulttuuri/satakunnanmuseo/teollisuustyonjaljilla.html*

Tuomaala, S., Holhouksenalaisuudesta koulutetuksi ja vapaaksi kansalaiseksi—*helsinki.fi/sukupuolentutkimus/aanioikeus/artikkelit/tuomaala.htm*

Vanhat Velot ry.—*vanhatvelot.org*

Picture sources

Cawthorne, N. 1998. *Sixties Source Book*. Grange Books.

Häggman, K. (ed.). 2007. *Suomalaisen arjen historia 2: Säätyjen Suomi* [The history of Finnish everyday life 2: Finland of the estates]. [Helsinki]: Weilin Göös.

Häggman, K. (ed.). 2007. *Suomalaisen arjen historia 3: Modernin Suomen synty* [The history of Finnish everyday life 3: The birth of modern Finland.] [Helsinki]: Weilin Göös.

Häggman, K. (ed.). 2008. *Suomalaisen arjen historia 4: Hyvinvoinnin Suomi* [The history of Finnish everyday life 4: The Finland of prosperity]. [Helsinki]: Weilin Göös.

Heimann, J. (ed.). 2003. *All-American Ads 60s*. Köln: Taschen.

Killinen, K. (ed.). 1964. *Maailman tapahtumat 1964* [World events 1964]. Helsinki: Kirjayhtymä.

Killinen, K. (ed.). 1966. *Maailman tapahtumat 1966* [World events 1966]. Helsinki: Kirjayhtymä.

Killinen, K. (ed.). 1967. *Vuoden ihmisiä: Maailman tapahtumat 1967* [People of the year: World events 1967]. Helsinki: Kirjayhtymä.

Magnus, O. 2002. *Suomalaiset Pohjoisten kansojen historiassa I* [Finns in the history of Nordic people I]. Helsinki: Tammi.

Magnus, O. 2002. *Suomalaiset Pohjoisten kansojen historiassa II* [Finns in the history of Nordic people II]. Helsinki: Tammi.

Niemelä, J., Nieminen, K. 2007. *Tampereen kuvia: Ennen ja nyt* [Pictures of Tampere: Then and now]. Tampere: Tampere-Seura.

Ojanen, R. (ed.). 1987. *Tampereen kasvot: Kuvateos Tampereesta* [The face of Tampere: An illustrated work]. Tampere: Tampere-Seura.

Seppälä, R., Jansson, J., Kauppila, E. 1997. *Oli puutalo, keittiö ja kamari* [A wooden house, a kitchen, and a parlor]. Tampere: Tampere-Seura.

Siiri, Tampereen museoiden kokoelmatietokanta [The collective database of Tampere museums]—*http://siiri.tampere.fi*

Sinisalo, H. (ed.). 1984. *Suomalainen perinnekuvasto* [Illustrated work of Finnish heritage]. [Kuopio]: VK-Perinnetieto Oy.

Sinisalo, U. (ed.). 1955. *Vanha Tampere* [The old Tampere]. Tampere-Seura, Tampere-Seuran kuva-arkisto.

Vapriikin kuva-arkisto [Vapriikki picture archives].

ACKNOWLEDGMENTS BY THE AUTHOR

Thank you, Mikko. For everything.

Thank you to those who answered my questions: Katja Solla, Simo Ollila, Pasi Toivonen, Merja Määttänen, Leena Ahonen, Emma, Terttu Mäkelä, Ante Anttila, and Sanna.

Thank you to those who allowed me to use their own archives. I will return them soon!

A huge thank-you to all those former residents who helped to keep Annikki alive by renovating, taking care, believing in dreams, fighting.

Thank you to my current neighbors.

Thank you to Matti Huhta for the song lyrics.

Thank you to the photo archives of Vapriikki and the Tampere Society.

Thank you to the sewing circle of the Blue House.

Thank you, friends.

Thank you for our years together to my studio mates, Elina and Heta.

Thank you to Patu and Juha for computerizing.

Thank you for financial help to:

Sarjakuvantekijät ry (The Finnish Comics Professionals), The City of Tampere, and Pirkanmaantaidetoimikunta (Arts Promotion Centre Pirkanmaa).

Thank you and apologies to those who had to participate in this graphic novel without knowing about it.

If you have memories of Annikki and would like to share them with others, you may contact the block's tenant community via email: *annikkimuistot@gmail.com*. We are pleased to receive stories and pictures having to do with the history of the block, and we will be happy to preserve them.

. . . .

TRANSLATION ACKNOWLEDGMENTS

Michael Demson and Helena Halmari

Helena and Michael would like to thank the Finnish Literature Exchange (FILI) for awarding us a translation grant to help us complete this project. Without the financial support of Dr. Abbey Zink, dean of the College of Humanities and Social Sciences, and Dr. Jacob Blevins, chair of the Department of English at Sam Houston State University, this project would never have been completed, and we are deeply thankful to them. Pam Berkman, Louis Swaim, Susan Bumps, and other members of the team at North Atlantic Books were wonderful—they brought tremendous energy to this project. And we would like to thank Maureen Forys and her team at Happenstance Type-O-Rama, who took on the laborious work of relettering the English translation. Helena thanks her colleague and husband, Robert Adams, who, throughout the project, has been readily available for quick feedback on appropriate turns of language. Michael would like to thank his wife, Audrey Murfin, to whom he dedicates his work.

ABOUT THE AUTHOR

Me, Mikko, and Annikki is an autobiographical love story and a renovation diary. At the same time, it depicts the struggle for old buildings and communal residential culture. Annikki, a wooden block in the Tammela section of the city of Tampere, Finland, becomes the main protagonist. It still remains as the only reminder of the old industrial city's historic working-class neighborhood.

TIITU TAKALO is a graphic book author, artist, and small-scale publisher who grew up in the Hervanta neighborhood in Tampere, Finland. Her most important works include *Tyhmä tyttö* [Stupid girl], *Kehä* [Ring], *Jää* [Ice], *Tuuli ja myrsky* [Wind and storm], and *Ottopoikia ja työläistyttöjä* [Foster sons and cotton girls], for Pauli Kallio's text.

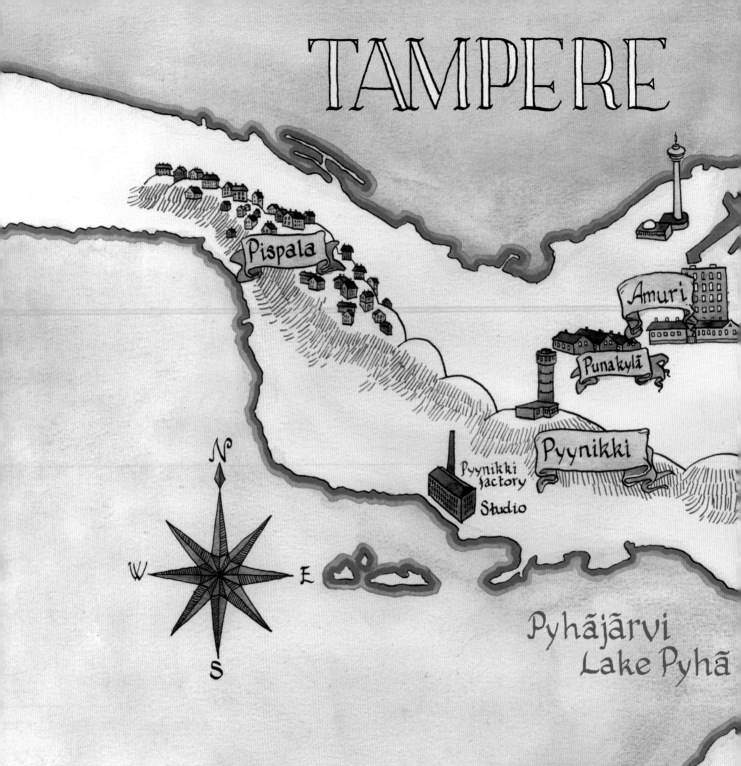

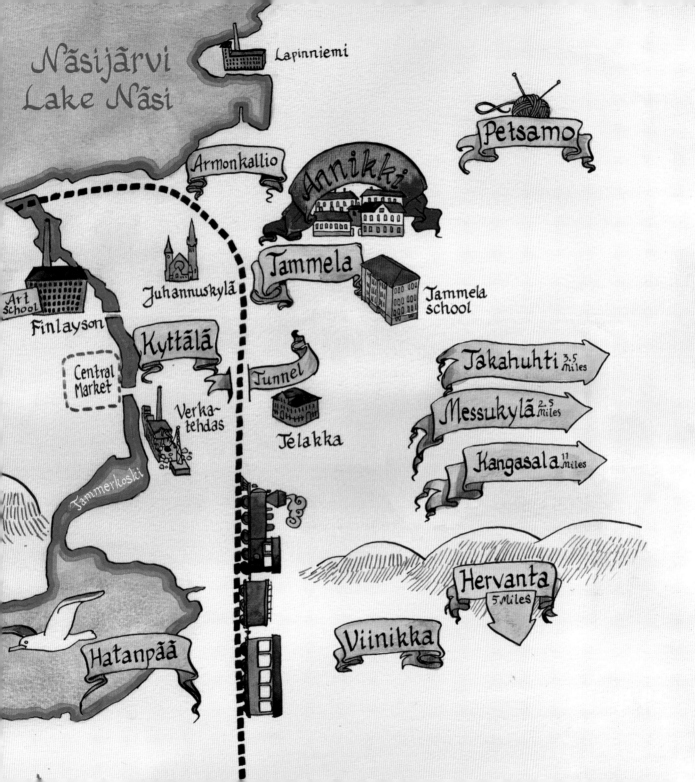

About North Atlantic Books

North Atlantic Books (NAB) is an independent, nonprofit publisher committed to a bold exploration of the relationships between mind, body, spirit, and nature. Founded in 1974, NAB aims to nurture a holistic view of the arts, sciences, humanities, and healing. To make a donation or to learn more about our books, authors, events, and newsletter, please visit www.northatlanticbooks.com.

North Atlantic Books is the publishing arm of the Society for the Study of Native Arts and Sciences, a 501(c)(3) nonprofit educational organization that promotes cross-cultural perspectives linking scientific, social, and artistic fields. To learn how you can support us, please visit our website.